RUSSIA, THE COUNCIL OF EUROPE AND THE EUROPEAN CONVENTION ON HUMAN RIGHTS

A Troubled Membership and Its Legacy

Ed Bates
Kanstantsin Dzehtsiarou
Andrew Forde

With a Foreword by
Daniel Tarschys

First published in Great Britain in 2025 by

Bristol University Press
University of Bristol
1–9 Old Park Hill
Bristol
BS2 8BB
UK
t: +44 (0)117 374 6645
e: bup-info@bristol.ac.uk

Details of international sales and distribution partners are available at bristoluniversitypress.co.uk

© Bristol University Press 2025

British Library Cataloguing in Publication Data
A catalogue record for this book is available from the British Library

ISBN 978-1-5292-3279-0 hardcover
ISBN 978-1-5292-3280-6 paperback
ISBN 978-1-5292-3281-3 ePub
ISBN 978-1-5292-3282-0 ePdf

The right of Ed Bates, Kanstantsin Dzehtsiarou and Andrew Forde to be identified as authors of this work has been asserted by them in accordance with the Copyright, Designs and Patents Act 1988.

All rights reserved: no part of this publication may be reproduced, stored in a retrieval system, or transmitted in any form or by any means, electronic, mechanical, photocopying, recording, or otherwise without the prior permission of Bristol University Press.

Every reasonable effort has been made to obtain permission to reproduce copyrighted material. If, however, anyone knows of an oversight, please contact the publisher.

The statements and opinions contained within this publication are solely those of the authors and not of the University of Bristol or Bristol University Press. The University of Bristol and Bristol University Press disclaim responsibility for any injury to persons or property resulting from any material published in this publication.

Bristol University Press works to counter discrimination on grounds of gender, race, disability, age and sexuality.

Cover design: Liam Roberts Design
Front cover image: Sandro Weltin

Contents

Table of Cases		viii
List of Abbreviations		xi
About the Authors		xii
Acknowledgements		xiii
Foreword by Daniel Tarschys		xv

1   Introduction — 1
   1 Opening remarks — 1
   2 Rationale for the book — 4
   3 Key themes — 6
   4 A realist underpinning — 8
   5 Structure of the book — 11
   6 Limitations — 14

2   'Therapeutic Admission' (1992–1998) — 16
   1 Introduction: Russia's CoE obligations and its promise to progressively realise CoE values — 16
   2 Russia's CoE obligations and commitments; and CoE monitoring procedures — 18
      2.1 CoE statutory obligations — 18
      2.2 Russia's accession commitments — 19
      2.3 Post-accession monitoring — 21
          2.3.1 The Vienna Declaration (1993) and the CM's Declaration on Compliance with Commitments — 22
          2.3.2 Monitoring by PACE and other CoE actors — 23
      2.4 Monitoring Russia: some reality checks for the CoE — 24
   3 Russia's 'therapeutic admission': the promise to progressively realise CoE values — 28
      3.1 Should law or politics prevail? — 28
      3.2 Russia joins the CoE (1996) and ratifies the ECHR (1998) — 31
      3.3 Early concerns and forewarnings — 33
   4 Conclusion — 36

3	**The Council of Europe and Russia (1998–2013)**	**39**
	1 Introduction: from 'therapeutic admission' to Russia 'at a crossroads'	39
	2 Impunity for serious violations in Chechnya, the North Caucasus and Georgia	42
	2.1 Impunity for grave human rights violations in Chechnya and the North Caucuses	42
	2.1.1 PACE as the guardian of the CoE's values: human rights mandates act on Chechnya, but what of the CM?	43
	2.1.2 After 2005: the ECtHR as the last hope?	49
	2.1.3 'Unresolved impunity': Russia's failure to implement the Chechnya judgments	51
	2.2 Zones of special influence? Transnistria, and the Georgian–Russian conflict of 2008	55
	2.3 Unhappy marriage? Serious violations of the CoE Statute: PACE and the CM's roles	59
	2.3.1 PACE as a guardian of CoE values, but lacking power	61
	2.3.2 The CM: power but lack of political will?	62
	3 Willing patient of 'therapeutic admission'? (1998–2013)	64
	3.1 The path to democracy and the rule of law: the turning tide (2004–2005)	65
	3.2 The turning tide (2004–2005) highlighted at the CoE, and the significance of PACE monitoring	67
	3.3 Digression? Russia, the ECHR and the ECtHR (1998–2012)	70
	3.3.1 The ECtHR's limitations	70
	3.3.2 Russia and the ECHR: initial room for some positivity?	72
	3.3.3 Russia and the ECtHR after 2005: strained relations	75
	4 Russia 'at a crossroads, confronted with the choice of its own future' (2012–2013) and the path adopted	80
	4.1 2012: a 'window of opportunity' for Russia's 'democratic future'	81
	4.2 The choice adopted by the Russian government: the view from 2016 (20 years after accession to the CoE)	84
	4.3 Potentially limiting the influence of the ECHR internally	87
	5 Conclusion	89

4	**The Council of Europe and Russia (2013–2022)**	91
	1 Introduction: Russia's increasing ritualism toward CoE values after 2013 until its expulsion	91
	2 Russia's invasion and annexation of Crimea (2014) and its repercussions (2015–2019): defining moments for the CoE?	93
	2.1 The CoE condemns Russia's actions: Russia precipitates a non-participation crisis	95
	2.1.1 PACE's (April 2014) internal sanctions: did PACE go too far?	97
	2.1.2 Russia boycotts PACE and suspends payments to the CoE	99
	2.1.3 The accountability and human rights case for appeasing Russia	103
	2.2 The ending of the non-participation crisis in June 2019	104
	2.3 Russia's ritualistic return to PACE copper-fastening its impunity for Crimea	108
	2.4 Ruxit avoided, but at what cost to the CoE?	109
	2.4.1 Capitulation?	110
	2.4.2 Russia's bad faith membership	111
	3 After 2019: ritualism?	113
	3.1 'Better in than out': 2019?	113
	3.2 Russia's human rights ritualism at the CoE after 2019–2022: a continuation of before	114
	3.2.1 The European Convention on Human Rights	114
	3.2.2 PACE monitoring (human rights)	117
	3.3 Russia's transition to 'de facto dictatorship'	120
	4 Over to the Court as 'last resort'? Inter-state cases brought against Russia before the ECtHR	121
	4.1 Inter-state cases brought by Ukraine	122
	4.2 Inter-state cases brought by Georgia	125
	4.3 Accountability under the ECHR: to what end?	127
	5 Conclusion	129
	5.1 Russia's persistent breach of CoE obligations, and its damaging membership	130
	5.2 Better in than out? Or, in fact, ritualism?	132
	5.3 The role of the CoE's human rights actors	134
	5.4 Reykjavík rhetoric?	137
5	**The Suspension and Expulsion of Russia: Legality and Legitimacy**	139
	1 Introduction	139
	2 Expulsion of states from international organisations	141

		3 The process of expulsion	145
		3.1 Immediate expulsion	151
		3.2 Phased expulsion ('complementary joint procedure')	151
		4 Comparable cases in the CoE's history	154
		4.1 Greece's exit from the CoE in 1969	154
		4.2 Turkish military action in Cyprus (1974) and military coup (1980)	160
		5 Analysing Russia's expulsion from the CoE	164
		5.1 Russia's invasion and the CM's immediate triggering of Article 8 (24 February 2022)	164
		5.2 PACE's emphatic response: 'the Committee of Ministers should request the Russian Federation to immediately withdraw' (14–15 March 2022)	168
		5.3 Russia's purported withdrawal under Article 7, as the Assembly debates its expulsion (15 March 2022)	170
		5.4 The CM expels Russia under Article 8 (16 March 2022)	173
		5.5 Russia's initial reaction to expulsion	174
		5.6 Criticisms of the CM Resolution of 16 March 2022	176
		5.6.1 Relevance of Russia's notification of withdrawal under Article 7	177
		5.6.2 Failure of the CM to 'request' that Russia withdraw	181
		6 Conclusion	183
6		**The Legacy of Russia's Expulsion on the European Court of Human Rights**	**185**
		1 Introduction	185
		2 The ECtHR and its impact on the legal system in Russia	187
		3 The ECtHR and its continued engagement with the ongoing human rights violations	190
		4 The legal aspects of Russia ceasing to be a party to the ECHR	194
		4.1 Interpretation of Article 58 ECHR adopted by the ECtHR and the CM	194
		4.2 Legal analysis of the chosen solution and alternative perspectives on Article 58	198
		5 Adjudication of the pending cases	201
		5.1 The 'business as usual' model	203
		5.2 The 'pick and choose' model	208
		5.3 The 'radical' model	209
		6 Execution of the judgments against Russia	210
		7 Conclusion	214

7	**Conclusion: A Legacy of Bad Faith**	**216**
	1 Introduction	216
	2 The core argument of the book	218
	3 A dominant legacy of bad faith?	219
	4 Democratic decay, aggressive military actions and the 'Triple Fault' scenario	224
	4.1 Original fault: Russia's bad faith and rejection of CoE values	226
	4.2 Abject failure of the CoE political leadership	227
	4.3 Conditional failure of the CoE system	231
	5 Limiting scope for repetition and adapting to post-peace Europe	236
	5.1 Dealing with the past	237
	5.2 Political renewal based on standards and realism	238
	5.3 Future relationship with Russia	240
	6 Conclusion	242
Index		244

Table of Cases

A.L. (X.W.) v. Russia, no. 44095/14, 29 October 2015
Abakarova v. Russia, no. 16664/07, 15 October 2015
Alekseyev and Others v. Russia, no. 14988/09, 27 November 2018
Alekseyev v. Russia, nos. 4916/07 and 2 others, 21 October 2010
Ananyev and Others v. Russia, 42525/07, 10 January 2012
Ananyev v. Russia, no. 20292/04, 30 July 2009
Anchugov and Gladkov v. Russia, no. 11157/04, 4 July 2013
Aslakhanova and Others v. Russia, no. 2944/06, 18 December 2012
B v. Russia, no. 36328/20, 7 February 2023
Bayev and Others v. Russia, nos. 67667/09 and 2 others, 20 June 2017
Burdov v. Russia, no. 59498/00, 7 May 2002
Burdov v. Russia (no. 2), no. 33509/04, 15 January 2009
Burmych and Others v. Ukraine (striking out) [GC], nos. 46852/13 et al, 12 October 2017
Carter v. Russia, no. 20914/07, 21 September 2021
Catan and Others v. the Republic of Moldova and Russia [GC], nos. 43370/04 and 2 others, ECHR 2012 (extracts)*Cyprus v. Turkey (I)*, no. 6780/74, 10 July 1976
Cyprus v. Turkey (I), no. 6780/74, 26 May 1975
Cyprus v. Turkey (II), no. 6950/75, 10 July 1976
Cyprus v. Turkey (III), no. 8007/77, 4 October 1983
Cyprus v. Turkey (IV) (just satisfaction) [GC], no. 25781/94, ECHR 2014
Denmark, Norway and Sweden v. Greece, no. 4448/70, Commission (plenary) decision, 16 July 1970
Denmark, France, Norway, Sweden and the Netherlands v. Turkey, no. 9940/82 to 9944/82, 7 December 1985
Ecodefence and Others v. Russia, nos. 9988/13 and 60 others, 14 June 2022
Estemirova v. Russia, no. 42705/11, 31 August 2021
Fedotova and Others v. Russia [GC], nos. 40792/10 and 2 others, 17 January 2023
Finogenov and others v. Russia, no. 18299/03, 20 December 2011
Frumkin v. Russia, no. 74568/12, 5 January 2016

Georgia v. Russia (I) [GC], no. 13255/07, 3 July 2014
Georgia v. Russia (II) [GC], no. 38263/08, 21 January 2021
Georgia v. Russia (IV), no. 39611/18, 9 April 2024
Greece v. United Kingdom, no. 176/56, 26 September 1958
Gusinskiy v. Russia, no. 70276/01, 19 May 2004
Ilaşcu and Others v. Moldova and Russia, no. 48787/99, 8 July 2004
Ivanţoc and Others v. Moldova and Russia, no. 23687/05, 15 November 2011 (follow-up case)
Ilgar Mammadov v. Azerbaijan, no. 15172/13, 22 May 2014
Ilgar Mammadov v. Azerbaijan (infringement proceedings) [GC], no. 15172/13, 29 May 2019
Isayeva v. Russia, no. 57950/00, 24 February 2005
Isayeva, Yusupova and Bazayeva v. Russia, no. 57947/00, 24 February 2005
Jehovah's Witnesses of Moscow and Others v. Russia, no. 302/02, 10 June 2010
Kalashnikov v. Russia, no. 47095/99, ECHR 2002-VI
Kavala v. Turkey, no. 28749/18, 10 December 2019
Kavala v. Türkiye (infringement proceedings) [GC], no. 28749/18, 11 July 2022
Khashiyev and Akayeva v. Russia, no. 57942/00, 24 February 2005
Khodorkovskiy v. Russia, no. 5829/04, 31 May 2011
Khodorkovskiy and Lebedev v. Russia, no. 11082/06, 25 July 2013
Klyakhin group v. Russian Federation, no. 46082/99, 30 November 2004
Kogan and Others v. Russia, no. 54003/20, 7 March 2023
Kononov v. Latvia, no. 36376/04, 17 May 2010
Konstantin Markin v. Russia [GC], no. 30078/06, ECHR 2012 (extracts)
Konstantin Markin v. Russia, no. 30078/06, 7 October 2010
Kutayev v. Russia, no. 17912/15, 24 January 2023
Latvia v. Denmark (dec.), no. 9717/20, 9 July 2020
Magnitskiy and Others v. Russia, nos. 32631/09 and 53799/12, 27 August 2019
Mazepa and Others v. Russia, no. 15086/07, 17 July 2018
Mikheyev v. Russian, no. 77617/01, 26 January 2006
Mozer v. the Republic of Moldova and Russia [GC], no. 11138/10, 23 February 2016
Navalnyy and Yashin v. Russia, no. 76204/11, 4 December 2014
Navalnyy and Ofitserov v. Russia, nos. 46632/13 and 28671/14, 23 February 2016
Navalnyye v. Russia, no. 101/15, 17 October 2017
Navalnyy v. Russia (No. 3), no. 36418/20, 6 September 2023
Nemtsova v. Russia, no. 43146/15, 6 September 2023
OAO Neftyanaya Kompaniya Yukos v. Russia (just satisfaction), no. 14902/0, 31 July 2014
OAO Neftyanaya Kompaniya Yukos v. Russia (merits), no. 14902/04, 20 September 2011

Ossewaarde v. Russia, no. 27227/17, 7 March 2023
Philis v. Greece, no. 15264/89, 10 February 1993
Rakevich v. Russia, no. 58973/00, 28 October 2003
Rasul Jafarov v. Azerbaijan, no. 69981/14, 17 March 2016
Russia v. Ukraine (dec.), no. 36958/21, 18 July 2023
Ryabykh v. Russia, no. 52854/99, 24 July 2003
Shamayev and Others v. Georgia and Russia, no. 36378/02, 12 April 2005
Svetova and Others v. Russia, no. 54714/17, 24 January 2023
Tagayeva and Others v. Russia, no. 26562/07, 13 April 2017
Tunikova and Others v. Russia, 55974/16, 14 December 2021
Ukraine v. Russia (re Crimea) (dec.) [GC], nos. 20958/14 and 38334/18, 16 December 2020
Ukraine v. Russia (IX), no. 10691/21
Ukraine v. Russia (VIII), no. 55855/18
Ukraine v. Russia (X), no. 11055/22
Ukraine and the Netherlands v. Russia (dec.), nos. 43800/14, 8019/16 and 28525/20 [GC], 20 November 2022
Volodina v. Russia, no. 41261/17, 9 July 2019
Yuriy Nikolayevich Ivanov v. Ukraine, no. 40450/04, 15 October 2009
Zhdanov and Others v. Russia, no. 12200/08, 16 July 2019

List of Abbreviations

CAHDI	Committee of Legal Advisers on Public International Law
CDDH	Steering Committee for Human Rights
CLAHR	Committee on Legal Affairs and Human Rights
CM	Committee of Ministers
CoE	Council of Europe
CPT	European Committee for the Prevention of Torture and Inhuman or Degrading Treatment or Punishment
ECHR	European Convention on Human Rights
ECtHR	European Court of Human Rights
EHRAC	European Human Rights Advocacy Centre
LGBTI	Lesbian, Gay, Bisexual, Transexual and Intersexual
MFA	Ministry of Foreign Affairs
MRT	Moldavian Republic of Transnistria
NATO	North Atlantic Treaty Organisation
OSCE	Organization for Security and Co-operation in Europe
PACE	Parliamentary Assembly of the Council of Europe
RCC	Russian Constitutional Court
USSR	Union of Soviet Socialist Republics
VCLT	Vienna Convention on the Law of Treaties
WECL	Well-established case law

About the Authors

Ed Bates is Associate Professor at the University of Leicester. He has been a co-author of Harris, O'Boyle and Warbrick, *The Law of the European Convention on Human Rights* for its second, third, fourth and fifth editions (Oxford University Press, 2009, 2014, 2018 and 2023) and is the author of *The Evolution of the European Convention on Human Rights* (Oxford University Press, 2010). He is currently writing a monograph entitled *The European Convention on Human Rights at 75: Its Post-2010 Transformative Era – Decline, Further Evolution, and Realistic Future?* to be published by Oxford University Press.

Kanstantsin Dzehtsiarou is Professor in Human Rights Law at the University of Liverpool. He is an author of three books and over 100 academic articles, review pieces and comments. His research interests spread between interpretation of the European Convention on Human Rights, reform of the European Court of Human Rights, administration of international justice, and comparative and constitutional law. Kanstantsin is a co-founder and co-editor-in-chief of the *European Convention on Human Rights Law Review*.

Andrew Forde is Assistant Professor in Law at Dublin City University (DCU), Adjunct Lecturer at the Irish Centre for Human Rights (University of Galway) and Commissioner on the Irish Human Rights and Equality Commission. He is the author of *European Human Rights Grey Zones: The Council of Europe and Areas of Conflict* (Cambridge University Press, 2024). He spent more than a decade working for the Council of Europe including as human rights advisor and political advisor.

Acknowledgements

It is not an easy task to write a co-authored monograph. It takes a lot of coordination and a lot of trust between the co-authors. Preparation of this monograph required long weekly meetings to discuss, disagree, find compromises and move forward with this project. There are still a few points on which we disagree, so we tried to present various views and perspectives, and the different possible legal solutions that were available. This means that some parts of the monograph do not provide one clear position but a range of them.

This monograph originated from our own exchanges on Twitter ('X') in March 2022. We thought that the most dramatic events in the recent history of the Council of Europe, namely Russia's expulsion from the organisation, and the wider context to that, raised so many important legal issues that it deserved to be addressed in a book. We discussed the framing of our arguments, wrote a book proposal, and submitted it to Bristol University Press. We are hugely grateful to Helen Davis and Grace Carroll from Bristol University Press for their ongoing support and guidance, and their patience given some inevitable delays.

Although the predominant mode of our conversation was via videoconferencing, we managed to meet three times in Liverpool and these meetings proved to be crucial for the development of the project and its ultimate result. We are grateful for the support of the University of Liverpool for partially funding these meetings. Ed Bates would like to acknowledge the support of the Centre for European Law and Internationalisation (Leicester Law School) in relation to the writing of Chapters 2–4. Andrew Forde would like to thank the Irish Centre for Human Rights at the University of Galway for providing a platform to develop several arguments in this book at the 'Lighting the Shade' conference in September 2022.

There are numerous colleagues who helped us with advice, materials, guidance and direction. It will be difficult to mention everyone, so we will list just a few names. We wanted to specifically thank Isabella Risini (Professor, Technical University Georg Agricola, Germany) for her impact and influence over this book at the beginning of the project. Some of the arguments were formed with her priceless help. We are deeply grateful to

Andrew Drzemczewski (former head of the Legal Affairs and Human Rights Department of the Parliamentary Assembly), Jörg Polakiewicz (Director of Legal Advice and Public International Law, Legal Adviser of the Council of Europe), Vassilis Tzevelekos (Reader in Law, University of Liverpool), Lauri Mälksoo (Professor of International Law, University of Tartu) and Philip Leach (Professor of Human Rights Law, Middlesex University). Finally, special thanks to Daniel Tarschys (Secretary General of the Council of Europe, 1994–1999) for his help during the course of this project. Of course, any opinions expressed are our own, as are any errors made. We also wish to thank Daniel Höltgen, the Council of Europe's Director of Communications, for permission to use the cover image which captures a seminal moment in the history of the Council of Europe.

Finally, we wanted to thank our families. This monograph required many hours of extra work, and without their support it would not have been possible to complete it. We thank our partners, children, and extended families for their enormous contribution to this book.

We hope that this book will be useful not only for those who are interested in the history of Russia's membership of the Council of Europe but also for those who study broader questions related to the integrity of international organisations, the role of member states, the law of membership sanctions and the legitimacy of decision-making in such organisations.

Foreword

*Daniel Tarschys,
Secretary General of the Council of Europe,
1994–1999*

In Central and Eastern Europe, the 1990s was a decade of chaos and hope. The Soviet economy had collapsed, and with it Moscow's grip on the satellite countries and its own society. Some dozen new states emerged on the map of Europe, and another scant dozen went from formal to genuine sovereignty. Amid this turmoil there was a deep longing to join Western Europe, to partake of its material wealth but also of its spiritual values and social systems.

In consequence, there were many knocks at the doors of the various European organisations. Foremost among these were the North Atlantic Treaty Organisation (NATO) and the European Union (EU), but these were distant dreams. The Council of Europe (CoE) was more accessible and therefore became the first port of call, along with the Organization for Security and Co-operation in Europe (OSCE), where geography was a sufficient entrance ticket, and the newly established Partnership for Peace, a much lighter version of NATO, with a generous open-door policy.

What made the CoE so attractive was not least its staunchly democratic profile. It had long been at loggerheads with the Kremlin, which had blocked the membership of any state under its control. Even Finland with its more limited dependence on Moscow had been prevented from joining the CoE, though it had long taken part in many of its activities.

The relatively meagre benefits of CoE accession certainly did not satisfy the great hunger for European inclusion and integration, but it was at least an early appetiser. For many politicians, experts and bureaucrats from Central and Eastern Europe, its byzantine network of committees, working parties and specialist projects provided the first opportunities for encounters with Western European colleagues.

For the CoE itself, the great Eastern enlargement was a game-changer. It was, as this excellent book reminds us, a very poor organisation. In economic terms, its budget was about a fifth of 1 per cent of the European Union's. It also continued to be resource-constrained by its member states.

Year after year, the stern message from the capitals was zero nominal growth. In contrast, the expectations pinned to the organisation grew all the more expansive over time.

Nevertheless, a lot was achieved on this shoestring budget. The staff members of the CoE had their precious black books of contacts with committed and enterprising colleagues in the member states who were often allowed to give help and advice at no cost to the organisation.

Some parts of Council expanded in response to external pressure, not least the various systems of monitoring mechanisms. In the early decades of the CoE, the European Commission of Human Rights and the European Court of Human Rights (ECtHR) had hardly been overburdened with work. The commissioners and the judges lived serenely at home, with only occasional visits to Strasbourg to inspect their half-empty in-trays. This changed, gradually, with the growing awareness of the European Convention on Human Rights among European citizens and particularly with the influx of the new member states.

A fusion of the two supervisory bodies became necessary, as did the elevation of the supreme functions to full-time judges working from Strasbourg-based offices. A new edifice was erected and several reforms were also undertaken to help the judges cope with their mounting workload. Meanwhile, separate oversight systems were also set up for many other treaties. Though some conventions were dead on arrival and others succumbed along the way, the total number of such instruments is now 224.

The authors in the present volume emphasise the different messages that can be heard from various institutions and bodies within the CoE. This is an important observation. The literature on international organisations in general often suffers from the unitary actor fallacy. We are incessantly told that the EU says this, that the Organisation for Economic Co-operation and Development (OECD) advocates that, or that the UN has taken or refrained from certain positions. But in actual fact each of these conglomerates is a choir of many voices, fora where governments and individual professionals take many different stands. And governments, in turn, are not always so consistent or unambiguous either.

In the CoE there have long been tensions between an activist Parliamentary Assembly, a normally reticent Committee of Ministers (CM) and a highly qualified professional staff with many politically astute members. The dynamics of the organisation owes much to the interplay between these three forces. Add to that the often enterprising and innovative ECtHR and the panoply of other supervisory bodies, and what comes out is a mixture of statements bound to raise the blood pressure in several capitals.

The enlargement of the CoE was always controversial. Cautious governments, a sizable minority in the Parliamentary Assembly, and many members of the staff kept warning that the various candidate countries were far from mature enough to assume the obligations of membership. The monitoring system, also called the Halonen mechanism, was introduced to convert the one-shot entrance examination into a process of enduring oversight and continued support to the new member states.

Nobody will contest that the Russian Federation with its long and tragic history of human rights violations and aggressive behaviour towards its neighbours presented a particular challenge in this respect. Ultimately, its transgressions made its continued membership impossible. For now.

The contours of Russia's membership in the CoE are very well covered in this volume. What remains for future research may be a more thorough mapping of its impact in particular policy areas and through particular decisions at the individual level. We know little about the personal chemistry that its accession generated. Thousands of applications were submitted to the ECtHR. Outrageous practices in the criminal system were examined by the European Committee for the Prevention of Torture and Inhuman or Degrading Treatment or Punishment (CPT). Many important encounters were organised. A high-level conference indelibly imprinted in my memory was held in Moscow on 3–4 June 1999 and devoted to the abolition of capital punishment. Solemn messages from President Yeltsin, Prime Minister Stepashin and the Speakers of the Duma and the Senate were read out. On this occasion it was also announced that in the first half of 1999, 716 prisoners on death row had had their sentences converted to prison terms.

What remains from Russia's membership of the CoE are many paper trails, but our knowledge about its deeper effects is limited. There is still work for many historians.

1

Introduction

1 Opening remarks

This book analyses the troubled history of a complex relationship between Russia and the Council of Europe (CoE), a story of failed hopes, bad faith and false promises. We examine matters comprehensively, offering a fresh perspective on events in the light of Russia's expulsion from the CoE. We hope that this book will not only present an overview of the events spanning three decades, but that it will also be read and considered by decision-makers to avoid repeating the mistakes that were made during Russia's troubled membership of the CoE.

The Statute of the CoE[1] was opened for signature on 5 May 1949 and by 1989, when Finland joined, the CoE included all states of Western Europe.[2] The CoE Committee of Ministers (CM) faced a profound question at the end of the 1980s: should the former communist countries of Central and Eastern Europe be integrated into the collaborative, normative framework that the CoE offered? We know now that the CoE's leadership answered this question affirmatively. At its core this was rather a matter of *realpolitik* and the balancing of risks than one of moral righteousness. The road to membership was cleared when Mikhail Gorbachev, then Chairman of the Supreme Soviet of the Soviet Union, made his interest to significantly strengthen association with the CoE in a landmark address to the Parliamentary Assembly of the Council of Europe (PACE) in 1989.[3] He pointed to the potential to create a European legal space and emphasised the notion of the

---

[1] Council of Europe Statute, ETS No. 1, 5 May 1949.
[2] For a full list of members as of 1 February 2024, see www.coe.int/en/web/about-us/our-member-states [Accessed 13 June 2024].
[3] Speech made by Mikhail Gorbachev, as President of the Supreme Soviet of the Soviet Union to the Assembly, 6 July 1989, available from: www.cvce.eu/en/obj/address_given_by_mikhail_gorbachev_to_the_council_of_europe_6_july_1989-en-4c021687-98f9-4727-9e8b-836e0bc1f6fb.html [Accessed 13 June 2024].

CoE being 'a common European home'⁴ which 'rules out the probability of an armed clash and the very possibility of the use or threat of force in Europe'.⁵ These words resonated in the CoE's 1993 Vienna Declaration,⁶ with its references to the 'end of the division of Europe' as hope for a new era, one in which Europe could 'become a vast area of democratic security'. Given that Russia was expelled from the CoE in 2022 as a direct result of its full-scale aggression against Ukraine and having occupied great portions of its neighbour's territory, history has shown the spirit of these words to be, ultimately, short-lived. Nevertheless, Gorbachev's speech and the fall of communism in Eastern Europe from the late 1980s onwards turned out to be a decisive point for the CoE as it then embarked on a major phase of eastward enlargement.⁷

Russia applied to join the CoE on 7 May 1992 after almost two decades of varying degrees of informal engagement in areas such as youth policy and environmental protection.⁸ On 28 February 1996 Russia became the 39th member state of the CoE, despite legitimate questions being asked about its readiness for this normative revolution. Russia's integration into the family of European democracies was seen as an opportunity, albeit one replete with challenges. The German Chancellor at the time, Helmut Kohl, observed that not only would the CoE have to adapt to this new reality but 'one of the great challenges of the years ahead will be getting Russia, too, to see its future in European terms'.⁹

---

4   The first time the idea of a 'common European home' was touted was by French member of parliament and later Secretary General of the Council of Europe Catherine Lalumière in her capacity as rapporteur for the last of three debates held at PACE on East–West relations from 1986 to October 1988, after which she stated as follows: 'The Council is also best placed to explore with the countries of eastern Europe, the potential for a European awareness, a European identity, a "common European home", first with one country, then with another, until it finally extends from the Atlantic to the Urals.' For a related discussion, see Haller, B. (5 May 2019) 'Mikhail Gorbachev's historic visit to the Council of Europe', available from: https://70.coe.int/visite-historique-gorbatchev-en.html [Accessed 13 June 2024].
5   Gorbachev, n 3.
6   Council of Europe Vienna Declaration, Vienna, 9 October 1993.
7   See Huber, D. (1999) *A Decade Which Made History: The Council of Europe 1989–1999*, Strasbourg: Council of Europe Press.
8   See 'History of the Russian Federation's Participation in the Council of Europe', archived site of the Permanent Representation of Russia to the Council of Europe, 15 March 2022, available from: https://coe.mid.ru/en_GB/istoria-ucastia-rossii-v-sovete-evropy [Accessed 13 June 2024].
9   Kohl, H. (1995) Speech made to the Parliamentary Assembly of the Council of Europe, 28 September 1995, available from: https://assembly.coe.int/nw/xml/Speeches/Speech-XML2HTML-EN.asp?SpeechID=120&a1=3&p2=3 [Accessed 13 June 2024].

Russia's 26-year membership of the CoE was, to say the least, a troubled one. As set out in Chapters 2 and 3 of this book, after a controversial accession to the CoE in the 1990s, there was a short period of cautious optimism. At that time it was expected that, as part of a 'therapeutic membership' of the CoE, Russia would progressively realise the organisation's values. This hope was hard to reconcile with the atrocities occurring in Chechnya in the late 1990s. Although the initial optimism was not completely groundless, as there had been important (early) reforms in domestic law, these reforms did not bring a sustainable change in Russia. Another shift occurred in the mid-2000s, such that the initial optimism about Russia's 'socialisation'[10] was fading fast by the end of that decade. By then the Russian government's attitude to the CoE had become far more negative and at times confrontational such that there was even talk of its 'subversive' influence on the CoE.[11] The latter had to cope as best it could with an increasingly obstinate Russia, one that was prepared, in effect, to block vital reforms to the European Court of Human Rights' (ECtHR) functioning,[12] and ignore PACE's strong criticism of it in the context of the Georgian–Russian war of 2008.[13]

By 2012, PACE had expressed great concern about the anti-democratic path Russia was pursuing, urging change, hoping that there still was a 'window of opportunity' left for its democratic future.[14] However, it is now clear that the relationship between Russia and the CoE was regressing in a relatively slow but steadily downwards direction. The Russian authorities demonstrated that they did not feel constrained by the negative reactions of the CoE and chose its course, via military aggression against Ukraine, initially in Crimea and eastern Ukraine. When, in response to this, PACE sought to condemn and discipline Russia while keeping the channels of dialogue open, Russia manufactured a major political and financial crisis at the CoE which resulted in the latter, as viewed by many, appearing to capitulate in 2019.[15] Over the 2010s, then, Russia's engagement with the CoE was, on the one hand, essentially ritualistic and, on the other, marked by egregious bad faith, as it aimed to shake the very foundations of Europe's oldest inter-governmental organisation.

Could matters get any worse? In fact, the decision by the Russian government to launch a full-scale aggression against Ukraine on 24 February

---

[10] See Roter, P. (2017) 'Russia in the Council of Europe: participation a la carte', in L. Mälksoo and W. Benedek (eds) *Russia and the European Court of Human Rights: The Strasbourg Effect*, Cambridge: Cambridge University Press, pp 26–56.
[11] See Chapter 3.
[12] See Chapter 3 regarding Russia's refusal to ratify Protocol 14 to the ECHR.
[13] See Chapter 3.
[14] See Chapter 3.
[15] See Chapter 4.

2022 marked the decisive end of Russia's pretence of commitment to CoE standards and led directly to the CM's unprecedented decision on 16 March 2022 to expel Russia from the CoE with immediate effect, in accordance with Article 8 of the Statute.[16] The invasion was so profoundly incompatible with the Statute and values of the CoE, there was hardly any other option than expulsion. Secretary General of the CoE Pejčinović Burić commented that '[t]o have kept Russia within our Organisation would have strained our credibility past breaking point. The Russian Federation does not respect our standards. And some lines simply cannot be crossed.'[17]

The inglorious end to the story of building a 'common European home' that includes Russia, serves as one of the main inspirations for this book. It is a first attempt to consider how matters could reach such a dire state of affairs. In seeking to answer this question we try to find evidence in what occurred over the period leading up to its expulsion, during which the troubled CoE–Russia relationship was becoming progressively more obvious. Russia's membership and expulsion represents a bitter lesson for Europe and for the CoE in particular, but it offers lessons which, if acted upon, could make the institution stronger. We discuss the legacy of Russian membership and its expulsion, arguing that although the main and overarching responsibility for what happened lies with the Russian government, there were situations in which the CoE could have certainly acted more decisively and more quickly to defend its values. This case offers important lessons because of its unprecedented nature that no other state has been previously expelled from the CoE.

2 Rationale for the book

Some of the challenges just set out have received little or no treatment in academic literature to date, hence the ambition of this book is to provide an evidence-based response to them. This is the first comprehensive overview of the Russian membership since it was expelled. Chapters 2, 3 and 4 of the book look at the relationship between the CoE and Russia from the early 1990s until the eve of expulsion in 2022. Chapters 4 and 5 then examine the expulsion itself and the many issues arising from it.

On the one hand, the literature on Russia's membership of the CoE is remarkably sparse. It has tended to focus on individual events and episodes,

---

[16] CoE Statute, n 1, Article 8. Also see Chapter 5.
[17] Speech by Marija Pejčinović Burić, Secretary General of the Council of Europe, public event with the Institute of International Affairs of the University of Iceland, on the Future of Europe, 24 November 2022, available from: www.coe.int/en/web/secretary-general/-/public-event-with-the-institute-of-international-affairs-of-the-university-of-iceland-on-the-future-of-europe [Accessed 13 June 2024].

rather than considering the bigger picture in a more holistic manner.[18] Most academic pieces focus on Russia through the lens of the European Convention on Human Rights (ECHR),[19] usually in relation to specific judgments, and notably so in more recent years as regards certain inter-state cases. This book aims to fill this gap in the literature.

On the other hand, there is also a dearth of literature on the broader law, standards and systems of the Council of Europe,[20] and especially so in relation to the major issues arising in 2022: expulsion of members from this organisation, and the aftermath issues arising. Moreover, apart from some notable exceptions, at the time of writing there is remarkably little written about the process of expulsion of Russia from the CoE.[21] Chapters 5 and 6 of the book review the available literature and consider their relevance and applicability to what happened after 24 February 2022.

The inherent importance of such a study will, it is hoped, be self-evident. From one angle there is value in providing an account of Russia's membership of the CoE, given the significance of that state, the gravity of the events which came within the purview of the CoE over the period from 1996 to 2022, and the relevance of what occurred over those years to so many people in Russia *and* neighbouring territories. From another angle, there is a need to provide an overall account of this experience, so that the damage done to the CoE and the issues arising may be identified, as a first step in drawing lessons for the future.

Drawing on and seeking to make sense of a vast amount of material issued by CoE actors, the book aims to contextualise and provide perspective on Russia's troubled membership of the CoE over its entire period of membership, including its expulsion and the immediate aftermath of this. Such a wide-angle and long-term perspective allows one to take stock of

---

[18] The main exception is an edited collection by Malfliet, K. and Parmentier, S. (eds) (2010) *Russia and the Council of Europe: 10 Years After*, London: Palgrave. However, this was limited in its coverage, and does not take account of crucial events from the late 2000s onwards.

[19] See especially, Mälksoo, L. and Benedek, W. (eds) (2018) *Russia and the European Court of Human Rights: The Strasbourg Effect*, Cambridge: Cambridge University Press. This mainly focusses on Russia–ECtHR interactions from the perspective of 2016–2017.

[20] Some exceptions include Schmahl, S. and Breuer, M. (eds) (2017) *The Council of Europe: Its Law and Policies*, Oxford: Oxford University Press; Kleinsorge, T.E.J. (2015) *Council of Europe (CoE)*, Leiden: Kluwer Law International; Forde, A. (2024) *European Human Rights Grey Zones: The Council of Europe and Areas of Conflict*, Cambridge: Cambridge University Press.

[21] See, for example, Magliveras, K.D. (2023) 'Legal and procedural issues arising from the expulsion of the Russian Federation from the Council of Europe', *International and Comparative Law Review*, 23(1): 95–116; Drzemczewski, A. and Lawson, R. (2022) 'Exclusion of the Russian Federation from the Council of Europe and the ECHR: an overview', *Baltic Yearbook of International Law*, vol. 21(1), pp 38–98.

the overall story of Russia's failed 'socialisation' within the CoE context, and the extraordinarily negative pressures and influences it placed on the governing bodies of the organisation. No such account currently exists and, as such, the full extent of Russia's bad faith influence on the CoE has not been documented and analysed.

Commentators and academics will be most familiar with Russia's interactions with the European Court of Human Rights (ECtHR), as this is where the vast majority of literature is focussed. However, while the book includes coverage of the role performed by the ECtHR in relation to Russia, much of the attention, especially early in the book, focuses on the importance – and failings of – the far less well-known, yet crucially important, statutory organs of the CoE, above all PACE and the CM. It was these institutions – *not* the Court – which were at the forefront of managing Russia's overall relations with the CoE. As shall be seen, they struggled to cope with Russia, particularly when it acted in bad faith and arguably breached Article 3 of the CoE Statute in serious ways which would have merited action under Article 8 of the CoE Statute (according to which a state may be expelled from the CoE) much earlier than 2022. This book shines a light on this hitherto largely unappreciated aspect of Russia's relations with the CoE. It exposes Russia's broken promises to its rights-holders and to the CoE, how it breached its international legal obligations and commitments, and yet how it was not properly held to account by the appropriate institutions, in particular the CM. It is against that backdrop, that any assessment of the Court should be made. It should not become a scapegoat for the lack of normative progress generally.

In these ways, the analysis of the role of Russia within the CoE presents an excellent, however regrettable, opportunity to unpack the challenges of dealing with a powerful member state acting in bad faith. Having said that, we are not intending to extrapolate our analysis to each and every case of troubled membership, of which there are many. The case of Greece in the 1960s, discussed in Chapter 5, is very different to the expulsion of Russia, for example. There is no shortage of states expressing dissent or backlash towards the CoE, but their features are different and one must avoid conflating them. Our intention in this book is to identify certain systematic challenges which deserve significantly more consideration from the member states, statutory actors and the Secretariat of the CoE, if we are to ensure the CoE is ready for some of the challenges of the future.

3 Key themes

The overarching narrative of this book is that of Russia's attempted transition towards European liberal democratic standards within the CoE framework, and its gradual but dramatic retreat from that path. This is a long and multifaceted story but ultimately culminates in Russia's dramatic expulsion from the CoE and its legacy. The idea of applying membership sanctions against Russia only came to fruition in 2022 but had been discussed long before.[22] As we assess this experience, a major asymmetry becomes obvious between Russia, as the world's largest state and a geopolitical superpower, and the CoE, a relatively weak intergovernmental organisation with a staunchly collegiate culture within its main executive organ (the CM), a persistently inadequate budget and deliberately reductionist Statute. Such circumstances meant that the CoE was always likely to be strongly influenced by, if not beholden to, the interests of Russia – or indeed any major player for that matter – unless the other CoE member states actively defended the CoE's integrity and counter-balanced any emerging nefarious interests in the spirit of collective responsibility.

Our intention in this book is to document and analyse the experience of Russia's membership of the CoE in order to draw lessons and trigger further consideration on how the CoE, as a system, can be strengthened to ensure maximum effectiveness even in the face of bad faith in the future. This discussion may serve as a platform for further research into the structure and functioning of the CoE.

As we explore the dynamics between Russia and the CoE over almost 30 years of membership, we highlight significant systemic deficiencies including an apparent inadequate sense of collective responsibility of member states and a lack of consideration of effective membership sanctions. These systemic deficiencies were detectable in the CoE's inability to address the poor rate of execution of the ECtHR judgments or the inadequate follow-up to monitoring mechanism recommendations, but became especially obvious when the organisation was faced with major violations of the Statute such as in 2008 during the war in Georgia and in 2014 when Russia annexed Crimea. Our critical analysis of the CoE is intended to diagnose weaknesses as a first step to collectively considering how the organisation might build forward stronger. The story of expulsion of Russia is testament to the need for the CoE member states through the CM to exercise their collective responsibilities towards the CoE more consistently and decisively, including, for instance, by resourcing it properly.

It is important at the outset to clarify that when we discuss Russia, we refer primarily (unless we state otherwise) to the past and current Russian

---

[22] Dzehtsiarou, K. and Coffey, D.K. (2019) 'Suspension and expulsion of members of the Council of Europe: difficult decisions in troubled times', *International and Comparative Law Quarterly*, 68(2): 443–76.

political regime led by Vladimir Putin,[23] and not the many brave citizens, lawyers, human rights defenders, civil society activists and others who openly and directly opposed the country's retreat to authoritarianism.

Russia's democratic decay and expulsion from the CoE is deeply regrettable but was by no means inevitable. Instead, it was the result of deliberate choices made by the Russian authorities based on their increasingly protectionist worldview which developed a pattern of behaviour that systematically undermined basic rule of law and democratic principles for the people of Russia. The Russian authorities were presented with the opportunity to join the family of European states on an equal footing, discarding the most negative legacies of the Soviet Union with a view to enhancing its democratic order and transforming the quality of life for its people. This could only happen if Russia engaged with its membership obligations in good faith. We argue that it was clear for many years that this was not happening and that the CoE member states were not prepared to decisively respond to the deterioration of the situation in Russia until the cataclysmic events of February 2022 forced them to do so. Indeed, it is quite possible – perhaps even likely – that had the war in Ukraine not dramatically escalated in February 2022, Russia would still be a member state of the CoE today. But the question remains, could the CoE have done more to avert the decline of Russia into aggressive totalitarianism, which ultimately led to its expulsion?

4 A realist underpinning

One must approach such an analysis with a high degree of realism. The CoE is a political organisation with a restricted mandate and is necessarily limited in what it can achieve as regards influencing member state behaviour.[24] The organisation is built on the foundation of *pacta sunt servanda* (i.e. agreements must be kept) and the good faith of its member states. It does not have the power, for example, to impose significant fines on its states. If a particular state is not prepared to act in good faith, and if the CM is unwilling or unable to uphold the standards to which all have voluntarily subscribed, the CoE as a body corporate is effectively powerless.

There are various ways in which the CoE can seek to influence a member state: by expressing concern over the situation of human rights, the rule of

---

[23] Vladimir Putin came to power in Russia on 31 December 1999 when the outgoing President Boris Yeltsin unexpectedly appointed Putin as interim President. He was duly elected on 7 May 2000 and has been effectively ruling Russia since then. Having served as Prime Minister of Russia between 2008 and 2012 and as President thereafter, the majority of the Russian membership of the CoE took place with Putin in power in Russia.

[24] See Chapter 2, section 2.4.

law or democracy in that state, principally through adopted texts of the CM,[25] formal monitoring and advisory processes, and judgments of the ECtHR. The precise effect of these various means is not always immediately clear, but they should not be dismissed as insignificant. Recalcitrant states can choose to ignore any or all of these actions of the CoE if they are prepared to accept the political cost of being seen to do so, which is not particularly high. That said, the only definite sanction options available to the CoE are the refusal to ratify delegation credentials at PACE,[26] and suspension from rights of representation, or expulsion procedures under Statutory Article 8. Perennial financial constraints undoubtedly also have a certain 'chilling effect' on the effectiveness of the organisation, something which Russia, as a 'big payer' in the CoE context, exploited.[27]

In reality, one can argue that the system is not structurally equipped to ensure meaningful checks and balances. The CM is the key decision-making body of the CoE and it makes the most important decisions concerning the functioning of the CoE. It is composed of the representatives of the national governments, whereas members of national parliaments are represented in PACE, and local and regional representatives at the Congress. PACE has limited decision-making power but retains significant political and consultative authority. It also elects judges to the ECtHR. The Secretary General plays a representative role and leads on the day-to-day operational functioning of the organisation. The CM retains an extensive margin of manoeuvre. This level of near-exclusive authority is relevant in the context of our discussion on the expulsion procedure under Article 8 of the CoE Statute,[28] which is the exclusive province of the CM, and is problematic as it is an 'all or nothing' power. Paradoxically, though, as we will see, it is the other actors in the system, such as, especially, PACE and the Commissioner for Human Rights, which have arguably served as far more diligent and proactive guardians of the values of the ECHR and Statutory Article 3 than the CM.

Therefore, considering the function of various statutory and other institutions within the CoE is relevant not just with respect to Russia, but

---

[25] Most frequently in the form of Recommendations of the Committee of Ministers to member states, but also through other texts such as Decisions and Resolutions.

[26] In accordance with Rules 7, 8, 9, 10 of the Rules of Procedure of PACE, as set out under Resolution 1202 (1999), adopted on 4 November 1999, with subsequent modifications of the Rules of Procedure, available from: https://assembly.coe.int/nw/xml/rop/RoP-XML2HTML-EN.asp?id=ENtoc_N0A29C3B0N0A2D67E8 [Accessed 13 June 2024]. See Chapter 2.

[27] See Chapter 4, text accompanying n 61 and 231, on threats to withdraw funding and suspension of funding from 2017 onwards. For earlier, see Chapter 3, text accompanying n 31 and 141.

[28] See Chapter 5.

also in the context of broader tendencies towards democratic backsliding and challenges to the CoE's normative authority. It is also important to recognise that Russia has not been the only source of damaging dissent within the CoE in recent years, and that other factors have served to weaken this international organisation and, especially, its Court over recent years. The United Kingdom's drumbeat debate over whether or not to leave the ECHR,[29] Hungary's suggestion that the ECHR is a threat to European security,[30] Poland's questioning of the authority of the Court's jurisprudence,[31] Azerbaijan's protracted non-execution of the *Mammadov* judgment leading to the first engagement of Article 46(4),[32] Türkiye's withdrawal from the Istanbul Convention[33] and persistent non-execution of the *Kavala* judgment[34] are just some examples of national discourses and actions which have had or are having a corrosive effect on the integrity of the CoE and the Convention system. Already in 2018, Thorbjørn Jagland, then Secretary General of the CoE, observed that '[t]here have been attempts to undermine institutions at the European level, namely the Council of Europe and the European Court of Human Rights themselves'.[35] He went further still in 2019 to say that: 'In parts of the continent, its standards are often called into question and its institutions – the European Court of Human Rights in particular – attacked. For some, multilateralism is now the subject of suspicion, and the international rule of law regarded as an obstacle to action rather than the guarantor of individuals' rights.'[36]

Examining and criticising the work of the CoE is not something to be concerned with in itself. Indeed, the lack of visibility and democratic debate at national level about the positive or negative effects of the CoE is one of its greatest weaknesses, so such a debate should be embraced as a healthy feature of any democracy. However, questioning the status or the fundamental

---

[29] See Bates, E. (2024) 'UK withdrawal from the ECHR ('BrECHRit'): from taboo to tenable?', *European Convention on Human Rights Law Review*, 5(1): 24–49.

[30] See, for example, www.euractiv.com/section/global-europe/news/orban-attacks-the-european-court-of-human-rights-at-epp-congress/ [Accessed 13 June 2024].

[31] See, for instance, https://hudoc.echr.coe.int/app/conversion/pdf/?library=ECHR&id=003-7573075-10409301&filename=Non-compliance%20with%20interim%20measure%20in%20Polish%20judiciary%20cases.pdf [Accessed 13 June 2024].

[32] *Ilgar Mammadov v. Azerbaijan* (infringement proceedings) [GC], no. 15172/13, 29 May 2019.

[33] Available from: www.coe.int/nb/web/commissioner/-/turkey-s-announced-withdrawal-from-the-istanbul-convention-endangers-women-s-rights [Accessed 13 June 2024].

[34] *Kavala v. Türkiye* (infringement proceedings) [GC], no. 28749/18, 11 July 2022.

[35] Annual Report of the Secretary General of the Council of Europe (2018), Strasbourg: Council of Europe, p 4.

[36] Annual Report of the Secretary General of the Council of Europe (2019), Strasbourg: Council of Europe, p 13.

legitimacy of the CoE and the ECtHR per se is a different matter, as it is usually designed to expressly undermine the European system of human rights protection. This book emphasises, in stark terms, the importance of member states exercising their collective responsibilities for the integrity of the system both at the level of the CM, as well as in their national contexts.

5 Structure of the book

This book proceeds on the basis that Russia's relationship with the CoE may be divided into three broad periods, each with various phases of engagement: the first period covers 1992–2013 (accession, and the first decade or so of membership), the second from 2014 to 2022 (which includes the invasion of Ukraine and annexation of Crimea and the subsequent non-participation crisis induced by Russia), and finally the post-2022 phase (covering the expulsion, the issues arising and the aftermath). The aim in identifying successive periods is to try to illustrate the main trends as regards the Russia–CoE relationship over the term of its membership, often punctuated by very significant events. We acknowledge that the phases lack a certain amount of nuance, with aspects of each phase naturally running into the next while others may be identifiable throughout. Nonetheless, the structure of the book seeks to generally align with this chronology of events.

Our first substantive chapter, Chapter 2, focusses on the period 1992–1998, including the lead up to Russia's accession to the CoE in 1996, and the obligations it undertook when doing so, including ratification of the ECHR in 1998. The starting point for the analysis in this chapter, which we refer to as Russia's 'therapeutic admission', is to examine the obligations that Russia accepted to progressively realise as a member state of the CoE in the context of the strategic decision by the heads of states of the CoE to copper-fasten the institution's role as 'the pre-eminent European political institution capable of welcoming, on an equal footing and in permanent structures, the democracies of Europe freed from communist oppression'.[37] We note that Russia's CoE membership was principally secured to help galvanise the forces of democracy in Russia, and offer political support to the risks taken by its leaders. While we accept that decisions were made at a point in time based on prevailing and compelling political considerations, the chapter demonstrates that the euphoria surrounding CoE expansion and the enthusiasm for Russia to be part of it, may have detracted from the necessity to place much greater effort into pressing for reforms to ensure that the new-entrant state came close to CoE standards in the pre-accession phase when the organisation arguably had the greatest leverage. In some

---

[37] CoE Vienna Declaration, n 6.

ways, perhaps, the CoE was seen as a relatively low-risk arena to develop and gauge the potential for deeper relations with Russia in the longer term. The importance of leveraging progress in the pre-accession period, however, was all the more important given the very strong message of caution from PACE about Russia's lack of readiness to join the organisation in the period immediately prior to it being admitted.

In Chapter 3 we turn to the period after ratification of the ECHR in 1998 up to 2013. This chapter explores how Russia went from being, apparently, a 'willing patient of therapeutic admission' to choosing a different path based on a range of challenging considerations about its own future. In this respect, we consider to what extent it could be said that by 2012 the Russian authorities had engaged with the CoE in good faith. We argue that from 2005 it was evident that Russia was becoming increasingly authoritarian internally and this also affected its practice of engagement with the CoE. This reference period includes the second Chechen War as well as the 2008 war between Russia and Georgia. The inevitable outcome of these two conflicts, that by 2012 the Russian government was flouting many of its CoE obligations, was well documented by various CoE monitoring mechanisms. We conclude that the tolerance for impunity, enduring non-execution of judgments of the ECtHR domestically, the political apathy regarding the concerns of the CoE, and Russia's actions in Chechnya and the Caucuses were in many ways emblematic of the deepening crisis in the relationship between Russia and the CoE.

Though the reader will of course be aware that matters worsened significantly from 2014 when Russia's war in Ukraine began, Chapter 4 provides further context to the deteriorating relationship up to 2022, which is characterised by increasing ritualism toward CoE values as well as brazen bad faith engagement, right up to the point of expulsion. The key events in this period include the illegal annexation of Crimea and the 'non-participation crisis' which illustrated not only antagonism and implied threats emanating from Russia towards the CoE, but also a closing window of opportunity for democracy in Russia. This would culminate in a series of low points for the integrity of the CoE in terms of its responses to the important events occurring. The chapter examines the apparent consideration as to whether it was better for Russia to remain in the CoE, even as a bad faith actor, than outside. At a time when the organisation faced an existential crisis, member states failed to respond with the necessary strength, clarity and decisiveness that should have been expected in line with the object and purpose of the CoE Statute. A final section of this chapter examines the inter-state cases directed against Russia, including those concerning Ukraine, and particularly Crimea.

In Chapter 5 we consider the legality and legitimacy of the membership sanctions applied to Russia in 2022. We point out that the CoE acted with uncharacteristic speed and decisiveness in response to Russia's aggression against Ukraine in February 2022 and the CM suspended and initiated the expulsion procedure the day after the military attack took place. Accordingly, on 16 March 2022, after receiving an Opinion from PACE, the CM decided to expel Russia from the organisation. While we have no doubt this was the correct decision, justifiable legally, morally and politically, we discuss the procedure applied by the CM within the precise scope of the appropriate provisions in the Statute, in particular the absence of a formal 'request' for Russia to withdraw before it was expelled, as is prescribed by the Statute. We conclude that the unprecedented expulsion of Russia from the CoE is an important example of practice that demonstrates that a state can be expelled if it undermines the foundational principles of an organisation, though the threshold for deploying it remains, for now, exceptionally high.

We then turn to the legacy of Russia's expulsion on the ECtHR in Chapter 6. We observe that Russia's expulsion had a significant impact on the European human rights system, not least in terms of the number of former rights-holders no longer served by that system. We consider that although the Court was, in general, quite effective at the micro level in Russia, including providing 'just satisfaction' (in accordance with Article 41, ECHR) in ordinary cases, it was much less so in terms of fostering systemic changes in law, policy or practice in Russia. Now that Russia is no longer a member state, even these modest areas of influence have disappeared and the Court will not be able to make *any* meaningful impact on the human rights situation in areas under Russian jurisdiction, be that within or beyond Russian borders. In the second part of this chapter, we turn to the complexity of interpretation of Article 58 of the ECHR, which regulates how the Convention can be denounced. The key issue of contention here is whether Russia should have ceased being a party to the Convention from the moment of expulsion by the CM (16 March 2012) or six months later. It seems that the expulsion of Russia has created a precedent which clarifies the interpretation of Article 58 of the ECHR such that a state will continue to be a party to that instrument for a residual six months in effectively all circumstances. Finally, in this chapter we consider the challenge of implementation of the judgments which are still pending execution before the CM in respect of Russia and suggest the *sui generis* nature of this situation can provide a justification for innovation by the CM, subject to the political will of the remaining member states.

To conclude, in the final chapter we take stock of the overall experience of Russia's membership to draw out some possible lessons for the future. We note that although the authorities of Russia are exclusively responsible for their violations of the Convention and the Statute, the experience of engagement and the asymmetric responses by the CoE to the serious and egregious breaches of its norms point to a number of systemic and structural weaknesses within the CoE. We refer to these as the 'Triple Fault' scenario. Primary responsibility for this crisis rests with Russia, due to its pattern of behaviour and bad faith over many years, culminating in its gross violations of Statutory Article 3 in particular. A secondary failure relates to the inability, unwillingness or both, of the CM to effectively safeguard the Statute despite progressive democratic decay, verified deterioration of human rights and rule of law standards and increasing hostility towards international human rights law. The most obvious example of this is the lack of meaningful response to the illegal annexation of Crimea, which by any objective measure was a grave violation of the Statute and a sanctionable offence. And finally, a third more conditional failure is that of the CoE system to effectuate compliance with CoE values and standards.

The chapter then examines how the CoE might consider adapting to a post-peace Europe, such as establishing its own internal processes to deal with the past or exploring how the Statute might be refreshed to face 21st-century challenges. Finally, we note that consideration must be given to how and in what circumstances, formal relations with Russia can be pursued in the future, and to what ends. We argue that the reintegration of Russia into the CoE should remain a viable long-term proposition particularly for the democratic-minded people of Russia, subject to the CoE ensuring that it is structurally as well as politically ready to open a new chapter with Russia, and Russia demonstrating it is willing and capable of meaningful cooperation by, as a minimum, implementing the judgments of the ECtHR delivered against it.

6 Limitations

Although this book offers a comprehensive account of the troubled nature of the relationship between Russia and the CoE, it does not claim to be a complete and exhaustive examination of the relationship. To do so would be an even larger project than this one. The book does not focus in detail on the role of the ECtHR in relation to Russia's democratic backsliding, or provide a wider assessment of this topic, which would merit a separate study. Nor is this a systematic review of all of the actions and reactions of the CoE, and all of its many constitutive actors, vis-à-vis Russia.[38] Instead, our intention is to paint a picture of the membership journey, identifying what

---

[38] The CoE system comprises a vast range of standard-setting, monitoring, advisory and cooperation mechanisms, many of which are not considered by this book in detail. See, for example, the European Committee on Social Rights at www.coe.int/en/web/european-social-charter/russian-federation [Accessed 13 June 2024]; the Framework Convention for the Protection of National Minorities at www.coe.int/en/web/minorities/-/council-of-europe-body-regrets-russia-s-withdrawal-from-the-national-minorities-convention-millions-left-without-protection [Accessed 13 June 2024]; and the European Committee for

we consider to be the key milestones and drawing out the salient points for consideration. We are acutely aware that this forces us to discuss some issues in a rather more superficial manner than we would like, but it is necessary for the purposes of this particular book. We do so from a critical perspective in order to inform a wider debate, which is necessary in the context of ensuring the effectiveness and longer-term future of the CoE system.

Our desire is to see the CoE evolve from this low point in its history to a position of strength and effectiveness. We also hope that accounting for this experience will serve as food for thought should a future democratic Russian government seek to reintegrate into the CoE, providing again the human rights and rule of law standards and supports under the ECHR and other treaties that the people of Russia so rightly deserve. For the removal of doubt, our determined hope is that Russia will one day become a rights-respecting, democratic member of the CoE where its people have access to the ECtHR and the broader CoE system.

We end our detailed study on 16 March 2023 – the one-year anniversary of the expulsion of Russia from the CoE – but, as we finish drafting this book in June 2024, we are fully aware that many important events have taken place in the intervening period. While we have chosen not to extend the substantive timeframe covered by the book, we may make occasional references to some key subsequent events such as some progress of inter-state cases, and the Reykjavík Summit.[39] On this basis we do not examine in detail major efforts related to the establishment of a register of damages for Ukraine or certain developments in ECtHR case law, though these are very significant in their own right. Nor have we addressed the inter-state judgment in *Ukraine v. Russia (re Crimea)*,[40] which was delivered by a Grand Chamber of the Court on 25 June 2024.

---

the Prevention of Torture and Inhuman or Degrading Treatment or Punishment (CPT) at www.coe.int/en/web/cpt/russian-federation [Accessed 13 June 2024].

[39] Council of Europe 4th Summit (Reykjavík Summit), 16–17 May 2023, available from: www.coe.int/en/web/portal/fourth-council-of-europe-summit [Accessed 13 June 2024].

[40] *Ukraine v. Russia (re Crimea)* [GC], nos. 20958/14 and 38334/18, 25 June 2024.

2

'Therapeutic Admission' (1992–1998)

1 Introduction: Russia's CoE obligations and its promise to progressively realise CoE values

This chapter focusses on Russia's accession to the Council of Europe in 1996,[1] and its ratification of the European Convention on Human Rights (ECHR) in 1998.[2] Both need to be seen in the context of the CoE's 1990s enlargement,[3] and the various CoE Declarations and

---

[1] On Russia's accession to the CoE, see Chatzivassiliou, D. (2007) 'L'adhésion de la Russie au Conseil de l'Europe', in C. Schneider (ed) *Le Conseil De l'Europe Acteur De La Recomposition Du Territoire Européen*, Grenoble: CESICE, pp 27–59; Huber, D. (1999) *A Decade Which Made History: The Council of Europe 1989–1999*, Strasbourg: Council of Europe Press, pp 133–48; Bowring, B. (1997) 'Russia's accession to the Council of Europe', *European Human Rights Law Review*, 6: 628–43 and (2000) 'Russian accession to the CoE and the ECHR: four years on', *European Human Rights Law Review*, 4: 362–79; Janis, M. (1997) 'Russia and the "legality" of Strasbourg law', *European Journal of International Law*, 8: 93–9; Bindig, R. (2010) 'Russia's accession to the CoE', in K. Malfliet and S. Parmentier (eds) *Russia and the Council of Europe: 10 Years After*, Basingstoke: Palgrave Macmillan, pp 33–42; and Nussberger, A. (2008) 'The reception process in Russia and Ukraine', in H. Keller and A. Stone Sweet (eds) *A Europe of Rights*, Oxford: Oxford University Press, pp 603–74, 603–6.

[2] On Russia's accession contextualised to its relationship with the ECtHR (from 2017 perspective), see Mälksoo, L. (2017) 'Introduction', in L. Mälksoo and W. Benedek (eds) *Russia and the European Court of Human Rights: The Strasbourg Effect*, Cambridge: Cambridge University Press, pp 3–25, 3–4, and Roter, P. (2017) 'Russia in the Council of Europe: participation à la carte', in L. Mälksoo and W. Benedek (eds) *Russia and the European Court of Human Rights: The Strasbourg Effect*, Cambridge: Cambridge University Press, pp 26–56, 32–4 and 40–2.

[3] On the CoE's enlargement, see Weiß, N. (2017) 'Origin and further development', in S. Schmahl and M. Breuer (eds) *The Council of Europe: Its Law and Policies*, Oxford: Oxford University Press, pp 3–23, 18–20, and Huber, n 1.

instruments issued in relation to this, including, especially, the 1993 Vienna Declaration.[4]

Through its decision to join the CoE and to ratify the ECHR, Russia committed itself to clear, specific, and binding international law obligations. In essence, in 1996 Russia made a promise and a firm commitment to progressively realise the CoE's values. It aspired to join the European 'family of nations',[5] and associate itself with the ideas and philosophy of the CoE as a political project. Of course, subsequent chapters will reveal how Russia progressively reneged on this commitment, and then flagrantly breached its international legal obligations.

The chapter reveals that on the question of whether Russia should join the CoE, political factors prevailed over the compelling legal case against it doing so. The former included the 'geopolitical' case for Russia being in the CoE, and becoming a democracy in due course, to help establish a new era of 'democratic security' in Europe. Hence, the CoE's invitation for Russia to join it was based on a calculated risk and the optimism of its so-called 'therapeutic admission',[6] that is, the hope that Russia would *evolve* into a state that complied with Article 3 of the CoE Statute[7] *in the future*, boosted by CoE membership, it being appreciated that it was far from being compliant with that provision in 1996. The idea was that admission to the CoE itself would promote the cause of democracy, the rule of law and human rights in Russia, while loyal and good faith interactions by Russia with the CoE would provide further assistance and discipline for what was expected to be a long journey. This was a partnership which, ultimately, the Russian political leadership rejected.

The chapter proceeds as follows. It starts by setting out and analysing the international legal obligations that Russia voluntarily accepted and the specific commitments it made upon accession (section 2). It then focusses on how and in what circumstances Russia acceded to the CoE and ratified the ECHR (section 3 – Russia's 'therapeutic admission'). It is noted that there were early signs of problems, once Russia had joined (section 3.3).

---

[4] Text available at (1993) *Human Rights Law Journal,* 14: 352. On the Declaration, see Huber, n 1, 96–100 and Weiß, n 3, 19.

[5] See text of letter from President Yeltsin, as extracted in Bindig, n 1, 37, and see text accompanying n 84.

[6] The term was coined by Leuprecht, P. (1998) 'Innovations in the European system of human rights protection: is enlargement compatible with reinforcement', *Transnational Law and Contemporary Problems,* 8: 313–36. On 'therapeutic admission', see Huber, n 1, 128–33.

[7] On which, see section 2.1 of this chapter.

2 Russia's CoE obligations and commitments; and CoE monitoring procedures

The commitments made by Russia when it joined the CoE in 1996 can be examined under two headings. First, its CoE statutory obligations; second, those accession commitments applying specifically to Russia.

2.1 CoE statutory obligations

The obligations[8] that all CoE member states, and so Russia, are required to uphold under the CoE Statute are relatively few, but nonetheless profound and potentially transformative for a society transitioning from a communist past. Aside from matters such as paying CoE membership fees,[9] the main provision is Article 3, which has two limbs.

First, Article 3 states that the 'rule of law' and 'human rights' 'must [be] accept[ed]' by all CoE states. This obligatory provision needs to be seen in the context of the Preamble to the CoE Statute, which refers to the 'spiritual and moral values which are the common heritage of [the] peoples [of CoE states] and the true source of individual freedom, political liberty and the rule of law, principles which form the basis of all genuine democracy'. Given that wider setting and the clear political direction of the CoE over many decades, it can be now taken[10] that respect for 'pluralist democracy' is a condition of membership implied by Article 3, in addition to the 'rule of law' and 'human rights'.

The second limb to Article 3 is the requirement that CoE states 'collaborate' in the 'realisation of the aims of the Council as specified in Chapter I', and do so 'sincerely and effectively'. Chapter I includes Article 1(a), identifying a main aim of the CoE as 'achiev[ing] a greater unity between its members for the purpose of safeguarding and realising the ideals and principles which are their common heritage and facilitating their economic and social progress'. By necessary implication this provision involves a duty to settle disputes peacefully,[11] it also being obvious that acts against the sovereignty and integrity of other CoE states, let alone acts of aggression, breach it.

---

8   On CoE obligations generally, see Klein, E. (2017) 'Membership and observer status', in S. Schmahl and M. Breuer (eds) *The Council of Europe: Its Law and Policies*, Oxford: Oxford University Press, pp 41–92, 43–50.
9   See Article 9 CoE Statute and see Klein, n 8, 73. Alongside France, Germany, Italy and the United Kingdom, Russia, the largest CoE nation, would become one of the top five annual contributors to the CoE budget. Each would contribute nearly 11 per cent (total 55 per cent). On Russia's 'big payer' status/threats of non-payment, see Chapter 3, section 2.1.1; on its non-payment/financial 'blackmail' over 2017–2019, see Chapter 4, section 2.1.2.
10 See Klein, n 8, 47.
11 See Klein, n 8, 48.

The obligatory nature of Article 3 is underlined by Article 8, which is examined in detail in Chapter 5.[12] It states that the Committee of Ministers (CM) may take action, potentially leading to expulsion from the CoE, against a state which has 'seriously violated Article 3'.

2.2 Russia's accession commitments

Article 4 of the CoE Statute states that only 'European' states 'deemed to be able and willing to fulfil the provisions of Article 3 may be invited to' join the CoE.[13] In the 1990s Russia may have been 'willing' to adhere to Article 3, however, after decades of communism it was not 'able' to comply with the human rights and the rule of law aspect of it. The significant compliance gap helps us appreciate why the 1996 Parliamentary Assembly of the Council of Europe (PACE) Opinion[14] proposing that Russia be invited to join the CoE stated: 'the Assembly believes that Russia – in the sense of Article 4 of the Statute – is clearly willing and *will be able in the near future* to fulfil the provisions for membership' (emphasis added).

The wording, not used for other enlargement states joining the CoE in the 1990s, emphasised Russia's supposed prospective ability to become compliant with the first (rule of law and human rights) limb of Article 3, and was optimistic as to timeframes ('near future').[15] The phraseology alluded to the political nature of the decision to admit Russia, and indicated that great weight would put on the sustained willingness of Russia's government to commit the nation to a long journey of embracing CoE values.

The desire of the 1996 Russian government led by Boris Yeltsin to undertake that journey explained its willingness to accept the numerous commitments attached to Russia's accession.[16] These were perfectly normal, being required of all other post-communist states which joined the CoE in the 1990s.[17] In Russia's case, however, the extent and nature of its accession commitments reflected two things. First, as regards national structures and laws, how far outside the orbit of Article 3 values Russia's domestic regimes were in 1996, and so how much these needed to change; second, as regards international relations and actions, Russia's historical backdrop

---

[12] See Chapter 5.
[13] See Klein, n 8, 43–50.
[14] PACE, 'Opinion 193 (1996) on Application by Russia for membership of the Council of Europe', 25 January 1996, para 7.
[15] See PACE Resolution 1065 (1995) (26 September 1995), and see text accompanying n 89.
[16] On 'Commitments' at accession and their legal significance, see Klein, n 8, 87–8.
[17] See Djeric, V. (2000) 'Admission to membership of the Council of Europe and legal significance of commitments entered by new member states', *Zeitschrift für ausländisches öffentliches Recht und Völkerrecht*, 60: 605–29, 605.

as the largest part of the Union of Soviet Socialist Republics (USSR) and a former superpower. Here CoE membership required it to reject the territorial influences and ambitions it had with respect to its neighbours, in accordance with the second limb of Article 3 CoE Statute.

Focusing on the first aspect (national structures and laws), specific areas of reform were identified as initial steps for Russia's transition to full alignment with the principles of the rule of law and respect for human rights. Hence Russia's CoE membership application was endorsed on the understanding that legislation was in preparation as 'a matter of priority, with international consultation, on the basis of [CoE] principles and standards'[18] in a whole variety of fields related to criminal and civil law.[19] Relatedly, Russia gave undertakings to reform important fields of law in other areas, such as 'to revise the law on federal security services in order to bring it into line with [CoE] principles and standards'.[20] Further, Russia became subject to a political obligation to ratify the CoE's key human rights treaties within one year,[21] and to subject itself to the disciplines that they established. The treaties in question included: the ECHR (to include Protocols 1, 4 and 7) (ratified by Russia on 5 May 1998);[22] the European Convention for the Prevention of Torture and Inhuman or Degrading Treatment or Punishment (ratified on 5 May 1998);[23] and the European Framework Convention for the Protection of National Minorities (ratified on 21 August 1998).[24] In due course, more

---

[18] PACE, Opinion 193, n 14, para 7. On the application process for CoE membership, see Klein, n 8, 41–65.

[19] See PACE, Opinion 193, n 14, paras 7.1–7.12 (examples included: 'a new criminal code and a code of criminal procedure'; a 'new civil code and a code of civil procedure'; new laws on 'functioning and administration of the penitentiary system'; new laws on 'national minorities'; on 'freedom of assembly and on freedom of religion'; 'freedom of movement and choice of place of residence; and conditions of detention').

[20] The undertakings (see para 10) included: reducing incidents of ill-treatment and deaths in the armed forces outside military conflicts; action relating to 'the property of religious institutions'; 'to cease to restrict – with immediate effect – international travel of persons aware of state secrets'; 'to revise the law on federal security services in order to bring it into line with Council of Europe principles and standards'; and to revise a law by which a person suspected of involvement in organised crime could be detained for up to 30 days without charge.

[21] PACE, Opinion 193, n 14, paras 10.1–10.6.

[22] On Protocol 6 (ETS 114), see following discussion in n 105.

[23] The European Convention for the Prevention of Torture and Inhuman or Degrading Treatment or Punishment (ETS 126). On the CPT, see Chapter 3, section 2.1.1 and Chapter 7, section 4.3.

[24] European Framework Convention for the Protection of National Minorities (ETS 157). Russia also ratified the European Social Charter (revised) (ETS 163) on 16 October 2009 (not stipulated by Opinion 193).

than 80 CoE treaties[25] were ratified by Russia on matters such as local self-government, extradition, mutual assistance in criminal matters, the transfer of sentenced persons, and on the laundering, search, seizure and confiscation of the proceeds of crime, many as part of its post-accession commitments.[26]

As to Russia's accession commitments regarding its international relations and actions, essentially Russia undertook to reject an antagonistic European foreign policy. It would 'settle international as well as internal disputes'[27] exclusively by peaceful means … rejecting resolutely any forms of threats of force against its neighbour';[28] it undertook to 'settle outstanding international border disputes according to the principles of international law';[29] and 'to denounce as wrong the concept of two different categories of foreign countries, whereby some are treated as a zone of special influence called the "near abroad"'.[30] Russia committed to fulfil its 'obligations under the Treaty on Conventional Armed Forces in Europe'[31] and to ratify within six months an existing (21 October 1994) agreement between Russia and Moldova, leading to the withdrawal the Russian military stationed in Transnistria.[32] Finally, and in view of on-going events in Chechnya,[33] Russia committed 'to respect strictly the provisions of international humanitarian law, including in cases of armed conflict on its territory';[34] and it would 'co-operate in good faith with international humanitarian organisations' on its territory.[35]

2.3 Post-accession monitoring

Russia also promised to 'co-operate fully'[36] with regimes established by the CoE regarding compliance with member states' commitments, and monitoring of obligations.[37]

---

[25] Further details may be found on the CoE's website: www.coe.int/en/web/portal/russian-federation [Accessed 1 June 2024].
[26] Russia also undertook to accept the European Charter for Regional or Minority Languages (ETS 148). This was signed on 10 May 2001; however, Russia never ratified it.
[27] A reference to Chechnya.
[28] PACE, Opinion 193, n 14, para 10.7.
[29] PACE, Opinion 193, n 14, para 10.8.
[30] PACE, Opinion 193, n 14, para 10.11.
[31] PACE, Opinion 193, n 14, para 10.10.
[32] PACE, Opinion 193, n 14, para 10.9.
[33] On Chechnya, see n 74, and section 3.1 of this chapter.
[34] PACE, Opinion 193, n 14, para 10.24.
[35] PACE, Opinion 193, n 14, para 10.25.
[36] PACE, Opinion 193, n 14, para 10.23.
[37] On which, see Drzemczewski, A. (2017) 'Core monitoring mechanisms and related activities', in S. Schmahl and M. Breuer (eds) *The Council of Europe: Its Law and Policies*, Oxford: Oxford University Press, pp 618–33.

2.3.1 The Vienna Declaration (1993) and the CM's Declaration on Compliance with Commitments

Here one may note the wider CoE 'enlargement' backdrop of the 1990s to include the various Decisions and Declarations issued by CoE states. Enlargement inspired the first ever gathering of the CoE's Heads of State and Government and so the 'Vienna Declaration of 9 October 1993',[38] endorsing a reinvented CoE as the institutional focal point for the new post-USSR Europe.[39] Post-Soviet Russia had applied for full CoE membership in 1992,[40] and the Vienna Declaration's text evidenced this (its text being poignant today, given events thirty years on). The Declaration referred to the 'end of the division of Europe' as offering 'an historic opportunity to consolidate peace and stability on the continent': 'Europe' could 'become a vast area of democratic security'. Indeed, this terminology closely resembled language used by Gorbachev during his landmark address to PACE in July 1989.[41] The Vienna Declaration referred to Europe as 'a source of immense hope', one 'which must in no event be destroyed by territorial ambitions, the resurgence of aggressive nationalism, the perpetuation of spheres of influence, intolerance or totalitarian ideologies'. The CoE states saw the CoE as 'the pre-eminent European political institution capable of welcoming, on an equal footing and in permanent structures, the democracies of Europe freed from communist oppression'.

Russia was one of many post-communist states to join the CoE in the 1990s and 2000s, and there were many concerns that this enlargement would result in a watering-down of the CoE's values. The Vienna Declaration sought to placate that, as the CoE states underlined their resolve 'to ensure full compliance with the commitments accepted by all member States within the [CoE]'. Subsequently, in 1994 the CM – the executive organ of the CoE, made up of governments[42] – issued a Declaration on Compliance with Commitments, confirming dedication to: 'strict compliance ... by every member state' of 'the commitments to democracy, human rights and the rule

---

[38] See n 4.
[39] Huber, n 1, 97.
[40] The Vienna Summit included a 'Declaration on Russia', communicating a positive and reassuring message of support from the Heads of States and Governments of the CoE to the Yeltsin administration and the process of democratisation; see Huber, n 1, 99.
[41] Mikhail Gorbatchev (1989) Speech made to the Assembly, 6 July 1989, available from: www.assembly.coe.int/nw/xml/Speeches/Speech-XML2HTML-EN.asp?SpeechID=78 [Accessed 1 June 2024].
[42] Palmer, P. (2017) 'The Committee of Ministers', in S. Schmahl and M. Breuer (eds) *The Council of Europe: Its Law and Policies*, Oxford: Oxford University Press, pp 137–65.

of law' as set out under the 'Council's Statute, the European Convention on Human Rights and other legal instruments'.[43]

The Declaration envisaged that member states, the Secretary General or PACE could seize the CM with respect to questions of implementation of commitments concerning the situation of democracy, human rights and the rule of law in any member state. The procedure for the application of this confidential monitoring mechanism was adopted by the CM in 1995.[44] It assumed that member states would take seriously their responsibilities of collective enforcement.[45]

2.3.2 Monitoring by PACE and other CoE actors

Meanwhile PACE[46] enhanced its procedures (which go back to the 1960s) for the continued monitoring of new entrant states,[47] to ensure that CoE obligations and accession commitments were adhered to. All states, including Russia, accepted this in the 1990s (although Russia would contest aspects of them in the 2010s).[48] Monitoring would be led by PACE's Committee on the Honouring of Obligations and Commitments (the 'Monitoring Committee').[49]

There were other forms of specialist monitoring within the CoE, notably with respect to human rights and the protection of effective political

---

[43] The Declaration on Compliance with Commitments, Accepted by Member States of the Council of Europe on 10 November 1994, was viewed as a major development at the time, and important for the future; see Huber, n 1, 113 and 'Editorial' (1996) *Netherlands Quarterly of Human Rights*, 1: 3–4. See, however, Drzemczewski noting some views at the CoE that considered this 'an artificial mechanism ... created to justify – retroactively – the precipitated decision to invite countries with suspect democratic credentials to join the [CoE]': Drzemczewski, A. (2012) 'Reflections on a remarkable period', in O. Delas (ed) *Liber Amicorum Peter Leuprecht*, Bruxelles: Bruylant, pp 105–15, 113.

[44] Procedure for Implementing the Declaration of 10 November 1994 on Compliance with Commitments Accepted by Member States of the Council of Europe (20 April 1995).

[45] On the CM's monitoring, see Drzemczewski, A. (2002) 'Monitoring by the Committee of Ministers', *Baltic Yearbook of International Law*, vol. 2, pp 83–103. Regarding the CM's failure to apply the 1994 Declaration, see Chapter 3, section 2.1.1.

[46] On PACE (including its monitoring role), see Leach, P. (2017) 'The Parliamentary Assembly of the Council of Europe', in S. Schmahl and M. Breuer (eds) *The Council of Europe: Its Law and Policies*, Oxford: Oxford University Press, pp 166–208.

[47] Full details are found within, PACE Order 508 (1995); and PACE Resolution 1115 (1997).

[48] See Chapter 4, section 2.1.

[49] Post-expulsion, a five-page document was issued by the Monitoring Committee providing a comprehensive list of documentation related to Russia's monitoring before PACE; see 'Parliamentary Monitoring Procedure with Regard to the Russian Federation [1996–2022]', AS/Mon/Inf (2022) 09, 7 April 2022.

democracy. So, for example, as a member of the CoE, Russia would become subject to the mandate of CoE Commissioner for Human Rights[50] when that office was created in 1999. Most importantly, there was a form of monitoring 'par excellence'[51] in terms of Russia's ratification of the ECHR. As is well known, it established specific legal obligations on the part of its member states,[52] and created a regime or system for the 'collective enforcement' of the selected human rights it protects.

2.4 Monitoring Russia: some reality checks for the CoE

Standing back, one may pause to consider how remarkable it was that Russia, a former superpower in the 1990s, was prepared to commit itself to the international legal obligations noted previously, given the historical backdrop. By doing so, Russia was, at least in theory, locking itself into international regime of monitoring (principally led by PACE and the CM) with respect to those obligations, and as regards the ECHR, agreeing to be bound by the many, various and far-reaching international legal obligations it created, as well as to submit itself to the final binding authority of its Court,[53] which could act in a quasi-constitutional way. In the past, the idea that the USSR could do this would have been dismissed as utopian. In turn that underlines how ambitious and optimistic it would have been to assume that Russia would instantly transition into a fully-fledged, rights respecting CoE state. But that was not expected in 1996,[54] no one being in any doubt that the transition would take many years. Nevertheless, slowly, but surely, and with enough political will, Russia was expected to progressively evolve into a compliant CoE state, with laws, policies and practices in line with European standards.

Of course, that was not the story that unfolded. Over time, Russia both tested the boundaries set by its CoE obligations, and exceeded them in manifest and quite outrageous ways.[55] It breached certain of the individual

---

[50] On the Commissioner's role, see Dörr, O. (2017) 'Commissioner for Human Rights', in S. Schmahl and M. Breuer (eds) *The Council of Europe: Its Law and Policies,* Oxford: Oxford University Press, pp 296–310. In relation to Russia, see Chapter 3, section 3.1, and latterly, Chapter 3, section 4.2 and Chapter 7, section 4.3.
[51] Drzemczewski, n 37, 623.
[52] For an up-to-date account, see Harris, D., O'Boyle, M., Bates, E. and Buckley, C. (2023) *Law of the European Convention on Human Rights,* Oxford: Oxford University Press.
[53] On the significance of Russia submitting to the jurisdiction of the Court, see Mälksoo, L. (2019) 'Introduction', in L. Mälksoo and W. Benedek (eds) *Russia and the European Court of Human Rights: The Strasbourg Effect,* Cambridge: Cambridge University Press, p 3.
[54] See section 3 of this chapter.
[55] See Chapters 3 and 4.

and specific obligations related to its CoE membership (as documented by PACE),[56] and violated the ECHR on many occasions, having a poor record when it came to the implementation of European Court of Human Rights (ECtHR) judgments directed against it.[57]

As such, certain political realities became clear as regards Russia's relationship with the CoE, and with respect to the implementation and enforcement of its international legal obligations, plus its accession commitments. Compared to the heady optimism of the mid-1990s what followed in the 2000s and 2010s constituted a type of 'reality check' in two respects.

First, it was evident just how much compliance with CoE obligations was reliant on the enduring good faith and cooperation of the state concerned. In short, the good faith underpinning the promises made on Russia's behalf in 1996 needed to endure – but did not. On the contrary, in fact, bad faith approaches evolved and took hold in the 2000s,[58] at which point the disciplines that the CoE could impose would be all important.

However, the second point relates to the weakness and so partial ineffectiveness of the CoE's enforcement mechanisms in the absence of good faith on the part of a state, and in the face of its unwillingness to cooperate. Put simply, the CoE could not force compliance from a state, hence the importance of that state being willing to act itself, if necessary, further to monitoring from CoE actors exposing the states' shortcomings and failures.

Unpacking this second point,[59] power within the CoE resides with the CM,[60] a political organ made up of government representatives from CoE states. It may suspend and then expel a state from the CoE (Article 8, CoE Statute);[61] however, aside from political criticism, or threats of expulsion, the CM has hardly any intermediary power to, for example, issues fines. Further, the threshold for the application of Article 8 is high (a 'serious violation' of Article 3 is required), while there are strong disincentives to employ it unless the situation is beyond hope: the state is ejected from the organisation altogether, ending opportunities for dialogue and monitoring, which will

---

[56] For a table analysing this, albeit from the perspective of 2012, see Appendix to PACE Monitoring Committee, 'The honouring of obligations and commitments by the Russian Federation', Doc. 13018, 14 September 2012.
[57] See Chapter 4, section 3.2. Of course, it was not alone in having a poor record of implementation; see Chapter 1.
[58] See Chapters 3 and 4.
[59] See further Chapter 7, sections 4.2 and 4.3. On the CoE's lack of enforcement powers, see Muižnieks, N. (2019) 'The Council of Europe's response to recent democratic backsliding', in P. Czech, L. Heschl, K. Lukas, M. Nowak and G. Oberleitner (eds) *European Yearbook on Human Rights 2019*, pp 3–31.
[60] See Palmer, n 42.
[61] On Article 8, see Chapter 5.

not be constructive if the aim is improved human rights protection, or to obtain reconciliation with another CoE state.[62] The 'all or nothing' nature of Article 8 therefore underlined the importance of the CM taking robust stances in other contexts, such as the 1994 Declaration on Compliance with Commitments, and in relation to Article 46 ECHR (regarding the supervision of the implementation of ECtHR judgments).[63] However, the former in particular requires collective political will to confront the state concerned, and in Russia's case – a big and powerful state – this appeared to be lacking. In this connection, the CM's failures with respect to Russia are noted throughout Chapters 3 and 4.

The story told, then, is one of the CM having power but being unwilling to use it against Russia, while PACE was a willing guardian of the CoE but lacked meaningful power. So, PACE could recommend to the CM that action be taken under Article 8 of the CoE Statute[64]; however, this brings us back to the problems just referred to, as the sanctions that PACE had at its own disposal for a state that was slow, failed to honour – or indeed, flagrantly violated – its commitments and CoE obligations were ultimately weak. Resolutions could be passed criticising the state, and if serious problems arose, under its Rules PACE could vote on an application to refuse to accept a national delegation's credentials;[65] or it could deny voting rights of

---

[62] See Chapter 5, section 2. The CM did not take or even threaten to take any Article 8 action against Russia until 2022.

[63] The ECHR does not provide for sanctions against a respondent state for non-execution of a judgment, even if, in exceptional cases, infringement proceedings may be brought by the CM under Article 46(4). On Article 46, see Harris et al, n 52, 185–202, and see Chapter 7.

[64] Prior to 2022, PACE only did this once, in relation to the situation in Chechnya in 2000 (see Chapter 3). PACE passed Resolutions deeming that Russia had breached Article 3 CoE Statute (but did not recommend action under Article 8), first in the context of the Georgia–Russia war of 2008 (see Chapter 3), and second after the military aggression against Ukraine in 2014 (see Chapter 4).

[65] See Rules 8–9 of PACE's Rules of Procedure concerning contestation of a national parliamentary delegation's credentials (the capacity to contest being triggered by a 'serious violation of the basic principles' of the CoE or 'persistent failure to honour obligations and commitments'), available from: www.assembly.coe.int/nw/xml/RoP/RoP-XML2H TML-en.asp [Accessed 1 June 2024]. On the role of PACE regarding general monitoring and the possibility of the sanction of non-ratification of credentials, see Klein, n 8, 70–2; Leach, n 46, 191–5; Drzemczewski, n 37, 618–22, and Ailincai, A. (2024) 'The Parliamentary Assembly of the Council of Europe is at it again: on the non-ratification of the credentials of Azerbaijan's Parliamentary Delegation', *Strasbourg Observers* [Blog], 8 March 2024, available from: https://strasbourgobservers.com/2024/03/08/the-parlia mentary-assembly-of-the-council-of-europe-is-at-it-again-on-the-non-ratification-of-the-credentials-of-azerbaijans-parliamentary-delegation/ [Accessed 1 June 2024].

a delegation.[66] Yet such measures were not necessarily effective: first they targeted parliamentarians, not the government itself; second, they risked ostracism, when dialogue was required.[67] Even so, via these mechanisms PACE would have a vital role in standing up for CoE values in relation to Russia. While the Russian PACE credentials were never rejected,[68] the challenge to credentials procedure was used regularly against it after 2008 in the context of serious (alleged) violations of the CoE Statute, occasionally leading to denial of voting rights.[69] In the 2010s Russia would contest PACE's powers here,[70] its delegation boycotting the institution, with Russia using this as a pretext for causing a crisis at the CoE.

The picture that would emerge over the 2000s and 2010s, then, was as follows. Objectively Russia should have been ejected from the CoE years before 2022, based on repeated serious violations of the Statute (sometimes in outrageous and premeditated ways), breach of numerous accession commitments, and other reasons. However, owing to the limitations of the CoE regimes in practice – including a tendency towards the logic of 'better in than out', and a lack of political will from the member states to employ any form of meaningful sanction (above all the CM) – Russia would be able to stay in the CoE.

That picture was not changed by the fact that Russia had ratified the ECHR, and was regularly found in breach of this too, including via human rights violations that were manifestly incompatible with effective political democracy and the rule of law.[71] Of course, the ECHR establishes legal obligations, including under Article 46(1); however, it has no power to force a state to comply with its rulings. The ECtHR only had jurisdiction with respect to the ECHR, *not* the CoE Statute, or accession commitments.

---

[66] See Chapter 4, section 2.1. Suspension of voting rights by PACE is rare, only ever occurring three times since 2000, all in relation to Russia: in 2000 (Chapter 3); and over 2014–2015 both in relation to Crimea (Chapter 4).

[67] See Chapter 3, section 2.2 re Chechnya and Georgia–Russia. For a leading political scientist's perspective on the CoE's need for dialogue with states, see MacMuller, A. (2004) 'Intergovernmental functionalism? The Council of Europe in European integration', *Journal of European Integration*, 26(4): 405–29.

[68] The Russian delegation boycotted PACE after 2016, until 2019; see Chapter 4. Rejection of a delegation's credentials is an exceptional measure. It has only ever occurred for Greece in 1969, Türkiye in 1981 and Azerbaijan in 2024. Regarding Türkiye, see Chapter 5, section 4.2.

[69] The Russian delegation's voting rights were denied in 2000; see Chapter 3 (re Chechnya) and in 2014, see Chapter 4 (re Crimea).

[70] Chapter 4, section 2.1. See also Chapter 3 (response in 2000, section 2.1.1).

[71] Russia was not the only state in this regard; see the various contributions to the 2021 edition of the *European Convention on Human Rights Law Review*, 2(2): 165–335, with references to serious violations by Türkiye, Azerbaijan, Poland and Hungary, in addition to Russia.

Questions of non-implementation are essentially a matter for the CM under Article 46.

An understandable frustration with the situation just described as regards lack of enforcement should not change the fact that what was in issue at the relevant times with respect to Russia were international legal obligations undertaken, ostensibly, in good faith by it. It broke these because its government was prepared to prioritise what it saw as national aims and commitments over its original, 1996 ambitions of transitioning to democracy and the rule of law.

With that in mind, the account that now follows of Russia's admission to the CoE highlights how it would not have been allowed to join the CoE had it not entered into the legal obligations referred to and made the accession commitments noted. It equally reveals that there was a very strong legitimate expectation on the CoE's behalf that Russia would not just fulfil the promises it made upon accession but do so according to the spirit in which they were made in 1996. That spirit was, as we shall see, one in which great compromises were made to facilitate Russia's entry in the first place, and for the benefit of the nurturing of democracy and human rights.

3 Russia's 'therapeutic admission': the promise to progressively realise CoE values

Russia applied to join the CoE on 7 May 1992,[72] soon after the end of the USSR had been announced by Mikhail Gorbachev in December 1991; however, it did not accede to the CoE until 28 February 1996. The account that follows reveals that, from a legal perspective, this accession was inappropriate, underlining how far the CoE extended itself by admitting Russia, and, importantly, the politics involved. It also provides some insights into the risks taken by the CoE on the understanding that Russia would live up to the promises it was making, and repay the faith that the former showed in it.

3.1 Should law or politics prevail?

The overwhelming 'legal' case against Russia's admission in February 1996 was set out in October 1994 via a thorough and detailed report from 'eminent lawyers'.[73] Nevertheless, PACE proceeded with its consideration of Russia's

---

[72] A warming of relations between the CoE and the then USSR was in evidence in July 1989, when Mikhail Gorbachev delivered a speech at the CoE, see n 41.
[73] Bernhardt, R., Trechsel, S., Weitzel, A. and Ermacora, F. (1994) 'Report on the conformity of the legal order of the Russian Federation with Council of Europe standards', *Human Rights Law Journal*, 15: 249–300.

request for membership, only to suspend it in February 1995 on account of indiscriminate and disproportionate use of force and the 'mass violations of human rights' occurring in Chechnya.[74] The atrocities highlighted by PACE were so serious that it was surprising that the CoE was in any sort of dialogue with Russia about membership.

However, Russia would be admitted just over a year later. This was a reflection of the politics involved, and the strong desire that Russia join the CoE on the part of the governments of its leading states, upon a 'better in than out' approach.[75] The geopolitical realism of Russia's entry was evident in the Vienna Declaration of 1993, as noted earlier.[76] There was an understandable emotional desire to seize the opportunity to help the Russian people,[77] and to support Russia's fragile democracy, and the risks taken by its then leaders. As for the CoE, with Russia on board it would be made relevant to the new post-USSR era.

A report issued by PACE's Committee on Legal Affairs and Human Rights (hereafter the 'Bindig Report',[78] after its rapporteur, Rudolf Bindig) just prior to admission, highlighted the 'therapeutic' nature of Russia's accession. It made it clear that Russia was not in a position to join the CoE,[79] given its failure to adhere to the rule of law[80] and respect human rights.[81] However, it asked whether Russia's accession to the CoE could 'in itself help to create conditions in conformity with CoE standards', via two aspects in particular. First, 'through the commitments to be entered into by Russia upon accession and the subsequent monitoring procedure'. Second, 'as a result of the mandatory judgments of the [ECtHR]'. Those considerations, plus 'other political arguments', might 'speak in favour of

---

[74] PACE Resolution 1055 (1995), 2 February 1995 (referring to 'indiscriminate and disproportionate use of force' against civilians, para 2; 'grave violation[s]' of the CoE's 'most elementary human rights principles', para 3).

[75] See Huber, n 1, 128. For example, Irish Prime Minister, John Bruton, spoke in favour of Russian admission: 'If Russia is within the [CoE], all problems, including human rights problems, can be talked through. If Russia is left outside the Council, momentum in the painful and necessarily gradual task of extending western-style constitutional order in Russia will be lost' (cited from Huber, n 1, 135).

[76] Text accompanying n 39.

[77] See Huber, n 1, 135. The PACE debates on potential accession came at a crucial time as regards internal developments in Russia, to which end the support that the CoE could give to the democratic forces in that state was important, Huber, n 1, 134.

[78] Committee on Legal Affairs and Human Rights, 'Russia's application for membership of the Council of Europe', Doc. 7463, 18 January 1996 (Bindig Report).

[79] Bindig Report, n 78 at 'VIII. Conclusion and recommendation'.

[80] See Bindig Report, n 78, under heading II (Rule of Law), III (The organisation of the judiciary), and IV (Criminal law and proceedings).

[81] Numerous problems were listed, including many fundamental inconsistencies with the ECHR.

Russia's accession',[82] the question being which approach should prevail: 'a critical assessment of the current [1996] legal and human rights situation or a political evaluation of the chances and perspectives for improvement of this situation following ... admission [?]'.

PACE and the CM pursued the 'political' route, and here it is reasonable to assume that a letter of January 1995 written to the CoE and signed by the then Russian President (Yeltsin), Prime Minister (Tchermomyrdin), the chair of the Federation Council (Shumeyko) and the chair of the Duma (Rybkin) was of real influence.[83] Essentially this was a promise at the highest level that Russia was committed to CoE values. So, the letter referred to the 'historical importance' of Russia's admittance to the CoE and how that would lead to 'new important prerequisites for the creation of the greater Europe with common humanitarian, legal, social and cultural space'. It was said that, '[t]he transformation of the Council into an organisation comprising the whole of Europe will make it possible to defend together common values shared by all European nations, to ensure in a consistent manner the [sic] democratic security.'[84]

Russia's desire to join the Council was said to be 'a logical consequence of our current policy aimed at establishing a rule of the law state in Russia, strengthening democracy and securing human rights'. Providing an upbeat and positive account of the direction of Russia as a nation, this 'Yeltsin letter' stated, 'we are sure that taking into account development trends in our society Russia's joining the family of European democracies will not result in the lowering of the high standards of your organisation but will help turn them into generally accepted and applied norms throughout our continent.' This 'Yeltsin letter' was referred to explicitly in the all-important PACE Opinion of January 1996 inviting Russia to join the CoE.[85] It had been cited too in a September PACE Resolution,[86] which saw PACE resume the procedure for an Opinion on Russia's request for membership after the suspension of its application in February 1995, on account of the situation in Chechnya.

The September PACE Resolution noted that Russia was 'seeking a political solution to the Chechnya conflict'.[87] Its basic message was that it was appreciated that Russia was making efforts towards democracy,[88] and

---

[82] See Bindig Report, n 78.
[83] The text is extracted from Bindig, n 1, 37 (also highlighting influence of this, given anxieties about Russia).
[84] Bindig, n 1, 37.
[85] Opinion 193, n 14, para 6.
[86] PACE Resolution 1065 (1995) (26 September 1995).
[87] PACE Resolution 1065 (1995), n 86, para 4.
[88] PACE Resolution 1065 (1995), n 86, para 5.

that accession should help to support and even stimulate that. It highlighted the historical, geopolitical significance of the fact that Russia was seeking membership of the CoE in the first place. It called for pragmatism given the Russian situation: it was 'in a state of radical transition', the 'timescale' for which was 'quinquennia, even decades', and its 'pace [would] vary', while '[p]olicies of the state authorities will fluctuate'.[89] This was only to be expected, 'because of immense social and economic difficulties, including the fight against organised crime'. Hence, with '[t]ragic errors of policy in dealing with the Chechnya conflict' now 'recognised' by Russia,[90] the Resolution stated that 'the Assembly has no wish to throw in doubt the long-term direction of this transition: towards democracy, the rule of law, and human (including social) rights and freedoms'. It added, that '[g]reat personal risks' had been taken by those who had 'steered the transition towards these values, with support (which must continue) from international and European institutions'. The Resolution referred to signs of improvement in the constitutional and legislative basis for human rights protection in Russia;[91] however, realism was called for: '9. ... The actual state of this protection across the country depends on a broad awareness of, and respect for, the rule of law. Such a "culture" must be developed in all its aspects: political, legal and administrative – and at all levels: national, regional and local.'

3.2 Russia joins the CoE (1996) and ratifies the ECHR (1998)

The September PACE Resolution further highlights PACE's attitude toward Russia's 'therapeutic admission', and its understanding that '[p]rogress measurable against the highest European standards [would] not be constant and [would] take many years'.[92] By comparison, the PACE Opinion of January 1996 was very business-like. It endorsed Russia's application to join the CoE but included serious expressions of concern about continuing issues in relation to Chechnya (including just the month before in December 1995). It stressed that the procedure for admission had only been 'resumed on the grounds that Russia was henceforth committed to finding a political solution and that alleged and documented human rights violations were being investigated'.[93] It became an accession commitment that '7.7 those found

---

[89] PACE Resolution 1065 (1995), n 86, para 8.
[90] PACE Resolution 1065 (1995), n 86, para 8.
[91] PACE Resolution 1065 (1995), n 86, para 9.
[92] PACE Resolution 1065 (1995), n 86, para 9.
[93] Opinion 193, n 14, para 4, see Bindig, n 1, 36.

responsible for human rights violations will be brought to justice – notably in relation to events in Chechnya'.[94]

With the Chechnya issue addressed in that way, PACE took the view that 'Russia ... *[was] clearly willing and will be able in the near future to* fulfil the provisions for [CoE] membership' (emphasis added).[95] The join-now-comply-later nature of the Opinion was only accepted '[o]n the basis of ... assurances and of ... considerations and commitments' provided by Russia in the context of the accession process.

Regarding the 'commitments', these were the around 25 accession commitments referred to earlier.[96] The 'assurances' were political signals or indications of Russia's willingness and good faith at that juncture,[97] express reference being made to the 'Yeltsin letter'.[98] Finally, the aforementioned 'considerations' related to certain steps already taken by Russia, reflecting its readiness to date to engage with the CoE and its values. It was noted that that was a significant departure from Russia's (more accurately the USSR's) past attitudes to such international initiatives, and signalled good intentions going forward.[99]

PACE Opinion 193 (1996), passed on 25 January 1996, was soon followed by a CM Resolution[100] inviting Russia to join the CoE (8 February 1996).

---

[94] On the accession process and Chechnya, see Merlin, A. (2010) 'The CoE and the war in Chechnya', in K. Malfliet and S. Parmentier (eds) *Russia and the Council of Europe: 10 Years After*, Basingstoke: Palgrave Macmillan, pp 137–64, 140–1. For contemporary criticism, see *The Economist*, 'Chechnya: baffled victims', 2 March 1996, 49.

[95] Opinion 193, n 14, para 7 (emphasis added). The timeframe ('near future') is hard to square with PACE's September Resolution.

[96] Text accompanying n 18, and see paras 10.1–10.25, Opinion 193, n 14. By commitment 10.16, Russia undertook to 'ensure that the application of the CIS Convention on Human Rights [did] not in any way interfere with the procedure and guarantees of the [ECHR]'. This important proviso had in mind The Convention on Human Rights and Fundamental Freedoms of the Commonwealth of Independent States, signed by Belarus, Russia and Ukraine in 1991, and adopted in 1995. Reports commissioned expeditiously in the CoE context expressed strong concerns about this regime (for example, the independence of its supervisory body), and the problems that could arise given its coexistence alongside the ECHR, prompting the proviso. For further background details, see Decision on the Competence of the Court to Give an Advisory Opinion, 2 June 2004, GC (Advisory Opinion ECtHR [under [Protocol No 2]), paras 7–15.

[97] PACE observed that, 'political, legal and economic reforms have been sustained', even if (and surely as a major understatement) '[t]he legal system continue[d] to show shortcomings'; the Opinion then added: '[n]onetheless, there is progress towards a general awareness of – and respect for – the rule of law', Opinion 193, n 14, para 5.

[98] Opinion 193, n 14, para 6.

[99] See Opinion 193, n 14, paras 7.1–7.3. The Opinion listed various new laws that were being proposed 'on the basis of Council of Europe principles and standards'.

[100] CM Resolution (96) 2, 8 February 1996.

It too was clear that the CoE's invitation to Russia was made in, 'light of the commitments entered into and the assurances for their fulfilment given by the Russian Government in its contacts, both with the [CM] and [PACE]'. The CM Resolution also gave prominence to Russia's obligation to ratify the ECHR 'as soon as possible'.

3.3 Early concerns and forewarnings

Russia became the 39th full member of the CoE on 28 February 1996, when it ratified the CoE Statute, and signed the ECHR.

As to the immediate post-accession period, it had been inauspicious that a debate in the Duma approving Russia's membership focussed on the national interest of joining the CoE,[101] as opposed to a deep commitment to it. It seemed to downplay Russia's obligations (its accession commitments being viewed by some as 'provocative attempts to keep Russia out of the [CoE], and which could be adopted or discarded at will').[102] Of greater concern were serious problems that would soon evolve related to Chechnya.[103] Russia's failure to uphold its accession commitments was also evidenced in a series of executions which were carried out in 1996, to which PACE responded forcefully referring to a 'flagrant violation' of Russia's '[accession] commitment to put into place a moratorium on executions'.[104] A moratorium was announced in August 1996. This was followed by a moratorium on death sentences pronounced on 2 February 1999, which was confirmed by the Constitutional Court of the Russian Federation on 19 November 2009. However, contrary to its accession commitments, Russia never did ratify the ECHR Protocols on the death penalty,[105] after Russia's ratification of the ECHR.[106]

---

[101] Bowring, n 1, 632.

[102] Bowring, n 1, 634, although also citing an impressive number of legislative changes made over the first year of Russia's membership (pp 639–41). Moreover, it was pointed out that the ECtHR influenced the text of the 1993 Constitution of Russia; see https://pravo.ru/story/245128/ [Accessed 14 June 2024].

[103] See Chapter 3.

[104] Resolution 1111 (1997), 'Honouring of the commitment entered into by Russia upon accession to the Council of Europe to put into place a moratorium on executions of the death penalty', 28 January 1997, paras 1–6. See Nussberger, n 1, 607.

[105] Protocol 6 (exemption in time of war) was signed by Russia on 16 April 1997, but rejected by the Duma on 6 August 1999, and never ratified. Russia never signed Protocol 13 (complete abolition of death penalty; ETS 187); however, see *A.L. (X.W.) v. Russia*, no. 44095/14, 29 October 2015 para 64 (ECtHR ruling that capital punishment contravenes Article 2 and 3 applied to Russia).

[106] The Duma had voted to ratify the main ECHR on 28 February 1998; see www.consultant.ru/document/cons_doc_LAW_18263/ [Accessed 1 June 2024]. In the State Duma, 65.3 per cent voted in favour of the ratification, see https://pravo.ru/story/245128/ [Accessed

A contemporary expert of CoE–Russia relations, Bill Bowring, saw Russia's ratification of the ECHR as having 'profound consequences',[107] for, by Article 15(4) of the 1993 Constitution as it was then, treaties ratified by Russia took priority over federal laws, so there was a real prospect that the ECHR could dynamically influence Russian law.[108] He observed that there was good knowledge of the ECHR among young lawyers, who could be expected to take many applications to the ECtHR,[109] albeit 'human rights violations will only be impeded and finally prevented by the growth of a vital civil society of non-governmental activists and monitors'.[110]

Indeed, over the 2000s Russia became one of the biggest 'client' states before the ECtHR,[111] while ECHR membership and the disciplinary force of 'mandatory [ECtHR] judgments'[112] had been seen as critical to Russia's 'therapeutic admission'. Yet, of course, this made great assumptions about what the ECtHR could reasonably do in its residual capacity as a long-stop, external reviewer of Russia's ECHR commitments. After all, Russia had been permitted to join the CoE without bringing domestic law into line with the ECHR, because this was not possible to do so in time. This was another reflection of how it was *not* one of the 'like-minded countries of Europe' (CoE Statute).[113] So, was this 'better to include than exclude' approach destined to backfire?[114] And, if so, what would be the cost to come

---

14 June 2024]. Two reservations were entered (concerning Article 5(3) and 5(4), related to an aspect of criminal procedure, and in the context of Armed forces discipline), on these reservations, and ratification of the ECHR see Nussberger, n 1, pp 606–10.

[107] Bowring, n 1, 643.

[108] For a very upbeat account, see the speech delivered at the ECtHR by the President of the Constitutional Court: Zorkin, V. (2005) 'The Constitutional Court of Russia in the European law landscape' (21 January 2005), Strasbourg: Council of Europe (available from: www.echr.coe.int [Accessed 1 June 2024]). For Zorkin's hostile attitude to the ECHR after 2010, see Chapter 3, section 4.3. For an excellent account of the interaction between ECHR law and Russian national law (as of 2009), see Nussberger, n 1, 615–26, noting a major gap between theory and practice as regards ECHR application. On later (hostile to ECHR) amendments to the Constitution, see Chapter 3, section 4.

[109] Bowring, n 1, 643. On application in the 2000s, see Chapter 3.

[110] Bowring, n 1, 643. For the state's attacks on civil society, see Chapter 3, section 4 and Chapter 7.

[111] See Chapter 3, section 3.3.2.

[112] See Bindig Report, n 78.

[113] The same expression ('like-minded') is employed in the ECHR's Preamble.

[114] See especially, Leuprecht, n 6. In 1997, Peter Leuprecht resigned as Deputy Secretary General of the CoE (1993–1997), 'because of disagreement with dilution of [CoE] Europe standards and values' (p 313). The resignation was not solely because of Russia's admission; however, this was clearly a very significant factor, Russia's admission (during the Chechnya war) being viewed as a 'telling example of the opportunistic and unprincipled "Realpolitik"' (p 329).

to the ECtHR and CoE? For academic commentators, Russia was seen as a major threat to the ECtHR success story, questions arising as to how it could cope with Russia and whether it could reasonably be expected to assimilate to the CoE, even given a fair wind and a long transitional period. Russia was not the only enlargement state with these problems inevitably on the horizon, but, of course, it was by far the biggest and most influential, and with the greatest capacity to cause harm.

With such issues in mind Mark Janis argued[115] that no matter how politically rational it may have been to include Russia within the CoE in 1996, it came with major risks. The obvious compliance gap between ECHR commitments on paper, and the reality on the ground was bound to result in 'important and probably negative consequences for the "legality" of the Strasbourg human rights law system', for it 'increase[d] the possibility that European human rights law will both be disobeyed and be seen to be flouted'.[116] The evident non-compliance would damage the 'sense of legal obligation'[117] arising under the ECHR, giving rise to a type of 'two-tier' system in which efforts to accommodate Russia would weaken the Strasbourg-based institutions more generally.[118] And here Janis suggested, if problems did arise, 'the same political importance of Russia that has prompted the [CoE] to accept its admittance will make it especially difficult for Strasbourg to force the Russian government to comply with adverse findings.'[119]

These words have proved prophetic, not just as regards the ECHR, but as regards Russia's overall CoE membership, in the context of its growing bad faith after 2005, that is, one decade on from admission, at which stage Russia was finding new confidence in its role and status. Then under new leadership a pattern was emerging of it flouting its obligations in national contexts and its aggressive actions against its neighbours (particularly from 2008). At that point, Russia's size and influence would be significant for the leeway the CoE would give it, and which Russia would abuse in the wider CoE context in later years, as the 'reality checks'[120] related to CoE enforcement became apparent.

---

[115] Janis, n 1, 98.
[116] Janis, n 1, 98. See also 'Editorial' (1996) *Netherlands Quarterly of Human Rights*, 1: 3–4, fearing 'dramatic devaluation' of ECHR, 4 (suggesting decision to admit Russia to be 'regretted', 3).
[117] Janis, n 1, 94.
[118] Janis, n 1, 99 (it would 'give the governments of the existing member states all the more latitude in weakening their own commitment to the Strasbourg system').
[119] Janis, n 1, 98.
[120] See section 2.4 of this chapter.

4 Conclusion

In this chapter Russia's CoE obligations and commitments were analysed, although its main focal point has been on its therapeutic accession, and the overall promise it made to progressively realise CoE values. Given that promise, Russia was allowed to join the CoE on the basis that it proved its potential Article 3 (CoE Statute) credentials after admission, not before. This placed enormous emphasis on the 'willing[ness]'[121] of Russia's future leaders to sustain that state's fragile first steps in its transition toward acceptance of CoE values and obligations.

Of course, it is a huge understatement to say that Russia failed to become a rights-respecting, democratic state consistent with CoE values. Rather, looking back the perspective today would be, as we will discuss in more detail in Chapter 4,[122] no state has breached its CoE obligations more than Russia, its membership having had a very damaging effect on the CoE.

Hindsight therefore allows us to make various observations about Russia's accession.

First, it is clear that Russia's membership had been granted before adequate guarantees for improvement had been obtained. A 'better in than out' attitude prevailed. Though many states were not normatively aligned upon accession, it appears there was too much willingness to accept Russia's pledges of reform, rather than actual reform, as the political case for accepting Russia into the CoE trumped the compelling legal case against. It should of course be recognised that similar latitude was afforded to all aspiring states, but in the case of Russia, it seems clear the scope of latitude was disproportionate.

Relatedly, and second, in the 1990s within the CoE context there was great misplaced complacency in Russia's enduring good faith,[123] and as regards the CoE's capacity to exert appropriate external influence and pressure on it if things did not go to plan. The disciplining force of CoE monitoring bodies was overestimated by some politicians, as was the capacity of instruments such as the ECHR to stimulate change on its own, as a type of top-down, and external influence. Of course, over the course of the decades to come this was largely because of the Russian authorities' (especially President Putin's) lack of receptivity, if not resistance to the same, and so their bad faith on the overall matter of CoE membership.

In that last connection, and thirdly, sight should not be lost of how over the 1990s there had been clear and unambiguous collective statements from the CoE governments to the effect that new CoE states such as Russia

---

[121] Cf text accompanying n 14 (PACE Opinion: Russia 'clearly willing').
[122] Chapter 4, Conclusion.
[123] However, see n 114 (Leuprecht's resignation).

would be required to fully uphold their obligations and commitments. Here reference has been made earlier to the reality checks that would follow as regards Russia's compliance with its obligations and commitments, and how, in later years, the CM was very cowed and supine with respect to Russia's breach of CoE obligations,[124] including (it seems) because of the latter's 'political importance' (to quote Janis). The CM's Declaration on Compliance with Commitments of 1994 gave rise to a legitimate expectation that, if Russia did not adhere to its obligations, it would be held to account by the CM as guardian of the CoE. However, ostensibly[125] that did not occur. As shall be observed in Chapters 3 and 4, there was a lack of political will to meaningfully confront Russia, let alone act decisively against it on the part of the CM as executive organ of the CoE, even after PACE had attempted to do so and in light of major transgressions.

Summing up, then, the long view enables us to reflect upon how much the CoE as an independent entity has been let down given what occurred since the 1990s starting point. From the perspective of 2022, it is hard to resist the conclusion that the CoE was failed by its states (in the guise of the CM), as custodians of that institution and all that it stood for. Having encouraged Russia's accession, did those states do all they could to maintain the integrity of the CoE's values, when Russia tested them?[126] Yet, of course, first and foremost, the CoE was let down – putting it charitably – by Russia (more accurately, successive Russian governments). It did not just renege on the promises and commitments it made in 1996, it breached its CoE obligations in manifest and egregious ways, all with a very negative impact on the CoE's credibility and standing.[127]

Accordingly, the calculated risk of Russia's 'therapeutic admission' backfired badly. However, noting the situation there today, and across wider Europe after February 2022, sight should not be lost of a key reason why the gamble was taken. Russia's CoE membership was secured to help galvanise the forces of democracy in Russia, offer political support to its leaders given the risks taken to that point, and so it showed solidarity in the sense highlighted by Vladimir Lukin.[128] In 1996, he warned that if PACE did not admit Russia, 'there is a danger the iron curtain may come down again'.[129] However, he

---

[124] See Chapters 3 and 4.
[125] Ostensibly – for there is no way of measuring (and perhaps one should not underestimate) the ameliorating effect of inter-governmental pressure brought to bear on Russia, especially in the 2000s (at least outside the Chechnya context).
[126] See Chapter 4, Conclusions.
[127] See Chapter 4, Conclusions.
[128] Lukin had been Russian Ambassador to the United States from 1992 to 1994, and served as Human Rights Commissioner of Russia from February 2004 to March 2014.
[129] Cited from Huber, n 1, 136.

said, were Russia admitted to the CoE, there was hope. True, there were risks but if Russia was admitted it would be, 'showing solidarity with a great country which, for the first time in its history, has embarked on a path to the rule of law and had guaranteed freedoms that Russians have never had before.'[130] Further, the CoE would be admitting not Russia as such but 'millions of young people who are no longer afraid and who say what they think, [and] retired people who curse democracy but are willing to defend their voting rights'.[131]

So, it was for such causes, and to promote 'democratic security' in Europe, that Russia was permitted to join the CoE in 1996. And once Russia was in, keeping such hopes alive was one reason why the CoE did so much to accommodate it, notwithstanding the harm that was done to the latter by doing so.

---

[130] Huber, n 1, 136.
[131] Huber, n 1, 136.

3

The Council of Europe and Russia (1998–2013)

1 Introduction: from 'therapeutic admission' to Russia 'at a crossroads'

This chapter covers the period from 1998 to 2013, although its conclusion looks a little beyond that, to 2016. Inevitably the coverage must be selective: the focus is on *aspects* of an evolving and increasingly troubled relationship over the 2000s and into the 2010s. The chapter demonstrates how, under its government, Russia was not a willing patient of 'therapeutic admission' over the period examined. It observes that at no point did Russia ever come close to being a fully-fledged democracy, even if it may have been taking steps along a democratic path up to around 2004–2005. However, things changed then, with Russia regressing from that point and thereafter. This is reflected towards the endpoint of the chapter which highlights the critical juncture reached by 2012, when, in the words of a Parliamentary Assembly of the Council of Europe (PACE) Monitoring Committee report, Russia was at a 'crossroads, confronted with the choice of its own future'.[1]

To help frame what occurred, a few words about the changing approach/ increasing belligerence of Russia's political leadership towards the Council of Europe (CoE) may be useful. This may be seen in terms of three phases. First a generally positive, but short-lived approach toward the CoE, associated with accession in the late-to-mid 1990s and the period immediately after. Second, a phase associated with the mid-2000s and after, up to around 2013, when the Russian authorities were, at best, ambivalent toward the CoE and the European Court of Human Rights (ECtHR),[2] and as the phase progressed,

---

[1] PACE Monitoring Committee, 'The honouring of obligations and commitments by the Russian Federation', Doc. 13018, 14 September 2012, para 536.
[2] See Fura, E. and Maruste, R. (2017) 'Russia's impact on the Strasbourg system, as seen by two former judges of the European Court of Human Rights', in L. Mälksoo and

far more negative, as it started to turn away from the CoE. A third phase occurred after 2013–2014, when there was a much greater distancing from, and an aggressive approach toward the CoE in evidence.[3]

Commentators have noted that 'the relationship between Russia and the West started to change after Putin came to office in March 2000'.[4] At this stage, 'Russia still considered itself to be European, though different from Western Europe'.[5] Then, over the 2000s, Russia found 'new strength as an energy power',[6] a trend which inspired a new confidence, even assertiveness from it. After 2004–2005, under Putin, Russia was determined to push its 'national values above all else', including above democratic values, as it resisted 'foreign supervision and meddling'.[7] Slowly but surely, Russia 'rhetorically, stopped positioning itself as a Western-oriented country'.[8]

It seems that there was receptivity for this in certain quarters domestically. Luc Van den Brande (member of the PACE Monitoring Committee and a co-rapporteur on Russia), commented in the late 2000s on how the turbulence of the 1990s and early 2000s was such that the Russian experience of 'democracy' was associated with chaos on the political scene as far as the public was concerned.[9] That gave rise to a 'lost trust in politicians and institutions' and to the popularity of parties that could offer stability and radical measures. This was 'why 70% of Russians were prepared to accept whoever President Putin earmarked as his successor [President Medvedev, in 2008]',[10] this as 'the restoration of relative order and economic growth and stability' associated with Putin's leadership over the 2000s, reinforced 'the population's confidence in Russia becoming a strong

---

W. Benedek (eds) *Russia and the European Court of Human Rights: The Strasbourg Effect*, Cambridge: Cambridge University Press, pp 222–51.

[3] See Chapter 4. See also Roter, P. (2017) 'Russia in the Council of Europe: participation à la carte', in L. Mälksoo and W. Benedek (eds) *Russia and the European Court of Human Rights: The Strasbourg Effect*, Cambridge: Cambridge University Press, pp 26–55, emphasising the post-2014 period.

[4] Busygina, I. and Kahn, J. (2020) 'Russia, the Council of Europe, and "Ruxit," or why non-democratic illiberal regimes join international organizations', *Problems of Post-Communism*, 67(1): 64–77, 70.

[5] Busygina and Kahn, n 4, 70.

[6] Massias, J.-P. (2007) 'Russia and the Council of Europe: ten years wasted?', *Russie.Nei. Visions*, Institut Français des Relations Internationales, available from: www.ifri.org/en/papers/russia-and-council-europe-ten-years-wasted [Accessed 1 June 2024], 13.

[7] Massias, n 6, 14.

[8] Busygina and Kahn, n 4, 70.

[9] Van den Brande, L. (2010) 'Democratic reforms in Russia: the role of the monitoring process of PACE', in K. Malfliet and S. Parmentier (eds) *Russia and the Council of Europe: 10 Years After*, Basingstoke: Palgrave Macmillan, pp 43–56, 50. See also Busygina and Kahn, n 4, 70.

[10] Van den Brande, n 9, 51.

and "self-sufficient" actor'. This 'resulted in the assertiveness of Russian foreign policy', including as regards its neighbours. Relatedly, in the late 2000s Russians felt that 'during the period of democratic transformations in the 1990s, the country was "abused" by the West and its "allies" from the liberal and democratic domestic elite'.[11] The outcome was 'more and more people [felt] that Russia should go its own way and build its own and "unique" democracy'.[12]

Against this backdrop, this chapter analyses the key interactions between Russia and the CoE in such diverse areas as the situation in Chechnya and the North Caucuses, the Georgian–Russian war, and as regards the domestic influence of the European Convention on Human Rights (ECHR). The picture revealed is one in which it was axiomatic that Russia's 'therapeutic admission' did not work, the CoE not only struggling to cope with a more hostile Russia, but suffering as a consequence as its continued membership started to have unacceptable implications for the CoE. As Malfliet and Parmentier put it (in 2010), '[i]nstead of learning democracy, Russia has started to undermine the authority of an eminent institution for the protection of European values and norms'.[13] Russia was too often playing the role of 'spoiler, hindering the institutions of the [CoE]', especially PACE and the ECtHR, and 'frustrating their attempts to effectively protect liberal values'.[14] Malfliet and Parmentier's pessimism and concern was evident in the rhetorical question they posed: back in the 1990s had 'the [CoE] let in a Trojan horse, or an undercover subversive member?'[15]

The chapter is now divided into three sections. Section 2 looks to two stand-out areas relevant to the period up to the late 2000s/early 2010s, when it was arguable that breaches of Article 3 of the CoE Statute were in issue, but no effective action was taken against Russia by the Committee of Ministers (CM). First, the exceptional matter of Chechnya is examined in detail, to include consideration of the very large number of extremely serious human rights violations that took place over many years. Secondly, the section looks to the Georgian–Russian conflict of 2008, and its aftermath, a further example of Russia's flouting of its CoE and ECHR obligations, that tested the CoE once again.

---

[11] See Massias, n 6, 13 and Busygina, n 4, 70–1.
[12] Van den Brande, n 9, 51.
[13] Malfliet, K. and Parmentier, S. (2010) 'Russia's membership of the CoE: ten years after', in K. Malfliet and S. Parmentier (eds) *Russia and the Council of Europe: 10 Years After*, Basingstoke: Palgrave Macmillan, pp 7–32, 26.
[14] See Malfliet and Parmentier, n 13, 11.
[15] Malfliet and Parmentier, n 13, 9–10. Cf Massias, n 6, 15–16, questioning whether the CoE was being 'undermined from the inside'.

Section 3 examines the domestic situation, in terms of Russia's receptivity to the CoE and the ECHR for the period from 1998–2013. Here we observe how what occurred fitted with Russia's changing attitude toward the CoE, as noted previously. That is, initially there were some signs of positivity; however, after 2005 relations with the CoE and ECtHR grew strained, as the tide was turning decisively away from pluralist democracy in Russia, the domestic political situation being crucial.

This takes us to section 4 of the chapter, and the 'crossroads' choice then confronting Russia. Of course, we know the path adopted, as reflected in Chapter 4, which looks to Russia's annexation of Crimea, and the aggressive approach Russia adopted toward the CoE in that context.

2 Impunity for serious violations in Chechnya, the North Caucasus and Georgia

If Russia's membership of the CoE had meant one thing in 1996 it was that the state's freedom of action should be restricted in certain fields related to the CoE's values and principles, and that corresponding boundaries would be set on Russia's actions. However, this was not so looking to events in relation to Chechnya and the North Caucuses from 1999 to 2009, and to the war between Georgia and Russia in 2008, and its aftermath. While what occurred in relation to these affairs was subject to some accountability at the CoE, it proved to be rather feeble in that it did not seem to significantly affect Russia's actions.

In the following sections, the focus is first on Chechnya (section 2.1). After this, the situation as regards Georgia is examined (section 2.2). A further section (2.3) reflects on this, suggesting that the CM's weak reaction was prescient of the troubled relationship between Russia and the CoE for the years to come.

2.1 Impunity for grave human rights violations in Chechnya and the North Caucuses

In June 2022, Dunja Mijatović, the then CoE Commissioner for Human Rights, highlighted the 'unresolved impunity for the grave human rights violations stemming from the war in Chechnya'[16] as an exemplar of Russia's broken CoE promises.

---

[16] Mijatović, D. (2022) 'At the crossroads: democracy, human rights and the rule of law', Strasbourg, 24 June 2022 (available from: www.echr.coe.int [Accessed 1 June 2024]), 2. For the comments/criticisms of a former CoE Commissioner (2012–2018) re Chechnya, see Muižnieks, N. (2023) 'Using the Summit to breathe new life into the Council of Europe', *European Human Rights Law Review*, 2: 126–34, 132–3.

Indeed, what occurred in relation to Chechnya and the North Caucuses is one of the emblematic issues of the troubled relationship between the CoE and Russia.[17] Russia's unacceptable action during the first Chechnya war prompted the suspension of its accession,[18] and it was only permitted to join after promising to secure accountability for the violations occurring.[19] That promise was totally reneged upon, including with respect to the second Chechnya war (1999–2009), which eclipsed the first in terms of the scale and severity of human rights violations occurring. Indeed, the authors are conscious that they cannot provide an account that appropriately reflects the extent of human suffering and atrocities occurring in the context of the extreme violence and gross human rights violations committed by the parties to the conflict,[20] that is, Russian forces and rebel groups on the Chechen separatist side. The latter included shocking terrorist attacks. However, for Russia's part there were uses of clearly disproportionate force (the bombing and shelling of inhabited areas with devastating effects on the civilian population), situations of regular 'disappearances' and deaths, and many allegations of extra-judicial executions, arbitrary detention and torture as well as a persistent failure to investigate many of these crimes effectively.

The account that follows proceeds in three steps. First, the period 1999–2005, which evidenced the *in*effectiveness of CoE statutory bodies, especially the CM. Second, after 2005, focussing on the role of the ECtHR. And thirdly, the overall issue of unresolved impunity.

2.1.1 PACE as the guardian of the CoE's values: human rights mandates act on Chechnya, but what of the CM?

As for the first period, this encompassed the start of the second Chechen war in the late summer of 1999. By December 1999, when the siege of

---

[17] On Russia and the Chechnya and the North Caucasian region issue, see Merlin, A. (2010) 'Gambling, misunderstanding or compromising? The Council of Europe and the war in Chechnya', in K. Malfliet and S. Parmentier (eds) *Russia and the Council of Europe: 10 Years After,* Basingstoke: Palgrave Macmillan, pp 137–64; Lemaitre, R. (2010) 'Can the European Court of Human Rights provide justice for victims of Russian human rights abuses in Chechnya?', in K. Malfliet and S. Parmentier (eds) *Russia and the Council of Europe: 10 Years After,* Basingstoke: Palgrave Macmillan, pp 165–86; Leach, P. (2017) 'Egregious human rights violations in Chechnya: appraising the pursuit of justice', in L. Mälksoo and W. Benedek (eds) *Russia and the European Court of Human Rights: The Strasbourg Effect,* Cambridge: Cambridge University Press, pp 255–94.

[18] Chapter 2.

[19] Chapter 2.

[20] For moving and tragic accounts of the issues and impunity, see Lemaitre, n 17, 166–7, and especially Gilligan, E. (2010) *Terror in Chechnya: Russia and the Tragedy of Civilians in War*, Princeton, NJ: Princeton University Press.

Grozny began, there was overwhelming evidence of indiscriminate and disproportionate assaults on Chechen civilians on a scale that *The Economist* described as 'worthy of a marauding medieval bully, or a latter-day war criminal such as Slobodan Milosevic'.[21] The lack of any real reaction from the CoE drew accusations that its 'cherished moral authority ha[d] been undermined'[22] by Russia's admission.

With the CM unwilling to place Chechnya in its agenda, after some delay the recently appointed Secretary General, Walter Schwimmer, acted, as did PACE. In December 1999, the former employed Article 52 of the ECHR, its first ever use in relation to a specific situation in a state. Russia, which at no point derogated from the ECHR[23] in relation to Chechnya, was asked 'to furnish, in the light of the case-law of the [ECtHR], explanations concerning the manner in which the Convention [was] implemented in Chechnya, and the risk of violation which [might] result therefrom'.[24] Over protracted correspondence Russia argued that what was occurring was an 'anti-terrorist operation'. An independent report commissioned by the Secretary General for the CM's attention examined the case file and concluded that the 'replies given [by Russia] were not adequate'; Russia had 'failed in its legal obligations as a Contracting State under Article 52 [ECHR]'.[25] The Secretary General referred the matter to the CM, encouraging action under the Committee of Ministers' 1994 Declaration on Compliance with Commitments.[26] The CM declined, stating instead that it would monitor matters.[27] The step may have been understood by Moscow as indicative of the unlikelihood of any major consequences at the CoE even in the face of objective evidence of serious transgressions.

---

[21] *The Economist*, 'Russia's brutal war: letting Russia get away with murder diminishes the West too', 11 December 1999, 17 (calling for Russia's suspension from the CoE; Western governments needing to correct the 'impression' that they would 'overlook behaviour from Russia … they would not have tolerated from the Soviet Union').

[22] *The Economist*, 'Walter Schwimmer, timid moral policeman', 27 November 1999, 56

[23] Cf Article 15, ECHR. For discussion see Merlin, n 17, 147–8 (Russia's unwillingness to acknowledge severity of matter as a 'war').

[24] The language echoed Article 52, which states that, if requested by the Secretary General, the state 'shall furnish an explanation of the manner in which its internal law ensures the effective implementation of any of the provisions of the Convention'. On this Article 52 action, see 'Consolidated report containing an analysis of the correspondence between the Secretary General of the Council of Europe and the Russian Federation under Article 52 of the European Convention on Human Rights prepared by Mr Tamas Bán, Mr Frédéric Sudre and Mr Pieter van Dijk', SG/Inf(2000)24, 26 June 2000. See also Merlin, n 17, 145, and 148–9.

[25] Consolidated report, n 24, para 32.

[26] See Chapter 2, section 2.4. Any CoE state could trigger this mechanism, but none did.

[27] By June 2000, and importantly, the CoE had established a permanent human rights office in Chechnya, the mission lasting 30 months, see Gilligan, n 20, 169–72.

The same message would have been communicated by PACE–CM interactions on Chechnya over the 2000s. This also illustrated the robust position Russia was prepared to take, both generally and before the CM, with the latter failing to support PACE.

So, from the late 1990s, PACE passed a succession of Resolutions condemning Russia's extreme violence and disproportionate actions.[28] After Russia had ignored requests for a ceasefire and for action to be taken by way of political resolution, in April 2000 PACE resolved that what was occurring (widescale attacks on civilian populations by Russian federal troops in the Chechen Republic) amounted to a 'grave violation of Article 3' of the CoE Statute.[29] It called for the CM to suspend Russia under Article 8 of the CoE Statute, unless '[24.2] … substantial, accelerating and demonstrable progress' was made 'immediately'. As an exceptional measure, the voting rights of the Russian delegation in PACE were suspended.[30] This prompted the Russian delegation to walk out, and threaten that Russia would not pay its CoE budgetary contributions.[31] The State Duma adopted a Declaration 'deeply regret[ting]' PACE's position as 'unjust and unfounded', and referring to the decision as 'discriminatory'.[32] The Russian delegation refused to participate in the work of the Assembly and its committees until such time as their voting rights were restored.[33] For its part, the CM[34] declined to invoke either its 1994 Declaration procedures, let alone Article 8 CoE Statute, instead calling for intensified dialogue with Russia. PACE saw this weak response, including the fact that the CM had not even 'denounced' Russia's conduct, as 'totally unacceptable'.[35]

---

[28] There were many such Resolutions (ten between 1999 and 2005), and Recommendations (13 between 1999 and 2005).

[29] See Recommendation 1456 (2000), 'Conflict in the Chechen Republic – Implementation by Russia of Recommendation 1444 (2000)', 6 April 2000, para 25 (PACE deploring, among other things: '9.1. the total and wanton destruction of … Grozny' including 'indiscriminate and disproportionate military action', resulting in the loss of 'hundreds, if not thousands of civilian lives'; 'murder and rape of civilians', attacks on civilian populations and aerial bombardment of densely populated areas [para 9.2]).

[30] See Merlin, n 17, 143.

[31] Massias indicated that the Russian side was aggrieved at the CoE's unilateral approach, there being two sides to the war, Massias, n 6, 7.

[32] See report (Political Affairs Committee, PACE), 'Credentials of the delegation of the Russian Federation', 23 January 2001, para 4.

[33] Cf Chapter 4, section 2.1 (Russian PACE delegation's reaction to PACE's withdrawal of voting rights in 2014).

[34] CM, 'Conflict in the Chechen Republic – implementation by the Russian Federation of Recommendation 1444, Reply to Recommendation 1456 (200)', 27 June 2000.

[35] PACE Resolution 1221 (2000), 'Conflict in the Chechen Republic? Follow-up to Recommendations 1444 (2000) and 1456 (2000) of the Parliamentary Assembly', 29 June 2000, para 20. See also n 27.

Nonetheless, the Russian PACE delegation's voting rights were restored in January 2001, reflecting, apparently, the PACE delegation's readiness to use its influence to improve the human rights situation in the Chechen Republic.[36] The relevant Resolution referred to PACE remaining 'gravely concerned' about the human rights situation, but believing that the Russian parliamentary delegation 'deserve[d] to be given another chance to prove that it is willing – and able – to influence the situation in the Chechen Republic for the better'.[37] There was sharp criticism from non-governmental organisations (NGOs).[38] However, a newspaper report pointed to the dilemma PACE faced: the Russian PACE delegation's return was an acknowledgement that the CoE 'had exerted only limited influence over Kremlin policy in Chechnya', and that 'in casting Russia away ... it had only restricted its own ability to monitor and help the region'.[39]

Over 2001–2005, PACE–CM relations became almost adversarial, with strong criticism of Russia from PACE, and the CM unwilling to publicly condemn it, let alone act under Article 8,[40] preferring dialogue and cooperation. Specially appointed PACE rapporteurs were able to visit Chechnya on numerous occasions, a positive for the CoE in that few other international monitoring bodies had access to the region.[41] Further, the Russian delegation in PACE took part in various working groups on Chechnya.[42] But did any of this make much of a difference?[43] Apparently not, according to the plethora of PACE Resolutions and Recommendations deploring the human rights violations occurring at the hands of Russian security forces and the lack of prosecutions in relation to them.[44] In parallel, robust criticism was directed

---

[36] Resolution 1241 (2001), 'Credentials of the delegation of the Russian Federation', 25 January 2001.
[37] Resolution 1241 (2001), n 36, para 3.
[38] Leach, n 17, 260.
[39] Baker, P. (2001) 'European Council restores Russia's rights', *Washington Post*, 25 January 2001.
[40] For strong criticism of the CM, see Merlin, n 17, 144.
[41] Jordan suggested that the Putin government chose interaction with the 'weakest institution ... in terms of clout, in an effort to avoid an international backlash', see Jordan, P. (2003) 'Does membership have its privileges?', *Human Rights Quarterly*, 25(3): 660–88, 683.
[42] See Bindig, R. (2010) 'Russia's accession to the CoE', in K. Malfliet and S. Parmentier (eds) *Russia and the Council of Europe: 10 Years After*, Basingstoke: Palgrave Macmillan, pp 33–42, 38.
[43] For Jordan such measures were really an 'excuse' for the CoE not to take more serious action, Jordan, n 41, 684.
[44] For an overview up to late 2005, see Committee on Legal Affairs and Human Rights (PACE), 'Human rights violations in the Chechen Republic: the Committee of Ministers' responsibility vis-à-vis the Assembly's concerns', Doc. 10774, 21 December 2005 (Rapporteur Bindig – hereafter 'Bindig 2005 Report').

at Russia by various PACE committees,[45] and other CoE actors,[46] including the European Committee for the Prevention of Torture and Inhuman or Degrading Treatment or Punishment (CPT).[47] It was able to visit affected areas,[48] and in 2001, 2003 and 2007 it took the exceptional measure of issuing public statements concerning the Russian authorities' failure to cooperate in relation to the climate of impunity in Chechnya, and with respect to the persisting torture and ill-treatments of prisoners.[49]

With Russia seemingly impervious to such criticism, PACE appealed to CoE states to bring an inter-state case before the ECHR,[50] and create an ad hoc criminal tribunal to try war crimes and crimes against humanity committed in the Chechen Republic.[51] Neither option was pursued, but the calls highlighted both how desperate and serious matters were, how PACE lacked appropriate powers itself, and the general inadequacy of the CoE's response.

A stand-out issue here was the CM's exceedingly passive stance. Unlike PACE, it operated in complete confidentiality. It is, of course, a political institution, comprising ministers of foreign affairs (or their representatives). Unsurprisingly, then, it acts 'politically', as it did via its decision to operate on the basis on consensus,[52] which, of course, restricted its capacity to act very significantly. More generally, following the 11 September 2001 attacks, the context was one in which 'Europe and the United States sought a strategic rapprochement with'[53] Russia. This gelled with the

---

[45] See, for example, Committee on Political Affairs and Democracy: Doc. 8585 and Resolution 1201 (1999); Doc. 8630 and Recommendation 1444 (2000); Doc. 8697 and Recommendation 1456 (2000); Doc. 8785 and Resolution 1221 (2000); Doc. 8840 and Resolution 1227 (2000); Doc. 8929 and Resolution 1240 (2001).

[46] The CoE Human Rights Commissioner issued reports in 1999, 2000 and 2001 following visits to Chechnya; for further details, see www.coe.int/en/web/commissioner/home [Accessed 14 June 2024].

[47] Full documentation regarding the CPT and Russia may be found at www.coe.int/en/web/cpt/russian-federation [Accessed 14 June 2024].

[48] Its reports remained confidential, as Russia refused to give permission for their publication, as was permissible under the Convention.

[49] See 'Public Statement of 10 July 2001' [CPT/Inf (2001), 15], 'Public statement of 10 July 2003' [CPT/Inf (2003), 33], and 'Public Statement of 13 March 2007' [CPT/Inf (2007), 17]. See Merlin, n 17, 146. For later interactions with the CPT, see n 259 and Chapter 7, text accompanying n 80.

[50] See Bindig 2005 Report, n 44, para 95, and Gilligan, n 20, 173.

[51] PACE, Recommendation 1600 (2003), 'The human rights situation in the Chechen Republic', 2 April 2003, para 3.5.

[52] Cf Bindig 2005 Report, n 44, para 89 ('gentlemen's agreement' not to vote, but act by 'consensus'). See Merlin, n 17, 145 (as such it was 'impossible to be surprised by [its] great feebleness' on Chechnya).

[53] Cf Nager, N. and Zwaak, L. (2008) 'The Russian Federation and human rights', *Netherlands Quarterly of Human Rights* 26(3): 4; see Gilligan, n 20, 177–9.

latter's rhetoric that Chechnya was another front in the so-called 'war on terrorism',[54] such that its actions against Muslim separatists in Chechnya were not an attack on the population generally, the widespread harm to civilians being unfortunate collateral damage. In the domestic context, the Chechnya affair was also an opportunity for President Putin to show strong leadership, and an unyielding approach given terrorist atrocities within Russia itself.

The pressures this placed on the CoE internally were in evidence in December 2005, via an extensive and detailed report produced by PACE's Committee on Legal Affairs and Human Rights (CLAHR), and a related PACE Recommendation.[55] The report[56] admonished the CM as 'executive organ' of the CoE, having 'primary responsibility for maintaining the Organisation's credibility', in that it was not showing sufficient 'determination' and 'courage' in monitoring Russia's human rights commitments.[57] The CM was accused of failing the CoE overall,[58] and of not taking or considering 'seriously' PACE's proposals on Chechnya, most of its Recommendations being treated as a 'dead-letter', even though matters on the ground had not improved significantly. Specifically, the CM was criticised for neglecting PACE's request, set out in a 2003 Recommendation,[59] to act under its (the CM's) 1994 Declaration on Compliance with Commitments.[60] This was 'unacceptable'.[61] The CM was further accused of inconsistency and double standards, for the 1994 Declaration had been initiated in relation to Ukraine, Georgia and Moldova,[62] yet not Russia. It was implied that Russia was receiving preferential treatment because of its size, status and financial clout,[63] even that the CM was scared of it.[64]

---

[54] See especially Merlin, n 17, 147–50.
[55] Recommendation 1733 (2006), 'Human rights violations in the Chechen Republic: the Committee of Ministers' responsibility vis-à-vis the Assembly's concerns', 25 January 2006.
[56] Bindig 2005 Report, n 44.
[57] Bindig 2005 Report, n 44, para 97.
[58] See Bindig 2005 Report, n 44, paras 81–98.
[59] Recommendation 1600 (2003), 2 April 2003, para 4.
[60] Cf Doc. 9821, 'The human rights situation in the Chechen Republic/ Recommendation 1600 (2003)/Reply from the Committee of Ministers', 3 June 2003. The CM explained it was monitoring the human rights situation.
[61] Resolution 1479 (2006), 'Human rights violations in the Chechen Republic: the Committee of Ministers' responsibility vis-à-vis the Assembly's concerns', 25 January 2006, para 14.2. See also criticism of governments, member states and the CM, para 2.
[62] See Bindig 2005 Report, n 44, para 85.
[63] Bindig 2005 Report, n 44, para 96.
[64] Bindig 2005 Report, n 44, fn 61, citing newspaper reports (*Le Monde*, 30 June 2005) referring to CoE diplomats who had a 'fear [of] Russia', and that 'nobody dare tell anything' about Chechnya.

PACE exhorted the CM 'to confront its responsibilities', as its inaction risked 'seriously threaten[ing] the credibility' of the CoE overall.[65] It was urged to pursue monitoring under the 1994 Declaration,[66] and to stop hiding behind its consensus/unanimity stance.[67] In effect, then, PACE urged the CM to act upon its CoE commitments and responsibilities,[68] and publicly call out Russia.[69] However, the CM's Reply[70] to PACE's Recommendation only seemed to endorse the criticism of it, for it was unclear as to whether it was even employing the 1994 Declaration at all with respect to Russia, stating that no 'specific action' was required under that regime as it was following matters closely in the context of ECHR and CPT procedures. The Reply emphasised how the CM was supporting the implementation of practical programmes in Chechnya as well as cooperation activities. However, this and what followed (apparently no further references to action under the 1994 Declaration as regards Russia) only seemed to confirm the thrust of the CLAHR's criticism that, in effect, the CM had (apparently) unofficially agreed 'to stop' monitoring Russia with respect to Chechnya (at least under the 1994 Declaration), such that the main responsibility was being left, by default, to other CoE actors, and especially the ECtHR.[71] But, it was warned, prophetically, if the nettle was not grasped by the CM now (2005), it would 'face potentially insurmountable difficulties in future, when supervising the execution of judgments of the [ECtHR] with regard to Chechnya'.[72]

2.1.2 After 2005: the ECtHR as the last hope?

What then of the prospect that the ECtHR would succeed where PACE had not, and given the CM's apparent unwillingness to confront Russia? As *Human Right Watch* put it, the ECtHR, which delivered its first judgments on Chechnya in 2005, had become the 'Last hope for victims' there.[73]

---

[65] Recommendation 1733 (2006), n 55, para 2.
[66] Recommendation 1733 (2006), n 55, paras 5.1–5.2.
[67] Recommendation 1733 (2006), n 55, para 6.
[68] Cf Bindig 2005 Report, n 44, para 92 (the CM 'reneg[ing] on its responsibilities' to PACE and 'its own commitments' under the 1994 Declaration).
[69] Passages in the Bindig 2005 Report implied that Russia had worked hard to ensure that effective monitoring or action/further action under the 1994 Declaration would not occur, see n 44, paras 87–8.
[70] CM Reply to Recommendation 1733 (12 May 2006).
[71] Bindig 2005 Report, n 44, para 86.
[72] Bindig 2005 Report, n 44, para 86.
[73] Human Rights Watch, 'Chechnya: European Court last hope for victims', 8 June 2008 (available from: www.hrw.org/news/2008/06/08/chechnya-european-court-last-hope-victims) [Accessed 10 June 2024].

The ECtHR is, of course, a court of law, not to be influenced by politics. Then again, its President in the early 2000s (Luzius Wildhaber) must have been left in no doubt about the political pressures bearing down on the Strasbourg judges. Apparently, the Russian ambassador to the CoE personally threatened Wildhaber after the imposition of interim measures in a case (*Shamayev and Others v. Georgia and Russia*)[74] concerning the extradition of persons of Chechen origin to Russia.[75]

The ECtHR's case law on Chechnya is vast,[76] and so only an illustration of some of the issues occurring can be offered here, using the first three cases decided by the Court, on 24 February 2005: *Khashiyev and Akayeva v. Russia*;[77] *Isayeva, Yusupova and Bazayeva v. Russia*;[78] and *Isayeva v. Russia*.[79]

In these judgments the ECtHR held that there had been a range of serious human rights violations, including Article 2 (the right to life) and Article 3 (the prohibition of torture).[80] The cases highlighted the plight of civilians caught up in the conflict, the Convention duties Russia was subject to in that regard, and how these had been manifestly ignored. For example, *Isayeva v. Russia* was brought by an applicant whose son and three nieces had been killed in 2000. In issue was the bombardment by Russia's forces of a village (Katyr-Yurt) apparently being held hostage by well-equipped and well-trained fighters, a Russian fighter jet air attack on a refugee convoy, and the total inadequacy of the ensuing Article 2 investigations. Among other things, the Court criticised the employment of heavy free-falling (indiscriminate) high-explosion aviation bombs with a damage radius exceeding 1,000 metres in a populated area, outside wartime and without prior evacuation of the civilians. This was 'impossible to reconcile with the degree of caution expected from a law-enforcement body in a democratic society'.[81]

In such cases, the message of the judgments was that the primary aim of operations like those in issue should be to protect lives from unlawful violence

---

[74] Cf *Shamayev and Others v. Georgia and Russia*, no. 36378/02, 12 April 2005 (violations of Article 3 and 5, but also of Articles 34 (hindering right of individual petition/ignoring Rule 39 interim order to suspend extradition) and 38 (obstacles to Court's fact-finding mission)).

[75] *The Guardian*, 'I was poisoned by Russians, human rights judge says', 1 February 2007 (also referring to Wildhaber's fears that he had been poisoned during a trip to Russia, although official ECtHR communiques stated illness was not suspicious).

[76] For an account of the Chechen case law up to 2009, see Lemaitre, n 17, 170–5.

[77] *Khashiyev and Akayeva v. Russia*, no. 57942/00, 24 February 2005 (allegations of killing and ill-treatment of civilians).

[78] *Isayeva, Yusupova and Bazayeva v. Russia*, no. 57947/00, 24 February 2005 (bombing of convoy by Russian military jets; loss of civilian life).

[79] *Isayeva v. Russia*, no. 57950/00, 24 February 2005 (air attack on convoy).

[80] As well as the right to an effective remedy and the peaceful enjoyment of possessions.

[81] *Isayeva*, n 78, para 191.

(or, ill-treatment), and that there should be effective accountability when things had gone wrong. The point was reiterated in numerous subsequent judgments, brought by civilian victims of military actions in places such as Grozny, and elsewhere. In 2017, Phillip Leach, who led EHRAC[82] at the time, commented on the nature of issues arising, the cases concerning, 'the torture of detainees, deaths in custody, enforced disappearances, extrajudicial executions, deaths caused by aerial bombardment, artillery shelling or other armed attack or operation, or the failure to de-mine, and the destruction of, or damage to, homes and other property caused by aerial attacks or other operations'.[83] The relevant judgments saw the ECtHR establish important human rights law principles in relation to what was, in effect, a zone of armed conflict (albeit Russia would not acknowledge this), and the ECHR's interaction with international humanitarian law.

2.1.3 'Unresolved impunity': Russia's failure to implement the Chechnya judgments

With the ECtHR issuing judgments years after events, and in relation to scenarios where the rule of law was non-existent, a central feature of its case law was the imperative that there be proper, effective Articles 2, 3 and 5 investigations into the alleged violations that had occurred. In other words, and just as PACE had required in 1996,[84] that there be proper human rights accountability – and that a culture of impunity should not prevail.

Evidently such an outcome could only be achieved in the national context, and required political will, plus good faith and cooperation from Russia. This was in very short supply, if it existed at all, as evidenced by a 2007 PACE Resolution referring to a 'significant number of cases' in which it was evident that there was a basic 'lack of willingness to effectively investigate the allegations' of murder, disappearance, beatings and so on, and 'in some cases the intention of whitewashing [was] clearly apparent'.[85] Relatedly there were reprisals against applicants to the ECtHR, harassment of human rights defenders on the ground,[86] and other forms of intimidation and obstruction

---

[82] The European Human Rights Advocacy Centre was founded in 2003, working with partners in Russia and the region to challenge serious human rights abuses before the ECtHR, see https://ehrac.org.uk/en_gb [Accessed 14 June 2024].
[83] Leach, n 17, 261.
[84] Chapter 2, sections 2.2 and 3.2.
[85] PACE Resolution 1571 (2007), para 5 (para 7 noting that this mainly concerned Russia/Chechnya). See Gilligan's account highlighting false cooperation from Russian authorities, n 20, 183–5 (opening cases but 'then "playing ping-pong" with investigation files'/leaving file 'open indefinitely' to avoid judicial scrutiny, 183).
[86] PACE Resolution 1571 (2007), n 85, referring to trumped-up criminal charges, discriminatory tax inspections and threats of prosecution for 'abuse of office'. This had

contrary to Article 34 ECHR.[87] Meanwhile, the Russian authorities constantly frustrated the Strasbourg litigation, employing delaying tactics,[88] and failing to disclose relevant documents. In due course the ECtHR felt compelled to make evidential assumptions,[89] and adopted a more robust stance to what was required of Russia.[90] By this stage, Leach came to the depressing conclusion that there was 'no discernible improvement in the quality of investigations carried out into cases emanating from the North Caucasus region raising issues under Articles 2 or 3'.[91]

Indeed, Dunja Mijatović's quotation about 'unresolved impunity'[92] may be illustrated by the aforementioned *Khashiyev and Akayeva v. Russia* case of 2005.[93] The CM's Department for Execution of Judgments uses this as a Leading Case for 324 repetitive cases,[94] resulting in serious violations of Articles 2, 3, 5, 6, 8, 13, 38 and of Article 1 of Protocol No. 1.[95] These remain pending before the CM to this day,[96] having been examined by the

---

led to claims not being taken up or their withdrawal. For analysis of the intimidation of applicants and lawyers, see Lemaitre, n 17, 175–7.

[87] A 'HUDOCs' search indicates Russia breached Article 34 on over 40 occasions during its ECHR membership (cases *not* confined to Chechnya context). There were 25+ violations of Article 38 (failure to furnish all necessary facilities to the ECtHR).

[88] Leach, n 17, 273.

[89] Leach, n 17, 277–83. For details of the Russian government's lack of cooperation with the court, see Lemaitre, n 17, 178.

[90] See *Aslakhanova and Others v. Russia*, no. 2944/06, 18 December 2012 (Article 46 used to indicate necessity of creating a single, sufficiently high-level body in charge of solving disappearances); also, *Abakarova v. Russia*, no. 16664/07, 15 October 2015 (the bombing of Katyr-Yurt in 2000; Article 46 direction highlighting (in additional to criminal law measures) need for non-judicial mechanisms to ensure similar occurrences do not recur, and applicant's rights adequately protected in new proceedings).

[91] Leach, n 17, 272.

[92] Mijatović, n 16.

[93] *Khashiyev and Akayeva v. Russia*, n 77.

[94] Full details available from: https://hudoc.exec.coe.int/eng?i=004-9 [Accessed 14 June 2024] (see further at https://hudoc.exec.coe.int).

[95] That is, 'killings or presumed killings notably as a result of indiscriminate bombings and failures to properly organise safe passages for civilians; unjustified use of force; disappearances; unacknowledged detentions; torture; unlawful search and seizure operations; destruction of property; and failure to co-operate with the Convention organs'. The ECtHR rulings had also identified issues related to 'the mental suffering of the victims' relatives, the lack of effective investigations into the alleged abuses and absence of effective domestic remedies in this respect', n 94.

[96] The process of attempted execution still goes on, see 9 May 2022 submission received from the European Human Rights Advocacy Centre (EHRAC) (available from: https://hudoc.exec.coe.int/eng#{%22execdocumenttypecollection%22:[%22CEC%22]}) [Accessed 14 June 2024]. A Memorandum issued by Department for the Execution of Judgments of the European Court of Human Rights (H/Exec(2023)12: 'Judgments of the European Court of Human Rights against the Russian Federation: measures required in the pending

CM at 44 meetings, with two interim resolutions being adopted,[97] critical of the lack of meaningful action by the Russian authorities. The *Khashiyev* group concerned 668 persons missing mostly between 1999 and 2006, the disappearances for which were attributable to state agents, such that effective investigations were required. However, only two missing persons had been found (the last in 2015) there being an absence of progress on all others. Regarding criminal investigations, '[n]one of the investigations of suspected perpetrators in these cases [had] led to decisive results'.[98]

This devastatingly negative insight raises many questions, first and foremost for Russia, itself, of course. We have seen how it reneged on clear and specific promises made on accession, compounding that by its subsequent actions, to include its wilful and premeditated obstructive conduct in relation to the ECtHR, and, for example, its lack of cooperation with the CoE's European Committee for the Prevention of Torture (CPT).[99] The history records will therefore show that Russia preferred a path associated with a lack of accountability and impunity, even after the end of the war. This is further evidenced, beyond 2010, by numerous statements made by the CoE Commissioner for Human Rights in the 2010s regarding attacks on civil society actors in Chechnya even in later years.[100]

What, then, could be said of the CoE and the ECtHR?

Due to Russia's obstinance, of course, Bindig was correct to say that, ultimately, 'PACE and the [CoE] could not exert real influence on the development of the conflict' or on Russia's approach in the region. Instead, 'at most' the PACE reports 'could inform the … public about the real situation in the region'.[101] However, that was important because collectively the various CoE documents, and the ECtHR judgments constitute a record of historical fact as to what occurred, entailing that the events in question in Chechnya could not be 'buried'. Instead, the CoE shone a light of matters in terms of Russia committing manifest human rights violations of an order and scale that saw PACE call for Article 8 action, and the creation of a war crimes tribunal. Here PACE, the CPT and the ECtHR stood up for core CoE principles and values, including: the notion that the rule of law should apply, regardless of the exceptional context; the sanctity of human life and

---

cases', 8 December 2023), highlights many individual and (profound) general measures still required of Russia as regards Chechnya.
[97] CM/ResDH(2011)292 and CM/ResDH(2015)45.
[98] 1436th meeting (8–10 June 2022), Department for Execution of Judgments' Notes (*Khashiyev and Akayeva v. Russia*, no. 57942/00), n 94.
[99] See n 49.
[100] For example, see Statement from CoE Commissioner, 'Human rights abuses in Chechnya should be investigated, not covered up', 18 March 2021.
[101] Bindig, n 42, 38.

dignity of individuals; the avoidance of impunity for serious human rights violations; and a system for their prevention, investigation and accountability including when lethal force is used by state officials, and when individuals were ill-treated.

The importance of the CoE's role here is highlighted further when one considers how investigative journalists who sought to publicise alleged violations of human rights in Chechnya were murdered in suspicious circumstances,[102] the ECtHR later upholding violations of Article 2 based on inadequate investigatory steps to find the person or persons who had commissioned the murder.[103] Consider also the case of *Tagayeva and Others v. Russia*[104] in the context of state attempts to whitewash its own actions. It concerned an atrocious terrorist attack on a school in Beslan, North Ossetia (Russia) in September 2004, which led to the deaths of some 334 civilians, including 186 children, who had been taken hostage in a school. The case at Strasbourg highlighted the culpability of Russia for aspects of the terrorist attack, drawing attention to the failures of the Russian authorities in multiple respects, including regarding preventing the situation from occurring and the management of the security operation (excessive and indiscriminate use of force), which resulted in unnecessary deaths.[105] At the time (2004), there had been major harassment (death threats) and intimidation of journalists trying to report on the issues.[106]

Regarding the ECtHR, as a lawyer acting for applicants in the first Chechnya case commented, the judgments helped establish what many had desperately wanted (often in the face of Russia's denials): judgments confirming the 'incontrovertible truth of what had happened to them and their families'.[107] Further, even though they were much delayed, the ECtHR judgments offered not just an element of moral justice for applicants, but

---

[102] See Merlin, n 17, 149.

[103] For example, see *Mazepa and Others v. Russia*, no. 15086/07, 17 July 2018 (contract killing of Anna Politkovskaya in Moscow (2006); criminal convictions without concluding who had ordered the killing).

[104] *Tagayeva and Others v. Russia*, no. 26562/07, 13 April 2017. See also *Finogenov and others v. Russia*, no. 18299/03, 20 December 2011 (Russian theatre hostage-rescue operation case – 125 hostages died; procedural violations of Article 2). Neither judgment has been closed by the CM (they remain unimplemented).

[105] *Tagayeva*, n 104: Russia required to reform law of use of force to ensure adequate legal framework during security operations, see para 640 of the judgment.

[106] PACE, 'Honouring of obligations and commitments by the Russian Federation', 3 June 2005, Doc. 10568, paras 387–8.

[107] Bowring, B. (2019) 'The crisis of the European Court of Human Rights in the face of authoritarian and populist regimes' in A. Kent (ed) *The Future of International Courts*, Abingdon: Routledge, pp 76–93, 78.

also financial compensation, for Russia tended to pay the just satisfaction awarded by the ECtHR in required deadlines.[108]

However, in turn, that highlighted a further issue. Russia's readiness to pay such just satisfaction gave the appearance of cooperation, but distracted from its true attitude, which was a steadfast refusal to address the underlying issues.[109] The bigger issue, of course, was the CoE's and the ECtHR's lack of impact and influence on Russia as regards Chechnya; that plus the CM's failure to confront Russia.

2.2 Zones of special influence? Transnistria, and the Georgian–Russian conflict of 2008

The preceding account demonstrated how the Russian government was prepared to ignore, blatantly and wilfully, fundamental CoE values, and criticism from its institutions. In section 3 of this chapter, we will see that that observation did not necessarily apply to all of Russia's interactions with the CoE and the ECtHR over the 2000s. However, the attitude was in evidence in other respects early on, including as regards certain key accession commitments Russia made when joining the CoE (including the commitment not to treat neighbouring states as zone of special influence).[110] Here Russia's actions in relation to Moldova, and the separatist 'Moldovian Republic of Transnistria' (MRT), may be highlighted, before turning to the Georgian–Russian conflict of 2008.

Regarding Moldova, upon accession Russia agreed to withdraw its troops from the disputed region of the MRT.[111] However, they remained there through the duration of its CoE membership, a PACE report of 2012 stating that 'Russian leaders [had] sought to condition' troop withdrawal to the 'resolution of Transnistria's status'.[112] The CoE seemed unable to affect this, although ECtHR rulings highlighted Russia's ECHR responsibilities in relation to the activities of the MRT, given Russia's continued military presence and support for the regime there. For example, while not concerning Russia's accession commitment to withdraw troops, the Grand Chamber ruling in *Ilaşcu and Others v. Moldova and Russia*[113] concluded that Russia, and to varying degrees,

---

[108] See Lemaitre, n 17, 179–80.
[109] Cf Merlin, n 17, 156.
[110] See Chapter 2, section 2.2.
[111] See Chapter 2, section 2.2. As of 2012, approximately 1,500 Russian troops remained on Transnistrian territory; for details, see PACE report, n 1, paras 153–62.
[112] PACE report, n 1, para 159.
[113] *Ilaşcu and Others v. Moldova and Russia* [GC], no. 48787/99, 8 July 2004. See also *Ivanţoc and Others v. Moldova and Russia*, no. 23687/05, 15 November 2011 (follow-up case).

Moldova, had violated Article 3 and 5(1)(a) ECHR in relation to the individual applicants, who had been detained and ill-treated by the MRT authorities. The Court established that Russia had 'jurisdiction' under Article 1 ECHR as at relevant times the MRT 'remain[ed] under the effective authority, or at the very least under the decisive influence', of Russia, including as it survived 'by virtue of the military, economic, financial and political support given to it' by Russia, including after its ratification of the ECHR.[114] According to the Court, then, Russia was responsible for the applicants' fate, and made no effort to put an end to their situation (although it did not have direct control over the MRT subsequently).[115] The judgment required their release.[116]

President Putin was reported to have stated that in *Ilaşcu*, 'Russia was accused of something which [it] had nothing to do with',[117] dismissing the judgment as 'a clear political decision', one which 'undermine[d] confidence in the international court system'.[118] The judgment was not implemented for several years,[119] although Russia's failure to adhere to its accession commitment regarding the MRT (and, for example, as regards the legal abolition of the death penalty) did not prevent it taking up the rotating chair of the CM in 2006.[120] *Ilaşcu* is but one of a litany of cases against Russia related to Transnistria that Forde argues are all-but inexecutable given Russia's intransigence regarding its occupation of the region and failure to engage meaningfully with the execution process.[121]

We turn now to the Georgian–Russian war, a comparatively short conflict in 2008 which ended with Russia effectively occupying parts of Georgian

---

[114] *Ilaşcu*, n 113, para 392. Cf the dissenting opinion of Judge Kovler ('Russian' judge) arguing that MRT was not controlled by Russia or Moldova, and so the 'objective impossibility' of enforcing the judgment.

[115] *Ilaşcu*, n 113, para 393. See also later rulings confirming the 'MRT's' high level of dependency on Russia, and so potential ECHR 'jurisdiction' of the later: *Catan and Others v. the Republic of Moldova and Russia* [GC], no. 43370/04, 19 October 2012, para 121; *Mozer v. the Republic of Moldova and Russia* [GC], no. 11138/10, 23 February 2016, para 110. Neither judgment has been closed by the CM (they remain unimplemented).

[116] *Ilaşcu*, n 113, para 490. The *Ilaşcu* and *Ivanţoc* cases were closed in 2014, after the adoption of five Interim Resolutions, as the respective applicants had been released and just satisfaction paid: CM/ResDH(2014)37.

[117] Reuters, 'European court rulings that have irked Russia', 21 January 2007, available from: www.reuters.com/article/idUSL11705682/ [Accessed 14 June 2014].

[118] On the controversy caused ('major dispute' between CoE and Russia), see Nussberger, A. (2008) 'The reception process in Russia and Ukraine', in H. Keller and A. Stone Sweet (eds) *A Europe of Rights*, Oxford: Oxford University Press, pp 603–74, 644–5.

[119] See n 116.

[120] On which see Massias, n 6, 5–16 (criticism of the CoE by key Russian figures).

[121] Forde, A. (2024) *European Human Rights Grey Zones: The Council of Europe and Areas of Conflict*, Cambridge: Cambridge University Press, pp 130–6.

territory.¹²² There was a long backdrop to this, of course. Tensions between the two nations had been in evidence via an inter-state case brought by Georgia in 2007, concerning collective expulsion of Georgians from Russia. The judgment in *Georgia v. Russia (I)* was delivered in 2014, upholding most of Georgia's claims.¹²³

The armed conflict of August 2008 was the first time since the 1970s, when Türkiye invaded Cyprus, that two CoE states had been at war with each other¹²⁴ (in this chapter we will use the contemporary name 'Türkiye' in all situations except when the title of the case or article or a quote uses the old name of 'Turkey'). Acting under 'Rule 39' the ECtHR called upon both sides to respect Articles 2 and 3 of the Convention. For its part, PACE assessed that *both* Russia and Georgia had seriously violated the Statute of the CoE¹²⁵ and their obligations and commitments as member states of the CoE, plus their accession commitments. It was documented that Georgia started the military action by shelling Tskhinvali (the capital of South Ossetia) without warning.¹²⁶ Russia counter-attacked with large-scale military actions in central and western Georgia and in Abkhazia, these also 'fail[ing] to respect the principle of proportionality and international humanitarian law' (according to PACE), and constituting 'a violation' of CoE principles'.¹²⁷ A significant part of Georgian territory (estimated at 20 per cent) was then occupied by Russia, and there were attacks on its economic and strategic infrastructure, which PACE regarded as, potentially, 'a direct attack on' Georgia's 'sovereignty', and so a further violation of the CoE Statute, or at least 'an attempt by Russia to extend its influence over a "near abroad" state in violation of its accession commitment to denounce such a concept'.¹²⁸ A Russian presidential decree (26 August 2008) officially recognised the independence of the breakaway regions of South Ossetia and Abkhazia (regions within Georgia's internationally recognised borders, and where Russia troops were deployed), in itself a further 'violation of international law' and CoE 'statutory principles', according to PACE.¹²⁹ It

---

[122] Much of the relevant factual background is set out in PACE Resolution 1633 (2008), 'The consequences of the war between Georgia and Russia', 2 October 2008.
[123] *Georgia v. Russia (I)* [GC], no. 13255/07, 3 July 2014 (administrative practice of collective expulsion of Georgian nationals by Russian authorities from October 2006 to January 2007: violation of Article 4 of Protocol 4).
[124] See Chapter 5.
[125] Resolution 1631 (2008), 'Reconsideration on substantial grounds of previously ratified credentials of the Russian delegation', 1 October 2008 (for both states, a 'serious violation of the Statute' and of accession commitments, para 2). On interim measures issued by the ECtHR, see Chapter 6, section 3.
[126] Resolution 1633 (2008), n 122, para 5.
[127] Resolution 1633 (2008), n 122, para 6.
[128] Resolution 1633 (2008), n 122, para 6.
[129] Resolution 1633 (2008), n 122, para 9.

further expressed its grave concerns at the human rights and humanitarian law violations committed by both sides in the context of the war.[130] In the course of all this large numbers of people had been displaced on potentially a permanent basis.[131]

Even though Article 3 had been breached in PACE's view, it neither imposed internal sanctions (for example, restrictions on voting rights) nor raised the possibility of Article 8 action under the CoE Statute. Instead, cooperation was seen as better than confrontation, because the latter would not achieve anything: a PACE rapporteur conceptualised Russia's continued CoE membership in 2008 as one according to which the CoE was 'not so much the "House of Democracy" but a kind of European hospital of democracy'.[132] No Article 8 action should be called for, for 'a healing process cannot be based on the expulsion of the sick and wounded'.[133] Dialogue and mutual trust were the only hope and would 'enable the Russian authorities to engage in a meaningful and constructive dialogue with a view to addressing all the issues mentioned in the Assembly resolutions on the consequences of the war between Georgia and Russia'.[134] So, 2008–2009 saw political criticism of Russia in PACE occurring in relation to unsuccessful challenges to the credentials of the Russian Delegation to PACE. However, no sanctions were imposed, even though the 2009 challenge highlighted Russia's lack of compliance with most of the demands PACE had formulated the previous year.[135]

Subsequently, the Russian government ignored PACE's exhortations, and those of the international community that it rescind its recognition of South Ossetia and Abkhazia, and withdraw its troops. In fact, the ominous path being followed was in evidence in September 2008, when President

---

[130] Resolution 1633 (2008), n 122, paras 11–12.
[131] Resolution 1633 (2008), n 122, para 15 ('192 000 persons ... displaced as a consequence of the war').
[132] PACE Monitoring Committee, 'Reconsideration on substantive grounds of previously ratified credentials of the Russian delegation', Doc. 12045, 29 September 2009, para 17.
[133] PACE Monitoring Committee, n 132.
[134] PACE Resolution 1687 (2009), 'Reconsideration on substantive grounds of previously ratified credentials of the Russian delegation', 1 October 2009, para 6, also para 7. Apparently, the leader of Russian delegation in PACE said he would recommend Russia's withdrawal from the CoE if the credentials of the delegation were withdrawn, see Malfliet, K. and Parmentier, S. (2010) 'Introduction', in K. Malfliet and S. Parmentier (eds) *Russia and the Council of Europe: 10 Years After,* Basingstoke: Palgrave Macmillan, p 24.
[135] See also Resolution 1683 (2009), 'The war between Georgia and Russia: one year after', 29 September 2009, referring to Russia's 'non-compliance' with PACE's demands as 'underscor[ing] a lack of political will on Russia's part to address the consequences of the war in a manner incumbent on' a CoE member state, para 11.

Medvedev and Foreign Minister Lavrov gave interviews referring to geographical 'regions of our privileged interests'. Lavrov called on 'the rest of Europe to recognise that "new reality"'.[136] This was the pattern thereafter. Russia insisted that it had bilateral agreements with the two new republics of South Ossetia and Abkhazia to keep its troops there. PACE representatives were told that Russia would ignore and did not feel bound by any PACE Resolutions or Recommendations related to Georgia, rejecting any political dialogue related to them.[137]

As for other CoE actors, the CM did not strongly criticise Russia (or Georgia) as regards the events associated with the August 2008 war, or its aftermath.[138] Meanwhile, the Secretary General declined to act under Article 52 ECHR, notwithstanding an appeal from PACE.[139] By this stage, Georgia had lodged an inter-state application against Russia (in fact, on 12 August 2008), the start of what turned out to be an exceptionally long and drawn-out process lasting over a decade and a half, the relevant judgments not being delivered until the early 2020s.[140]

2.3 Unhappy marriage? Serious violations of the CoE Statute: PACE and the CM's roles

The focus on Chechnya, the MRT and Georgia has been detailed for it reveals much about the CoE–Russia relationship over its first decade, and the CoE's response was rather prophetic for what followed.

A decade or so on from accession, these affairs had been powerful and unambiguous demonstrations of how Russia, stronger and more confident than in the 1990s, was prepared to flout its CoE commitments and obligations if this suited it, and how it would extend its regional influence. Accompanying this was the idea at the time that dialogue with Russia

---

[136] See PACE report, 'The honouring of obligations and commitments by the Russian Federation', Doc. 13018, 14 September 2012, paras 134–5. He was speaking in Poland.

[137] PACE Monitoring Committee, 'Consequences of the war between Georgia and Russia', AS/Mon (2013) 14 rev/Information note, 27 June 2013, para 70.

[138] The CM effectively operates on the basis of consensus, so strong criticism was highly unlikely. The informal meeting of Ministers of Foreign Affairs in September 2008 described the conflict as 'a serious challenge to the organisation and the values it stands for' and called for enhanced monitoring of both Russia and Georgia. See Chairman's Summing-up, SecCM/Inf(2008)21, 24 September 2008, available from: https://search.coe.int/cm?i=09000016805d291a [Accessed 28 June 2024].

[139] Resolution 1633 (2008), n 122, para 28.

[140] See Chapter 4, section 4. A subsequent inter-state case concerned Russia's so-called 'borderisation' of Abkhazia and South Ossetia and the Georgian government-controlled territory after 2009 (that is, the erection of physical barriers and measures such as surveillance and patrolling), see Chapter 4, section 4.

could yield results. In fact, however, there would be little or no substantive progress in relation to these matters over the remaining years of Russia's CoE membership.

Yet Russia had no intention of withdrawing from the CoE, as it could have under Article 7 CoE Statute. Instead, it pushed back on criticism of it, doubtless confident that it could do so, and stay within the CoE. As Bindig noted in 2010, '[w]hen confronting criticism of its record Russia regularly threatens that it could cut its [financial] contribution (as one of the five main payers) to the [CoE] budget'.[141]

Meanwhile, it was evident that Russia was not going to be expelled from the CoE despite its serious transgressions. The CM was clearly unwilling to face up to Russia, let alone threaten it with Article 8, notwithstanding the credible, even convincing, case that Article 3 had been seriously violated over the 2000s, and the ominous rhetoric from Lavrov as just noted. One can only assume that this emboldened Russia. Presumably its action in relation to Georgia reflected its growing confidence and power by the end of the 2000s, as suggested in the introduction to this chapter.

So, Russia would not leave, and the CM would not force it to do so. As Nussberger suggested, 'for both sides it is clear that the marriage, even if unhappy, should continue',[142] for both sides had something to gain. For the CoE – that is to say, the member states – it was of 'utmost importance to continue the dialogue with Russia in order to justify [its] role as a decisive political player in the relationship between Eastern and Western Europe'.[143] For Russia, CoE membership, entailed: 'reintegration into the legal and cultural European space'; leaving the CoE would be interpreted as a step towards a new isolationism.[144]

However, if the political reality was that the CoE needed Russia, and it needed the CoE,[145] that did not mean that the relationship was mutually beneficial on an even basis. As noted,[146] by 2010 commentators were comparing Russia to a Trojan horse, with ever-more negative effects on the CoE (further details of which are noted in sections 3 and 4 of this chapter). Citing Russia's actions in relation to South Ossetia and Abkhazia, concern was expressed that it was using the CoE 'as a political forum for its own

---

[141] Bindig, n 42, 40.
[142] Nussberger, n 118, 605–6.
[143] Nussberger, n 118.
[144] Nussberger, n 118, cf Massias, n 6, 13 (referring to the CoE as part of 'Moscow's search for recognition and international respectability'. As of the late 2000s, the Kremlin was 'absolutely not considering the possibility of quitting'. Russia was 'very self-conscious of its image abroad').
[145] See further Roter, n 3, 46.
[146] See text accompanying n 15.

foreign policy'.[147] More generally, it was evident that Russia and the CM were putting the CoE's credibility under major pressure: the former for its open and manifest breach of its obligations; the latter for its failure to even threaten Article 8 action.[148] The reality was, then, that by 2010 the CoE was coming off far worse in the relationship. So, was this being endured because the CoE had no choice and lacked the capacity to handle the emergent force that Russia had become?

2.3.1 PACE as a guardian of CoE values, but lacking power

On the last question, the 2000s had revealed PACE's role as a guardian of the CoE's values by calling out and acting against Russia for breach of its CoE obligations. However, it had also demonstrated that it lacked real power in relation to this.

Essentially PACE could name and shame, via passing Resolutions (as with those on Chechnya, calling for the CM to act under Article 8 CoE Statute), or provide criticism from one of its expert bodies, including its Monitoring Committee on honouring of obligations and commitments. Otherwise, the most relevant 'disciplinary' power it had arose in relation to its Rules allowing for challenges to be made to the credentials of a PACE delegation either at the start of a year, or during it, for a 'serious violation of the basic principles of the Council of Europe mentioned in Article 3 of, and the Preamble to the Statute'.[149] Challenges of that type occurred following the Georgian war[150] and would be resorted to again in 2014–2015, in relation to Crimea,[151] and over 2019–2022.[152] However, as noted, over 2008–2009 the PACE Russian delegation's credentials were not rescinded (they never would be over Russia's entire CoE membership), even though they were challenged. One problem here was that expulsion of a PACE delegation risked closing dialogue when it was needed most,[153] and, of course, that measure was targeted at Parliamentarians (potentially cooperative and sympathetic voices),[154] and so not the real culprit, namely the government. Hence, it was acknowledged over 2008–2009, that PACE could: '[16] …

---

[147] Malfliet and Parmentier, n 13, 26.
[148] Nager and Zwaak, n 53, 7–8.
[149] See Rules of Procedure of the Assembly, Rule 8.2.a (and generally Rules 8–10 generally). See Chapter 2, section 2.4 and Chapter 4, section 2.
[150] See n 125 and 132.
[151] Chapter 4, section 2.
[152] Chapter 4, section 3.
[153] See PACE Monitoring Committee report 2009, n 132, para 22.
[154] Roter, n 3, 45 (citing the important role of Russian delegates within PACE).

only try to convince those who do not share our convictions and ideas', that is, Russia, because 'we have *no means to impose them on to anyone*'.[155]

The dawning of this reality by the late 2000s, plus that of Russia's increasing power and preparedness to exploit it, might help us to appreciate the contrast between the relatively robust stance taken in relation to Chechnya, back in 2000, and PACE's handling of the Russia/Georgia situation over 2008–2009. The changing dynamic was reflected in the 2008 reference to the CoE as 'hospital of democracy' as far as Russia was concerned, the hope (if not expectation) being that, if kept in the CoE, Russia could be persuaded to change: so, it was better to keep Russia in than push it out. But was it? Only if Russia was a willing patient of the hospital. The reality, of course, was that the Russian government was not. It was uninterested in the dialogue PACE sought. It ignored PACE's criticism, and demands for action, both in the short[156] and longer term.[157]

2.3.2 The CM: power but lack of political will?

As regards the CM, unlike PACE it had power under the CoE Statute (Article 8).[158] However, while it was prepared to strongly criticise Russia in the context of its Article 46 duties related to the supervision of the execution of judgments, it clearly lacked political will to adopt a head-on stance against it. This mirrored Western nations' attitudes towards Russia generally over the 2000s;[159] nonetheless, the CM's inaction reflected badly on the CoE.

The CM's proceedings are confidential; hence one can perhaps assume, but cannot say, that a robust dialogue took place behind closed doors. Then again, and as noted previously, there was strident criticism of the CM by PACE actors over 2004–2005,[160] including on the basis that the latter was abdicating its responsibilities both generally and in the context of its own 1994 Declaration. In fact, the latter mechanism appeared to go

---

[155] PACE Monitoring Committee report 2009, n 132, para 16 (emphasis added).
[156] See text accompanying n 137, and see PACE Monitoring Committee report 2012, n 1, para 18 (referring to opening of polling stations in Abkhazia (Georgia), South Ossetia (Georgia) and Transnistria (Republic of Moldova) without the explicit consent of the *de jure* authorities; also to the 'passportisation' of populations in these territories).
[157] Cf PACE referring, in 2022, to 'no progress' made on the demands and requests it issued in the context of the 2008 war: PACE Resolution 2422 (2022), 'Challenge, on substantive grounds, of the still unratified credentials of the parliamentary delegation of the Russian Federation', 26 January 2022, para 8 (or, then, with regard to Crimea).
[158] See Chapter 5. For further criticism of the CM, see Chapter 7, section 4.3.
[159] Cf *The Economist* (2010) 'Be critical, not hypocritical; dealing with Russia', 397(8712): 14.
[160] See text accompanying n 55.

into dormancy after the mid-2000s (for all states, not just Russia),[161] the CM being prepared, it appeared, to let regimes such as the ECHR play the leading role, with subsequent input from the CM. That seemed to confirm a view apparently held by some at Strasbourg in the mid-1990s that the 1994 Declaration had only ever been 'an artificial' mechanism created 'to justify – retroactively – the precipitated decision to invite countries with suspect democratic credentials to join the [CoE]'.[162] So, this would be a further indictment of the CM – and so the CoE member states – given that the enlargement process of the 1990s had clearly been on the basis that subjection to the ECHR would *not* be enough, and that effective political monitoring by the CM could be required (as was clearly the context to Russia's admission), due to the political nature of the issues arising. That, however, assumed the states' willingness to take up their responsibilities, and that of collective enforcement, seriously, which, on the face of it, they did not.[163] The unwillingness of any state to initiate an ECHR inter-state case against Russia in respect of Chechnya was also notable.

Did the ECHR become a type of 'fig leaf' for CoE states to justify their inaction at a time when a very strong stance by the CoE executive organ was required most to help prevent further major violations of human rights? Furthermore, while there may have been critical words from the CM in the context of its Article 46 duties, the very poor record of implementation of the ECtHR 'Chechnya judgments' noted earlier was placed in further perspective by Leach (lawyer for many Chechen applicants) who maintained that in many instances, 'CoE states [had] not seriously attempted to enforce [the Chechen] judgments or ensure that the victims [were] redressed'.[164] Leach referred to there being a general lack of receptivity to the sustained efforts he and others made in that regard, 'speaking to state representatives, [and] trying to persuade them to take up [Chechnya] cases properly', and so 'exert real pressure' on Russia, and 'use the legal or diplomatic tools available to them'. While there was some 'personal interest from some individual diplomats', 'the overwhelming state response has been that of complacent

---

[161] See Palmer, S. (2017) 'The Committee of Ministers', in S. Schmahl and M. Breuer *The Council of Europe: Its Law and Policies*, Oxford: Oxford University Press, 2017, pp 137–65, 158–9.

[162] See Drzemczewski, A. (2012) 'Reflections on a remarkable period', in O. Delas (ed) *Liber Amicorum Peter Leuprecht*, Bruxelles: Bruylant, pp 105–15, 113.

[163] See also 'Action Plan' (CM(2005)80 final 17 May 2005) emanating from the *Third Summit of Heads of State and Government of CoE* in Warsaw (16–17 May 2005): 'We will continue our common efforts to ensure strict compliance with the commitments of member states to the common standards to which they have subscribed' (heading 4).

[164] Leach, P. (2022) 'A time of reckoning? Russia and the Council of Europe', *European Human Rights Law Review*, 3: 219–27, 226.

disinterest – as the states were not directly affected, it was seen to be too "difficult" (or even too "political") to take action, and much else besides was far more pressing'.[165]

The situation leaves one asking many questions. Over the 2000s (and beyond) were the CoE states able to hide behind the CM as a collective (consensus-based), confidential institution?[166] If so, would it be going too far to say that the CoE was a victim first and foremost of Russia's attitude toward it, but also that of its other member states' failure to stand up to Russia? Or perhaps the stance adopted was reflective of a political realism, namely the need to cooperate with Russia? But if so, was this cooperation at any price, including sacrifices to the values and the sense of *obligation* found in Article 3 CoE Statute? As for the ECtHR, was its role as a fall-back relevant? But to what extent did its presence mask the failures of the CM to act in the first place? Was this a type of passing the buck of responsibility to the ECtHR, a kind of kicking matters down the line? Or perhaps this all reflected the eternal hope that Russia would change, at which point the ECtHR's positive influence would be witnessed.

3 Willing patient of 'therapeutic admission'? (1998–2013)

So, could it be argued that the matters discussed previously (Chechnya and Georgia) were exceptional, and to be tolerated, for patience was needed with Russia? That is, the 'long game' was that Russia would come good as a CoE state, and, therefore, not engage in the type of behaviour witnessed in relation to Chechnya and Georgia, and, in due course, resolve the issues arising. Even if that were so, this would not have justified the excessively tolerant approach towards Russia over the 2000s. Moreover, the following account will suggest that, as of the late 2000s, such a 'long game' argument would have been increasingly unrealistic. By then, Russian authorities were clearly and unambiguously moving further and further away from CoE values, not closer to them, despite the best efforts of an increasingly determined (albeit repressed) civil society in Russia. The problem for the CoE was what to do about that; it failed to grasp the nettle.

Russia's 1996 'therapeutic admission' to the CoE was not on the naïve expectation that it would become a flourishing democracy in just a few

---

[165] Leach, n 164. For very strong criticism of the CM, see also Merlin, n 17, 144–5, and 155. After 2010, when Protocol 14 entered into force, the Chechnya cases might have been worthy of infringement proceedings under Article 46(4) ECHR (on the basis that Russia 'refuse[d] to abide by a final judgment'). However, the CM declined to act here.

[166] Recall too PACE's unsuccessful plea to the states to bring an inter-state case in respect of Chechnya, n 50.

years. Still, the first decade or so would have been viewed as a type of grace period for the nurturing of CoE values in Russia, the expectation being that significant progress would be made on the road to democracy.

With that in mind, the following account attempts to stand aback and assess what occurred over the period from 1998 to 2013,[167] and the role that the CoE and the ECtHR played in national settings. It picks up on the political narrative set out in the introduction to this chapter, that is, regarding changes in the Russia government's attitudes to the CoE. A first section describes how, up to around 2005, there were some signs of promise within the national context, but how the tide turned after and, in fact, soon after President Putin was elected for a second presidential term (2004). By then, around ten years after accession, a new, more emboldened Russia was in evidence, and, as PACE and other CoE actors highlighted in 2005, regressive steps were being taken in the national context, contrary to the expectations of Russia's progressive realisation of CoE values. One may see how this fitted with the strained relations reflected in accusations (by the Russian government) that the ECtHR was anti-Russian after the *Ilaşcu* ruling,[168] the Georgian war of 2008, and the 'new reality' of Russia's regional influence. And, of course, this timing also coincided with the CM's timid stance with respect to Chechnya.

3.1 The path to democracy and the rule of law: the turning tide (2004–2005)

The perspective in the early 2000s might have been that, putting Chechnya aside (if that was possible), there were early signs of positivity as regards Russia's progressive realisation of CoE values. In 2000, Bowring listed many changes made in the national context, together providing 'convincing grounds for concluding that Russia is under-going genuine and profound transformation as a direct result of accession, especially in the application of the rule of law'.[169] Meanwhile important steps had been taken in terms of laws passed and other initiatives adopted in Russia's efforts to honour many of its accession commitments, notably so in terms of ratifying the human

---

[167] See also Leach, P. (2007) 'Strasbourg's oversight of Russia: an increasingly strained relationship', *Public Law*, 4 (Winter): 640–54; Jägers, N. (2008) 'The Russian Federation and human rights', *Netherlands Quarterly of Human Rights*, 26(1): 3–4, 3.
[168] *Ilaşcu*, n 117.
[169] Bowring, B. (2000) 'Russia's accession to the Council of Europe and human rights: four years on', *European Human Rights Law Review*, 4: 362–79, 363. Although see Massias, noting (in 2007), 'criticism also abounds in regard to Russian criminal law. The public prosecution authority needs to be reformed so that the Prokuratura conforms to democratic standards', n 6, 12.

rights treaties identified. As regards internal reforms the situation was also relatively positive initially, even if not perfect: for example, responsibility for the prison system was transferred to the Ministry of Justice;[170] however, reforms to the Prosecutor's office took much longer, and, for example, there was little progress in relation to ill-treatment in the military.[171]

Still, early interactions with CoE actors were constructive as regards national law. The PACE monitoring procedure resulted in detailed reports on Russia in 1998,[172] 2002[173] and 2005,[174] and for these its rapporteurs visited Russia on numerous occasions where there was a willingness for dialogue on all matters. This 'include[ed] at one point a long meeting with President Putin'.[175] The PACE–Russian interaction was cooperative.[176] In 2002, a PACE Resolution 'welcome[d] the undoubted progress made by Russia towards the rule of law and democracy, and the building of a democratic multi-party state, which is resulting in increased political and economic stability'.[177] Meanwhile, with respect to the earliest (non-Chechnya) ECtHR judgments delivered against Russia (from 2002 and 2003, to be discussed later), there was evidence of Russia's willingness to engage with the CM in the enforcement process.[178]

Cause for some positivity was also found in a CoE Commissioner for Human Rights report[179] published in 2005. Over 100 pages long, it highlighted significant reforms, and how Russia had taken 'a great step forward in radically reforming some of its legislation to bring it into line with European standards'.[180] Legislation once based on totalitarianism ideals had been replaced with that which aspired to 'liberal, democratic' values.[181]

---

[170] Bindig, n 42, 39.
[171] Bindig, n 42, 39.
[172] PACE, 'The honouring of obligations and commitments by the Russian Federation – Information report', Doc. 8127, 26 June 1998.
[173] PACE, 'The honouring of obligations and commitments by the Russian Federation', 23 April 2022; Resolution 1277 (2002); Recommendation 1553 (2002).
[174] PACE, 'The honouring of obligations and commitments by the Russian Federation', 26 June 2005; Resolution 1455 (2005); Recommendation 1710 (2005).
[175] Bindig, n 42, 38–9.
[176] Bindig, n 42, 38–9.
[177] Resolution 1277 (2002), 'Honouring of obligations and commitments by the Russian Federation', para 1.
[178] See CM Reply to PACE Recommendation 1710 (2005), Doc. 10760, 9 December 2005, para 8. For a positive review of Russia's involvement in the CM, and in PACE over this time, see Roter, n 3, 45.
[179] 'Report by Mr Alvaro Gil-Robles, Commissioner for Human Rights, on his visit to the Russian Federation, 15 to 30 July 2004, 19 to 29 September 2004', CommDH(2005)2, 20 April 2005, available from: https://rm.coe.int/16806db7be [Accessed 14 June 2024]. See Roter, n 3, 37–9.
[180] Commissioner's report, n 179, para 8.
[181] Commissioner's report, n 179, para 10.

There had been a potential whole shift in the direction of the state,[182] there being a 'far from perfect' 'fledgling democracy' in Russia, but one whose 'existence and its successes'[183] could not be denied.

As such, over the early 2000s there may have been a cause for guarded optimism, given the extent of the transformation required.[184] However, it was equally clear that, after decades of authoritarian rule, these were early days, with matters hanging in the balance. Hence the Commissioner on Human Rights' report of 2005 identified concerns related to implementation on the ground, that is whether the new laws could be or would be applied in practice, and whether the reforms had been introduced too quickly, with a lack of clarity and without training and broader understanding.[185] Likewise, it was evident early on that it would not be enough for Russia just to ratify instruments such as the ECHR, and initiate the internal reforms identified. What was required was sustained political will in relation to them, and here matters were taking a negative turn in the mid-2000s.

3.2 The turning tide (2004–2005) highlighted at the CoE, and the significance of PACE monitoring

The Commissioner's report of 2005 had followed two visits to Russia soon after President Putin had been elected President for a second term (March 2004), with more than 70 per cent of the vote. It referred to recent and proposed reforms, which 'elicited concern ... as to whether' the progress made to date in Russia would 'remain in place', and in relation to which, the 'misgivings of civil society' had been 'very much in evidence'.[186]

The PACE monitoring procedure of 2005 confirmed this diagnosis, the relevant PACE Resolution[187] referring to a 'package of reforms, introduced in the autumn of 2004 with a view to reinforcing "the vertical of power"' (sic),[188] and warning that effective democracy required that 'power must not only be vertically reinforced but also horizontally shared'.[189] As PACE put it, those

---

[182] Commissioner's report, n 179, para 10.
[183] Commissioner's report, n 179, para 6.
[184] Cf comments by Luc Van den Brande, n 9, 50–1 ('it would take generations to eradicate the former soviet-type concepts ... years to retrain former politicians and bureaucrats educated under the former regime').
[185] Commissioner's report, n 179, para 11.
[186] Commissioner's report, n 179, para 10.
[187] PACE Resolution 1455 (2005), see also Bindig, n 42, 39.
[188] PACE Resolution 1455, n 187, para 6.
[189] PACE Resolution 1455, n 187, para 6. On the significance of this (a 'decisive blow' for separation of powers), see Nussberger, A. (2022) 'Human rights and peace: disillusionment or hope? The Russian example', in J. Kjølbro, S. O'Leary and M. Tsirli Anthemis (eds) *Liber Amicorum Robert Spano*, The Hague: Eleven International Publishing, pp 511–22, 513.

reforms were 'a cause for considerable concern', for 'in many respects [they] may undermine[d] the system of checks and balances indispensable for the normal functioning of any democracy'. In issue were new laws concerning reforms to Russian federalism, changes to the electoral arrangements, and the regulation of the registration of political parties. Steps had also been taken to increase the state's influence over judicial appointments, dismissals and disciplinary procedures. Alongside that were new laws concerning the control of NGOs, and regarding the regulation of the media (ensuring that TV stations were brought under state control), as well as new laws on extremism. So, in 2005 and backed by the CoE Commissioner for Human Rights' report, PACE set out a long list of action points that Russia was urged to take in the field of effective political democracy,[190] the rule of law and the protection of human rights.[191] In essence, PACE exhorted 'the Russian authorities to improve the conditions for the normal functioning of pluralist democracy'.[192] It also urged Russia to take steps as regards improvement of its relations with other CoE states in the region, notably regarding Moldova and Georgia.[193]

According to Malfliet and Parmentier, the steps adopted by Russia in the mid-2000s started to promote a type of 'competitive normative agenda'[194] to the CoE. It was one that was contrary to European standards and norms, as Russia pressed for 'its own – be it not so different from Europe – concept of democracy and human rights'.[195] The Russian version, however, lacked the normal checks and balances required for the actual effective functioning of democracy.[196] It was a form of so-called 'managed' or 'guided' democracy, and that it was incompatible with CoE values was self-evident,[197] and reflected

---

[190] PACE Resolution 1455, n 187, para 12, including 'strengthen[ing] legal, administrative and political conditions in which a democratically elected and genuinely pluralist parliament will be able not only to support but also to control the executive power'; plus other important reforms regarding separation of powers; independence of the media and freedom from state interference functioning of private nation-wide broadcasting media, which must be free of; and 'immediately end the harassment and intimidation of members of civil society critical of the authorities'.

[191] PACE Resolution 1455, n 187, para 13.

[192] PACE Resolution 1455, n 187, para 12. See also Recommendation 1710 (2005) (22 June 2005) and the very limited, business-like response of the CM, see Doc. 10760, 9 December 2005.

[193] PACE Resolution 1455, n 187, para 14.

[194] Malfliet and Parmentier, n 13, 11.

[195] Malfliet and Parmentier, n 13, 11.

[196] See Bindig, n 42, 39.

[197] In Malfliet and Parmentier's words, 'since the second Putin term, from 2004 on, no reasonable observer can qualify what is happening in Russian politics as a process of "democratisation"', Malfliet and Parmentier, n 13, 11.

in critiques from PACE and the Commissioner on Human Rights. Today one may say that the roots to an authoritarian Russia may be traced back to 2005. However, here two sets of points may be made.

The first concerns the lack of receptivity to the CoE's messages *within Russia* by the mid-2000s. Of course, one cannot be definitive on this; however, we refer back to the introduction to this chapter[198] in terms of what were, apparently, changing attitudes towards the CoE in Russia, and the growing popularity of President Putin. Massias's 2007 study – evocatively entitled 'Russia and the Council of Europe: ten years wasted?'[199] – suggested that under Putin Russia had transitioned from progression to stagnation to regression. However, and most importantly, the regression was 'not perceived' as such in much of Russia, 'where, on the contrary, the elite and the population believe they are living in an era of improved economic and political living conditions',[200] especially considering the backdrop and disappointments of the 1990s. President Putin stepped down from the presidency in 2008 but his status and influence was such that it was widely agreed that he identified his successor (Medvedev). The elections of 2007 (parliamentary) and 2008 (presidential) were ostensibly free, but *not* fair, as pointed out by CoE actors.[201] The war with Georgia followed soon after, accompanied by increasing anti-CoE narratives from Moscow.

The second set of points concerns how all this was highlighted, but not tackled in an effective way at the time in the CoE context; 'highlighted', for credit should go to PACE as a watchdog and peer-reviewer of Russia in the context of the monitoring procedure.[202] In that regard, the 2005 report was an impressive document, almost 50,000 words in length, following multiple visits to Russia,[203] and drawing on many resources. It provided detailed and important insights related to the declining health of democratic institutions, the rule of law and human rights in Russia, trends confirmed by PACE monitoring of all Russian elections after 2003,[204] and important and detailed interventions from the CoE Commissioner for Human Rights.

---

[198] See section 1.1 of this chapter.
[199] Massias, n 6.
[200] Massias, n 6, 13.
[201] See PACE Election Observation report, 'Observation of the presidential election in the Russian Federation (2 March 2008)', Doc. 11536, 20 March 2008; PACE Election Observation report, 'Observation of the parliamentary elections in the Russian Federation (2 December 2007)', Doc. 11473, 20 December 2007.
[202] For a review of PACE monitoring of Russia up to 2010, see Van den Brande, n 9.
[203] Between 1999 and 2005, there had been nine visits to Russia by members of the Monitoring Committee; between 2006 and 2014, 14 further visits occurred: see PACE, 'Parliamentary Monitoring Procedure with regard to the Russian Federation [1996–2022]', AS/Mon/Inf (2022) 09, 07 April 2022, 3.
[204] An exception was 2017, when Russia refused to invite CoE monitors.

However, the main aim of PACE's monitoring was to support, not sanction, in the context of what was essentially a peer review process. So, it relied on the reviewed state being a willing partner, and constructive respondent, and here we know that, especially when it came to democratic reforms, the Russian government was not. Furthermore, it seemed that by the mid-2000s the CM had virtually given up its own form of monitoring under its 1994 Declaration. In short, then, with PACE and other CoE actors sounding alerts, there did not appear to be any real consequences for Russia other than the sanction of criticism which it routinely dismissed as ill-informed, biased or politicised. As a result, it seems that matters drifted such that, aside from the challenges to delegation's credentials in PACE occurring in relation to Georgia (associated, of course, with the 'hospital of democracy' narrative[205]), the next PACE monitoring of Russia occurred in 2012, by which stage matters were reaching a critical point as regards the functioning of pluralist democracy.[206] As with the 2012 report,[207] here PACE drew attention to growing – indeed, by then very significant – concerns as regards Russia's backward steps away from democracy. But by then was it too late to rescue the situation?

3.3 Digression? Russia, the ECHR and the ECtHR (1998–2012)

The role of PACE and the CM, plus the situation in Russia as just described, should be kept in mind as we now look to what today, with hindsight, could almost be seen as a secondary issue – or digression: the role played by the ECHR over the period from 1998 up to around 2012. Here we proceed in three steps. First, the ECtHR's limitations are discussed in section 3.3.1. After that, looking to Russia–Strasbourg relations, there is a similar narrative to the previous section. That is, there were some initial signs of positivity when it came to interactions between the ECHR and Russia (looked at in section 3.3.2). However, there were then causes for concern ('strained relations' after 2005 (section 3.3.3)), fitting the turning of the tide in the mid-2000s.

3.3.1 The ECtHR's limitations

Regarding the ECtHR's limitations, arguably it was never going to be at the vanguard of challenges to, for example, the new, regressive laws passed in Russia after 2004. That responsibility fell to other CoE actors, who could proceed on a wider footing, and more contemporaneously than the ECtHR,

---

[205] See text accompanying n 132.
[206] See section 4 of this chapter.
[207] See n 1.

notably the Commissioner for Human rights, plus PACE and, theoretically (but not in practice) the CM. By comparison the ECtHR's role was limited, having jurisdiction with respect to the ECHR only (and so not Article 3, CoE Statute, let alone Article 8, or Russia's accession commitments). More generally, the ECtHR operated in a residual, long-stop role in relation to an instrument, the ECHR, which protected a limited range of rights. The latter was not a guarantor of the democratic constitutional structures of the state, while the ECtHR could only respond to individual applications brought to it by (potential) victims, after exhaustion of potentially effective domestic remedies. So, there could be significant time lags between events in Russia, and resulting ECtHR judgments, the matter made worse in the 2000s by long delays in case processing because the Court was thoroughly overloaded with work from over 40 states.

In fact, it transpired that over the 2000s and up to 2012–2013 there were few, if any, ECtHR judgments related to authoritarianism or democratic backsliding, or which threw into doubt fundamental features of the national legal order in terms of effective political democracy. However, cases were brought by high-profile financial figures alleging, in essence, foul play and political motivation in criminal proceedings that had been brought against them. This included judgments in cases brought by Mikhail Khodorkovskiy, an exceptionally wealthy Russian businessman, and opposition activist (plus Platon Lebedev, another businessman). Khodorkovskiy was one of the few 'oligarchs' to stand up to the Putin administration, and, it was contended, was subject to politically motivated prosecutions. He and Lebedev had strong connections to the Yukos oil company, whose shareholders also brought proceedings before the Court.[208] In relation to the *Khodorkovskiy* cases, the Court found various violations of certain Convention Articles, but not of the all-important Article 18,[209] as regards bad faith and foul play in the prosecutions themselves.[210] A former Vice-President of the ECtHR has argued, with hindsight, that the Court should have been stronger in these cases, and risked condoning unacceptable behaviour via its failure to find an Article 18 violation.[211]

---

[208] *OAO Neftyanaya Kompaniya Yukos v. Russia* (just satisfaction), no. 14902/0, 31 July 2014; 20 September 2011 (merits), n 321.

[209] Cf *Gusinskiy v. Russia*, no. 70276/01, 19 May 2004 (media tycoon exempt from prosecution under national law detained in violation of Article 5(1)(c) read with Article 18; the first ever violation of the latter provision).

[210] *Khodorkovskiy v. Russia*, no. 5829/04, 31 May 2011 (violation Article 5(1)(b)); see also *Khodorkovskiy and Lebedev v. Russia*, no. 11082/06, 25 July 2013 (violation of Article 6 and 8). Khodorkovskiy was released in 2013 after President Putin pardoned him.

[211] Nussberger, n 189, 513–14.

3.3.2 Russia and the ECHR: initial room for some positivity?

Regarding these early interactions between Russia and the ECtHR, the following account does not purport to be exhaustive.[212] Its main purpose is to highlight how, and again putting aside the Chechnya situation, a case could be made as to a level of receptivity to European human rights control on Russia's part, and for some positive influence.[213]

If the number of notable (non-Chechnya related) cases concerning Russia over the period up to 2012–2013 was relatively small, the actual number of applications made,[214] and judgments delivered[215] was not. That said, the high figures[216] reflected how many of the 'Russian' cases related to repeated violations in relation to certain systemic, structural problems identified in initial cases from around 2002–2003 onwards.[217] These concerned, among others: non-enforcement of domestic judicial decisions in relation to social

---

[212] For a detailed account (up to 2006), see Nussberger, n 118, 631–45.

[213] For reviews of the influence of CoE norms on legal reforms in Russia over the 2000s, see Feldbrugge, F. 'Russian and the rule of law', in K. Malfliet and S. Parmentier (eds) *Russia and the Council of Europe: 10 Years After*, Basingstoke: Palgrave Macmillan, pp 57–64; Fogelklou, A. 'Russian legal reforms and the CoE: three steps forward, two steps back', in K. Malfliet and S. Parmentier (eds) *Russia and the Council of Europe: 10 Years After*, Basingstoke: Palgrave Macmillan, pp 83–106; and Kahn, J. 'Adversarial principles and the case file in Russian criminal procedure', in K. Malfliet and S. Parmentier (eds) *Russia and the Council of Europe: 10 Years After*, Basingstoke: Palgrave Macmillan, pp 107–35.

[214] Approximately 5,000 applications were lodged each year in the early 2000s; however, there was a dramatic increase after this. By the end of 2006 more applications were pending against Russia that any other state: Russia (19,300), after which: Romania (10,850), Türkiye (9,000) and Ukraine (6,800), ECtHR, 'Analysis of statistics 2006' (available from: www.echr.coe.int), 4. The figure for Russia represented 21.5 per cent of the Court's total case-load. Russia was the highest 'case-count' state over the following years: 2007 (26 per cent of total case load); 2008 (28 per cent); 2009 (28.1 per cent); 2010 (28.9 per cent [40,300 applications]); 2011 (26.6 per cent); 2012 (22.3 per cent [28,600 applications]), and 2013 (16.8 per cent).

[215] There was a dramatic uptick over the 2000s. In 2002 and 2003, there were two and five 'Russian' judgments respectively. The figures rose as follows: 2006 (105 judgments); 2007 (211 judgments); 2008 (269); 2009 (575); 2010 (430); 2011 (199); 2012 (216); 2013 (257).

[216] See Nussberger, n 118, 631, noting that the Russian Constitutional Court did not act as a filter in that it had no competence to rectify human rights violations occurring via wrong application of a law (it controlled constitutionality of the law).

[217] For example, a ECtHR report noted that at the end of 2006, applications related to Russia concerned: 'non-execution of judgments (about 190 applications); events in Chechnya (about 200 applications); conditions of detention (about 40 applications); excessive length of civil proceedings (about 25 applications); excessive length of pre-trial detention without sufficient grounds (about 55 applications); quashing of final judgments in supervisory review proceedings (about 60 applications); method of calculating military pensions (about 300 cases); method of calculating wages in a steel works in Karelia (about 300 applications)', ECtHR, 'Analysis of statistics 2006', n 214, 19.

benefits, including from the Chernobyl disaster (the *Burdov* case, 2002);[218] the so-called 'supervisory review procedure' (*nadzor*) which allowed for the quashing of final judicial decisions in violation of the principle of legal certainty (the *Ryabykh* case, 2003);[219] and dire conditions of detention on remand (severe overcrowding, confinement, lack of private toilet facilities, ventilation problems, lack of access to natural light and basic sanitation and so on, entailing a violation of Article 3 (degrading treatment)) alongside excessively long pre-trial detention periods, based on flawed grounds (lack of relevant and sufficient reasons (the *Kalashnikov* case, 2003)).[220]

In relation to these cases, and as noted,[221] in 2005 the CM referred to some initial signs of promise in their enforcement, general measures being required to prevent new violations similar to those found by the Court. That said, a PACE Resolution of 2007 (following a detailed CLAHR report on 'Implementation of judgments of the European Court of Human Rights') was less upbeat, citing 'major shortcomings'[222] that remained to be rectified as regards the areas identified. With very large numbers of so-called clone cases in the field identified contributing to the overwhelming of an already overburdened Court, the onus was placed on Russia to do more, and promptly.

Progress was very slow indeed. Then again, as the following examples demonstrate, over time dialogue and engagement entailed that meaningful reform could be secured, albeit in certain limited fields only – and so *not* in relation to democratic structures and issues.[223]

For example, in *Burdov v. Russia (no. 2)*[224] the ECtHR adopted a pilot judgment (violation of Article 6(1) and Article 1 of Protocol No. 1), given Russia's prolonged failure to enforce three domestic judgments ordering monetary payment. Applying Article 46(1), Russia was required to introduce an effective remedy securing redress for non-enforcement or delayed

---

[218] *Burdov v. Russia*, no. 59498/00, 7 May 2002. See Nussberger, n 118, 636–7.

[219] *Ryabykh v. Russia*, no. 52854/99, 24 July 2003.

[220] *Kalashnikov v. Russia*, no. 47095/99, 15 July 2002, see notably paras 93–4 re Article 3 (plea by Russia that there was no intention to ill-treat, that the dire conditions of detention were endemic in Russia, and due to economic reasons/lack of resources). Ill-treatment in police custody was a further recurrent issue, cf *Mikheyev v. Russia*, no. 77617/01, 26 January 2006 (ill-treatment during police custody amounting to torture), see PACE report, n 1, para 385.

[221] CM reply to 2005 PACE Recommendation, n 178.

[222] Resolution 1516 (2006), 'Implementation of judgments of the European Court of Human Rights', para 10.2.

[223] See further the discussion in Chapter 4, section 3.2.1.

[224] *Burdov v. Russia (no. 2)*, no. 33509/04, 15 January 2009. See Leach, P. (2010) 'Can the European Court's pilot judgment procedure help resolve systemic human rights violations? Burdov and the failure to implement domestic court decisions in Russia', *Human Rights Law Review*, 10(2): 346–59.

enforcement of judgments and to grant redress to all victims in the numerous 'Burdov-like' cases pending before it. On 4 May 2010, the Duma adopted amendments to the Civil Code aimed at remedying the situation. The case was finally closed by the CM in 2016.[225]

As for the condition of detention (*Kalashnikov*) cases, a pilot judgment[226] was delivered in 2012, focussing on a recurrent structural problem in the Russian prison system, and its insufficient legal and administrative safeguards. Russia was required to take general measures to alleviate conditions of detention in remand prisons, steps that required considerable investment of resources. It took until 12 December 2018 for the CM to adopt a final resolution closing its supervision of the individual measures in 136 cases of this group (related to many applicants),[227] although other issues remained.[228]

These examples of long-delayed implementation, of which others could be cited,[229] illustrate that it would be incorrect to assume that Russia was totally unreceptive to the influence of the ECHR, even if, of course, there were major problems in the general CoE–Russia relationship.[230] This demonstrated that – perhaps after very long delays – valuable changes could be made to improve human rights protection in Russia, with positive effects for a significant number of people.[231] Recall here, too, how on 19 November 2009 the Russian Constitutional Court (RCC) confirmed a moratorium on the death penalty. This was a reminder that the ECHR could have a positive impact within the domestic legal landscape, if key national constituencies including, of course, judges were receptive to that. On the latter, the 'Russian' judge on the ECtHR for 1999–2012, Anatoly Kovler,

---

[225] CM/ResDH(2016)268, Execution of the Judgments of the European Court of Human Rights, two hundred and thirty-five cases against Russian Federation.

[226] *Ananyev and Others v. Russia*, no. 42525/07, 10 January 2012. See also PACE Monitoring Committee report of 2012 (n 1) recognising that Russia was making genuine efforts in this field, para 384.

[227] See CM/ResDH(2018)455.

[228] See *Ananyev and Others v. Russia*, no. 42525/07, case description and status of execution, available from: https://hudoc.exec.coe.int/eng?i=004-14142 [Accessed 14 June 2024].

[229] See Chapter 4, section 3.2.1. See further Department for the Execution of Judgments of the European Court of Human Rights, 'Country Fact Sheet: Russia' (15 March 2021). See also Memorandum by Russian human rights defenders, 'Addressing the crisis in relations between the Council of Europe and Russia: uphold the values and fulfil the mission to protect rights across all of Europe', November 2018 (on file with author; available from: www.nhc.nl/assets/uploads/2018/12/Memorandum-on-Russia-and-CoE_November_2018_eng_signatures-as-of-30.11.18.pdf [Accessed 1 June 2024].

[230] See also Nussberger, n 118, 645, referring to cases of lack of cooperation between Russian authorities and the Court.

[231] See Memorandum, n 229.

gave an upbeat and positive account of how the Plenum of the Russian Supreme Court encouraged proper and uniform application of the ECHR by domestic courts and state officials.[232] Counter to the narrative noted previously regarding disaffection with the ECHR, in 2008 Judge Kovler spoke of 'the growing popularity' of the ECHR, one which had 'created a situation of "no return" in public opinion'. For him, that was 'the most important result' of ten years of ECHR membership for Russia.[233]

3.3.3 Russia and the ECtHR after 2005: strained relations

Yet as we know, there was another, far more negative face to Russia's interactions with the CoE. As reactions to the *Ilascu* ruling might have indicated,[234] there appeared to be an emergent post-2005 Moscow initiative to criticise the ECtHR on the basis that it was 'Russia-phobic'. Newspaper reports highlighted confidential statements made by Court 'officials' who 'conceded ... that the Kremlin had been annoyed by a series of judgments by the court and regarded it as pathologically anti-Russian and biased'.[235] Over 2006–2010, after all other ECHR states had ratified Protocol 14, the Duma effectively blocked its entry into force by refusing to ratify it. The Protocol was part of a package of rescue measures for the ECtHR, which was facing a case overload crisis that was almost paralysing it, and needed reforms to enable it to work with economy of procedures to address the enormous number of ill-founded applications emanating from ECHR states, and great numbers of repetitive cases reaching it. And, by the mid-2000s, Russia was consistently in the top three states in terms of judgments finding at least

---

[232] Kovler, A. (2010) 'The impact of the ECHR on Russian legislation and judicial practice', in K. Malfliet and S. Parmentier (eds) *Russia and the Council of Europe: 10 Years After*, Basingstoke: Palgrave Macmillan, pp 65–82, 66–7. He also noted that many ECtHR judgments were translated into Russian, 81, n 21. For a far more negative account of reception by the national judiciary in general, see Burkov, A. (2007) *The Impact of the European Convention on Human Rights on Russian Law*, New York: Columbia University Press.

[233] Kovler, n 232, 79.

[234] See n 117.

[235] *The Guardian*, n 75. The Chechnya cases were referred to, as were the dismissal of cases of discrimination by ethnic Russians in Latvia. For a review of other cases which had prompted negative reactions in Russia, see Mälksoo, L. (2014) 'Concluding observations', in L. Mälksoo, *Russia and European Human-Rights Law: The Rise of the Civilizational Argument*, Leiden: Brill, pp 222–4 (noting strong criticism of *Kononov v. Latvia* [GC], no. 36376/04, 17 May 2010, when, in effect, the GC held that 1993 legislation on war crimes committed in the Second World War, used to convict a Soviet partisan, did not breach Article 7).

one violation against it.²³⁶ The debate in the Duma²³⁷ and media reactions, revealed that the refusal to ratify Protocol 14 was 'a response to perceived discrimination against Russia', aggrieved at the loss of ECtHR cases.²³⁸ The Vice-Speaker of the Duma complained that Russia's 'voluminous membership fees' were 'being used for attacks on our country'.²³⁹ The *Kommersant* newspaper described the rejection of Protocol 14 as 'The Duma "gives it" to the European Court'.²⁴⁰

Evidently, even if the ECHR had some popularity in some quarters in Russia, as Judge Kovler suggested, what really counted was the attitude of key actors (parliamentarians, or the government itself) who took decisions impacting on that instrument. Here two former Strasbourg judges have suggested that from the mid-to-late 2000s a change of approach to the ECHR was discernible from the Russian state itself. Prior to 2007, there was 'a genuine interest in cooperating and implementing the judgments and doctrine of the Court';²⁴¹ after that there emerged 'a critical approach to the Court's law making, putting the Russian constitutional order and Orthodox values above Convention values and opting for selective implementation of the Court's rulings'.²⁴²

Two ECtHR rulings illustrate this. Both concerned anti-discrimination matters and reflected the potential for friction between Strasbourg and some stakeholders in Russia in relation to social policy and human rights issues.

In *Konstantin Markin v. Russia*²⁴³ the Grand Chamber adjudged that there had been discrimination (in breach of Article 14) given the difference in treatment between male and female military personnel regarding access to parental leave. This was the first occasion, when, in effect, the ECtHR ruling superseded that of the RCC on a specific legal matter, the latter having held

---

²³⁶ In 2007, the highest number of judgments finding at least one violation of the Convention was delivered in respect of Türkiye (319), followed by Russia (175), then Ukraine (108). In 2008 the figures were Türkiye (257), Russia (233), and Romania (189).

²³⁷ December 2006 (138 votes against, 27 in favour and a (very large) 286 abstentions). For further information, see the Memorandum prepared by the PACE's Committee on Legal Affairs and Human Rights: 'The Russian Federation's non-ratification of Protocol 14 to the ECHR', AS/Jur (2008) 45.

²³⁸ Bowring, B. (2010) 'The Russian Federation, Protocol No. 14 (and 14bis), and the battle for the soul of the ECHR', *Goettingen Journal of International Law*, 2: 589–617.

²³⁹ Bowring, B. 'Submission to House of Commons Foreign Affairs Committee: inquiry into global security – Russia', available from: https://publications.parliament.uk [Accessed 24 June 2024], 18.

²⁴⁰ Bowring, n 239 (citing, at fn 19, www.kommersant.com/p732043/r_500/State_Duma_European_Court/).

²⁴¹ Fura and Maruste, n 2, 251. See also 244–50 for discussion of changes in attitudes of various political and judicial leaders.

²⁴² Fura and Maruste, n 2, 251.

²⁴³ *Konstantin Markin v. Russia* [GC], no. 30078/06, 22 March 2012.

that the difference of treatment *could* be justified under the constitution of Russia (including due to the unique legal status and role of the military). The case sparked a reaction from the Chairman of the RCC, Judge Valery Zorkin,[244] who argued that the ECtHR had overreached itself. He adopted a hostile, nationalistic approach to the ECtHR thereafter.[245] An unsuccessful legislative proposal was put to the Duma to the effect that certain ECtHR judgments might be rendered unenforceable.[246] Just satisfaction was paid by Russia to the applicants in *Konstantin Markin*, but the judgment was never implemented.

Another illustration of potential resistance from national actors and strong differences of outlook was *Alekseyev v. Russia*,[247] concerning the Moscow mayor's repeated refusals to authorise gay-pride parades. The ECtHR found a violation of Article 11 and Article 14 read with Article 11, contrary to the Russian government's remarkable plea that the event(s) in question 'should [have been] banned as a matter of principle, because propaganda promoting homosexuality was incompatible with religious doctrines and the moral values of the majority and could be harmful if seen by children or vulnerable adults'.[248] The Moscow authorities defied the judgment,[249] as with, on 18 May 2011, when 18 peaceful demonstrators were arrested and attacked. PACE identified this as part of a broader issue of discrimination against LGBTI people in Russia. In 2013 the Duma passed legislation prohibiting 'propaganda of non-traditional sexual relations' among minors, subsequently criticised strongly by the Venice Commission,[250] and found to

---

[244] See Provost, R. (2015) 'Teetering on the edge of legal nihilism: Russia and the evolving European human rights regime', *Human Rights Quarterly* 37(2): 289–340, 309, noting that President Medvedev also spoke against the ruling in blunt terms. See also Mälksoo, n 235, 222.

[245] For discussion, see Antonov, M. (2017) 'Philosophy behind human rights: Valery Zorkin vs. the West?', in L. Mälksoo and W. Benedek (eds) *Russia and the European Court of Human Rights: The Strasbourg Effect*, Cambridge: Cambridge University Press, pp 150–87, and Yudkivska, G. (2022) ' "And the work of justice shall be peace —": when human rights are not the path to peace and security', in J. Kjølbro, S. O'Leary and M. Tsirli Anthemis (eds) (2023) *Liber Amicorum Robert Spano*, The Hague: Eleven International Publishing, pp 759–70, 764.

[246] Provost, n 244, 309.

[247] *Alekseyev v. Russia*, no. 4916/07, 21 October 2010.

[248] *Alekseyev v. Russia,* n 247, para 78.

[249] According to the PACE 2012 report, n 1, paras 487–91.

[250] Venice Commission, 'Opinion on the Issue of the Prohibition of So-called "Propaganda of Homosexuality"', CDL-AD(2013)022),14–15 June 2013 (also focused on Moldova and Ukraine). See further 'Statement by the Secretary General of the Council of Europe on legislation in the Russian Duma prohibiting "propaganda of non-traditional sexual relations" among minors' (DC082 – DOC13/06/2013English).

be in violation of the ECHR (Article 10, also read with Article 14) by the ECtHR in *Bayev and Others v. Russia*.[251]

The reaction to *Alekseyev* pointed to the Duma's willingness to act in conscious defiance of the CoE to supposedly emphasise traditional 'family' values, helping to create a 'rhetorical distance between Russia and the West'.[252] This galvanised populist opinion against the ECtHR, which was discredited as overly concerned with gay rights issues.[253]

As to the Duma's obstinance in relation to Protocol 14, this was outflanked by a new Protocol (14bis). It entered into force (1 October 2009), soon after which Russia ratified the main Protocol 14. Prior to this, over 2008–2009, Bowring referred to a rhetorical offensive against the Court and the ECHR system by the Russian Ministry of Justice, its Deputy Minister, and the Russian (Agent) representative before the ECtHR.[254] Apparently a key target was the Court's decision to declare the *Yukos* case admissible (29 January 2009), the application concerning a claim for compensation by shareholders, one connected to wider allegations about inappropriate expropriation of assets for political reasons. The hearing on the merits was put back to 4 March 2010, just after Russia's belated acceptance of Protocol 14 (February 2010).[255] Bowring referred to 'intense speculation by informed Russian commentators' that Russia raced to ratify the Protocol before the *Yukos* hearing 'in the hope of obtaining from the Court a *quid pro quo* in the form of a more favourable judgment'.[256] Around this time too there was a 'true sensation'[257] when a PACE Resolution highly critical of Russia on Chechnya[258] was passed without opposition from the Russian delegation. Subsequently, in January 2011, Russia announced its intention to follow the general practice of

---

[251] *Bayev and Others v. Russia*, no. 67667/09, 20 June 2017 (such laws, 'reinforce[d] stigma and prejudice' and 'encourage[d] homophobia', hence were 'incompatible with the notions of equality, pluralism and tolerance inherent in a democratic society', para 83). See further Chapter 4.

[252] Mälksoo, L. (2017) 'Introduction', in L. Mälksoo and W. Benedek (eds) *Russia and the European Court of Human Rights: the Strasbourg Effect*, Cambridge: Cambridge University Press pp 3-26, 23. On the anti-propaganda laws as illustrating the lack of ECHR's 'socialising' effect, see Bartenev, D. (2017) 'LGBT rights in Russia and European human rights standards', in L. Mälksoo and W. Benedek (eds) *Russia and the European Court of Human Rights: the Strasbourg Effect*, Cambridge: Cambridge University Press, pp 326–52.

[253] See Nussberger, n 189, 519–20.

[254] See Bowring, n 238, 608–12.

[255] Russia also ratified the Revised European Social Charter on 16 October 2009.

[256] Bowring, n 238, 612.

[257] Bowring, n 238, 614.

[258] PACE Recommendation 1922 (2010), 'Legal remedies for human rights violations in the North Caucasus region', 22 June 2010.

lifting the confidentiality of all the reports on visits by the CPT and authorise their publication.[259]

The schizophrenic nature of Russia's interactions with the CoE around the late 2000s and early 2010s underlines how multi-dimensional issues were. As we have seen, relations between the CoE and Russia in the first 15 years of membership were complex, and not easily distilled into a black and white account, even if, taking account of Chechnya and Georgia, there was far more darkness than light.

In their 2010 study, Malfliet and Parmentier offered a gloomy forecast: Russia had developed into a subversive member of the CoE.[260] Based on section 2 in this chapter, one can understand why this was said. However, other views were possible. That of Judge Kovler, noted earlier,[261] was more in keeping with Luc Van den Brande in 2010, the PACE rapporteur on Russia. Writing in his personal capacity, Van den Brande expressed guarded optimism 'about the future of democracy in Russia', expressing the hope that 'day after day, over the years, the democratic process will take root in Russian society'.[262]

This glass half-full perspective was based on a longer view of matters, and had in mind the scale of change required of Russia given the starting point. Indeed, if one took 2010 as a specific year to take stock, one could argue that such an exercise should have regard to how less than a generation before Russia (then the Union of Soviet Socialist Republics (USSR)) had been a totalitarian state for many decades, ideologically opposed to the CoE and what it stood for. From that perspective, even if Russia's membership casts a long shadow, some of the more positive achievements noted previously could be regarded as spectacular. They reflected the notion,

---

[259] See text accompanying n 48. This new policy of openness was put into practice with respect to a CPT report produced following its visit to the North Caucasus occurring from 27 April 2011 until 6 May 2011. See 'Council of Europe Secretary General welcomes publication of anti-torture Committee report on the Russian Federation – 24 January 2013', DC006(2013). The same applied to the CPT's report on its periodic visit to the Russian Federation occurring over May and June 2012. However, reports in relation to 2013, 2014, 2016 (North Caucus), 2016 and 2017 (North Caucus) were not published. The report in relation to a 2018 visit was published on 24 September 2019 after the end of the non-participation crisis. On 11 March 2019 the CPT issued a 'Public Statement' concerning the Chechen Republic and other republics of the North Caucasian region. Documentation available from: www.coe.int/en/web/cpt/russian-federation [Accessed 24 June 2024].

[260] See text accompanying n 15.

[261] See text accompanying n 232.

[262] Van den Brande, n 9, 52. The former rapporteur (Bindig) was far less upbeat in his account ('The Russian authorities have clearly walked away from the promises that were made upon entry'), Bindig, n 42, 40.

apparently, that Russia 'in principle accept[ed] human-rights norms on both the level of its own constitutional law and of its international legal commitment',[263] even if, of course, translating this into a reality on the ground was a different matter.

The optimistic view also leaned into the notion that to some extent Russia's courts were giving effect to Convention law in national contexts. A very positive step was adopted here in June 2013, when a resolution of the plenary of the Russian Supreme Court advanced the reach of the ECHR by stipulating that when interpreting Russian legislation all courts in Russia should take into account the ECtHR's jurisprudence generally (that is, in all relevant ECtHR cases, not just those in which Russia was respondent).[264] Meanwhile, of course, ratification of the ECHR entailed that individuals within Russia jurisdiction were able to petition the ECtHR, and, as we have seen, this could have positive effects, eventually. Hence, as Provost put it: 'What we can hope is that the ratification of the ECHR was a significant milestone in a continuous process of thickening normative commitments to the idea of human rights and the rule of law by a wide range of public and private actors in Russia.'[265]

4 Russia 'at a crossroads, confronted with the choice of its own future' (2012–2013) and the path adopted

CoE–Russia relations would change forever in 2014 when Russia invaded Ukraine and illegally annexed Crimea. That and the crisis occurring over 2014–2019 are addressed in the next chapter. In the final section of this chapter, we look to the national context which preceded this and then existed in parallel to it. That is, we note Russia's unequivocal and decisive shift away from CoE values from around 2012 onwards, as had been feared and threatened by events and action occurring since 2005. We proceed in three steps. First, how PACE identified 2012 as a critical year for Russia – the crossroads juncture referred to in the Introduction of this chapter. Second, the choice adopted by the Russian government under President Putin, as evidenced by how things were in 2016. And third, how new powers for the RCC reflected the implied threat that Russia was prepared to wield at the CoE.

---

[263] Mälksoo, n 235 (2013), 224.
[264] Kovler, A. and Chernishova, O. (2013) 'The June 2013 Resolution No. 21 of the Russian Supreme Court: a move towards implementation of the judgments of the European Court of Human Rights', *Human Rights Law Journal*, 33(7): 263–7.
[265] Provost, n 244, 340.

4.1 2012: a 'window of opportunity' for Russia's 'democratic future'

The extent to which matters hung in the balance over 2012–2013 was reflected in a report[266] produced by PACE in 2012 as part of the on-going process of monitoring Russia's obligations and commitments. The rapporteurs had visited Russia several times and were clear that the 'overall state of democracy in Russia raise[d] concern', while 'progress in the fulfilment of the country's obligations and commitments [had been] slow'.[267] They saw their task as 'assessing the democratic progress in a country which seem[ed] to be at a crossroads, confronted with the choice of its own future'.[268]

The rapporteurs explained that their report should be not delayed any further,[269] referring to a slowly closing 'window of opportunity' for 'Russia's democratic future' after the December 2011 parliamentary elections. The latter had 'created a new political situation'.[270] Demonstrations occurred following the elections, based on concerns about allegations of fraud in favour of the ruling party. There had been similar protests, and again many arrests, following the March 2012 election, when Putin returned to the presidency,[271] following an election which the International Election Observation Mission considered had been held in conditions which were clearly skewed in favour of the then *Prime Minister* Putin.[272] According to the PACE rapporteurs, over 2011–2012 '[a] broadly engaged civil society ha[d] emerged, the existence of which even surprised the Russians', the view being that it 'created a specific moment of crucial importance and opportunity'[273] for the process of democratisation, one recognised by sections of Parliament.[274] As the related PACE Resolution put it, the new movement was creating 'a momentum for change',[275] and 'in order to realise this unique political potential, Russian society need[ed] concrete reforms'.[276] However, here there were mixed messages emanating from Russia. Certain reforms (on political parties, electoral law and direct elections of governors) suggested possible liberalisation, and the incoming President Putin had promised to

---

[266] PACE monitoring report, n 1.
[267] PACE monitoring report, n 1, para 532. An appendix to the report listed the steps taken/not taken by Russia in the (non)fulfilment of its accession commitments.
[268] PACE monitoring report, n 1, para 536.
[269] Cf PACE monitoring report, n 1, para 4 on the delayed nature of the report.
[270] PACE monitoring report, n 1, para 11.
[271] PACE monitoring report, n 1, paras 45–97.
[272] PACE monitoring report, n 1, para 84.
[273] PACE monitoring report, n 1, para 11.
[274] PACE monitoring report, n 1, para 12.
[275] PACE Resolution 1896 (2012), 2 October 2012, para 3.
[276] PACE Resolution 1896, n 275, para 4. PACE 'urge[d] the newly elected President Putin to democratise the system', para 8.

democratise Russia. However, various laws passed by the Duma in June and July 2012 – on the criminalisation of defamation, on the amendments to the law on assemblies and on NGOs, among others – had the potential to be clearly authoritarian in their application, and lead to a deterioration of the conditions for genuine political pluralism.[277] They created a far more unfavourable climate for the operation of civil society organisations by placing significant and alarming limits on the rights to freedom of association, expression and assembly.

The narratives just noted were reflected in the Resolution adopted by PACE, by 161 to 41 votes (with 7 abstentions), setting out (as in 2005) a very long list of reforms that Russia needed to make in the domain of the functioning of pluralist democracy and regarding human rights and fundamental freedoms.[278] The Resolution referred to the 'unique moment' arrived at in Russia's 'short history of democratic development'.[279] There was 'the awakening of a very engaged civil society and the [apparent] willingness of the authorities to hear the call for reforms [which] could create a momentum for change'.[280] If the authorities were willing to live up to their promised actions to restructure, then 'a window of opportunity' was 'still open'.[281] However, echoing PACE's 2005 report,[282] concern was raised at the continuation of reforms concentrating power in the presidency (reinforcing 'the verticality of power'), including in relation to power and influence over the judiciary. The trend was viewed 'as fundamentally undermining in many respects the system of checks and balances indispensable for the proper functioning of pluralistic democracy'.[283] Furthermore, the laws of June and July 2012 were clearly 'potentially regressive in terms of democratic development', and so the authorities were 'urge[d] ... not to make use of them in this harmful way'.[284]

Other CoE actors endorsed these messages. For example, the Commissioner on Human Rights inputted his own critique on various aspects of the

---

[277] PACE Resolution 1896, n 275, paras 22–3.

[278] The PACE Resolution, n 275, proceeded to identify a whole series of major issues with the functioning of pluralist democracy in Russia, making 18 recommendations for action (paras 25.1–25.11). With regard to fundamental aspects of the rule of law, a further 16 recommendations for action were made (paras 25.12–25.21), and with respect to human rights and fundamental freedoms, a further 11 recommendations for action (paras 25.22–25.32).

[279] PACE Resolution 1896, n 275, para 3 ('[t]o realise this unique political potential, Russian society needs concrete reforms, para 4).

[280] PACE Resolution 1896, n 275, para 3.

[281] PACE Resolution 1896, n 275, para 20.

[282] See text accompanying n 174.

[283] PACE Resolution 1896, n 275, para 8.

[284] PACE Resolution 1896, n 275, para 21.

2012 law reforms, notably the law regulating NGOs.[285] As for the Venice Commission, at the request of the PACE Monitoring Committee, it provided its own assessment (and so, an independent voice), in various Opinions highlighting a whole range of concerns related to, respectively, the Federal Law on the election of the Deputies of the State Duma of the Russian Federation;[286] the law on political parties of the Russian Federation;[287] the law on assemblies and demonstrations,[288] and laws relating to combatting extremism.[289] In each instance there were significant criticisms, reflecting problems from the perspective of effective political democracy.

Returning to the 2012 PACE monitoring report on Russia, its authors explained how they felt that the report needed publication so that it could contribute to the improvement of democracy in Russia'.[290] The idea was that the CoE 'voice its position, engage in an honest and fair analysis and actively support all those who work in the country for its democratic and European future'.[291]

These words were indicative of the limited role PACE could perform, akin to the 'hospital for democracy' labelling used in 2008 (Russia/Georgia).[292] The reality, of course, was that, under the Putin regime, there was no attempt to democratise the system after 2012. Rather than being relaxed or rescinded, several of the relevant laws were reinforced. So, for example, regarding the law regulating assemblies, in June 2012 new laws were passed which ignored the Venice Commission's advice of March 2012, and established an even

---

[285] See, for example, Commissioner for Human Rights (Nils Muižnieks), 'Opinion: Russia: legislation and practice on NGOs should be revised', 15 July 2013, and 'Opinion: Commissioner for Human Rights reiterates his call to bring Russian NGO legislation in line with European standards', 9 July 2015.

[286] Venice Commission, 'Opinion on the Federal Law on the Election of the Deputies of the State Duma of the Russian Federation', 657/2011, 19 March 2012.

[287] Venice Commission, 'Opinion on the Law on Political Parties of the Russian Federation', 658/2011, 20 March 2012 (the Russian law '[52] … established[d] important obstacles to the very existence of political parties'; a situation 'not in line with European standards and, particularly, Articles 10 and 11' of the ECHR).

[288] Venice Commission, 'Opinion on the Federal Law No. 54-FZ of 19 June 2004 on Assemblies, Meetings, Demonstrations, Marches and Picketing of the Russian Federation', 659/2011, 20 March 2012.

[289] Venice Commission, 'Opinion on the Federal Law on Combating Extremist Activity of the Russian Federation', CDL-AD(2012)016, 20 June 2012 (being critical of broad and imprecise wording, giving too wide a discretion in its interpretation and application, thus leading to arbitrariness (para 74), needing amending to bring compliance with Articles 10 and 11 ECHR (para 76) and infringing 'principles of legality, necessity and proportionality' (para 77)).

[290] PACE monitoring report, n 1, paras 15 and 13.

[291] PACE monitoring report, n 1, para 15.

[292] See text accompanying n 132.

more restrictive framework.[293] Added to that there were new laws on so-called 'foreign agents' (13 July 2012) and related to treason (21 February 2014), which raised 'several serious issues' for the Venice Commission,[294] and 'seen in context mutually reinforc[ed] the chilling effect on the exercise on freedom of expression along with freedom of association', which were 'crucial rights for the viability of an effective political democracy'.[295] The law related to foreign agents, regarding undesirable activities of foreign and international non-governmental organisations, was extended further still in 2016[296] and in 2020.[297]

4.2 The choice adopted by the Russian government: the view from 2016 (20 years after accession to the CoE)

By then, of course, Crimea had been illegally annexed, and there was no doubt whatsoever that Russia was far down a path of authoritarianism. Hence, as the next chapter will argue, its membership of the CoE became increasingly ritualistic over the 2010s.

As before, the serious decline in the human rights and democracy situation in Russia was highlighted by CoE actors. So, for example, in 2015, a year on from the invasion of Crimea, a PACE Resolution condemned the rapidly deteriorating internal human rights situation in Russia, and, in effect, the government's determination to attack the newly engaged civil society.[298] PACE 'encourage[d]' the Secretary General of the CoE 'to prepare a report

---

[293] Venice Commission, 'Opinion on Federal Law No. 65-FZ of 8 June 2012 of the Russian Federation Amending Federal Law No. 54-FZ of 19 June 2004 on Assemblies, Meetings, Demonstrations, Marches and Picketing and the Code of Administrative Offences', CDL-AD(2013)003, 11 March 2013 (para 59 ... 'firmly convinced' the new law was 'a step backward for the protection of freedom of assembly' potentially infringing 'fundamental right to peaceful assembly', and 'strongly recommend[ing]' repeal).

[294] 'Opinion on Federal Law No. 121-FZ on Non-Commercial Organisations ("law on foreign agents"), on Federal Laws No. 18-FZ and No. 147-FZ and on Federal Law No. 190-FZ on Making Amendments to the Criminal Code ("law on treason") of the Russian Federation', 27 June 2014, CDL-AD(2014)025-e, para 132.

[295] Venice Commission, n 294, para 139.

[296] 'Opinion on Federal Law No. 129-FZ on amending certain legislative acts (Federal Law on undesirable activities of foreign and international non-governmental organisations)', 13 June 2016, CDL-AD(2016)020.

[297] Cf Venice Commission, 'Opinion on the Compatibility with International Human Rights Standards of a Series of Bills Introduced to the Russian State Duma between 10 and 23 November 2020, to Amend Laws Affecting So-called "Foreign Agents"', CDL-AD(2021)027, 18 June 2021.

[298] Resolution 2063 (2015), 'Consideration of the annulment of the previously ratified credentials of the delegation of the Russian Federation (follow-up to paragraph 16 of Resolution 2034 (2015))', 24 June 2015, para 4.

on the situation of human rights and democracy' in Russia, in order to assess 'the conformity of these recent developments with [CoE] standards'. By 2016, however, the Russian delegation to PACE was boycotting that body as Russia de facto withdrew itself from the monitoring procedure.[299] A planned visit by the Commissioner for Human Rights in October 2016 was cancelled due to unacceptable restrictions imposed to his programme.[300]

The boycott of PACE meant that an official PACE monitoring report in Russia could not be produced. Instead the Monitoring Committee issued an 'Information Note' (October 2016) on the 'functioning of democratic institutions'[301] in Russia. It made for gloomy reading on the 20th anniversary year of Russia's accession to the CoE.

First, the co-rapporteurs referred to a justice system which was 'biased in favour of the prosecution', and which raised questions as to 'equality of arms between prosecution and defence and thus the fairness of trials'.[302] They referred to 'concern about the lack of independence of the judiciary and its vulnerability to external and internal pressure and interference', highlighting recent controversial high-profile trials raising issues in that regard, and suggestions they were 'politically motivated'.[303]

Second, reference was made to severe restrictions on the right to freedom of association made possible by regressive legislative reforms, which facilitated disproportional police responses, including the use of force and routine arrests. There had been a clear and obvious deterrent to the exercise of this right ('[p]ermission to hold street rallies ha[d] often been denied or only granted in non-central locations'; 'violation[s] of the bans ... resulted [in] steep fines and detention').[304] Strong concerns were expressed about freedom

---

[299] See Chapter 4, section 2.1.2.

[300] Statement, 'Russia: Commissioner cancels visit to the country because of unacceptable restrictions imposed to his programme', 11 October 2016 (available from: www.coe.int/en/web/commissioner [Accessed 1 June 2024]). For further details and context see Chapter 7, text accompanying n 76–9.

[301] PACE Monitoring Committee, 'Information note on the functioning of democratic institutions in the Russian Federation', AS/Mon (2016) 29, 11 October 2016.

[302] PACE Monitoring Committee, n 301, para 57.

[303] Para 55. See also Commissioner on Human Rights, 'As long as the judicial system of the Russian Federation does not become more independent, doubts about its effectiveness remain', 25 February 2016 (joint statement issued by Nils Muižnieks (then Council of Europe Commissioner for Human Rights), Thomas Hammarberg (former Commissioner, 2006 to 2012) and Álvaro Gil-Robles (former Commissioner, 1999–2006)), and, before, Commissioner for Human Rights, 'Report following visit to the Russian Federation from 3 to 12 April 2013', CommDH(2013)21, 12 November 2013.

[304] PACE Monitoring Committee, n 301, para 63. See also PACE Resolution, 'Urgent need to prevent human rights violations during peaceful protests', Resolution 2116 (2016), 27 May 2016.

of assembly and so the opportunity to campaign freely in the context of the State Duma elections of September 2016.[305]

Thirdly, as regards the broader democratic environment the October 2016 Information Note referred to a significant narrowing of the space for the operation of opposition parties and their capacity to express dissent. There had been 'systematic harassment and intimidation of opposition leaders and opposition activists by the authorities, as well as by civil groups that are seen as connected to the authorities'.[306] Relatedly the rhetoric aimed at non-conformist views had become harsh and inflammatory, 'resulting in an increasingly polarised and confrontational political environment'.[307]

The 2016 Information Note raised further alarm bells as regards freedom of expression and of the media, and with respect to civil society and association. On the former, there was analysis of the restrictions on dissenting opinions and pressure on independent media facilitated by the extremism laws criticised by the Venice Commission back in 2012. The laws in issue gave the authorities 'broad powers to close down any media organisation deemed to spread extremist information'. The relevant laws 'hampered independent media' including via 'restrictions on foreign ownership of news outlets, warnings, revocation of licences, closure of news outlets and blockage of websites and online platforms'.[308] The highly unfavourable climate for the operation of civil society organisations was also highlighted, especially laws directed to the branding of NGOs as 'foreign agents'. These stigmatised independent human rights institutions, purportedly based on their 'political activity' and foreign funding, including by requiring prior registration with the Ministry of Justice if overseas funding was to be received and by the obligation to state 'foreign agent' on all their publications and material.[309] The co-rapporteurs further observed that 'criminal prosecutions are increasingly being used against NGO activists and political parties and movements that are critical of the authorities and their policies'. They drew attention to the fact that in October 2015 the highly respected Russian human rights organisation, the Memorial Human Rights Centre, had produced a non-exhaustive list of what it considered to be 50 political prisoners (that is, individuals detained or imprisoned on politically motivated charges).[310]

---

[305] PACE Monitoring Committee, n 301, para 70.
[306] PACE Monitoring Committee, n 301, para 24.
[307] PACE Monitoring Committee, n 301, para 26.
[308] PACE Monitoring Committee, n 301, para 44.
[309] The co-rapporteurs referred to 'harsh action, seemingly aimed at preventing and dissuading civil society organisations from carrying out their work, often forcing them to shut down or face harassment and persecution at the hands of the authorities', PACE Monitoring Committee, n 301, para 12.
[310] PACE Monitoring Committee, n 301, para 55.

4.3 Potentially limiting the influence of the ECHR internally

What then of Provost's hope, noted earlier,[311] that the ECHR would lead to a 'thickening normative commitments to the idea of human rights'?

In fact, the quote was extracted from the conclusion to Provost's 2015 article, the title of which – 'Teetering on the edge of legal nihilism: Russia and the evolving European human rights regime'[312] – spoke volumes. Clearly there had not been enough force and presence for the ECHR in the domestic context to prevent the developments just noted. In that regard, a detailed analysis[313] of how the ECHR was employed in Russian courts authored in 2017 highlighted the disparity between the apparently progressive approach implied by the Constitution, and the reality in practice, which was often to ignore the ECHR. There was a '[l]ack of judicial will to implement international human rights guarantees that Russia [was] obliged to abide by', one evident at all levels, including the RCC, while the jurisprudence of the Supreme Court resembled 'an attempt to demonstrate' the application of the ECHR, rather than actual implementation in fact.[314] More generally, under the chairmanship of Zorkin,[315] the RCC operated in a pragmatic, politically expedient way: submissive to the Putin regime in politically important cases, yet prepared to prioritise constitutional considerations in others.[316]

---

[311] See text accompanying n 244.

[312] Provost, n 244.

[313] Burkov, A. (2017) 'The use of European human rights law in Russian courts', in L. Mälksoo and W. Benedek (eds) *Russia and the European Court of Human Rights: The Strasbourg Effect*, Cambridge: Cambridge University Press, pp 59–92, 91–2. On the RCC's relations with the ECHR (2017 perspective), see Mälksoo, L. 'Introduction', in L. Mälksoo and W. Benedek (eds) *Russia and the European Court of Human Rights: The Strasbourg Effect*, Cambridge: Cambridge University Press, and chapters 2–5 of L. Mälksoo and W. Benedek (eds) *Russia and the European Court of Human Rights: The Strasbourg Effect*, Cambridge: Cambridge University Press.

[314] Burkov, n 313, 92. For similar analysis, see Nussberger, n 118, 667 (contrasting the apparent 'remarkable openness' of Russian national law to the ECHR with a reality of 'lip service' paid to it and an absence of 'an important impact' on the outcome of cases). For more upbeat analysis, see Bowring, B. (2017) 'Russia's cases in the ECtHR and the question of implementation', in L. Mälksoo and W. Benedek (eds) *Russia and the European Court of Human Rights: The Strasbourg Effect*, Cambridge: Cambridge University Press, pp 188–221, 188.

[315] On whom, see n 245.

[316] See Trochev, A. and Solomon, H. (2018) 'Authoritarian constitutionalism in Putin's Russia: a pragmatic Constitutional Court in a dual state', *Communist and Post-Communist Studies,* 51(3): 201–14. See further Podoplelova, O. (2024) 'Legitimizing authoritarian transformation: Russia's Constitutional Court and the cost of compromise', *VerfBlog* [Blog], 2 October, available from: https://verfassungsblog.de/legitimizing-authoritar ian-transformation [Accessed 1 June 2024] ('RCC has never really been an independent institution. It did not condemn a single law that undermined the democratic government and curtailed the political participation of the general public').

In keeping with this disingenuous position, the Russian Constitution had been essentially reconfigured by the Duma on 15 December 2015,[317] to enable *potential* defiance of the ECtHR by the RCC. The latter was equipped to: (i) declare that an ECtHR judgment directed against Russia directly conflicted with the 'foundations of the constitutional system of [Russia]', and, as such, (ii) to additionally declare that judgment 'non-executable'. While (i) was highly unwelcome, it left open the possibility of a re-reading of an incompatible provision in line with the Convention. Hence the real concern was (ii), for the prospect of declaring a judgment 'non-executable' (and paralysing 'all measures of execution' (including payment of the just satisfaction)) was *potentially* in direct contradiction of Russia's ECHR (Article 46(1)) obligations.[318]

To be clear, then, the powers gained by the RCC in 2015 did not amount to a wholesale rejection of ECHR in the national context or a type of open warfare against the ECtHR. The RCC's treatment of the Russian 'prisoner voting' case of *Anchugov and Gladkov v. Russia*[319] demonstrated this, given its openness to dialogue on the compatibility question, one that ultimately resulted in compliance (perhaps controversially)[320] without defiance of the ECtHR. So, the real, immediate motivation for the RCC's new powers was seen when, on 19 January 2017, the procedure was used to provide an ostensibly legitimate basis (under national law) to prevent the payment of

---

[317] See Venice Commission. 'Interim Opinion on the Amendments to the Federal Constitutional Law on the Constitutional Court of the Russian Federation', CDL-AD(2016)005, 11 March 2016; and 'Russian Federation – Final Opinion on the Amendments to the Federal Constitutional Law on the Constitutional Court' CDL-AD(2016)016, 13 June 2016.

[318] Final Opinion, n 317, para 42 (the 'no execution measure' provision 'conflict[ed] with Russia's international obligations under the Vienna Convention on the Law of Treaties and Article 46 ECHR and should be removed'). See Kuijer, M. (2019) 'The perspective of the Venice Commission', in M. Breuer (ed) *Principled Resistance to ECtHR Judgments: A New Paradigm?*, Berlin: Springer, pp 275–98.

[319] *Anchugov and Gladkov v. Russia*, 11157/04, 4 July 2013 (Article 32(3) of the Constitution: automatic and indiscriminate ban on convicted prisoners' voting rights, violated Article 3 Protocol 1).

[320] In the relevant case, the RCC affirmed that the ECtHR's judgment could not be executed but also indicated to the federal legislator how domestic law could be amended to secure potential compatibility. The legislation was amended such that community work would count as a criminal punishment involving placement in correctional centres, but without automatic disenfranchisement. On the basis the CM considered the judgment fully executed, see CM/ResDH(2019)240. See also Dzehtsiarou, K., Golubok, S. and Timofeev, M. (2016) 'The Russian response to the prisoner voting judgment', *ECHR Blog* [Blog], available from: www.echrblog.com/2016/04/the-russian-response-to-prisoner-voting.html [Accessed 14 July 2024].

just satisfaction (nearly two billion euros (EUR 1,866,104,634))[321] in the *Yukos* case.[322] The ECtHR judgment has never been implemented.

5 Conclusion

So, perhaps the new 2015 procedure was best seen as presenting a clear statement to the CoE: a sovereign Russia was willing, if necessary, to create a constitution that could 'legitimately' defy the ECtHR. This was a far cry from events associated with Russia's 1996 'therapeutic admission' 20 years before.

As we have seen across this chapter, after some initial signs of positivity the 1990s dream of Russia as part of the European family of nations had already started to fade by the mid-2000s. The CoE had been able to highlight the issues arising here, but it was soon evident that it could not do much more in the face of an unwilling government. In short, the CoE could offer assistance from a top-down, European perspective; however, that was not enough. Rather, the rule of law, and a judiciary able to apply Convention standards, was required, as was a strong dedication to the value of effective political democracy, as part of a bottom-up approach. More than that, however, good faith and cooperation, and a sustained political will, were necessary. And after 2005, it was clearly absent in Russia's case, and especially so as the 2000s gave way to the 2010s. As we have seen, after 2012, the point in which PACE had clearly identified how Russia was at a critical juncture, it was an open secret that Russia was wilfully violating aspects of the CoE's founding principles.

By then, not only was it becoming evident that the socialising effect of CoE membership had not worked – because the Russian government did not want it to – but it was also clear too that the CoE was unable to discipline Russia in matters affecting its credibility and standing as an international organisation. In this way, Russia's membership had an increasingly negative effect on the CoE itself. The Chechnya issue was very dark indeed and did not turn out to be an exceptional matter staining Russia's otherwise improving record, as might have been hoped for. Its legacy – that of impunity – endures to this

---

[321] *OAO Neftyanaya Kompaniya Yukos*, n 208. For analysis, see Starzhenetskiy, V. (2017) 'Property rights in Russia: reconsidering the socialist legal tradition', in L. Mälksoo and W. Benedek (eds) *Russia and the European Court of Human Rights: The Strasbourg Effect*, Cambridge: Cambridge University Press, pp 295–325, 320–3, and for wider analysis of the RCC's new power as a 'blocking mechanism', see Starzhenetskiy, V. (2019) 'The execution of ECtHR judgments and the 'right to object' of the RCC', in M. Breuer (ed) *Principled Resistance to ECtHR Judgments: A New Paradigm?*, Berlin: Springer, pp 245–72.

[322] On this case, see Dzehtsiarou, K. and Fontanelli, F. (2018) 'Unprincipled disobedience to international decisions: A primer from the Russian Constitutional Court', in C. Strohal and S. Kieber (eds) *European Yearbook on Human Rights 2018*, pp 319–41.

day. The CoE's inability to contain Russia had been apparent then, as it was with respect to Georgia, when Russia was determined to express its regional influence and power. The European hospital for democracy narrative was then employed in PACE, exposing how cooperation had to be preferred over confrontation in such scenarios, for PACE could not force Russia to do anything, and the CM was unwilling to confront it. The same political realities – those of the weakness of the CoE in the face of a more hostile and aggressive Russia – would be seen over 2014–2019, as the Crimea crisis reverberated around the CoE.

4

The Council of Europe and Russia (2013–2022)

1 Introduction: Russia's increasing ritualism toward CoE values after 2013 until its expulsion

Although the preceding chapter focussed on the period 1998–2013, it concluded by looking ahead to 2016, recounting how dark the picture had then become in Russia as regards human rights protection, democracy and the rule of law. That overlaps with this chapter, which spans from 2013 until the eve of Russia's expulsion in February 2022. The standout issues of this period relate to Russia's invasion and annexation of Crimea and illegal activities in eastern Ukraine from 2014, and, following this, how Russia manufactured a major crisis at the Council of Europe (CoE) over 2014–2019. In effect, Russia positioned itself such that the CoE faced a stark choice: either the crisis was resolved in Russia's favour, effectively resulting in impunity for its actions in Crimea, or it would leave the CoE. Here Russia exerted its considerable bargaining power as a major power and 'big payer'[1] in the CoE context – and it seemed to prevail in 2019, when somewhat ritualistic, arguably deceptive arrangements were made for it to remain in the CoE. The return of Russia created the impression that an appropriate resolution to the crisis had been reached with Russia committed to the CoE, when the reality was far darker. Russia had evaded accountability as it remained in the CoE without any meaningful statutory action being taken against it (or to come) in relation to its manifest and ongoing breaches of the CoE Statute, principally through its illegal annexation of Crimea and military action in eastern Ukraine. In that regard the CoE had effectively capitulated to Russia, allowing it to remain in the CoE with it openly in continuous breach of Article 3 CoE, flouting numerous of its accession

---

[1] See Chapter 2, n 9, and discussion around text accompanying n 61 in this chapter.

commitments, and with a progressively deteriorating internal human rights record to boot, for the 2019 arrangements tended to conceal the extent of democratic backsliding that had taken hold in Russia at that point. For such reasons 2019 was a defining moment in CoE–Russia relations, setting the seal on what had by then become Russia's evermore *ritualistic* membership of the CoE.

Regarding the notion of 'ritualism', inspiration is taken from Charlesworth[2] and Davies'[3] work in relation to United Nations human rights monitoring. The former envisages 'ritualism', as 'involv[ing] the formulaic or perfunctory acceptance of norms or values in the absence of a more substantial commitment' to them. She explains that '[r]ights ritualism is a more common response than outright rejection of human rights standards and institutions'.[4] This maps neatly on to Russia's relations with the CoE. It was a member state for 1996–2022, when it benefitted from association with its values, including by the appearance of being subject to its highly respected human rights regimes, even though after the mid-2000s the true extent of the depth and sincerity of its commitment to the CoE's values was very doubtful, and in later years almost non-existent.[5] Yet, Russia made no effort to exit the CoE under Article 7 CoE Statute.

In terms of perpetuating ritualism, on the one hand, there were some achievements as with the 2009 moratorium on the death penalty, and implementation of certain European Court of Human Rights (ECtHR) judgments.[6] Worth mentioning too is Russia's active engagement in other areas of CoE standard-setting and cooperation activities over several years. In these senses, it was possible to argue that Russia's CoE membership could yield some positive outcomes, keeping hopes alive for engagement, change and improvement. On the other hand, this contrasted dramatically with features which exhibited Russia's complete defiance of core values of CoE membership: Russia's actions with respect to Georgia and especially

---

[2] See Charlesworth, H. (2021) 'Rituals and ritualism in the international human rights system', in N. Bhuta (ed) *The Struggle for Human Rights: Essays in Honour of Philip Alston*, Oxford: Oxford University Press, pp 16–29.

[3] Davies, M. (2021) 'How regional organizations respond to human rights?', *Journal of Human Rights*, 20: 245–62.

[4] Charlesworth, n 2, 19.

[5] Here Russia gained 'the positive reputational benefits or legitimacy associated with human rights commitments' (or CoE membership), Charlesworth, n 2, 19. This membership fitted Charlesworth's conceptualisation of ritualism to 'include ratifying human rights treaties without implementing their provisions domestically ... failing to provide remedies for human rights breaches or to develop policy to prevent violations, and, in some circumstances, invoking claims of culture to undermine international standards', 19.

[6] But were these judgments insignificant when seen from the wider perspective, especially those *not* implemented? See text accompanying n 124 and n 126.

Crimea (and its hostility to the CoE in the aftermath), and trends such as the clear and unequivocal authoritarian and anti-democratic tendencies on display in the national context, especially after 2012. As such, the truer picture of Russia's membership was a lack of meaningful commitment to CoE values, indeed gross breaches of the same, accompanied by a pretence that there was such a commitment, even that the CoE rules were being unfairly applied against it.[7]

This fits with ritualism, which does not necessarily mean that institutions of control are totally ignored. There can be apparently 'great respect paid to these formal institutions even as the realization of goals retreats into the background'.[8] The context can be one of organisations that establish instruments which 'suggest a commitment to human rights', but have institutions 'tied to intergovernmentalism', which are then 'often undermined by their own rules, procedures, and guidelines, which further retard their proactivity and oversight'. The following account will reflect this, documenting the CoE's apparent 'tolerance for behaviour that contradict[ed] nominally agreed standards, with human rights violations sometimes of egregious extent, usually prompting at best weak criticism'.[9]

The ritualism narrative runs through this chapter, section 2 of which looks in detail at the crisis created at the CoE by Russia's annexation of Crimea, and how this was concluded in 2019. Section 3 then looks to the situation after 2019, addressing the human rights and the rule of law situation in Russia, and how this was overseen by the CoE. Section 4 provides an overview of the inter-state cases directed against Russia, to include those concerning Ukraine. The final section offers some general reflections.

2 Russia's invasion and annexation of Crimea (2014) and its repercussions (2015–2019): defining moments for the CoE?

As noted in Chapter 2,[10] to pave the way for enlargement, the heads of state and government of the CoE member states issued the Vienna Declaration in 1993. It eyed a future era of 'democratic security' in Europe, a notion that Russia approved of during the accession process.[11] Over 2008–2009, Russia's actions in Georgia severely threatened this whereas its illegal annexation of Crimea and broader military action in Ukraine from 2014 shattered it.

---

[7] Cf the Russian delegation's boycott of the Parliamentary Assembly of the Council of Europe (PACE), text accompanying n 46.
[8] Davies, n 3, 249.
[9] Davies, n 3.
[10] See Chapter 2, text accompanying n 38.
[11] See Chapter 2, text accompanying n 84.

In February 2014, the outcome of the 'Revolution of Dignity' in Kyiv was the removal of the Russia-friendly President of Ukraine (Viktor Yanukovich), after which Russian troops intervened in Ukraine's Crimea region.[12] Russia subsequently illegally annexed Crimea following a hastily organised referendum (16 March 2014) condemned by many nations, actions which led to sanctions being imposed by the United States and the European Union (the CoE has no such powers, nor the ability to fine its member states).[13] After this a pro-Russian separatist uprising emerged in eastern Ukraine apparently backed by Russia, an estimated 13,000 people dying in the process, including many civilians. There were allegations of killings, torture and enforced disappearances.[14] It was estimated that one and a half million people were displaced. The outcome was that separatists were left controlling significant parts of Ukrainian territory, backed by Russia. In July 2014, from those territories a Malaysia Airlines flight from Amsterdam to Kuala Lumpur was shot down, allegedly by Russian-controlled forces, killing 298 people.

Russia's accountability (or lack thereof) for this in the CoE context may be seen from legal and political perspectives. The former involves allegations of serious human rights violations in the context of the European Convention on Human Rights (ECHR), and various inter-state cases brought before the ECtHR. These were submitted by Ukraine against Russia in 2014, and are discussed later.[15] By contrast, the focus over the next few pages is on political accountability, in relation to the very serious breach of Article 3 CoE Statute that Russia's actions represented, and the events related to this occurring between 2014 and 2019 at the CoE.[16] This may be broken

---

[12] For a detailed account of the events of 2013–2014 up to 2022 see, among others, Arel, D. and Driscoll, J. (2023) *Ukraine's Unnamed War: Before the Russian Invasion of 2022*, Cambridge: Cambridge University Press.

[13] See Chapter 2, section 2.3.

[14] See admissibility decision in *Ukraine v. Russia (re Crimea)* (dec.) [GC], no. 20958/14, 16 December 2020, for a detailed factual account, plus allegations of human rights violations put by Ukraine (paras 105–41), and Russia's response (paras 142–97). See also issues highlighted by United Nations (UN) bodies (paras 225–30) and non-governmental organisations (NGOs) (paras 231–2).

[15] See section 4 of this chapter. On interim measures issued by the ECtHR, see Chapter 6, section 3.

[16] For relevant materials see: Roter, P. (2017) 'Russia in the Council of Europe: participation à la carte', in L. Mälksoo and W. Benedek (eds) *Russia and the European Court of Human Rights: The Strasbourg Effect*, Cambridge: Cambridge University Press, pp 26–56, 47–51; Glas, L. (2018) 'The Assembly's appeasement towards Russia', 27 September, and (2019) 'Russia left, threatened and won: its return to the Assembly without sanctions', 2 July, *Strasbourg Observers* [Blog], both available from: https://strasbourgobservers.com [Accessed 1 June 2024]; Dzehtsiarou, K. and Coffey, D. (2019) 'Suspension and expulsion of members of the Council of Europe: difficult decisions in troubled times', *International and Comparative Law Quarterly*, 68(2): 443–76; Drzemczewski, A. (2020) 'The (non-) participation of

down into two episodes. First, the Committee of Ministers' (CM's) and the Parliamentary Assembly of the Council of Europe's (PACE's) initial reaction to the illegal annexation of Crimea over the period of 2014–2015 and Russia's response through to May 2019 (section 2.1).[17] Second, the 'resolution' of the matter in that year (sections 2.2 and 2.3). 'Resolution' – in that the crisis was concluded on very dubious terms, indeed at some cost to the CoE's credibility, as shall be seen (section 2.4).

2.1 The CoE condemns Russia's actions; Russia precipitates a non-participation crisis

February to April 2014 saw the CM and PACE respond to Russia's actions in relation to Crimea. True to form, the CM's initial response was weak as regards action, even if it was firm in terms of criticism of what had occurred as being totally unacceptable. So, over February to April 2014[18] (and subsequently) the CM adopted several Decisions on the 'Situation in Ukraine'. These expressed solidarity with its people,[19] 'condemned' the referendum held in Crimea on 16 March 2014, and 'deplored' President Putin's signature of treaties making Crimea and the city of Sevastopol part of Russia, plus his appeal to the Parliament of the Russian Federation to adopt a law to complete this process. In April 2014, the CM referred to the 'illegal referendum', and stated that the 'illegal annexation' of the territories by Russia could not 'form the basis for any alteration of [their] status'.[20]

One could perhaps understand a cautious initial reaction in February as events were actively unfolding, but by March 2014 the facts on the ground spoke for themselves. However, over 2014 – and at no point ever – did the CM call out what occurred as a breach of Article 3 of the CoE Statute, let alone did it threaten resort to Article 8. Instead, it 'recalled the duty of

---

Russian parliamentarians in the Parliamentary Assembly of the Council of Europe: recent developments', *Revista do Instituto Brasileiro de Direitos Humanos*, 20: 49–57; Steininger, S. (2020) 'With or without you: suspension, expulsion, and the limits of membership sanctions in regional human rights regimes', *Zeitschrift für ausländisches öffentliches Recht und Völkerrecht*, 81(2): 533–66; Demir-Gürsel, E. (2021) 'The former Secretary General of the Council of Europe confronting Russia's annexation of the Crimea and Turkey's state of emergency', *European Convention on Human Rights Law Review*, 2(2): 303–35.

[17] On this, see PACE Monitoring Committee, 'Challenge, on substantive grounds, of the still unratified credentials of the parliamentary delegation of the Russian Federation', Doc. 14922, 26 June 2019 (hereafter 'PACE Monitoring Committee (Gale) report').

[18] CM Decision, 26 February 2014, Item 1.2; CM/Del/Dec(2014)1194/1.7, 19–20 March 2014; CM/Del/Dec(2014)1196/1.8, 2–3 April 2014.

[19] CM/Del/Dec(2014)1194/1.7.

[20] CM/Del/Dec(2014)1196/1.8, 2–3 April 2014, para 1. The point was made repeatedly in subsequent Decisions.

all member States to comply with the commitments undertaken'[21] under the CoE Statute and, in September 2014, 'stressed' that the crisis in Ukraine 'can only be resolved ... on the basis of the principles of the peaceful settlement of disputes, the full respect of the territorial integrity of Ukraine within its internationally recognised borders and the protection of human rights'.[22] It called on Russia to 'use its influence over the separatist movement in eastern Ukraine with a view to de-escalating tensions'[23] and it 'urged' it to:

> withdraw all its troops from Ukraine and refrain from any further military interference in Ukraine, including the supply of military assets to other parties, and to secure the border to avoid the illegal transfer of such assets, in full respect of the United Nations' Charter and its commitments within the Council of Europe, regarding in particular the principles of the peaceful settlement of disputes and the full respect of the territorial integrity, sovereignty and independence of States, rejecting any forms of threats of force.[24]

In contrast, PACE was stronger, even if conciliatory (it did not call for Article 8 action either). Its Resolution of 10 April 2014[25] (occurring in the context of a challenge to the Russian PACE delegation's credentials)[26] was its initial response to Russia's annexation of Crimea, and events in eastern Ukraine. Passed by a large majority,[27] it condemned the 'flagrant violation' of Russia's CoE obligations and commitments that had occurred.[28] Russia's actions constituted, '[3] ... beyond any doubt, a grave violation of international law, including of the United Nations Charter', and were '[4] ... in clear contradiction' with the CoE Statute, 'in particular its preamble, and the obligations resulting from Article 3'. Russia had '[6] ... created a threat to stability and peace in Europe', '[5] ... persistently reject[ing]' 'diplomatic efforts ... aimed at the de-escalation of the situation'. The Russian Parliament's condoning of the invasion was criticised, as was action taken by Russia against PACE members who had spoken out against it.[29] Deep

---

[21] CM/Del/Dec(2014)1194/1.7, para 4. In May 2014, the CM Chair's Conclusions did refer to a breach of the CoE Statute, see Chapter 7, text accompanying n 48.
[22] CM/Del/Dec(2014)1207/1.5, 17 September 2014, para 1.
[23] CM Decision, n 22, para 3.
[24] CM Decision, n 22, para 4.
[25] Resolution 1990 (2014), 'Reconsideration on substantive grounds of the previously ratified credentials of the Russian delegation', 10 April 2014.
[26] On challenges to credentials, see Chapter 2, text accompanying n 65.
[27] 145 in favour, 21 against, 22 abstentions.
[28] Resolution 1990 (2014), n 25, para 13.
[29] Resolution 1990 (2014), n 25, para 7 ('blacklisting' of 89 European personalities, including certain current and a former members of PACE).

concern was expressed at the lack of free expression and political freedoms in Russia as a means of criticising or challenging what had occurred.[30]

PACE sought a balance between a 'strong signal of disapproval'[31] of Russia's action, while communicating the need for 'political dialogue', resolution, and reconciliation. There should be '[14] … no return to the pattern of the Cold War'; that had to be avoided. Then again PACE was compelled to 'confront face-to-face' Russia 'with questions and facts and to demand answers and accountability'.[32]

So, to help foster dialogue, the 18 person Russian PACE delegation's credentials were confirmed in April 2014, the threat of their rejection being held in reserve, if Russia did not '[16] … de-escalate the situation and reverse the annexation of Crimea'. However, 'to mark [PACE's] condemnation'[33] at events, internal sanctions were imposed on the Russian PACE delegation until the end of the 2014: in particular, voting rights were suspended.[34]

2.1.1 PACE's (April 2014) internal sanctions: did PACE go too far?

Had PACE gone too far? The reader might be surprised that the question is asked. However, three distinct points need to be made.

The first relates to whether PACE's actions in 2014 were justifiable on the facts and merits: were they a proper and appropriate response to what had occurred? On that the answer was surely yes. Russia's action in Crimea in 2014 constituted by far and away the most serious breach of Article 3 of the CoE Statute for 40 years,[35] if not since the formation of the CoE (prior to Russia's full-scale invasion of Ukraine, in 2022, of course). As such, it was perfectly understandable that PACE acted as it did in April 2014 by denying voting rights to the Russian PACE delegation. Further, the sanctions imposed were by virtue of PACE's Rules,[36] which had been in place since the early

---

[30] Resolution 1990 (2014), n 25, paras 9 and 10–1.
[31] Resolution 1990 (2014), n 25, para 13.
[32] Resolution 1990 (2014), n 25, para 14.
[33] Resolution 1990 (2014), n 25, para 15.
[34] Additionally, so were the right to be represented in the Bureau of the Assembly, the Presidential Committee and the Standing Committee; also, Russian PACE delegates were not able to 'participate in election observation missions'.
[35] The only comparison being Türkiye's invasion of Cyprus, in 1974, see Chapter 5, section 4.2.
[36] Notably Rule 9.4.c (as it then was) allowing for confirmation of credentials but with 'depriving or suspending the exercise of some of the rights of participation or representation' in PACE. The CoE Statute (Article 28) gives PACE the capacity to set its own Rules.

1960s,[37] and had been accepted by Russia when it joined ('therapeutically') the CoE. Their application had become 'recognised practice'.[38]

The second point, however, concerns the validity of such internal (PACE) sanctions from the perspective of the CoE Statute. Arguably it gives the CM exclusive competence to sanction states by suspending any voting rights (under Article 8 and 9). On that footing Russia contested the legitimacy of the April 2014 sanctions, maintaining that PACE did not have the power to impose withdrawal of voting rights, that this created an unacceptable imbalance between the two statutory organs of the CoE, and insisting on the need for equality of the delegations of all CoE member states, including in PACE.[39] Furthermore, Russia referenced the risk that such a – as it saw it – unilateral move by PACE would effectively deprive a member state of its right to, *inter alia*, vote for new judges on the ECtHR, the Secretary General or the Commissioner for Human Rights.[40] This argument is not entirely devoid of merit, *if* the perspective was solely that of the CoE Statute.[41] However, seen in the wider context of PACE's post-1990s role (including Russia's entry to the CoE in 1996), and in relation to an egregious breach of Statute, the deprivation of voting rights of the offending state was, without a shadow of doubt, justifiable in the sense noted in the previous paragraph. Furthermore, as shall be noted later, with respect to Russia's lack of input into elections for new judges after 2016 and so on, this was the result of the delegation's own decision to boycott PACE.[42]

---

[37] See Drzemczewski, n 16, 50.
[38] Klein, E. (2017) 'Membership and observer status', in S. Schmahl and M. Breuer *The Council of Europe: Its Law and Policies*, Oxford: Oxford University Press, pp 41–92, 72. For further discussion, see Drzemczewski, n 16, and Drzemczewski, A. and Dzehtsiarou, K. (2018) 'Painful relations between the Council of Europe and Russia', *EJIL:Talk!* [Blog], 28 September, available from: www.ejiltalk.org/painful-relations-between-the-council-of-europe-and-russia/ [Accessed 1 June 2024].
[39] See especially 'Foreign Minister Sergey Lavrov's interview with Euronews, Moscow, October 16, 2018', available from: https://coe.mid.ru/en_GB/-/interv-u-ministra-inos trannyh-del-rossii-s-v-lavrova-informacionnomu-agentstvu-evron-us-moskva-16-okta bra-2018-goda?inheritRedirect=true [Accessed 9 March 2024] ('anti-Russia fervour' at the CoE from 'a small, but very loud and aggressive group', who acted in 'punishment for the free expression of will by Crimea residents, who voted in favour of reintegration with Russia at a referendum'. PACE had adopted 'illegitimate actions that violate the Statute and seek to deprive the Russian delegation of their equal rights').
[40] Lavrov interview, n 39 (referring to resultant 'dubious' 'legitimacy' of Commissioner's position/the ECtHR and citing 24 judges elected without Russia's voting input).
[41] See, for example, de Salvia, M. (2018) 'Role and responsibilities of the CoE's statutory organs with special emphasis on limitation of membership rights', *Human Rights Law Journal*, 38: 468–80.
[42] See text accompanying n 54.

One therefore observes a tension between two approaches, one accepting wider powers for PACE in the light of its evolved monitoring role, the other focussing on the strict terms of the Statute. However, even if the second perspective is accepted, proportionality considerations would apply.

Hence the third point concerns just that, and the bad faith employed by Russia in relation to its position with respect to PACE. That is, even if there was some validity to its point about the legitimacy of PACE's sanctions power (regarding voting rights), this did not remotely justify Russia's response, and especially so when seen in the round. The alleged illegitimacy of PACE's sanctions became the pretext for the Russian government to claim that the CoE was anti-Russian,[43] and, more importantly still, for it exert major, clearly inappropriate pressure on the CoE. It effectively manufactured a crisis and intensified it to ensure the focus remained off its egregious breach of the Statute in Crimea, raising the stakes to a point when Russia appeared ready to leave the CoE unless it (Russia) prevailed not just on the issue of sanctions but effectively on the Crimea issue itself. And that outcome occurred in 2019, when arrangements were made to reintegrate Russia into PACE, on the basis (supported by the CM)[44] that it amended its Rules such that deprivation of voting rights was not a sanction available to it (although rejection of a delegation's credentials overall remained[45] possible).

2.1.2 Russia boycotts PACE and suspends payments to the CoE

How did all this unfold?[46] The victimisation claims from Russia were immediately in evidence, and, given what had occurred in Crimea, unashamed. *The Guardian*[47] reported the Russian PACE delegation's reaction

---

[43] See 'Interview of Russia's Permanent Representative to the Council of Europe Ivan Soltanovsky with Rossiyskaya Gazeta (19 January 2018)', available from: https://coe.mid.ru/en_GB/vystuplenia/-/asset_publisher/8AU4kd9Kwq6u/content/nterv-u-postoannogo-predstavitela-rossii-pri-sovete-evropy-i-d-soltanovskogo-rossijskoj-gazete-opublikovannoe-19-anvara-2018-goda (referring to 'continuing attempts of the West to "give lessons" to Russia', and 'the scandalized politicization of human rights' by PACE; human rights 'a populist tool to combat geopolitical rivals') [Accessed 14 June 2024].

[44] See text accompanying n 84.

[45] On remaining controversies here, see especially Ailincai, A. (2024) 'The Parliamentary Assembly of the Council of Europe is at it again. On the non-ratification of the credentials of Azerbaijan's Parliamentary Delegation', *Strasbourg Observers* [Blog] 8 March, available from: https://strasbourgobservers.com/2024/03/08/the-parliamentary-assembly-of-the-council-of-europe-is-at-it-again-on-the-non-ratification-of-the-credentials-of-azerbaijans-parliamentary-delegation/ [Accessed 1 June 2024].

[46] See also Demir-Gürsel, n 16, 320–4.

[47] *The Guardian*, 'Russia delegation suspended from Council of Europe over Crimea', 10 April 2014.

to the April 2014 (PACE) internal sanctions, at 'a chaotic, ill-tempered press conference', when Alexey Pushkov, head of the Russian PACE delegation, said Russia would consider terminating its membership of the Assembly. Other Russian delegates 'launched a venomous attack on European countries that had moved to punish Russia'. According to *The Guardian* report members of the Russian delegation complained that: 'Some Europeans had adopted a "pathologically biased approach" and had treated Russia – a "great country" – in a scornful and condescending manner. "Since arriving here a year and a half ago I haven't heard a nice word said about the Russian Federation," one complained.' On 18 April 2014, the Russian Duma resolved not to participate in the work of PACE until all the rights of the Russian delegation had been restored.

In January 2015,[48] by which stage fighting had spread to eastern Ukraine, and the Malaysia Airlines flight had been shot down, PACE reiterated its condemnation of Russia's actions in relation to Crimea, repeated its demands (withdrawal from Crimea) and maintained the earlier internal sanctions.[49] By then the CM had been prepared to criticise Russia, in mild terms,[50] but no more. Against that backdrop, PACE encouraged dialogue and so relented on its earlier threat to annul the Russian delegation's credentials, even though Russia was in continuing violation of the CoE Statute (in respect of its actions in Georgia, as well as Crimea). The internal sanctions were confirmed, but it was indicated that they would be removed in June 2015 if progress was made on Crimea;[51] if not, the credentials would be annulled then. When June 2015 came, and there had been no progress, the restrictions remained in place, but to encourage dialogue the credentials were not annulled then either.[52]

---

[48] Resolution 2034 (2015), 'Challenge, on substantive grounds, of the still unratified credentials of the delegation of the Russian Federation', 28 January 2015.

[49] It reiterated its earlier demands: notably the immediate withdrawal of Russian military troops from eastern Ukraine, and the need to implement the Minsk Protocol and Memorandum.

[50] See text accompanying n 18 and following (earlier Decisions). In September 2014, the CM made no reference to Article 3 or 8 of the CoE Statute in a Decision (CM Decision 1207th meeting – 17 September 2014, Item 1.5) which 'called upon' Russia to 'use its influence over the separatist movement in eastern Ukraine', para 3; to 'withdraw all its troops from Ukraine and refrain from any further military interference in Ukraine', para 4; and 'reiterated that the illegal annexation by the Russian Federation of the Autonomous Republic of Crimea and the city of Sevastopol cannot form the basis for any alteration of their status', para 9. See also CM Decision 1225th meeting – 15 April 2015, Item 1.8.

[51] Resolution 2034 (2015), n 48, paras 15–6.

[52] Resolution 2063 (2015), 'Consideration of the annulment of the previously ratified credentials of the delegation of the Russian Federation', 24 June 2015.

In response, the Russian PACE delegation escalated matters, suspending all official contacts with PACE until the end of 2015, including all visits on behalf of PACE bodies.[53] Then, in 2016 it refused to submit its credentials to PACE,[54] the automatic effect of which was its exclusion from PACE – and, of course, the inability to criticise it in the context of any challenges to credentials.[55]

In effect, then, what occurred was a boycott of PACE by Russia, even though the internal sanctions had lapsed by early 2016, and the delegation's credentials had never been rejected at any point. It lasted for the next three and half years, entailing that PACE could not pass Resolutions challenging the delegations' credentials, and so criticise Russia's action in that context as with, for example, the serious alleged human rights violations occurring in the relevant territories, and Russia's efforts to integrate Crimea into Russia (elections to the Duma for that occupied region being held in September 2016). Over this time the Russian delegation refused to cooperate with the PACE Monitoring Committee (a de facto withdrawal from PACE's human rights monitoring processes, in breach of an explicit accession commitment).[56] There were allegations of major human rights violations – deaths, disappearances, and repression – against those opposed to Crimea's occupation.[57]

Claims from Russia[58] that ECtHR judges had been elected by PACE without Russia's say followed, thereby putting their legitimacy (and that of the Court) in doubt. The hypocrisy on display was seen in an exchange of letters between the Secretary General of the CoE (Thorbjørn Jagland) and Russian Foreign Minister Sergey Lavrov to coincide with the 20th anniversary of Russia's accession in 2016. The latter referred to the 'present challenging situation in our continent'. He considered it 'important' that the CoE 'carry out its activities without double standards and selective attitudes that undermine[d] its underlying principles' and gave rise to a 'lack of mutual trust'.[59]

---

[53] PACE Monitoring Committee (Gale) report, June 2019, n 17, para 9.
[54] See PACE Monitoring Committee (Gale) report, June 2019, n 17, para 9 (non-presentation 'reportedly anticipating' their challenge, and possible sanctions; Russian leadership adopting 'policy decision not to co-operate' with PACE until restoration of full rights).
[55] There were no further such challenges until 2019, when the delegation returned.
[56] See Chapter 2, n 36–7. On lack of cooperation with the CoE Commissioner for Human Rights, see Chapter 7, text accompanying n 75.
[57] See PACE Monitoring Committee (Gale) report, June 2019, n 17, paras 21–45.
[58] See *TASS*, 'Russia concerned about number of ECHR judges elected without its participation', 20 June 2018, available from: https://tass.com/politics/1010271 [Accessed 14 June 2024].
[59] See CoE Press Release, 'Lavrov, Jagland on Russia's membership in Council of Europe', 24 February 2016 (Ref. DC 023(2016)).

With the screw of political pressure slowly acting against the CoE, in 2017 the Russian government turned it significantly.[60] At the start of that year, alongside the UK, France, Germany, Italy and Türkiye, Russia was one of six major financial contributors to the CoE.[61] Referring to a 'rampant campaign ... launched to persecute [Russian] parliamentarians', on 30 June 2017 Lavrov suspended the payment of Russia's contribution to the CoE budget for 2017, until the 'unconditional restoration in full of powers of the [Russian] delegation'.[62] This step itself took advantage of circumstances in that, after 2016, the CoE's financial situation was already precarious following the CM's tight budgetary restrictions, and Türkiye's decision to cut back its funding (soon after the 2016 coup attempt). In fact, from 2017 onwards Russia froze all payments to the CoE, until (it transpired) July 2019, that is, when the crisis was resolved. The non-payment was linked to implied threats that Russia would withdraw from the CoE altogether – that is, 'Ruxit'.[63]

What was, arguably, a form of financial blackmailing of the CoE came soon after the CM had issued a Decision (May 2017) 'underlining' that the illegal annexation of Crimea by Russia was a violation of international law, and 'challeng[ed] peace and democratic security in Europe'.[64] The CM also 'reaffirm[ed] ... commitment to the principle of peaceful settlement of disputes, to the independence, sovereignty and territorial integrity of Ukraine within internationally recognised borders and to the respect for human rights and fundamental freedoms'.[65] However, the next two years would test the CM's resolve in this regard. Ostensibly the CM should have demanded payment from Russia, Article 9 CoE Statute giving it the power to suspend rights of representation (on the CM and PACE) for a state which

---

[60] See European Stability Initiative, 'From Russia with threats', 13 July 2017, available from: www.esiweb.org/pdf/ESI%20Note%20-%20From%20Russia%20with%20thre ats%20-%2013%20July%202017.pdf [Accessed 14 June 2024].

[61] In 2016, Russia's contribution was roughly 10–11 per cent of the budget: €32,801,563. On the influence Russia exerted as a big 'payer' and (unofficially) special status member of the CoE, see Roter, n 16, 46 and 52–3, and Fura, E. and Maruste, R., 'Russia's impact on the Strasbourg system, as seen by two former judges of the European Court of Human Rights', in L. Mälksoo and W. Benedek (eds) *Russia and the European Court of Human Rights: The Strasbourg Effect*, Cambridge: Cambridge University Press, pp 222–52, 228–30. On the CoE's budgetary crisis as of 2018, see PACE report, 'Modification of the Assembly's Rules of Procedure: the impact of the budgetary crisis on the list of working languages of the Assembly', Doc. 14511, 12 March 2018 and Recommendation 2124 (2018) (same title), and see Drzemczewski, n 71. See further comments in n 230 and 231.

[62] *The Independent*, 'Russia cancels payment to Council of Europe after claiming its delegates are being persecuted over Crimea', 30 June 2017.

[63] See PACE Monitoring Committee (Gale) report, June 2019, n 17, para 13, and *The Guardian*, 'Human rights body faces cash crisis after clash with Russia', 16 March 2018.

[64] CM/Del/Dec(2017)1285/2.1bisb, 3 May 2017 (Preamble paragraph).

[65] CM Decision, n 64.

'has failed to fulfil its financial obligation during such period as the obligation remains unfulfilled'.[66] However, relying on exceptional procedures, in 2017 the CM allowed Russia to suspend payment for two years – in effect until July 2019.[67] This drew strong criticism from PACE,[68] itself coming under great pressure to compromise on its Rules to appease Russia (including via proposals, rejected in 2018, that it significantly qualify its powers in relation to challenges to delegations' credentials).[69] It seemed as if the CM feared inflaming matters, it being suggested that Russia would withdraw from the CoE (under Article 7) rather than suffer the 'humiliation'[70] of threatened action under Article 9.

2.1.3 The accountability and human rights case for appeasing Russia

Here one may consider a further feature of the very strong hand Russia had to play (beyond the financial) in the unfolding game of geopolitical poker, and the cruel ironies involved.

Ruxit brought to the fore the prospect of Russia ceasing to be a member state not just to the CoE, but also a Contracting Party to the ECHR. The Russian political leadership was no doubt acutely aware that this 'caused considerable consternation'[71] at the CoE. As to what was in issue, a 'Memorandum by Russian human rights defenders' of November 2018, signed by 72 Russian human rights lawyers, argued how 'righteous anger' at Russia's behaviour risked playing into the hands of 'the Kremlin', where

---

[66] Payment of contributions is an obligation under Article 39 CoE Statute.
[67] See PACE Monitoring Committee (Gale) report, June 2019, n 17, para 11.
[68] Cf the criticism from PACE, Recommendation 2124 (2018), n 61, paras 4–5.
[69] On this, see procedural amendments proposed by Rapporteur Petra de Sutter in 2018 (Committee on Rules of Procedure, Immunities and Institutional Affairs, 'Strengthening the decision-making process of the Parliamentary Assembly concerning credentials and voting', Doc. 14621, 21 September 2018). Proposals to, for example, increase the required majority for challenges to credentials to two-thirds were rejected (Russia had been subject to such challenges over 2008–2009, 2014–2015 and would be in 2019–2022). See Steininger, S. (2018) 'Managing the backlash? The PACE and the question of participation rights for Russia, *VerfBlog* [Blog], 9 October, available from: https://verfassungsblog.de/managing-the-backlash-the-pace-and-the-question-of-participation-rights-for-russia/[Accessed 1 June 2024].
[70] Memorandum by Russian human rights defenders, 'Addressing the crisis in relations between the Council of Europe and Russia: uphold the values and fulfil the mission to protect rights across all of Europe', November 2018 (available from: www.nhc.nl/assets/uploads/2018/12/Memorandum-on-Russia-and-CoE_November_2018_eng_signatures-as-of-30.11.18.pdf [Accessed 14 June 2024].
[71] Drzemczewski, A. (2020) 'The (non-) participation of Russian parliamentarians in the Parliamentary Assembly of the Council of Europe: an overview of recent developments', 1, *Europe of Rights & Liberties*, 7–15, section B.

there may have been some who sought an excuse for Ruxit.[72] They also stressed how Ruxit would amount to a veritable disaster for human rights protection in Russia, and for the realisation of the ideals the CoE held dear. It was stressed that a CoE without Russia would not 'contribute to the resolution of the conflict in Eastern Ukraine and the return of Crimea under Ukrainian jurisdiction'. Rather it would 'turn a large territory in Europe into a legal "grey zone" for decades to come'. Nor would Ruxit 'stop human rights violations and halt the authoritarian backslide' in Russia. Rather, it 'would have irreversible consequences, putting an end to a difficult struggle of Russian society to make the country an important part of Europe on the basis of shared norms and values of democracy, rule of law and respect for human rights'. Hence, the real victims of Ruxit would not be the Putin regime, but the Russian public, deprived of access to the ECtHR as 'an ultimate hope for justice, which in many cases they cannot find in Russia'. In short, it was suggested Ruxit would see the end of 'the struggle for democracy and justice' in Russia, and the 'dismantling the common European legal framework and challenge the CoE's unique role and mission'.[73]

2.2 The ending of the non-participation crisis in June 2019

The stalemate arrived at by 2018–2019 could not endure, for the CM's two-year payment delay for Russia was due to expire in 2019, at which stage a new Secretary General was due to be elected.[74] By June 2019 Russia's dues to the CoE were in the region of €70 million, and the CoE was in not only a very substantial financial crisis, but also 'an unprecedented institutional and political' one.[75] Furthermore, there did not appear to be any appetite for other member states to plug to resourcing-gap that the CoE was facing at the time.

The CoE blinked first in the game of brinkmanship which tested the CoE's political will to uphold its values, against Russia's threat that if it did so it

---

[72] Memorandum, n 70 (Ruxit '[t]hreats … not just a bluff to raise the bargaining stakes' as were 'many influential people in the Russian political establishment in favour of isolationist policies' hoping for withdrawal, seeking detachment from 'obligations stemming from the CoE membership' and intent on presenting Ruxit as 'result of an "anti-Russian" plot').

[73] The outgoing Secretary General, Thorbjørn Jagland, read extracts from an earlier letter containing a very similar text ('irreversible consequences', 'grey zone', Russian citizens as real victims of Ruxit and so on) to PACE, in January 2019: see Verbatim Records, PACE, 22 January 2019 (afternoon), available from: https://pace.coe.int/en/verbatim/2019-01-22/pm/it [Accessed 1 June 2024].

[74] Russia had indicated it may not recognise the new Secretary General (elected by PACE) if its delegation had not been present in PACE, see n 39 (Lavrov, 2018).

[75] PACE Monitoring Committee (Gale) report, June 2019, n 17, para 14 ('unprecedented institutional and political crisis').

would leave the CoE. So, a resolution (of sorts) occurred over May–June 2019.[76] Russia would pay its outstanding contributions if voting rights were restored in PACE, and the Russian delegation would return. *However*, there were no sanctions or meaningful plan of action to address Russia's action in Crimea and the surrounding region.

Indeed, after it had induced a crisis at the CoE, the basis upon which Russia prevailed in 2019 risked seriously undermining the credibility of the institution, reflecting the ritualistic narrative set out in the introduction to this chapter. Essentially a blind eye was turned toward Crimea's annexation and related issues, on the basis that Russia pay its financial dues, return to PACE on the basis noted later and agree to cooperate with CoE monitoring mechanisms in PACE – and not carry out its threat to leave the CoE (and so the ECHR). The relevant CM Decisions gave an impression of respectability to what had occurred, which was in fact a deeply embarrassing retreat from its values, effectively succumbing to Russia's pressure and whitewashing its serious violations of the Statute in Ukraine.

There is no avoiding, then, that this was an ignominious climbdown for the CoE. It was led by the CM, which failed to support PACE, although the role of the CoE Secretary General, Thorbjørn Jagland, must not be underestimated.[77] So, in May 2019 in Helsinki, the CM issued several documents to include, a 'Declaration by the Committee of Ministers on the occasion of the 70th anniversary of the Council of Europe',[78] and a Decision on 'A shared responsibility for democratic security in Europe – Ensuring respect for rights and obligations, principles, standards and values'.[79] Given Russia's behaviour not only as regards Crimea, but its effective blackmailing of the CoE, both documents were remarkable.

The 70th anniversary Declaration, for example, was upbeat and self-congratulatory in its tone, referring to the CoE's 'strength' in terms of its 'periodic and thorough assessment of all member States, in line with established legal criteria'. It added: '[c]ompliance with the standards and commitments undertaken is an overriding priority'. Reference was made to 'our shared responsibility' to maintain the CoE system as the states reaffirmed their 'deep and abiding commitment to' the CoE Statute and the ECHR.

Given that Russia was continuing to violate the CoE Statute in relation to Crimea (and Georgia), plus its actions in eastern Ukraine (to include Donetsk

---

[76] *The Guardian*, 'Council of Europe votes to maintain Russia's membership', 17 May 2019 ('France and Germany had pressed to reinstate Russia').
[77] See Demir-Gürsel, n 16. On the Secretary General, see Chapter 7, section 4.3.
[78] Adopted by the CM on 17 May 2019 at the 129th Session of the Committee of Ministers, Decl (17/05/2019).
[79] CM/Del/Dec(2019)129/2.

and Luhansk),[80] the CM's Decision on 'A shared responsibility for democratic security' was equally ritualistic. It talked up the importance of the role and influence of the CoE, and the very values that Russia had acted in complete defiance of:[81] reference was made to the great importance the CoE attached to international law, including 'the principle of peaceful settlement of disputes, the independence, sovereignty and territorial integrity of all member States within their internationally recognised borders'. The Decision reaffirmed all CoE states had to accept the values reflected in Article 3, CoE Statute. It then alluded to Russia's claim that it had been treated unfairly by PACE, recalling 'that all member States shall be entitled to participate on an equal basis in the two statutory organs of the [CoE], as long as Articles 7, 8 or 9 of the Statute have not been applied'. One must remember that Decisions of this nature represent the lowest common denominator, the point at which *all* states agree. Russia was, of course, party to the negotiation of the draft Decision, and one can safely assume left no stone un-turned to water down its content. In any case, in effect the CM indirectly vindicated Russia's position on its PACE boycott. Next the CM's Decision highlighted the importance of member states paying their obligatory contributions to the CoE's Ordinary Budget,[82] and expressed a desire that delegations (that is, the Russian delegation) attend the June 2019 session of PACE, noting the 'importance of forthcoming elections of the Secretary General and of judges to the European Court of Human Rights'.[83]

Indeed, it was clear that that was the plan, and at its June 2019 session the Russian delegation returned to PACE.

To facilitate that, first a Resolution was passed on 25 June 2019 (118 votes to 62) entitled 'Strengthening the decision-making process of the Parliamentary Assembly concerning credentials and voting'.[84] Bizarrely it did nothing of the sort. In light of 'contacts between the leadership of the Russian Federation and the Parliamentary Assembly',[85] the latter agreed that it did not have the power to issue internal sanctions such as withdrawal of voting rights (minor sanction powers remained, for example denying the Russian delegation the ability to participate in election observation missions).[86] As

---

[80] Cf PACE Monitoring Committee (Gale) report, June 2019, n 17, paras 41–5. See also Russia's failure to cooperate with the CPT, in March 2019, Chapter 7, text accompanying n 81.

[81] Likewise, see 70th Declaration, n 78 ('[w]e remain concerned by confrontations and unresolved conflicts' affecting continent; 'shall work together for reconciliation and political solutions in conformity with the norms and principles of international law').

[82] CM Decision, n 79, para 2.

[83] CM Decision, n 79, para 4.

[84] Resolution 2287 (2019), 25 June 2019.

[85] PACE Monitoring Committee (Gale) report, June 2019, n 17, para 18.

[86] Resolution 2287 (2019), n 85, para 10. New rule Rule 10.1.c states that there should be no suspension/withdrawal of members' rights to vote, to speak and to be represented in the Assembly and its bodies, in the context of a challenge to or reconsideration of credentials.

such, the Resolution was not only a major blow to PACE's authority, 'it amputated itself of one of its key "internal sanctions"'.[87]

The next day (26 June 2019) PACE ratified the credentials of the Russian delegation without resort to even the minor sanctions that it retained (116 in favour, 62 against, 15 abstentions).[88] The absence of any sanction was strongly criticised by Sir Roger Gale, one of the PACE rapporteurs on Russia, who considered it 'unimaginable'[89] given Russia's open flouting of its CoE obligations, and its behaviour over the previous four years. The report produced by Gale also highlighted in detail the many serious human rights violations occurring in Russia, and by it in Crimea and related areas.[90] The same report also noted that 'the rejection of the Russian credentials ... could ultimately lead to'[91] Russia's withdrawal from the CoE. The importance of retaining the role that the ECHR might play was emphasised, reference being made to 'the needs of Russian citizens'.[92]

These last points highlighted the tough political choice facing PACE: either accept Russia back on its terms (despite the compelling case that it had no place in the CoE), or lose any realistic hope of holding it accountable (as Russia would leave the CoE). A 'better in than out' approach prevailed. Despite the major blow to PACE's credibility,[93] it prioritised favouring a re-launching of cooperation, and dialogue with Russia. Here PACE referred to itself as 'the most important pan-European platform where political dialogue' on Russia's CoE obligation could take place, and 'where

---

[87] Drzemczewski, n 71, section 4.
[88] PACE Resolution 2292 (2019), 'Challenge, on substantive grounds, of the still unratified credentials of the parliamentary delegation of the Russian Federation', 26 June 2019.
[89] PACE Monitoring Committee (Gale) report, June 2019, n 17, para 82. See further the statement issued by 38 human rights NGOs, 'Civil society warns CoE that the time is not ripe to lift sanctions against Russia' (undated), available from: www.iphronline.org/ [Accessed 14 June 2024] (return without sanctions would 'contradict' CoE principles/ Statute of the CoE, legitimise Russia's illegal actions in Crimea and be a 'threat not only for Ukraine but for the entire region', sending a 'strong signal' that 'most flagrant violations of the international law are accepted and tolerated by European states', and it would also be a 'detrimental precedent', given the threat of non-payment of membership fees, and show a 'blatant and total disregard of the suffering inflicted upon thousands of victims of Russian aggression').
[90] PACE Monitoring Committee (Gale) report, June 2019, n 17, paras 21–85.
[91] PACE Monitoring Committee (Gale) report, June 2019, n 17, para 75.
[92] PACE Monitoring Committee (Gale) report, June 2019, n 17, para 75.
[93] See interventions during (PACE) 'Debate: Challenge, on substantive grounds, of the still unratified credentials of the parliamentary delegation of the Russian Federation | According to Rule 8.3 of the Assembly's Rules of Procedure' (Wednesday, 26 June 2019, afternoon), available from: https://pace.coe.int/en/verbatim/2019-06-26/pm/en#theme-386 [Accessed 10 July 2024].

the Russian delegation can be held accountable on the basis of the [CoE's] values and principles'.[94]

2.3 Russia's ritualistic return to PACE copper-fastening its impunity for Crimea

The summer of 2019, therefore, saw the Russian delegation back in PACE, and in July 2019, Russia paid its financial dues, subsequently paying its arrears to the CoE (but not interest due, of 13 million euros (2019)).[95]

What then of the manifest violations of the CoE Statute committed by Russia in and around Crimea? And, what reassurance could be offered that the Statute would be enforced in the future, with Russia reintegrated into the CoE? The ritualistic nature of Russia's return to PACE is further brought out by the answers to these questions.

A new, proposed 'complementary joint procedure' was the CoE's response to the last question. During its May 2019 meeting, the CM agreed in principle to new working arrangements to address situations that may culminate in resort to Articles 8 and 9 of the Statute. It agreed to work with PACE to develop '[?] ... a clearly defined complementary procedure, which could be initiated by either' PACE, the CM or the Secretary General, 'in which all three of them would participate'.[96] The aim would be to establish '[?] a co-ordinated response, carried out in a constructive manner, encouraging member States, through dialogue and co-operation, to take all appropriate measures to conform with the principles of the Statute'.[97] On its face, then, the promised development of the complementary joint procedure appeared to be a basis to make the CoE more resilient and effective in the face of the type of breach of statutory obligations that had occurred in 2014. Presumably this was an attempt to restore some credibility to the CoE in terms of the enforcement and application of these provisions going forward, given the CoE's abject failure to do so over 2014–2019 (and before). However, as Donald and Speck observed, the procedure foresaw PACE and the CM, together with the Secretary General of the CoE, having to act in concert when

---

[94] PACE Resolution 2292 (2019), n 88, para 7.
[95] PACE Monitoring Committee report, Doc. 15216, 26 January 2021, para 56.
[96] CM Decision, n 79. This would be 'building on' the CM's 1994 Declaration on Compliance with Commitments (which had gone into dormancy by this stage; see Chapter 2 and Chapter 3).
[97] CM Decision, n 79, para 7. For detailed discussion, see Chapter 5, section 3.2.

considering sanctions, and that would 'effectively mean moving at the pace of the most cautious actor',[98] that is, the CM. The scheme seemed almost certain to prolong any putative decision on sanctions, rather than make them more effective. Ultimately matters still rested with the CM, which had been totally unwilling to even threaten, let alone take Article 8 or 9 action against Russia. Hence it was very clear that the proposed complementary joint procedure – established in February 2020[99] – would not be used against it on Crimea, and related issues.

So, in fact, in 2019 there was no real plan to address the manifest and continuing violations of the CoE Statute that had occurred and were still occurring in Crimea and the region. Or, at least, that which existed on the political level was entirely ritualistic. That is, via its 26 June 2019 Resolution PACE sought to set conditions to the Russian delegation's reintegration;[100] 'in return' for PACE's agreement to ratify the credentials of the Russian delegation, the '[11] … Assembly call[ed] on the Russian Federation to fulfil' all 'recommendations' included in its earlier, that is, 2014 and 2015 (January and June) Resolutions, and that included Russia's withdrawal from Crimea. Given all that had preceded 2019, it was utterly fanciful to think that Russia would do this.

2.4 Ruxit avoided, but at what cost to the CoE?

Having set out the events at the CoE over the period from 2014 to 2019 in some detail, let us now try to stand back and ponder on their significance. In what follows, two themes are pursued. First, why 2019 might be seen as the year that the CoE capitulated to Russia and was, as a consequence, a great cost to the former, thus making that year a defining moment. Second, how this was a product of Russia's bad faith, reflecting its harmful influence. Both go to the suggestion that Russia's 2019 reintegration was unacceptable.[101]

---

[98] Donald, A. and Speck, A. (2021) 'Time for the gloves to come off? The response by the Parliamentary Assembly of the Council of Europe to rule of law backsliding', *European Convention on Human Rights Law Review*, 2(2): 241–73, 252.
[99] CM/Del/Dec(2020)1366/1.7-app, 5 February 2020.
[100] PACE Resolution 2292 (2019), n 88, para 11. See also paras 12–13 (Russian delegation should 'engage in meaningful dialogue on the fulfilment of its commitments and obligations'; Russia called upon to: release 24 captured Ukrainian sailors, pay all CoE fees, fully cooperate with the joint investigation on Malaysia Airlines flight MH17, and so on).
[101] Dzehtsiarou and Coffey, n 16; for counter-arguments see section 3.1.

2.4.1 Capitulation?

As to arguments that the CoE capitulated to Russia, this is most compelling given that there were no undertakings as to the future regarding Russia's CoE obligations, either generally or as regards Crimea, there being no contrition from the Russian government. On the contrary, in practice Russia's return amounted to an unacknowledged impunity for its manifest transgressions toward the CoE. And what of the latter? At the risk of repetition, back in 2014 Russia breached – *manifestly* breached – the CoE Statute and numerous other CoE obligations, doing so on a scale unparalleled in the CoE's history (annexation of the territory of another state). In 2019 it was continuing to breach Article 3, via the annexation of Crimea, and supporting separatist breakaway regions of Luhansk and Donetsk. There were many allegations of serious violations of human rights related to that. *Nonetheless*, Russia was allowed back into the CoE fold with no plan for its withdrawal from Crimea (which was being integrated into Russia) and the region. For example, there was no threat of future Article 8 action, to be overseen by the CM, if Russia did not withdraw. Indeed, there was no meaningful plan for accountability as regards Russia's actions over 2014–2015 and beyond – unless the ECHR, by default, was expected to achieve this. Meanwhile, as will be noted later, Russia continued to commit serious human rights violations in the national context. On top of that, its actions had brought the CoE to a financial crisis unprecedented in its history. Non-payment of CoE fees was itself a breach of statutory obligations.

So, Ruxit had been avoided in 2019. However, what was the true cost to the CoE?[102]

The short answer is that the events of 2019 saw major damage done to the CoE's reputation, credibility and integrity as a human rights and rule of law organisation. The whole *raison d'etre* of the CoE, after all, was to defend those very values set out in Article 3 of the CoE Statute which it appeared to give up on in 2019 (by virtue of Russian pressure) via the lack of statutory accountability for Russia's actions. So, it was clear that under Article 8 Russia *should* have been expelled from the CoE in 2019 for numerous reasons (if not sooner), yet it was permitted to remain on a type of ritualistic or nominal basis, one that, worse still, came close to normalising its annexation of Crimea. This was so after CoE bodies, including the CM, had repeatedly stated that the annexation was illegal, the latter confirming (in 2017) its 'commitment to … the independence, sovereignty and territorial integrity of Ukraine within internationally recognised borders'.[103]

---

[102] Cf Drzemczewski, n 71, section 4.
[103] See text accompanying n 65.

2.4.2 Russia's bad faith membership

To prevail in the way it did in 2019, a key card played by Russia appeared to be the threat of Ruxit. It manoeuvred matters to a point when the return of its delegation to PACE would have to be on its terms, or not at all. A cruel irony here was that it was able to leverage its membership status to damaging effect, since that was inextricably linked to the need for human rights accountability, when, of course, the government had scant regard for the same, and flouted CoE values.

This brings us to the Russia government's bad faith and negative influence. Indeed, given how Russia was undermining the CoE from the inside, one might refer to its subversive influence.

The events of 2019 certainly sent a strong signal that a big state such as Russia could get away with the most flagrant breaches of the CoE Statute, the CoE being, apparently, not just unable to discipline states such as Russia, but unwilling to do so for fear of the consequences. On the face of it, what had been exposed was that Russian clout had been employed to outplay the CoE because it was a big and powerful state,[104] even that the former had caved in because of the latter's threats to deprive the CoE of significant funding.[105] Whether that was exactly so or not, it reflected the Russian government's harmful influence in that it used its membership of the CoE as a bargaining tool and threat, in effect presenting the CoE with a binary choice in 2019: fidelity to the CoE Statute and its values or Ruxit. The latter would have the major consequences referred to previously.[106] Ironically, then, the very reasons why Russia needed to be in the CoE (indeed, those that had promoted its accession in 1996) strengthened the bad faith hand of its government.

One may also reflect upon the hypocrisy and sophistry displayed by the Russian government as it gained this leverage regarding the denial of voting rights in PACE – and how it 'got away' with that. After it had invaded its neighbour and illegally annexed its territory, Russia cried foul as regards the internal application of PACE's established Rules, claiming PACE was discriminatory and unfair. The victimisation claims distracted from the fundamental breaches of Article 3, and further delegitimised the CoE for domestic audiences (enabling 2019 to be presented as a victory).[107] Russia

---

[104] Cf Glas, L.R. (2019) 'The European Court of Human Rights supervising the execution of its judgments', *Netherlands Quarterly of Human Rights*, 37(3): 228–44, n 16.
[105] (PACE) Debate, n 93 (Sir Roger Gale: impression that the CoE, 'needed [Russia's] money more than we needed the [CoE's] principles').
[106] See section 2.1.3 in this chapter.
[107] *The Guardian*, 'Ukraine walks out of Europe human rights body as Russia returns' 25 June 2019 ('Russia's establishment took a victory lap … "This is a victory of common sense," said Dmitry Peskov, the press secretary to Vladimir Putin').

also gained a supposedly respectable pretext for it to exert its leverage at the CoE; however, to reiterate, even if there was validity in Russia's initial point about PACE's Rules, its prosecution of it was out of all proportion to any original fault.[108] Nor did it justify Russia's non-payment, which itself weakened the CoE's capabilities, and constituted a form of financial blackmail in that the CoE was plunged into a major financial crisis.[109] And, of course, the outcome of 2019 was only possible because of the power and influence Russia could and did apply – abusively – demonstrating how it was *not* equal to other states in the CoE context.

Finally, Russia's subversive influence could be seen from the perspective of a devaluation of or degradation of CoE's sanctions. According to the former CoE Commissioner for Human Rights (2012–2018), Nils Muižnieks, the year 2019 signalled that 'it is virtually impossible' for a state to be excluded from the CoE, 'rendering the threat' to do so 'largely ineffective'.[110] And, of course, the Russian government's action saw PACE seriously weakened. The significance of that for the CoE will be appreciated in that across this study it has been observed that PACE was at the forefront of efforts to protect the integrity of CoE values, calling out Russia's behaviour in that regard. Its willingness to do so contrasted with the CM, hamstrung by its propensity to seek consensus rather than vote.[111] In that context, the importance of PACE, and its sanctions power – weak as that was – was clear to see. Yet when it used these measures against Russia to stand up for the CoE's values over 2014–2015, in very careful and measured ways, to retain hopes for dialogue on each occasion,[112] Russia unilaterally sought to change PACE's Rules and generally took on that institution. It provoked a type of internal 'constitutional' crisis within the CoE, resulting in the climbdown of 2019 which, as noted, reduced PACE's powers. Hence Russia diminished PACE as the political 'conscience of Europe'.[113] The result was to place more onus on the CM, an institution proven to be an unwilling guardian of the CoE, and an arena in which Russia could be confident it had an upper hand.

---

[108] See text accompanying n 43.
[109] On CoE budgetary issues, see n 61, 230 and 231.
[110] Muižnieks, N. (2019) 'The Council of Europe's response to recent democratic backsliding', in P. Czech, L. Heschl, K. Lukas, M. Nowak and G. Oberleitner (eds) *European Yearbook on Human Rights 2019,* pp 3–31, 9.
[111] Cf the CM's failure to act effectively in relation to Chechnya, see Chapter 3, section 2.1.1.
[112] To reiterate, the Russian delegation's credentials were never rejected; it was the Russian delegation itself which boycotted PACE from 2016 until June 2019.
[113] Cf comment made by the former Commissioner for Human Rights, Nils Muižnieks, cited in Donald. A. and Speck, A., 'Wholehearted? Half-hearted? The response from the Parliamentary Assembly of the Council of Europe to recent developments in Turkey', 30 August 2019 (on file with author).

Indeed, after May 2017 (following which Russia suspended its payments) the CM did not take another Decision on Crimea for four years.[114]

3 After 2019: ritualism?

It is impossible to know what kind of political calculus was at play in 2019 in CoE capitals. Perhaps a decision was made to seek to utilise any leverage vis-à-vis Russia through other forums.

3.1 'Better in than out': 2019?

In terms of justifying Russia's continued membership after 2019, once again, an argument might have been that of 'better in than out'. That is, Russia's membership was needed for a relaunching of political dialogue with it, and to keep alive the possibility of accountability based on CoE values and principles and under CoE regimes, including the ECHR, not only in relation to Crimea, but human rights in areas subject to Russia's jurisdiction overall. Simply put, in 2019 Russia's appeasement was the only means of achieving this, that is, retaining the goals just noted, for it seemed most likely that all hope of accountability would be lost were Russia outside the CoE (Ruxit).

But did this 'better in than out' justification stand up? The answer may have depended on whether one prioritised the integrity and credibility of the CoE, or the possibility (remote as it may have been) of continued accountability. Adopting the former line, 'better in than out' did not stand up in 2019 given the harm done to the CoE and Russia's repugnant stances towards it, including the very fact that it required appeasement on the enormous issues at stake in 2019. On similar bases to this it was argued[115] that in 2019 the CM and PACE should have drawn a line by standing up for CoE's values and not appeasing Russia.

Alternatively, painful as it was, 'better in than out' remained preferrable to the harm occurring were Russia no longer to be a member of the CoE, some hope of improvement being better than none. From this perspective what occurred in 2019 should be seen less about appeasement of the Russia leadership (a failure to punish its government), and more in terms of retaining CoE membership for the Russian people.[116] Relatedly, while

---

[114] See CM/Del/Dec(2021)1403bis/2.3 (11 May 2021), urging Russia to 'uphold all of its obligations under international law and restore the territorial integrity of Ukraine within its internationally recognised borders', para 1.1, also citing 'continuing disregard' by Russia 'as an occupying power for its obligations under international law and all its attempts to legitimise its illegal annexation of Crimea' (Preamble).
[115] Dzehtsiarou and Coffey, n 16.
[116] See section 2.1.3.

Russia remained 'in', CoE actors could continue to highlight issues and strive to hold Russia to account, including in the context of inter-state cases directed against Russia (concerning Crimea and Georgia), which were reaching important stages in 2019.[117] These could run their course with Russia in the CoE. That accountability aim was an end in itself, even if it was reasonable to argue in 2019 that it was far more ritualistic than real, given Russia's prior track record of disregard for its CoE obligations, and lack of respect for the ECHR.

Of course, any assessment of what occurred in 2019 must focus on the situation and circumstances then existing. So, in the account that follows, which looks to the situation after 2019, we must keep in mind that it was not known that Russia would exit the CoE in 2022 in the circumstances it did. Under section 3.2, the human rights situation in Russia is discussed. After that, in section 4, the focus is on the inter-state cases which were directed against Russia, where issues related to Georgia and Crimea were coming before the ECtHR in 2019.

3.2 Russia's human rights ritualism at the CoE after 2019–2022: a continuation of before

The discord associated with 2014–2019 might make it easy to forget that during this time Russia remained a full CoE member, the latter's institutions retaining their role in relation to the internal human rights and rule of law situation in Russia (albeit a role made far more challenging by its behaviour). Over 2014–2019 the ECtHR was still delivering rulings in relation to Russia, and, perhaps remarkably, certain of its judgments were being implemented over this time too. This pointed to the important role and influence that the ECHR could play.

3.2.1 The European Convention on Human Rights

'Could play', for examples could be listed of improvements to human rights laws in Russia, and individual human rights justice outcomes achieved, as a basis to justify the 'better in than out' argument.[118] However, on closer inspection it seemed that these reforms related to structural issues in specific contexts[119] (for example: legal certainty, and enforcement of judgments in certain civil cases;[120] compensation for excessive length of judicial

---

[117] See text accompanying n 169.
[118] See Memorandum, n 70, and PACE, 'Impact of the European Convention on Human Rights in states parties: selected examples', S/Jur/Inf (2016) 04 (8 January 2016), 32–3, see further n 215.
[119] See the discussion in Chapter 6, section 2.
[120] See Chapter 3, section 3.3.2, on *Ryabykh* and *Burdov*.

proceedings;[121] detention on remand;[122] conditions of detention;[123] rights in the context of psychiatric detention,[124] and so on). Important as that was, the reforms did not relate to crucial (populist) fields such as those related to the rights of homosexuals (where the authorities could exacerbate a disconnect between Russia and the CoE),[125] and the democratic decline of the state, and its authoritarianism. In those fields, and others, regrettably, there was little direct evidence of any real ECHR impact, a point which former ECtHR judges have been candid in making after 2022.[126] In keeping with the ritualism narrative set out in the introduction, commentators also noted Russia's tendency to pay just satisfaction in cases, thereby giving the impression of recognition and acceptance, but then ignoring totally the necessary general reforms required by the case.[127] Undoubtedly, overall Russia had a poor record of implementing important ECtHR judgments, indeed, according to an expert NGO, 'arguably the worst among all' CoE states.[128]

---

[121] See Resolution CM/ResDH(2017)168 'Execution of the judgments of the European Court of Human Rights – 106 cases against the Russian Federation concerning length of domestic judicial proceedings and remedies thereof, closing cases related to excessive length of civil and criminal proceedings and the lack of an effective domestic remedies'.

[122] See H46-32 *Klyakhin group v. Russian Federation*, no. 46082/99 (and many related cases), and legal reforms secured as set out in CM Interim Resolution CM/ResDH(2020)100 (although judgment not closed).

[123] H46-23 *Ananyev and Others and Kalashnikov group v. Russian Federation*, no. 42525/07; see CM/Notes/1348/H46-23, referring to improvements made.

[124] *Rakevich v. Russia*, 58973/00, 28 October 2003; see Resolution CM/ResDH (2020)333 'Execution of the judgments of the European Court of Human Rights, closing the case, but also highlighting further law reforms required in context of other cases'.

[125] See Chapter 3, section 3.3.3, and see n 133 in this chapter.

[126] See Nussberger, A. (2022) 'Human rights and peace: disillusionment or hope? The Russian example', in J. Kjølbro, S. O'Leary and M. Tsirli Anthemis (eds) *Liber Amicorum Robert Spano*, The Hague: Eleven International Publishing, pp 511–22, 517–19 (referring to reforms as 'bogus successes'); and Yudkivska, G. (2022) '"And the work of justice shall be peace –": when human rights are not the path to peace and security', in J. Kjølbro, S. O'Leary and M. Tsirli Anthemis (eds) *Liber Amicorum Robert Spano*, The Hague: Eleven International Publishing, pp 759–70, 765–7 (reforms not 'major achievement[s] of the "school of democracy"'). For criticism of the ECtHR, see text accompanying n 226.

[127] Mälksoo, L. (2017) 'Introduction', in, L. Mälksoo and W. Benedek (eds) *Russia and the European Court of Human Rights: The Strasbourg Effect*, Cambridge: Cambridge University Press, pp 3–25, 6 (Russian government 'coexist[ed] with the ECtHR according to the principle "we will (usually but not always) pay the fines but will otherwise continue to live in our own way"'). See further Yudkivska, n 126, 767 ('camouflaging with monetary compensation a deliberate failure to address systematic problems').

[128] European Implementation Network, 'Implementation of the judgments of the ECtHR: Russia' (January 2021), available from: www.einnetwork.org/russia-echr [Accessed 14 June 2024]. Also referring to 'strong resistance to change from the

The CM and PACE would have been fully aware of this and Russia's human rights trajectory in 2019. PACE had identified 2012 as a crucial 'crossroads' year for democracy in Russia,[129] but it was followed by a rapidly deteriorating situation regarding pluralism, human rights and fundamental freedoms, reflected in laws facilitating a crackdown on opposition politicians, independent civil society, dissenting voices and critical journalists. Notwithstanding criticism from CoE actors,[130] the measures in question were in many instances strengthened in their anti-democratic tendency. That had been the context to Russia's annexation of Crimea, and its ensuing non-participation tactics, which involved a de facto withdrawal from PACE human rights monitoring.[131] And these issues were there for all to see when the Russian delegation returned to PACE in June 2019, as were a whole host of other serious human rights issues related to Russia, and confirmed by the ECtHR via specific judgments such as (to name a few) those related to violence against women,[132] blatant discrimination against the LGBTI community,[133] deaths, torture or inhuman and degrading treatment while in police custody (and lack of effective investigations into such police brutality),[134] alleged political prisoners,[135] deaths of high profile figures,[136] and accusations of assassinations overseas.[137] Based on this apparent disregard and disrespect for the ECHR (reflected further in the 2015 amendments to

---

authorities', and indicating a Russian attitude that the judgment is duly implemented if just satisfaction had been paid.

[129] Chapter 3, section 4.
[130] Chapter 3, section 4.
[131] See text accompanying n 55.
[132] Cf *Tunikova and Others v. Russia*, no. 55974/16, 14 December 2021 (violations of Article 3 and 14; Russia required (Article 46) to take comprehensive measures to address structural and discriminatory lack of protection of women against domestic violence).
[133] Cf *Alekseyev and Others v. Russia*, no. 14988/0, 27 November 2018 (repeated refusals to authorise LGBT public assemblies: violations of Article 8 and 14; Russia required (Article 46) to take general measures in respect of repeated refusals to authorise LGBT public assemblies). Also, *Zhdanov and Others v. Russia*, no. 12200/08, 16 July 2019 (refusal to register LGBTI associations: violations of Articles 11 and 14).
[134] See, before the CM, H46-33 *Mikheyev group v. Russia*, no. 77617/01, detailed in CM notes: CM/Notes/1419/H46-33.
[135] See n 151, and n 155, and discussion of Alexei Navalnyy cases in Chapter 7, sections 3 and 4.2.
[136] Regarding Sergei Magnitskiy, see n 153; regarding Aleksandr Litvinenko, see n 137; regarding Anna Politkovskaya, see Chapter 3, n 103. See further *Estemirova v. Russia*, no. 42705/11, 31 August 2021 (human rights activist; procedural violation of Article 2; also violation Article 38 (government's failure to furnish all necessary facilities)).
[137] Cf *Carter v. Russia*, no. 20914/07, 21 September 2021 (targeted killing of a Russian political defector and dissident (Aleksandr Litvinenko) perpetrated in the UK by individuals acting as state agents and a lack of effective investigation: violations of Article 2). See n 180 (inter-state case brought by Ukraine against Russia re targeted assassinations).

the Russian constitution, and defiance in the *Yukos* case),[138] leading experts had suggested in 2017 that the nature of the overall relationship between Russia and the ECHR was such that it was 'difficult to avoid the question whether the Russian government still respects the [latter] as a binding international treaty or not'.[139]

3.2.2 PACE monitoring (human rights)

Based on this evidence it was arguable that Russia was 'seriously violating' (Article 8 CoE Statute) Article 3 CoE Statute under its human rights and rule of law limb in the late 2010s. By contrast, and with breath-taking understatement, the PACE Resolution of June 2019, approving the Russian delegation's credentials, merely referred to a 'concern over a number of exacerbating negative tendencies with regard to democracy, the rule of law and human rights'![140] More remarkable still was the CM's 'Declaration by the Committee of Ministers on the occasion of the 70th anniversary of the Council of Europe' of May 2019'.[141] Issued just before Russia's reintegration of June 2019, this Declaration 'reaffirm[ed]' the CoE states' commitment 'to securing the independent functioning of the judiciary and to continuously reinforcing the authority of the rule of law'. It stated that '[a] free and pluralist public debate is a precondition for democracy', and called for strong action to reverse the 'recent deterioration of freedom of expression in Europe'. The CoE states 'recognise[d] the key role of civil society and express our deep concern at its shrinking space'.

As was indicated in Chapter 3,[142] in the precise areas just referred to, Russia's human rights record was worse than ever in 2019. As such, the justification for allowing Russia's return to PACE appeared to be based on the premise that some human rights monitoring – and so some hope of dialogue and change – was considered better than none.[143] To this end, when the Russian delegation returned to PACE, the latter's' Monitoring Committee was asked to expedite a report on Russia, for receipt 'no later' than the April 2020.[144]

---

[138] Chapter 3, section 4.3.
[139] Mälksoo, L. 'Introduction', in L. Mälksoo and W. Benedek (eds) *Russia and the European Court of Human Rights: The Strasbourg Effect*, Cambridge: Cambridge University Press, pp 3–25, 6.
[140] Resolution 2292 (2019), n 88, para 6.
[141] See n 78.
[142] Chapter 3, section 4.
[143] Russia's return to PACE would (it was assumed) at least allow for human rights monitoring by PACE, see Resolution 2292 (2019), n 88, para 12.
[144] Resolution 2292 (2019), n 88, para 14.

Unfortunately, however, PACE interactions with Russia achieved little after 2019, other than to highlight the worsening state of human rights.

The report just referred to, which was the main focal point opportunity for PACE to hold Russia to account for its dire human rights record, never materialised. The COVID-19 pandemic played a part in its delay, but only in April 2022 – after Russia's expulsion – did the two co-rapporteurs for the PACE Monitoring Committee produce an Information Note[145] entitled 'State of the parliamentary monitoring procedure for the Russian Federation on 16 March 2022' (the date of Russia's expulsion). It made painful reading, including for how the co-rapporteurs seemed to have been led along by Russia. They explained how they had genuinely believed that there had been some hope for a change of direction. Meetings in Moscow and with the Russian PACE delegation over 2021[146] had resulted in the proposal that the co-rapporteurs 'draw up a Roadmap accompanied by a concrete timetable, based on recommendations by the Venice Commission, which would identify concrete measures aimed to address the identified concerns'.[147] The co-rapporteurs stated how encouraged they had been 'by the renewed commitment of the Russian authorities and members of the delegation to pursue the fulfilment of their commitments and obligations', and that they had 'confidence in their sincerity'. The agreement was to 'define in April 2022, concrete action translated into concrete changes to the legislation with deadlines for their accomplishment'. So, the co-rapporteurs were 'shocked' at the Duma's approval of the invasion of Ukraine in February 2022. They felt 'betrayed' by the Russian delegates in PACE.[148]

Had the CoE been taken in again, or was what occurred all part of 'ritualism'? The co-rapporteurs' (post-expulsion) Note itself showed how fanciful it had been to expect any change from Russia, as they documented its increasingly anti-democratic trajectory after 2019. The period had seen, a 'strengthening of the executive power, a reduction in parliamentary oversight and narrowing pluralism',[149] and all the trends noted in 2016 (and before) had continued (regressive laws on political parties, on freedom of assembly, on 'foreign agents', on extremism and the law on undesirable organisations; the systematic persecution of political opponents, and the creation of restrictive conditions for the media and harassment of any critics, and so on).[150]

---

[145] PACE Information Note, 'State of the parliamentary monitoring procedure for the Russian Federation on 16 March 2022', AS/Mon (2022) 09, 26 April 2022.
[146] PACE Information Note, n 145, para 37.
[147] PACE Information Note, n 145, para 38.
[148] PACE Information Note, n 145, para 39.
[149] PACE Information Note, n 145, para 17.
[150] PACE Information Note, n 145, paras 18–19.

The depressing reality was that the co-rapporteurs' post-expulsion indictment of Russia was typical of what had occurred before. The latter's atrocious human rights record had been set out in successive (but unsuccessful) challenges to the Russian PACE delegation's credentials over 2020–2022, and by other CoE mandates. Three examples suffice to illustrate this.

First, in January 2020, less than a year after the Russian delegation's return to PACE, a motion for a Resolution[151] was tabled highlighting political prosecutions of government opponents and calling for an examination of the 'growing crisis with politically motivated imprisonments' in Russia. There were 'more than 300 political prisoners' (a six-fold increase since 2015), including journalists, civil society activists, human rights advocates, participants in peaceful demonstrations, adherents of prohibited religious groups and members of 'undesirable' organisations. PACE instituted a rapporteur with a mandate to prepare a report on the issues. A damning report[152] followed in 2022, standing alongside several earlier Resolutions passed by PACE on the plight of individual political figures in Russia, such as Sergei Magnitsky,[153] Boris Nemtsov[154] and Alexei Navalnyy,[155] in relation to which it was observed that there had been a 'lack of co-operation'[156] from the Russian delegates in PACE.

Second, the period after 2019 saw a further dramatic crackdown on civil society. This was aided by laws enacted well before then, yet which were

---

[151] PACE Motion for a Resolution, 'Political prisoners in the Russian Federation', Doc. 15049, 28 January 2020.

[152] PACE report, 'Reported cases of political prisoners in the Russian Federation', Doc. 15545, 3 June 2022 (refers to 'sheer number' of political prisoners, and 'pattern of systematic repression against any and all opponents of the current authorities', para 64).

[153] See Resolution 2252 (2019), 'Sergei Magnitsky and beyond – fighting impunity by targeted sanctions', 22 January 2019 (and before: Resolution 1966 (2014), 'Refusing impunity for the killers of Sergei Magnitsky', 28 January 2014). See *Magnitskiy and Others v. Russia*, no. 32631/09, 27 August 2019 (violation Article 2).

[154] Resolution 2297 (2019), 'Shedding light on the murder of Boris Nemtsov', 27 June 2019. See *Nemtsova v. Russia*, no. 43146/15, 6 September 2023 (violation of Article 2: death in pre-trial detention following delays in providing emergency medical care and failure to conduct adequate and timely investigation).

[155] Resolution 2375 (2021), 'The arrest and detention of Alexei Navalny in January 2021', 22 April 2021; Resolution 2423 (2022), 'Poisoning of Alexei Navalny', 26 January 2022. There were many cases brought to the ECtHR by Navalnyy, including: *Navalnyy v. Russia (No. 3)*, no. 36418/20, 6 September 2023 (violation of Article 2: domestic authorities' refusal to investigate in criminal proceedings plausible claims of applicant's poisoning with a chemical nerve agent prohibited by the Chemical Weapons Convention). See discussion of Navalnyy cases in Chapter 7, section 4.2.

[156] PACE Resolution 2422 (2022), 'Challenge, on substantive grounds, of the still unratified credentials of the parliamentary delegation of the Russian Federation', 26 January 2022, para 10.

then strengthened after Russia's return to PACE. So, for example, the earlier 'foreign agents' law was reinforced via Bills introduced to the Duma in late 2020. The Venice Commission reported on this in 2021,[157] noting that the 'foreign agent' register in Russia listed 76 organisations, and an additional media register listed 20 media outlets and individual persons.[158] The new laws clearly violated basic Convention rights.[159] They enabled the authorities 'to exercise significant control over the activities and existence of associations as well as over the participation of individuals in civic life',[160] such that they had a 'significant chilling effect' for 'the free exercise of the civil and political rights which are vital for an effective democracy'.[161]

Third, various constitutional amendments made after 2019 had implications for effective political democracy in Russia. These removed presidential term limits,[162] enabling President Putin to remain in office until 2036. Also passed in 2020[163] was a successor to the law of late 2015 on possible constitutional defiance of the ECtHR,[164] potentially more broad ranging than its predecessor. Once again, the Venice Commission expressed significant concern,[165] it also being noted that amendments were being proposed to the Constitution empowering the dismissal of judges of the Russian Constitutional Court (RCC) at the request of the President, which made the RCC 'vulnerable to political pressure'.[166]

3.3 Russia's transition to 'de facto dictatorship'

Certain of the constitutional amendments just mentioned were relevant to a report issued by PACE's Committee on Legal Affairs and Human Rights

---

[157] Venice Commission, 'Russian Federation – Opinion on the Compatibility with International Human Rights Standards of a Series of Bills Introduced to the Russian State Duma between 10 and 23 November 2020, to Amend Laws Affecting "Foreign Agents"', CDL-AD(2021)027, 3 July 2021.
[158] Venice Commission, n 157, para 6.
[159] Venice Commission, n 157, para 92.
[160] Venice Commission, n 157, para 92.
[161] See generally the long-delayed ruling in *Ecodefence and Others v. Russia*, no. 9988/13, 14 June 2022, see further n 226.
[162] Cf Venice Commission, 'Interim Opinion on Constitutional Amendments and the Procedure for Their Adoption', CDL-AD(2021)005, 19 March 2021.
[163] See Venice Commission, 'Opinion on Draft Amendments to the Constitution (as Signed by the President of the Russian Federation on 14 March 2020) Related to the Execution in the Russian Federation of Decisions by the European Court of Human Rights', CDL-AD(2020)009.
[164] See Chapter 3, section 4.3.
[165] Venice Commission, n 163, para 65.
[166] Venice Commission, n 163, para 66.

(CLAHR) in 2023, which referred to how Russia had 'turned … into a *de facto* dictatorship'.[167]

In keeping with ritualism, no CoE actor had been prepared to make such direct statements in relation to Russia until after its expulsion, even though this description clearly applied to it well before 2023, arguably years before. In fact, prior to 2022 matters had only served to demonstrate how weak PACE had become in its relationship with Russia. It was able to highlight concerns, and thereby shine a light on how bad the human rights situation was in Russia, which served a purpose. Then again, it was unable to affect this, the CoE becoming, in effect, a bystander in relation to Russia's slide into ever-greater authoritarianism. Of course, PACE itself had been weakened by Russia. Over 2020–2022, its diminished role compared to 2014 (let alone 2000 in relation to Chechnya) was evident in the annual challenges to credentials of the Russian PACE delegation.[168] These events became focal points for criticism of Russia's human rights record; however, the credentials were approved by significant majorities, and the minor sanctions that PACE retained were never imposed.

4 Over to the Court as 'last resort'? Inter-state cases brought against Russia before the ECtHR

We turn now to the role played by the ECtHR after 2019, in relation to inter-state cases brought against Russia, to include those concerning Crimea and eastern Ukraine.[169] As we have seen, aside from the political criticism directed against Russia by PACE and the CM over 2014–2015, there was a failure to hold Russia truly accountable here in 2019. What then of the prospects of legal accountability under the ECHR?[170]

---

[167] PACE, Committee on Legal Affairs and Human Rights, 'Examining the legitimacy and legality of the ad hominem term limit waiver for the incumbent President of the Russian Federation report' (AS/Jur (2023) 25), para 6.

[168] Cf PACE Resolution 2363 (2021), 'Challenge, on substantive grounds, of the still unratified credentials of the parliamentary delegation of the Russian Federation', 28 January 2021.

[169] Details of the various inter-states decided and pending before the ECtHR may be found at www.echr.coe.int/inter-state-applications. For up-to-date accounts of inter-state cases, see Risini, I. and Eicke, T. (2024) 'Inter-state applications under the European Convention on Human Rights – situating the instrument in the current human rights landscape', *International Human Rights Law Review* (published online ahead of print 2024); Dzehtsiarou, K. (2022) 'The aggression against Ukraine and the effectiveness of inter-state cases in case of war', *European Convention on Human Rights Law Review*, 3(2): 165–73; and Lixinski, L. (2022) 'On the circumscribed and problematic resurgence of inter-state human rights cases', *European Convention on Human Rights Law Review*, 3(2): 174–84.

[170] On interim measures issued by ECtHR in connection with these inter-state applications, see Chapter 5, section 3.

Was this a factor in the way matters were resolved in 2019? Ruxit in 2019 would not have affected the ECtHR's *ratione temporis* jurisdiction with respect to events prior to that.[171] However, at least with Russia in the CoE it would not have an excuse to avoid the process of legal accountability under the ECtHR,[172] even if, of course, the enforceability of any its rulings would be a different matter.

The relevance of Russia's on-going ECHR membership was clearly in evidence as the 2014–2019 crisis started to come to a head. As will be noted later, over 2018–2019 there had been important developments in the inter-state cases brought by Georgia against Russia. Meanwhile, over 2019 the Grand Chamber of the Court started to address one of the key inter-state cases brought by Ukraine (back in 2014) against Russia concerning Crimea, in relation to which an administrative practice of breaches of many human rights was alleged (*Ukraine v. Russia (re Crimea)*).[173] An admissibility hearing had been scheduled for this on 27 February 2019, although it was put back to 11 September 2019. Accordingly, Russia's 2019 reintegration into the CoE and the failure of the CoE's statutory organs to hold it accountable in relation to Crimea coincided with important stages in the ECtHR's role in doing so, albeit in the very different, and more limited context of the ECHR.

4.1 Inter-state cases brought by Ukraine

As might have been predicted (based on established ECHR jurisprudence at the time), in an admissibility decision of 16 December 2020 (*Ukraine v. Russia (re Crimea)*)[174] the Court concluded that from 27 February 2014 Russia had 'jurisdiction' over Crimea under Article 1 of the Convention based on the 'effective control' it exercised.[175] Accordingly, and with the CM taking note,[176] this case proceeded to its merits phase.

---

[171] See Chapter 6, section 4.

[172] On Russia's non-participation/refusal to interact with the ECtHR after its expulsion in 2022, see Chapter 6.

[173] *Ukraine v. Russia (re Crimea)* (dec.) [GC], no. 20958/14 (also concerns transfer of Ukrainian 'convicts' to Russia/allegations of persecution of Ukrainian 'political prisoners').

[174] *Ukraine v. Russia (re Crimea)* (dec.) [GC], no. 20958/14, 16 December 2020, at para 349 (without prejudging the merits, see para 351).

[175] In its various Decisions related to Crimea over 2014–2017, the CM repeatedly expressed its concern about serious human rights issues/situations in Crimea and related regions. It also stressed the 'importance of the interim measure granted' by the ECtHR following an inter-state application lodged by Ukraine, and 'called on the two Parties concerned to comply with this measure without delay', CM/Del/Dec(2014)1194/1.7, para 5.

[176] CM/Del/Dec(2021)1403bis/2.3 (11 May 2021), citing the ECtHR's admissibility decision in *Ukraine v. Russia (re Crimea)* (2020), n 174, and expressing great concern over the human rights situation. The Secretary General was asked to 'report on a regular basis, at

The hearing was on 13 December 2023, and so, it transpired, after Russia's expulsion in March 2022.[177] Russia failed to appear, having been invited to do so. The Court proceeded with the hearing, in accordance with its Rules, and satisfied that such a course was consistent with the proper administration of justice.[178] The judgment is awaited at time of writing. In issue are allegations of the existence of an administrative practice breaching a whole range of fundamental rights, including Article 2 ECHR (enforced disappearances and of a lack of effective investigations), Article 3 (ill-treatment), Article 5 (unlawful detention), in relation to Article 6 (extending the Russian Federation's laws to Crimea and the resulting effect that as from 27 February 2014 the courts in Crimea could not be considered to have been 'established by law' within the meaning of Article 6 of the Convention), and Article 8 (alleged existence of an administrative practice of unlawful automatic imposition of Russian citizenship), and many other issues.

Meanwhile, the ECtHR's website[179] lists three other pending inter-state applications launched by Ukraine against Russia, and again judgments are waited for these. Of the three, two concern targeted assassinations by Russia[180] and specific cases related to naval incidents connected to Crimea,[181] while the other is a much bigger affair: *Ukraine and the Netherlands v. Russia*.[182] This concerns the alleged administrative practices by Russia in eastern Ukraine under separatist control, and the downing of Malaysian Airlines flight MH17,

---

least once a year, on the human rights situation in Crimea ... to provide' the CM 'with a basis for an assessment of the situation and possible decisions on action'. On the latter, see SG/Inf(2023)29 (31 August 2023).

[177] ECtHR Press Release, 'Grand Chamber hearing on inter-State case *Ukraine v. Russia (re Crimea)*', 13 December 2023. Note: judgment on the merits was delivered in *Ukraine v. Russia (re Crimea)* [GC], nos. 20958/14 and 38334/18, 25 June 2024.

[178] Cf The CM's 'Declaration by the Committee of Ministers on the effective processing and resolution of cases relating to inter-State disputes', 5 April 2023 ('welcomes the Court's approach to proceeding with examination of applications lodged against the Russian Federation even in the absence of co-operation from the Russian authorities, in order to best preserve the effective functioning of the Convention system').

[179] Details at n 169. This highlights an inter-state case brought by Russia against Ukraine, in 2021 (*Russia v. Ukraine* (dec.), no. 36958/21: allegations of an administrative practice in Ukraine of, among other things, killings, abductions, forced displacement). This was struck off the Court's list in July 2023 (the Russian government had repeatedly failed to reply to its correspondence; the Court concluded that Russia no longer wished to pursue the application).

[180] *Ukraine v. Russia (IX)*, no. 10691/21 (lodged on 19 February 2021), concerning allegation of an ongoing administrative practice by the Russian Federation consisting of targeted assassination operations against perceived opponents of the Russian Federation, in Russia and on the territory of other states.

[181] *Ukraine v. Russia (VIII)*, no. 55855/18 (lodged on 29 November 2018): concerns 2018 naval incident in the Kerch Strait and capture of three Ukrainian naval vessels and crews.

[182] *Ukraine and the Netherlands v. Russia* (dec.) [GC], nos. 43800/14, 8019/16 and 28525/20, 20 November 2022.

in respect of which the Netherlands intervened (the plane departed from Amsterdam, and 196 Dutch nationals died). Those cases were declared partially admissible by a Grand Chamber of the ECtHR on 30 November 2022,[183] when it decided that Russia had jurisdiction over parts of eastern Ukraine controlled by separatists (from 11 May 2014 and subsequently),[184] and declared allegations of administrative practices by Russia resulting in multiple potential Convention violations in eastern Ukraine partly admissible, plus those regarding the downing of Malaysian Airlines flight MH17 also admissible.[185] This case has now been joined[186] with *Ukraine v. Russia (X)*.[187] This concerns Russia's invasion of Ukraine and the latter's allegation of mass and gross human-rights violations committed by the former during its military operations on the territory of Ukraine since 24 February 2022.[188] A hearing on the merits took place in June 2024.[189]

Given the magnitude of the issues that form their backdrop, it is highly likely that these *Ukraine v. Russia* judgments will be the most important the Court has delivered across the Convention's entire 75-year life-span. Certainly, they will be among them. In addition to that, the allegations of human rights violations in issue are of a nature, breadth and scale that are unapparelled in the Court's history.[190] Here it is worth adding that in April 2023, the CM issued a Declaration[191] fully supporting the Court's work in relation to these and the other inter-state cases pending before the Court.

---

[183] *Ukraine and the Netherlands v. Russia*, n 182.

[184] *Ukraine and the Netherlands v. Russia*, n 182, para 695 (within Russia's ECHR jurisdiction ('effective control'): 'vast body of evidence' of 'Russia's military presence in eastern Ukraine' and of 'the decisive degree of influence and control it enjoyed over the areas under separatist control … as a result of its military, political and economic support to the separatist entities').

[185] *Ukraine and the Netherlands v. Russia*, n 182, paras 702–6 (within Russia's ECHR jurisdiction ('effective control'): 'ample evidence … firing of the Buk-missile and the consequent downing of flight MH17 occurred in territory which was in the hands of separatists', but under 'effective control' of Russia, para 702).

[186] See ECtHR Press Release, 'European Court joins inter-State case concerning Russian military operations in Ukraine to inter-State case concerning eastern Ukraine and downing of flight MH17', 20 February 2023.

[187] *Ukraine v. Russia (X)*, no. 11055/22.

[188] See ECtHR Press Release, 'Inter-State case *Ukraine v. Russia (X)*: receipt of completed application form and notification to respondent State', 28 June 2022.

[189] See the statement by the government of the Netherlands, 10 June 2024, available from: www.government.nl/latest/news/2024/06/10/flight-mh17-european-court-of-human-rights-the-netherlands-inter-state-application-russian-federation [Accessed 20 June 2024].

[190] See Chapter 5, section 4.2, for discussion of the inter-state cases Cyprus brought against Türkiye.

[191] CM Declaration, n 178.

Notably, the Declaration 'deplor[ed]' Russia's actions 'in various member states' which 'grossly violate[d] human rights' resulting in 'numerous interstate and individual applications'. The CM was conscious of 'the utmost importance of cases relating to interstate disputes' and recognised how this required the states and the CoE to support the Court, which should 'continue to prioritise [these cases] and take the steps necessary to ensure their effective and speedy examination and resolution'.

4.2 Inter-state cases brought by Georgia

On the assumption that findings are made against Russia in these cases, the question of enforcement of the judgments will arise. Here what has happened in relation to two, earlier inter-state cases brought by Georgia against Russia are indicative of what may occur.[192]

On 31 January 2019, at the height of the non-cooperation crisis, the ECtHR delivered its just satisfaction ruling in *Georgia v. Russia (I)*[193] (this in respect of the GC ruling of 3 July 2014, concerning the expulsion of Georgian nationals from Russia).[194] Russia was ordered to pay €10,000,000 in respect of non-pecuniary damage suffered by a group of at least 1,500 Georgian nationals.[195] No payment was made prior to Russia's expulsion from the CoE, after which the CM has underlined Russia's unconditional obligation in international law to comply with the judgments of the European Court against it.[196] Default interest has been added to the sum still owed.

The sums have been added to a 'public register of just satisfaction owing in all inter-state and individual cases against the Russian Federation' established

---

[192] For background, see Chapter 3, section 2.2. A further inter-state case was lodged in 2018: see *Georgia v. Russia (IV)* no. 39611/18, 9 April 2024 (chamber ruling concerned Russia administrative practices stemming from 'borderisation' between breakaway regions (Abkhazia and South Ossetia) and the Georgian government-controlled territory. Multiple Convention violations).

[193] *Georgia v. Russia (I)* [GC], no. 13255/07, 31 January 2019.

[194] See Chapter 3, n 123. The judgment remains unexecuted as regards the general measures required of Russia (obligation to prevent any further coordinated unlawful policy relating to migration/expulsion involving, *inter alia*, the police, the Federal Migration Service and the courts as was implemented in Russia at the relevant time, see Interim Resolution CM/ResDH(2022)146).

[195] The Court indicated (n 193, para 77) that these amounts should be distributed by the Government of Georgia to the individual victims under the supervision of the CM within 18 months of the date of the payment. To enable such payments via a Council of Europe bank account (held in escrow), the Russian authorities had signed a Memorandum of Understanding (on 17 December 2021).

[196] See CM/Del/Dec(2023)1468/H46-27 (June 23) (and Statement by the Committee of Ministers President – Committee of Ministers chairmanships, available from: www.coe.int).

by the CM.¹⁹⁷ The register highlights 'the issue' of non-payment, while the 'the sums due can remain under close public scrutiny and be available to the Committee in the light of any future developments'.¹⁹⁸

At the time of writing, the register includes 1,376 individual case entries with a combined total of €2,725,460,337 outstanding, although the majority of this concerns the *Yukos* case.¹⁹⁹ The register also includes €129,827,500 awarded by the Court (with accrued interest: €137,824,340) following the litigation in *Georgia v. Russia (II)*.²⁰⁰ This concerned the (Convention) jurisdiction of Russia over Abkhazia and South Ossetia during the active phase of hostilities during the Russia–Georgian conflict of 2008, and after their cessation. The Grand Chamber had held a hearing on this on 23 May 2018 (a decade on from when the application was lodged: 12 August 2008), the judgment on the merits finally being delivered on 21 January 2021, and the just satisfaction element not until 28 April 2023 (Russia failed to participate in the latter).²⁰¹ In the main case (and with significance for the forthcoming judgments related to Ukraine's invasion) the Court ruled that it did not have jurisdiction during the 'active phase of hostilities' (8–12 August 2008), as there was an absence of 'effective control' over territory at that stage.²⁰² However, it held that there had been administrative practices on the part of Russia, in violation of Articles 2, 3, 5 and 8 of the Convention and Article 2 of Protocol No. 4, and that it had failed to comply with its obligations under Article 38 ECHR. As to the execution of this judgment, in June 2023²⁰³ the CM called upon Russia to pay the just satisfaction awarded by the Court. It strongly urged the Russia authorities to submit a thorough and comprehensive action plan on the execution of the judgment. As indicated, this would require the Russian authorities to '[6]. ... take urgent and tangible measures to ensure cessation as well as elimination of the root cause of [the] violations [found by the ECtHR]

---

¹⁹⁷ See 'Register of just satisfaction concerning the Russian Federation – Department for the Execution of Judgments', available from: www.coe.int/en/web/execution/register [Accessed 20 June 2024].

¹⁹⁸ Text from CoE website, n 197. Separately, see Resolution CM/Res(2023)3 'Establishing the enlarged partial agreement on the register of damage caused by the aggression of the Russian Federation against Ukraine' (12 May 2023). For further details, see www.coe.int/en/web/human-rights-rule-of-law/register-of-damage-for-ukraine [Accessed 1 June 2024].

¹⁹⁹ 15 May 2024; the amount for *Yukos* case (*OAO Neftyanaya Kompaniya Yukos v. Russia*, no. 14902/04, 31 July 2014) is €2,523,385,527 (including interest)).

²⁰⁰ *Georgia v. Russia (II)* [GC], no. 38263/08, 21 January 2021. See Dzehtsiarou, K. (2021) 'Georgia v. Russia (II)', *American Journal of International Law*, 115(2): 288–94.

²⁰¹ *Georgia v. Russia (II)* [GC], no. 38263/08, 28 April 2023.

²⁰² *Georgia v. Russia (II)*, n 200, paras 125–44.

²⁰³ CM/Del/Dec(2023)1468/H46-28, *Georgia v. Russia (II)*, no. 38263/08, 7 June 2023.

and to avoid their repetition'. Relatedly Russia was '[7] … exhorted … to thoroughly, independently, effectively and promptly investigate the serious crimes committed during the active phase of hostilities as well as during the period of occupation, so as to identify all those responsible for the purposes of bringing the perpetrators to justice'. The CM also '[8]. firmly reiterated once again [its] profound concern about the inability of Georgian nationals to return to their homes in South Ossetia and Abkhazia', insisting that Russia, 'which has effective control over these regions, ensure without delay safe return of persons wishing to return to their homes'.

4.3 Accountability under the ECHR: to what end?

It is beyond the scope of this study to provide detailed examinations of these cases. However, the following general points about them and their overall significance may be worth reflecting upon.

First, with respect to both Georgia and Ukraine's applications, it is undeniable that the Court has taken a long time to address them (in the former cases almost a decade and a half, and around a decade (to date) for events related to 2014 (Ukraine)). With respect to both it is evident that by the time it did rule (in the cases brought by Georgia) and will rule on (the Crimea and related issues), the geopolitical situation had/will have changed dramatically. Then again, even if the Court had ruled earlier would Russia have respected these judgments?

With respect to the long delays, one should not underestimate how complex and multidimensional the cases are.[204] The challenges involved (made worse by Russia's non-cooperation) are significant for an institution not designed to address aspects of them yet required under the ECHR to do so. As the Court's Registrar once noted, 'the Court … cannot settle war-like conflicts between States',[205] and is 'not equipped to deal with large scale abuses of human rights'.[206] Indeed, the cases are a major drain on the Court's limited resources, as is, potentially, the thousands of individual petition cases

---

[204] See Contribution of CDDH [Steering Committee for Human Rights] to the evaluation provided for by the Interlaken Declaration, CDDH(2019), R92Addendum2 (29/11/2019) at para 11. See also para 233/4, referring to the 'particular complexity' of inter-state cases. See also 'Comment from the European Court on Human Rights on the CDDH contribution to the evaluation of the Interlaken reform process', 11 February 2020.

[205] CDDH, Committee of Experts on the Reform of the Court, Drafting Group 'F' on the Reform of the Court, Presentation to the 3rd Meeting by the Registrar of the European Court of Human Rights, Erik Friberg, GT-GDR-F(2014)021, 24 September 2014.

[206] Steering Committee, n 205. See also *Georgia v. Russia (II)*, n 200, paras 141–2 (Court's limitations in context of 'war and active hostilities').

connected to Russia's aggression against Ukraine.[207] Given that the Court comes to these matters following the failure of other CoE processes, it is sadly ironic to note that it has been under-resourced by the states for many years, even though it faces numerous challenges on multiple fronts.[208]

A second set of points relates to enforcement of the judgments. In relation to that the public register of just satisfaction is an important initiative. Presumably it will include any sums awarded by the ECtHR in the inter-state cases directed against Russia by Ukraine. However, the register is just a first step, of course. How it could be resourced,[209] how awardees in Russia could make use of it in the near future, and so the use to which it may be put generally remains to be seen. It, plus the inter-state cases, would surely assume great significance in the context of any application made by Russia for readmission to the CoE. After all, it would be inconceivable for Russia to re-join without plans for the settlement of the register plus a full and effective plan for the implementation of the inter-state judgments, and arguably a comprehensive process of domestic accountability and transitional justice.[210] This again underlines the significance of the judgments.

Of course, Russia's return to the CoE would require very different political circumstances in Russia compared to today, and may be many years away. As such a third collection of points relates to the importance of the role that the Court may play in terms of what it documents, the findings it makes and their legacy generally. On the latter, one must be realistic, it being necessary to appreciate the context and very difficult situation the Court is placed in. Then again, the Court's rulings, to be delivered by Grand Chambers, will constitute that institution's authoritative judgment on Russia's international obligations under the ECHR for events related to 2014 and after as regards Crimea and eastern Ukraine, and then for at least up to September 2022, as regards the full-scale invasion of Ukraine (in matters the Court has Article 1 jurisdiction

---

[207] See ECtHR Press Release, 'European Court joins inter-state case', 20 February 2023 (over 8,500 individual applications pending before the Court concerning the events in Crimea, eastern Ukraine and the Sea of Azov).

[208] On the general challenges facing the Court (over and above the handling of many inter-state cases), see Harris, D., O'Boyle, M., Bates, E. and Buckley, C. (2023) *Law of the European Convention on Human Rights*, Oxford: Oxford University Press, pp 39–43. On lack of resources, see n 230.

[209] The CM has 'invited the [CoE's] Committee of Legal Advisers on Public International Law (CAHDI) to explore all possible avenues consistent with international law aimed at securing the payment by the Russian Federation of just satisfaction awarded by the European Court of Human Rights, while respecting the immunities of States and their property', see CM/Del/Dec(2024)1488/10.5 (7 February 2024).

[210] Cf n 203 as regards execution of the judgment in *Georgia v. Russia (II)*.

over). The Strasbourg court's rulings have the potential to be an important historical record of what occurred (seen through the lens of the ECHR), and a vital legal record of Russia's liability under the ECHR, and so, more generally, what the CoE stands for. On this last point, as the Grand Chamber pointed out in its admissibility decision in *Ukraine and the Netherlands v. Russia*, inter-state cases such as those directed against Russia see the CoE states themselves seek a ruling on alleged violations of the 'public order of Europe'.[211] Here it is striking that 26 CoE states have been granted leave to intervene in relation to inter-state case concerning Russia's 2022 invasion of Ukraine.[212]

This last point leads to some final comments. A cynic might suggest that this apparent enthusiasm for ensuring there is legal accountability via the ECHR for Russia's action (albeit post the events of 2022) stands in contrast to the appeasement of 2019, and the lack of effective political responses by the CM at that time (and before). S/he might equally point out that the ECtHR's fall-back or 'last resort'[213] role here also occurred with respect to Chechnya and Georgia.

5 Conclusion

This chapter examined the crisis caused at the CoE by Russia after its aggression in Crimea and eastern Ukraine in 2014; it analysed how this was concluded in 2019, and what followed. Russia was reintegrated into the CoE in 2019, but on terms that came at a cost to the latter's credibility. What occurred added to the sense that the CoE Statute and instruments such as the ECHR only partially applied to Russia, the legal obligations they established not restraining it in practice. Indeed, Russia's open, blatant and continuing breach of its obligations was such that the impression is gained that over the 2010s there almost came to be an air of normalcy, rather than exceptionality, about it. This open disrespect, and even defiance of CoE values, fits with a key theme of this chapter, which has been to argue that Russia's CoE membership became essentially ritualistic over the 2010s, and into the 2020s. Until that is, the ritualism bubble burst with Russia's expulsion from the CoE following its full-scale invasion of Ukraine in February 2022.

---

[211] *Ukraine and the Netherlands v. Russia*, n 182, para 335.
[212] See ECtHR Press Release, 'Update on the third-party intervention requests granted in Inter-State case Ukraine and the Netherlands v. Russia', 17 March 2023.
[213] Cf Registrar Fribergh, n 205 ('the Court is seen as the last resort not only for individuals but also for some States').

5.1 Russia's persistent breach of CoE obligations, and its damaging membership

Given that endpoint one may now draw certain conclusions about Russia's 26 membership years of the CoE, as examined in Chapters 2–4 of this book.[214]

An initial set of points relates to Russia's record as regards its CoE obligations and commitments. It did not just breach its accession commitments on numerous occasions (for example, failing to withdraw troops from Transnistria) and have a very poor implementation record regarding ECtHR judgments,[215] it repeatedly violated Article 3 CoE Statute, in premeditated and blatant ways. Here (regarding Article 3), two strands may be noted.

First, there were aggressive acts against Russia's neighbours and occupation of their territory. This was so as regards Georgia over 2008–2009 (and continuing after),[216] and as regards Crimea and eastern Ukraine after March 2014 (and continuing after).[217] And, of course, there was the full-scale invasion of Ukraine in 2022. As the PACE Resolution of March 2022 put it, '[t]hrough its attitude and actions, the leadership of the Russian Federation poses a blatant menace to security in Europe'.[218] Connected to this, the scale

---

[214] For reflections on Russia's CoE membership (post-expulsion), see Leach, P. (2022) 'A time of reckoning? Russia and the Council of Europe', *European Human Rights Law Review*, 3: 219–27, 226; Nussberger, n 126; Yudkivska, n 126; and Brummer, K. (2024) 'The Council of Europe, Russia, and the future of European cooperation', *International Politics*, 61: 1–21. See further Spano, R. (2023) 'Inclusive democracy and the European Convention on Human Rights', *European Human Rights Law Review*, 2: 112–18, 116–18.

[215] See text accompanying n 119. Under instructions from the CM, the Department for the Execution of Judgments of the European Court of Human Rights has prepared a Memorandum of all leading cases grouped by Convention articles, see H/Exec(2023)12 Final (8 December 2023, 'Judgments of the European Court of Human Rights against the Russian Federation: measures required in the pending cases', available from: www.coe.int/en/web/execution/russian-federation [Accessed 24 June 2024]. At the end of 2022, there were 228 leading and 2,352 repetitive cases pending execution with regard to Russia: see 'Supervision of the execution of judgments and decisions of the ECHR. 16th Annual Report of the Committee of Ministers (2022)', 98 (a leading case is disclosing a new problem; repetitive cases relate to a problem already raised). On the continued role of the CM in supervising the execution of ECtHR judgments post Russia's ceasing to be a member of the ECHR, see Resolution CM/Res(2022)3, para 7, and see Chapter 6, section 6.

[216] PACE Resolution 2422 (2022), 'Challenge, on substantive grounds, of the still unratified credentials of the parliamentary delegation of the Russian Federation', 26 January 2022, para 8.

[217] Resolution, n 216.

[218] PACE Opinion, 'Consequences of the Russian Federation's aggression against Ukraine', Opinion 300 (2022), 15 March 2022, para 5.

and nature of the allegations of human rights violations related to Ukraine's inter-state cases before the ECtHR, would, if upheld, be among the worst in the CoE's history.

Second, arguably Russia breached Article 3 CoE Statute in the national context. On the one hand, there were the atrocities in Chechnya and the North Caucuses over the 2000s, Russia's disrespect for CoE values being compounded by the enduring impunity afterwards (entailing further breaches of its obligations). On the other, over the 2010s and into the 2020s, there were acts of authoritarianism which constituted serious violations of human rights, and other highly regressive measures contrary to effective political democracy: the detention of political prisoners, crackdowns on civil society, alleged assassinations and much more. The cumulative effect of this was, arguably, also a violation of Article 3 CoE Statute. Of course, it entailed significant numbers of serious violations of the ECHR.

Suffice to say, no state has come close to breaching its CoE legal obligations on the scale that Russia did. And, given that the CoE's very raison d'etre is to protect, defend and stand up for the values that Russia repeatedly flouted, one may say that no state has, by virtue of its continued membership in such circumstances, harmed the CoE's credibility more than Russia has.

This brings us to some comments on the damaging effect of Russia's membership. Here one recalls that already by 2010 commentators had labelled Russia a 'Trojan horse'[219] member of the CoE. That was *before* the events of 2014–2019, to include Russia's unilateral campaign against PACE for having the temerity to stand up for CoE values, its financial blackmail and threatened Ruxit, all to achieve CoE reintegration based on impunity regarding Crimea. The damage to the CoE, perceived as (once again) applying double standards, condoning totally unacceptable behaviour, and caving in to a big state, was discussed in detail previously. And to what end? The CoE's appeasement of and bending over backwards to reintegrate Russia in 2019 was met with latter's full-scale invasion of Ukraine. No wonder Marija Pejčinović Burić, Secretary General of the CoE, commented, '[t]o have kept Russia within our Organisation [after 2022] would have strained our credibility past breaking point. The Russian Federation does not respect our standards. And some lines simply cannot be crossed.'[220] While one could hardly disagree with the first sentence, had the CoE's credibility not already been taken to 'breaking point' – even beyond – by Russia, before 2022?

---

[219] Chapter 3, n 15.
[220] Speech, 'Public event with the Institute of International Affairs of the University of Iceland, on the future of Europe', 24 November 2022.

5.2 Better in than out? Or, in fact, ritualism?

Very credible arguments could be – and were[221] – made that Russia should have been expelled from the CoE in 2019. They look even more compelling from the perspective of 2024. Today there can be little doubt about the answer to the critical question that arose all through Russia's membership. Was it better to keep Russia in, or better to expel it? The hindsight perspective is certainly not a flattering one for the CoE.

Back in 1996, when politics prevailed over law in the decision over Russia's admission, the assumption must have been that political factors and 'better in than out' arguments would have influence for an initial grace period of a decade or so. Presumably the thinking was that the latitude would apply as regards the CoE's handling and accommodating approach toward Russia in mainstream human rights issues. Instead, after Russia's so-called 'therapeutic admission' failed, and the troubled (Trojan horse) nature of its membership became apparent, 'better in than out' prevailed time and again, and in relation to very serious human rights issues and in relation to major breaches of the CoE Statute.

Presumably the eternal hope was that things would change in Russia. However, in the light of the defining events of 2022 and Russia's expulsion, the multiple opportunities that CoE actors, especially the CM, had to bring Russia to account come into sharp focus, as does their failure in that regard, and so the consequential damage to the CoE. It is a sorry tale, one that now (with the benefit of hindsight) seems utterly predictable, as alarm bells rang loudly but appeared to be ignored, especially in the mid-2000s and over 2012–2013. Even if the Chechnya situation could be compartmentalised, CoE actors noted that a change occurred in Russia after around 2005 when measures were adopted that were profoundly undemocratic. After this there was the Georgian conflict, and the regressive laws and actions associated with 2012–2013, described by PACE as a 'crossroads' one for Russia, there still being, just about, a 'window of opportunity' for change at that point. It was firmly closed by Moscow via more regressive internal measures, and then the events related to Crimea.

All through Russia's membership PACE communicated strong signals as to the complete unacceptability of Russia's actions. However, the CM remained essentially passive, lacking commitment to its own 1994 Declaration on Compliance with Commitments in the 2000s, and apparently unwilling to confront Russia, at least not publicly. Instead, it seemed to let other CoE actors take the lead (passing the buck to them?). Of course, one cannot say what pressure was put on Russia behind the scenes at the CM, and what

---

[221] Dzehtsiarou and Coffey, n 16.

influence this may have had, and there were occasional strong words directed against Russia in the context of Article 46 ECHR. In the final analysis, however, it is evident that it was not enough to persuade Putin's Russia to change course, and even that the latter was allowed to abuse Russia's position as a big player within the CoE context. The zenith of this came in 2019. By then, given the lack of substantive results on numerous fronts,[222] and the negative, even subversive influence Russia was having on the CoE, it seemed like CoE actors had overestimated any leverage they had on Russia. Perhaps there had been over-confidence at the CoE in the notion that Russia would not dare leave it – or take action that would demand its expulsion[223] – for the international criticism this would entail. Numerous questions then arise as we look back to 2019. Was reintegration then courageous from the CoE in its efforts to secure accountability, including for the Russian people, or foolish (blind optimism) given all that was known of Russia? After 2019 did Russia remain in the CoE primarily because of the unwillingness of the CM to uphold the CoE statute, or because of the faint hope that some form accountability could be achieved in CoE circles, which was better than no such hope? A mixture of both?

The real criticism was the failure of the CoE, and the CM especially, to prevent matters reaching that stage. At the same time, certain points can be made in mitigation, reflecting the dilemma 'better in than out' inevitably throws up.

First, seen from the perspective of the desire for improvement in Russia and the region, and accountability in the CoE context (to include, for example, inter-state cases before the ECtHR), the Russian government held all the cards. From the perspective just referred to, up until 2022 there always was scope for the argument that *some* hope for improvement (and retention of monitoring/accountability) was better than the alternative, that is, the near certainty of no hope (Russia expelled, with all the consequences). True in 2019 the hope aspect of this equation must have been very low indeed, the CoE's capitulation to Russia having been driven by the latter's position that it be appeased. Such an aggressive approach, coupled with the prior track record of the Putin administration, entailed that 'better in than out' (if that is what really accounted for Russia's continued membership in 2019) was futile, and seeking cooperation (to retain hope) at almost any price (the CoE's credibility). Nonetheless, in 2019 perhaps it was a matter of opinion as to whether retention of some hope on those and other fronts (keeping

---

[222] See text accompanying n 104.
[223] In the context of the 2014–2019 crisis some leading CoE figures were (apparently) not shy in saying that the CoE needed Russia, but that Russia needed the CoE too, see Roter, n 16, 47 (citing interview with Ann Brasseur, former President of PACE between January 2014 and January 2016).

Russia in the CM room, within PACE, subject to the ECHR and other human rights regimes) was worth it given how bleak (no hope), certain and unthinkable (so-to-speak) the alternative was: a return to Cold War patterns,[224] and with parts of Europe left as a legal 'grey zone'.[225] This is the situation today, and expulsion in 2019 would not have stopped it.

Of course, this is not to condone what occurred in 2019; however, and secondly, matters must be seen in context. One would like to think that the events of 2019 were, genuinely, to avoid the 'unthinkable' alternative just referred to, rather than to appease Putin's Russia as such. To the extent that Russia's size and influence was a major factor in its appeasement, might this also be seen as a reflection of the magnitude and scale of the issues in relation to which hope for accountability and progress needed to be retained? So, we recall that the overall backdrop was the tireless effort of CoE actors and that of human rights defenders, civil society, academia, independent-minded media and other liberal actors to turn the tide of authoritarianism in Russia, and bring it closer to the European standards that it had voluntarily subscribed to in the 1990s. Obviously it is for those constituencies in Russia and its citizens, so deeply betrayed by their political leadership, as well as those in affected regions of Georgia and Crimea and seeking accountability for the same, that what has occurred is the greatest tragedy. Again, this would not have been prevented by Russia's expulsion in 2019, and what has occurred is because the Russian government chose the unthinkable alternative path previously noted.

Finally, and in terms of assessing *the CoE's role* in all this, let us recall that it is an international organisation with power focussed in the CM. The former should not be scapegoated, for it can be no stronger than the political will of the latter.

5.3 The role of the CoE's human rights actors

The point made in the preceding paragraph about scapegoating should be kept firmly in mind as we turn specifically to human rights issues. Here we recall that Russia was expelled from the CoE because of the full-scale invasion of Ukraine, not the major human rights issues related to Chechnya, Georgia, Crimea and in Russia itself. It is the CM which decides this, not other CoE actors.

By contrast for human rights, both generally and as regards Russia, the media and even academic literature focus overwhelmingly on the ECtHR,

---

[224] Cf PACE's April 2014 Resolution, n 25, and text accompanying n 31.
[225] Cf the plea from prominent human rights campaigners and lawyers in Russia, see text accompanying n 72.

almost as if it is the only actor that counts. While that is understandable, given the ECHR's legal nature as regards human rights monitoring (and wider issues to do with Russia's CoE membership), this study has highlighted the importance of less well-known CoE actors such as PACE, the CoE Commissioner on Human Rights and the Venice Commission. Unlike the Court these bodies offered contemporary, wide-ranging and direct critiques of the deteriorating democratic and human rights situation in Russia, and other major issues (Georgia and Crimea). It was the CoE institutions just referred to, not the Court, which raised the alarm with respect to crucial matters such as attacks on civil society in Russia, including, for example, the 'foreign agents' law, the suppression of dissent and as regards blatant attacks on political actors. The preceding chapters therefore underline why the non-Court actors referred to must be taken seriously by those who hold the power at the CoE – the CM and CoE states – plus be adequately resourced, and, ideally, empowered.

As for the ECtHR itself, space constraints have entailed that there has been relatively little attention paid to it in terms of its role in relation to Russia's shift to authoritarianism. For that a detailed study would be merited, it being evident that criticisms could be levelled at the ECtHR, especially as regards long delays experienced with respect to certain applications concerning attacks on civil society,[226] and examples of political persecution. The delays entailed that the ECtHR's contribution was 'too little too late' and in several instances frontline protectors of human rights and democracy within Russia did not get the ECtHR's protection when it was needed most, that is, in the critical, post-2012 years.[227] Why not? That question looms large over the Court,[228] even if, as noted, other CoE actors were highlighting major issues as regards Russia's clear shift to authoritarianism in a timely fashion, such that the shift itself was well known about.

That said, points may be made in mitigation for the Court.

---

[226] A stand-out example would be *Ecodefence and Others v. Russia*, no. 9988/13, 14 June 2022, when, after nearly ten years, and post-expulsion, the Court finally addressed the application of the 'foreign agents' legislation of 2012 (as amended in 2016), finding clear violations of Articles 11 and 34. See text accompanying n 161, and strong criticism by former ECtHR judges Nussberger, n 126, 514 (delays to be 'deplored') and Yudkivska, n 126, 768.

[227] Cf calls for the CoE to adopt a far more robust and holistic approach to protect effectively civil society and civic space; see Muižnieks, N. (2023) 'Using the Summit to breathe new life into the Council of Europe', *European Human Rights Law Review*, 2: 126–34, 127, and McBride, J. (2023) 'Protecting and engaging with civil society: a challenge for the Council of Europe', *European Human Rights Law Review*, 2: 119–25.

[228] Cf Speech by Síofra O'Leary, 'Opening of Judicial Year', 27 January 2023, 7 (need to be 'open and self-critical' about the Court's performance in relation to Russia; highlighting lack of resources). On the ECtHR's limitations, see Chapter 3, section 3.3.1.

Firstly, for years it has been overburdened by tens of thousands of individual petition cases from 47 CoE states, and a growing number of very complex, difficult and challenging inter-state cases[229] (many directed against Russia), yet it has been under-resourced.[230] This continued failure to properly support the Court, and, indeed, the CoE financially, is a responsibility of all states, and it strengthened Russia's (financial blackmailing) hand in the late 2010s.[231] It is out of step with the rhetoric of appreciation for the ECtHR repeatedly offered by the states in various Declarations issued by them and the CM. This, and, for example, the CM's failure to condemn Russia's 2016 anti-ECHR amendments to the constitution, are particularly unforgiveable given the second point.

This concerns the position the Court was placed in by the CM and doubts as to whether the latter sufficiently supported the former. On successive occasions the ECtHR appeared to be a fall-back option with respect to Russia, after the CM had failed to bring it to heel (under the CoE Statute), as with Chechnya and the inter-state cases.[232] Yet, of course, the ECtHR does not have a Midas touch. It cannot be expected to make up for the failures of the CM, and should not be a type of convenient fig-leaf for it, or the inadequacies of the Article 3 and 8 CoE Statute. Even so, the ECtHR needs fulsome political (and financial) support from the CM as part of a holistic CoE regime which includes PACE, the CoE's Human Rights Commissioner, and the Venice Commission. That this support was lacking, or was insufficient, fits with Leach's observations about the CM's

---

[229] See sources cited at n 169.

[230] See 'Speech by Robert Spano – 25 October 2021' (available from: www.echr.coe.int/home [Accessed 10 July 2024]), highlighting concerns about budgetary restrictions and, consequently, significant staff reductions, and implying that the Court was struggling to cope. See further 'Memorandum of the European Court of Human Rights: Fourth Summit of Heads of State and Government of the Council of Europe', 20 March 2023, pp 2–3, referring to loss of 51 posts over the preceding decade, and unstable finances (reliance on voluntary contributions). The Court's budget for 2022 was €74,510,300, although this was increased in 2024, to €85,163,700. The 2024 budget for the International Criminal Court is more than double this: €187,084,300; that for the Court of Justice of the EU (in 2022) was nearly six times greater (€464,800,000).

[231] As to the CoE's precarious financial situation, in parallel with the 2014–2019 crisis, the CM's budgetary policy was of zero nominal growth (in effect reducing the budget, given inflation). Further, in 2017 Türkiye withdrew its 'major contributor' status. Even so, the CoE states could have, but did not, help immunise the CoE from Russia financial blackmail by themselves making up appropriate financial contributions required to fill the deficit Russia created (or threatened to), see Glas, n 16. The sums concerned (approximately €70 m) were small in the scheme of things.

[232] Note also the number of CoE states joining as third-party intervenors in the inter-state case against Ukraine, n 212, in contrast to the failure of such states to bring cases against Russia while it was in the CoE.

failure to confront Russia on Chechnya in the context of ECtHR cases. For him, the lack of political will shown by the CM, a kind of preference to turn a blind eye it seems, reflected 'a much wider problem'.[233] This was the CoE states' 'inadequate backing for the Court and their failure to take the trouble to work diligently to ensure that its judgments (against all states) are properly implemented, within a reasonable time period'. This meant that '[f]or the Russian people' there had been a 'disastrous failure to double down on judgments highlighting the state authorities' alarmingly increasingly repressive measures', as occurred over the 2010s especially.

Speaking in January 2023, the Court's President, Síofra O'Leary, may have had some of these points in mind when she suggested that 'a misplaced complacency may have installed itself in certain states over the last decades regarding the Convention's success in supporting and preserving democracy itself'.[234] Might one even suggest that the 'misplaced complacency' referred to could actually have been wilful in some instances?

5.4 Reykjavík rhetoric?

These arguments point to wider systemic weaknesses related to the institutional set up of the CoE.[235] Here one may suggest that the events of 2014–2019 pointed to how problems that then arose were deep-rooted, and reflected in what occurred earlier – or did not occur – with respect to Chechnya and Georgia, when the CM failed to act.[236]

To be clear, when one criticises the CM, really this is a criticism of the CoE states who are collectively represented in this executive CoE organ, yet, might it be said, risk becoming anonymous, faceless and unaccountable in that context?[237] Back in the 1990s these states championed Russia's entry into the CoE, promising to uphold CoE values, amidst optimistic visions of a new era of 'democratic security' in Europe. Thirty years on, in May 2023, the Heads of State and Government of the CoE states gathered in Reykjavík, issuing a Declaration, to stand 'united against Russia's war of aggression against Ukraine and to give further priority and direction to the [CoE's] work',[238] and to support the sovereignty of Ukraine, Georgia

---

[233] Leach, P. (2022) 'A time of reckoning? Russia and the Council of Europe', *European Human Rights Law Review*, 3: 219–27, 226.
[234] O'Leary, n 228, 3.
[235] See Chapter 7, section 4.
[236] See Chapter 3, section 2.
[237] Cf Palmer, P. (2017) 'The Committee of Ministers', in S. Schmahl and M. Breuer (eds) *The Council of Europe: Its Law and Policies*, Oxford: Oxford University Press, pp 137–65 ('the CM do[es] not have an effective will of [its] own: [its] "will" is the sum of those of the participating governments', 165).
[238] Council of Europe, 'Reykjavík Declaration – United around our values', 16–17 May 2023.

and Moldova. The Declaration referred to the CoE's historical origins and philosophy as European countries had united in 'the common belief that true democracies that uphold the rule of law and ensure respect for human rights were the best defence against authoritarianism, totalitarianism and war on our continent'. Russia's 'war of aggression against Ukraine' was referred to as 'a violation of international law, but [also] an attack on our democracies'. As in 1993, at Vienna,[239] but in very different circumstances, the states maintained that 'democratic security' was an imperative that had to be pursued by the CoE, while also countering 'the undermining of human rights, democracy and the rule of law'.

The extracts from the Reykjavík Declaration quoted came under a sub-heading titled 'The Europe we want'. If the CoE states are sincere in their stated aspirations, what is required is that in European capitals governments now resolve to live up to their rhetoric. They must steadfastly and resolutely back the CoE so that it is robust and able to act ahead of major problems, rather than issue warm words (and join inter-state cases) after things have gone so badly wrong. Here a clear lesson from this study is that the CoE states must fully support (politically and financially) those CoE institutions which have proven faithful guardians of CoE values.[240] Could that have made a difference with respect to Russia in the early years, when there may have been more leverage over it than in the 2010s when authoritarianism really took hold?

---

[239] Chapter 2, section 2.3.1.
[240] For broader reflection on the need for the CoE to evolve, see Muižnieks, n 227 and Leach, P. and Donald, A. (2023) 'Responding to seismic change in Europe: the road to Reykjavik and beyond', *European Human Rights Law Review*, 2: 95–111.

5

The Suspension and Expulsion of Russia: Legality and Legitimacy

1 Introduction

This chapter looks at how membership sanctions can be applied by the Council of Europe (CoE) and specifically in the context of Russia's expulsion from the CoE in 2022. At the outset we wish to define what we mean by membership sanctions. Membership sanctions are any restrictions of participatory rights that are applied to a member state of an international organisation by its statutory bodies. These sanctions can range from restriction of the voting rights in a particular organ of the organisation to suspension and expulsion from the organisation. In this chapter, however, we focus on suspension and expulsion.

The narrative of this chapter moves from a more general consideration of membership sanctions to a more specific examination of the questions related to suspension and expulsion of Russia from the CoE. The chapter will demonstrate that the application of membership sanctions is a controversial issue under international law generally. Given the inextricable link between politics and law in this context, there is no consensus among academics even as to whether or not membership sanctions should be applied at all. This chapter will briefly summarise the risks associated with the application of such sanctions including severing the links with the expelled member state and possibly punishing the people of the relevant member state more than the offending authorities. This does not mean that we would argue that membership sanctions should never be applied, as the threat of their application as well as occasional justified application might act as a deterrent, which in turn could increase the credibility and legitimacy of the organisation. We will also highlight that the likelihood of application of membership sanctions depends on the geopolitical considerations and legal regulations that exist in a particular organisation.

It is important that the organisation applying membership sanctions follows the proper legal procedures. This chapter then explains what is required by the CoE Statute and other relevant documents in order to apply membership sanctions on the members of the CoE. We identify that there are two types of expulsion envisaged: phased and immediate. The former includes multiple stages, it is long and complex and can be used when the CoE perhaps retains some hope that the member state can be 'socialised'.[1] Immediate expulsion is more likely to be a response to a crisis of great magnitude caused by a member state. It can be assumed that whenever the statute of an organisation provides for a legal procedure for expulsion as in the case of the CoE, it enhances the legitimacy of the process but also limits, albeit not decisively, the discretion of the decision-makers in a crisis situation.

Then we consider how the membership sanctions were (or were not) applied in practice by the CoE. We note that expulsion is a highly political process and despite legal regulations, dependent on the collective political will of the member states, a matter which has been discussed in previous chapters. To that end, we examine two historical cases in which application of membership sanctions was possible. We first explore the withdrawal of Greece from the CoE in the late 1960s, and then we consider the case of Türkiye[2] in the 1970s and 1980s when the membership sanctions arguably could have been applied but were not. We conclude that although both of these cases offer certain interesting parallels, they are significantly different – to the extent that Russia was the first state ever to be expelled in accordance with Article 8 of the Statute – and direct comparison with the Russian case is neither appropriate nor particularly helpful.

Finally, we offer a detailed legal analysis of the expulsion of Russia from the CoE. We provide a step-by-step chronicle of the process of expulsion and offer our assessment of its legality, validity and legitimacy. We point out that the CoE acted swiftly and decisively in response to Russia's aggression against Ukraine in February 2022. The Committee of Ministers (CM) initiated the immediate expulsion procedure the next day after the military attack took place. On 16 March 2022, after receiving an Opinion from the Parliamentary Assembly of the Council of Europe (PACE), the CM decided to expel Russia from the organisation.

We note that this decision is substantively indisputable, morally justified and a legitimate execution of the CM's statutory functions. However, we

---

[1] On socialisation of Russia in the CoE, see Roter, P. (2017) 'Russia in the Council of Europe: participation à la carte', in L. Mälksoo and W. Benedek (eds) *Russia and the European Court of Human Rights: The Strasbourg Effect,* Cambridge: Cambridge University Press, pp 26–56.

[2] In this monograph we use the contemporary name 'Türkiye' in all situations except when the title of the case or article or a quote uses the old name of 'Turkey'.

identify at least two potential procedural concerns that can be levelled against the Resolution of the CM of 16 March 2022 according to which Russia was expelled. We stress that even if these are considered procedural shortcomings they do not question the validity and necessity of the final outcome. The first issue is related to the fact that the CM set aside the information from the Russian authorities claiming that they had initiated the process of withdrawal based on a letter received the day before Russia was in fact expelled. The second issue is related, in that the CM did not 'request' Russia to withdraw in accordance with the precise wording of Article 8 of the Statute. We provide multiple legal and political reasons that explain these decisions and justify the validity of expulsion.

2 Expulsion of states from international organisations

There is no consensus or even a predominant view among commentators as to whether or not membership sanctions, in particular suspension and expulsion of states from international organisations, are a justified punishment for failing to abide by the rules of the organisation. Some commentators oppose the idea of such sanctions, especially expulsion, because after using this 'clumsy weapon'[3] the organisation removes the 'recalcitrant member' from the pressures of the organisation.[4] This argument is made especially forcefully in relation to global organisations for which peace, integration and cooperation are the key objectives.[5] Indeed, there are very few examples of expulsion from such global organisations.[6] Broadly speaking, all these views are related to the 'better in than out' argument discussed in Chapter 4. It has also been argued that international organisations apply membership sanctions

---

[3] Jenks, C.W. (1965) 'Due process of law in international organizations', *International Organization*, 19: 166.
[4] Amerasinghe, C.F. (2005) *Principles of the Institutional Law of International Organizations* (2nd edn), Cambridge: Cambridge University Press, pp 123–4; Duxbury, A. (2011) *The Participation of States in International Organisations: The Role of Human Rights and Democracy*, Cambridge: Cambridge University Press. See also White, N.D. (1996) *The Law of International Organisations*, Manchester: Manchester University Press, p 64; Sohn, L.B. (1964) 'Expulsion or forced withdrawal from an international organization', *Harvard Law Review*, 77: 1381–425.
[5] Morgenstern, F. (1986) *Legal Problems of International Organizations*, Cambridge: Cambridge University Press, p 53; Amerasinghe, n 4, 123.
[6] The Union of Soviet Socialist Republics (USSR) was expelled from the League of Nations in 1939. It was more common that a transgressor state would take the initiative to leave than be expelled. Take, for example, Japan which took the initiative to withdraw itself in advance of a possible expulsion upon the publication of the Report of the Lytton Commission of Inquiry which considered the events leading to the Empire of Japan's seizure of Manchuria.

unevenly, and if the problematic member is important economically and politically, it is less likely that membership sanctions will be applied.[7]

In their recent study of membership sanctions for political backsliding, von Borzyskowski and Vabulas argue that the application of these sanctions depends on two factors: first, the geopolitical leverage and, second, the institutional rules.[8] Of course, the use of membership sanctions for a war of aggression, as in the case of the expulsion of Russia from the CoE, is influenced by a fundamentally different set of considerations than for democratic backsliding. Nevertheless, these two factors are useful to understand why membership sanctions were not applied to Russia until its full-scale military aggression against Ukraine. In what follows, first, we will briefly summarise the role that Russia played in the CoE in recent years. We will then discuss the institutional rules of application of membership sanctions within the context of the CoE.

As mentioned in the previous chapters, Russia is the biggest country in Europe both in terms of territory and population.[9] It was argued that '[r]emaining member states have incentives to suspend violators only when the benefits outweigh the costs.'[10] For many years, it seemed that the cost of applying membership sanctions to Russia was prohibitively high for two main reasons: first, the resource implications or in other words, the *realpolitik* argument in favour of Russian membership. Russia was a major budgetary contributor to the CoE[11] and an important player both politically and economically. It increased the scope and prominence of the CoE and the prestige of its operation. It has been argued that the value of international organisations is that they allow cooperation that would not

---

[7] See von Borzyskowski, I. and Vabulas, F. (2019) 'Credible commitments? Explaining IGO suspensions to sanction political backsliding', *International Studies Quarterly*, 63: 139–40.

[8] von Borzyskowski and Vabulas, n 7, 139–40.

[9] Russia is the biggest country in the World totalling over 17 million square kilometres and covering over 3 per cent of the Earth surface; see www.weforum.org/agenda/2021/01/earth-surface-ocean-visualization-science-countries-russia-canada-china/ [Accessed 12 June 2024]. It is also the biggest country in Europe on the basis of population with over 140 million people living there; see *Statista*: www.statista.com/statistics/685846/population-of-s150elected-european-countries/ [Accessed 12 June 2024].

[10] von Borzyskowski and Vabulas, n 7, 142.

[11] Alongside France, Germany, Italy and the United Kingdom, Russia was a major contributor to the CoE budget. The full budget in 2022 was €477 m. In 2022, the contribution of the Russian Federation was €34,343,923. See Russian Federation, member page, available from: www.coe.int/en/web/portal/russian-federation [Accessed 12 June 2024]. Between 1 January 2016 and 1 January 2018, Türkiye has been acting as a major contributor to the CoE budget. See status of Turkey and budgetary implications, available from: https://rm.coe.int/status-of-turkey-and-budgetary-implications/16808e474c [Accessed 12 June 2024]. See Chapter 4 for a more in-depth discussion of Russia's financial relations with the CoE over 2017–2019.

happen without these organisations[12] and cooperation with Russia was seen as one of the strategic priorities and unique added-value propositions of the CoE. Therefore, the value of maintaining some aspects of this cooperation was perceived as high. The fact that democracy, human rights and the rule of law in Russia was consistently deteriorating over the previous decade or longer did not seem to play a decisive role in this calculation. It seems that until a member commits a 'fatal blow' to the fundamental values of the organisation, such as the Russian aggression against Ukraine, it is quite unlikely that membership sanctions would be used to address the slow decline into dictatorship. If Russia did not start the war in Ukraine it would almost certainly still be a member of the CoE, despite its record of increasingly potent transgressions since, in particular, 2014, as discussed in Chapter 4.

The second reason why the cost of applying membership sanctions was prohibitively high is because it was the people of Russia who were ultimately punished by expulsion more than the authorities of Russia. Indeed, such sanctions almost inevitably freeze almost all collaborations with the expelled state and for many stakeholders the 'better in than out' argument was crucial.[13] When on 16 September 2022 the European Convention on Human Rights (ECHR) ceased to be applicable in Russia, more than 140 million people lost the protection of the European Court of Human Rights (ECtHR).[14] When in 2018 there was a real chance that Russia would withdraw from the CoE, the then Secretary General of the Council, Thorbjørn Jagland in his address to PACE stated:

> We must protect people's human rights wherever they live and regardless of political circumstances. All our bodies have taken a clear stance on the illegal annexation of Crimea and the conflict in eastern Ukraine. But under the current international order it is not for us to solve these conflicts. And they should not prevent us from protecting people's rights in Ukraine – including in Crimea and Eastern Ukraine – and in the Russian Federation.[15]

---

[12] Martin, L.L. (2017) 'International institutions: weak commitments and costly signals' *International Theory*, 9: 354.

[13] Dzehtsiarou, K. and Coffey, D.K. (2019) 'Suspension and expulsion of members of the Council of Europe: difficult decisions in troubled times', *International and Comparative Law Quarterly*, 68(2): 473–6.

[14] Secretary General: Millions of Russians no longer protected by the European Convention on Human Rights, available from: www.coe.int/en/web/portal/-/secretary-general-millions-of-russians-no-longer-protected-by-the-european-convention-on-human-rights [Accessed 12 June 2024].

[15] Address by Thorbjørn Jagland to the Parliamentary Assembly of the CoE (22 January 2018), available from: www.coe.int/en/web/secretary-general/-/address-by-thorbj-rn-jagland-to-the-parliamentary-assembly-of-the-council-of-europe [Accessed 12 June 2024].

This argument of influencing from the inside[16] and not punishing rights-holders rather than the state prevailed over 2018–2019 and Russia remained in the CoE. This argument was also eagerly supported by Russian civil society.[17] In a way, this argument is also closely connected to the geopolitical significance of the organisation: although the number of potential issues and applicants increase the workload of the CoE's bodies, they also provide opportunities to impact the human rights, democracy and the rule of law situation in a member state. For instance, the highest number of applications to the ECtHR were consistently submitted against Russia. At the same time, judgments against Russia developed the law of the ECtHR in many crucial areas. So, while the core of this argument is idealist in the sense that it focuses on the protection of human rights in Russia, it has a clear connection to the geopolitical standing of the organisation.

For organisations aiming to promote human rights and democracy while lacking financial sanctions such as the CoE, it is important that their members share common values and actively engage in achieving its aims in good faith.[18] Dzehtsiarou and Coffey argue that in some circumstances the desire of an international organisation to keep a state that clearly fails to comply with its statutory aims within the organisation can undermine the importance of this organisation, and, in such cases, expulsion is a healthier option for the legitimacy and effectiveness of the organisation.[19]

Article 1 of the Statute of the CoE is clear as to the aims of the organisation: they include safeguarding the ideals and principles which are the common heritage of the members. Moreover, the CoE was established to maintain and further realise human rights and fundamental freedoms. Article 3 of the Statute lists the conditions of membership which are important for the application of membership sanctions. Members should accept the principles of the rule of law, human rights and fundamental freedoms and 'collaborate sincerely and effectively in the realisation of the aim of the Council'.[20] Although some departures from these common values do not seem to lead easily to the 'nuclear option' of membership sanctions, an event or act of an order or magnitude that is manifestly in contradiction with Article 3 of the Statute of the CoE such as an aggressive war is more likely to be followed with suspension and/or expulsion. This may be because such a dramatic violation of the

---

[16] See Chapter 4 for more detail.
[17] Baranov, K. and Dzhibladze, Y. (2018) 'Don't let Russia leave the Council of Europe', *Open Democracy*, available from: www.opendemocracy.net/en/odr/don-t-let-russia-leave-council-of-europe/[Accessed 12 June 2024]. See also Chapter 4.
[18] Jenks, n 3, 160.
[19] Dzehtsiarou and Coffey, n 13.
[20] Article 3 the Statute of the CoE.

fundamental values of the organisation is far more likely to generate a very large majority, or even consensus, among CM member states whereas lesser transgressions are likely to be decisively influenced by bilateral considerations and an appraisal of the possible costs of such a reaction on individual member states.

We have demonstrated that membership sanctions can lead to some clear negative consequences: they can undermine the geopolitical standing of the organisation, there are *realpolitik* and idealist arguments against using them but there are also good reasons too for deploying such sanctions. Regular disregard of the values of the organisation undermines the efforts and effectiveness of the organisation. Conversely, the application of sanctions might demonstrate that such behaviour cannot be tolerated and so might have a certain deterrent effect.[21] Furthermore, if gross violations of the rule of law, democracy and human rights are left to go unpunished they might embolden a state to commit even graver violations. Moreover, sanctioning gross violations can enhance the credibility and legitimacy of the international organisation.[22] However, if membership sanctions are applied it creates an expectation that the same will be done in all other comparable situations, which underscores the importance of the legal requirements for application of membership sanctions being followed consistently by the organisation.

3 The process of expulsion

Apart from the factor of geopolitical importance, the internal institutional rules are significant in considering the possibility and likelihood of applying membership sanctions. It has been argued that the presence of a clause for suspension and expulsion increases the chances of application of membership sanctions albeit quite insignificantly.[23] Those organisations that do not have suspension clauses in their founding documents can still quite successfully suspend and expel members. For example, the Charter of the Organization of American States as adopted in 1948 did not explicitly provide for expulsion. After the Cuban revolution in 1958, notwithstanding the lack of provision, the remaining members declared that the government of Cuba 'placed itself outside the inter-American system'.[24] This creative

---

[21] Drezner, D. (2007) *All Politics Is Global: Explaining International Regulatory Regimes*, Princeton: Princeton University Press, pp 203–4.
[22] Barnett, M. and Finnemore, M. (2004) *Rules for the World: International Organizations in Global Politics*. Ithaca, NY: Cornell University Press.
[23] von Borzyskowski and Vabulas, n 7, 148.
[24] Resolution VI: 'Exclusion of the Present Government of Cuba from Participation in the Inter-American System', Final Act, Eighth Meeting of Consultation of Ministers of Foreign Affairs, Punta del Este, Uruguay, Doc. No. OEA/Ser.C/II.8, 22–31 January 1962.

reading of the founding document was not accepted by all member states[25] and academic commentators.[26] Fenwick, however, argued that if a member state violates a foundational document of an international organisation this organisation has an implied right to expel.[27] Serbia and Montenegro were suspended from the Organization for Security and Co-operation in Europe (OSCE) between 1992 and 2000[28] despite the fact that the OSCE founding documents do not contain mechanisms of suspension.[29] The OSCE had to develop a mechanism of 'consensus minus one' for suspension and expulsion of participating states. In the case of the OSCE it is unlikely that Russia will be suspended despite some calls for that[30] as a few members of this organisation can block it.

This consideration does not present a challenge for the CoE as its Statute clearly provides for the power to expel.[31] This should, in principle, make the application of membership sanctions less controversial, or at least more predictable, though this is not necessarily in fact the case.

The legality of application of membership sanctions is crucial for the reputation of the organisation. It has been argued that 'if used in a premature and most of all not strictly legal way, suspension or expulsion of a member may cause damage to the organization ... and even to the whole concept of organized international cooperation'.[32] The CoE has developed an array of measures that can warn the state in question that it may be seriously breaching its obligations and so may not be acting in line with Article 3 of the Statute, such as monitoring missions and reports,[33] PACE reports and associated documents, rejection of PACE delegation credentials,[34] comments

---

[25] See Sohn, n 4, 1418.
[26] See, for example, Duxbury, n 4, 174.
[27] Fenwick, C.G. (1962) 'The issues at Punte Del Este: non-intervention v. collective security', *American Journal of International Law*, 56: 474.
[28] Serbia and Montenegro suspended as a participating State (8 July 1992); see www.osce.org/node/58332 [Accessed 12 June 2024].
[29] See the Helsinki Final Act, available from: www.osce.org/files/f/documents/5/c/39501.pdf, and the Charter of Paris for a New Europe, available from: www.osce.org/files/f/documents/0/6/39516.pdf [Accessed 12 June 2024].
[30] (2022) 'Kuleba calls for setting up procedure to suspend Russia from OSCE' *Ukrinform*, available from: www.ukrinform.net/rubric-ato/3452657-kuleba-calls-for-setting-up-procedure-to-suspend-russia-from-osce.html.
[31] Article 8 of the Statute of the CoE.
[32] Makarczyk, J. (1982) 'Legal basis for suspension and expulsion of a state from an international organization', *German Yearbook of International Law*, vol. 25, p 477.
[33] The monitoring procedure of the Parliamentary Assembly, available from: https://assembly.coe.int/committee/MON/Role_E.pdf [Accessed 12 June 2024].
[34] See, for example, PACE's resolution not to ratify the credentials of Azerbaijan. PACE Resolution 2527 (2024), 'Challenge, on substantive grounds, of the still unratified credentials of the parliamentary delegation of Azerbaijan', available from:

by the Secretary General,[35] debates in the CM, and many others. These are the warning signs which might not lead to suspension or expulsion of membership but indicate that the state failing in its compliance with the statutory obligations of the CoE. When none of these warning signs make a positive impact, then the issue of suspension and expulsion may be considered provided that the transgressions reach the threshold established in Article 8 of the Statute of the CoE and, importantly, provided there is a political will on the part of the CM to do so.

Suspension and expulsion of members are regulated by Article 8 of the Statute of the CoE. This sets out when a state may be expelled (the threshold requirements for expulsion), and the procedure for this. Until Russia was expelled from the CoE in 2022, the provision has never been utilised by the CM.

Regarding the threshold requirements, Article 8 may be triggered when '[a]ny member of the CoE … has seriously violated' Article 3 of the CoE Statute. In turn, Article 3 establishes that all members of the CoE should 'accept the principles of the rule of law and human rights and they should collaborate sincerely and effectively in the realisation of the aims of the Council as specified in Chapter I'. As to the latter, Article 1(a) notes that the 'aim of the Council of Europe is to achieve a greater unity between its members for the purpose of safeguarding and realising the ideals and principles are their common heritage and facilitating their economic and social progress'.

The process of expulsion should follow a three-step procedure, first, suspension: the first part of the first sentence in Article 8 states that '[a]ny member of the Council of Europe which has seriously violated Article 3 may be suspended from its rights of representation'. Step two, as set out in the second part of the first sentence of Article 8, is that the state concerned is 'requested by the Committee of Ministers to withdraw under Article 7'. The third step arises if this 'request' is ignored, for the second sentence of Article 8 reads: 'If such member does not comply with this request, the

---

https://pace.coe.int/en/files/33333/html [Accessed 12 June 2024] or, previously, citing Crimea, PACE suspends voting rights of Russian delegation and excludes it from leading bodies. PACE Resolution 1990 (2014), 'Reconsideration on substantive grounds of the previously ratified credentials of the Russian delegation', available from: www.assembly.coe.int/LifeRay/APCE/pdf/Communication/2014/20140410-Resolution1990-EN.pdf [Accessed 12 June 2024].

[35] See, for example, Statement from CoE Secretary General Marija Pejčinović Burić on the military attack by the Russian Federation on Ukraine, available from: www.coe.int/en/web/portal/-/statement-from-council-of-europe-secretary-general-marija-pejcinovic-buric-on-the-military-attack-by-the-russian-federation-on-ukraine [Accessed 12 June 2024].

Committee may decide that it has ceased to be a member of the Council as from such date as the Committee may determine.'

When a state is 'request[ed]' to withdraw from the Council of Europe, it is in fact told to leave it, although the language used under Article 8 is more diplomatic: it is 'requested' to withdraw (the equally authentic French text uses the terms 'invité'/'invitation').[36] After all, the CM has the ultimate power to terminate the membership, for it may expel the state if the 'request' is ignored, that is to say not 'compl[ied] with.' Again, the language of Article 8 here is more diplomatic: 'may decide that [the state] has ceased to be a member of the Council as from such date as the Committee may determine'.

Article 8 does not create an obligation on the CM to suspend the member state even if it has 'seriously violated' Article 3; this ultimately comes down to a political decision. Moreover, if a state was suspended, it does not necessarily need to be subsequently expelled. It may be, for example, that step one of the process – that is, suspension, and the threat of imminent expulsion – has an influence on the state, such that it is met by an appropriate reaction. The CM might decide that it is unnecessary to move to step two, that is, the actual request to withdraw under Article 7. Similarly, there is no obligation on the part of the CM to proceed to step three after step two ('may decide', second sentence Article 8) if having issued its request to withdraw, the response of the state in question is deemed by the Committee to be appropriate for its continued membership. In such circumstances, presumably the CM would withdraw its own 'request' to withdraw. In both instances, the interruption of the application of the steps foreseen under Article 8 would be on the basis that a state faced with the prospect of expulsion has reacted in a certain way such that it may remain a member, presumably on certain conditions being fulfilled. However, if the state fails to react positively and persists in violating Article 3, the letter of Article 8 allows the CM to choose whether or not to initiate steps one, two or three. Article 8 does not seem to empower the CM to skip steps.

Article 8 makes the CM the exclusive decision-maker in the process of suspension and termination of membership. Having said that, there is a political requirement for PACE to be consulted on this issue.[37] PACE may also pass a Recommendation for the CM to consider action under Article 8, as occurred in relation to Chechnya in 2000, though in that case the CM did not follow the request.[38] The Rules of Procedure of the CM are quite limited in this area and do not offer much clarity as to how the decisions

---

[36] Cf Article 7.
[37] CM Resolution (51) 30 C, available from: https://rm.coe.int/revision-of-the-statute/168074f0c5 [Accessed 12 June 2024].
[38] Discussed in Chapter 3.

of suspension and expulsion should be made in practice. Article 26 of the Rules provides that:

> All consideration of the suspension of a member must begin by a proposal for suspension put forward by at least one representative. The proposal must have been included in the agenda of the session at which it is discussed. The member concerned shall receive through the Secretary General a notification of the decision reached in its case. This notification shall set out the legal and financial consequences of the decision.[39]

According to Article 27 of the Rules of Procedure, the same mechanism should be followed for step three, that is, when the CM is deciding whether the suspended member should cease to be a member or cease to be suspended. It seems that technically the process mirrors the accession procedure to the CoE: the CM is expected to request the Opinion of PACE and then decide by two-thirds majority.[40]

The CM is not bound by the Opinion of PACE, but it would seem politically very difficult to ignore, at least not without good reason (for example, a major change in circumstances). After obtaining an Opinion from PACE, the CM may decide on the application of membership sanctions. In the case of Russia, the CM and the President of PACE held an in-camera meeting on 25 February 2022 to coordinate a concerted reaction to the unprecedented crisis, which immediately preceded the decision by the CM to suspend Russia's rights of representation.

Finally, Article 7 must be mentioned. This grants to any member state a unilateral right of withdrawal from the CoE by a formal notification to the Secretary General. Such withdrawal does not take effect immediately, but depends on when the notification is delivered within the CoE's financial year.[41] Russia attempted to withdraw in accordance with Article 7 the day before the CM, acting under Article 8, expelled it from the CoE. A question that therefore arises is whether a state's right to rely on Article 7 is qualified or suspended once Article 8 has been triggered. This is discussed further later.

---

[39] Article 26 of the Rules of Procedure of the CM.
[40] See Article 20.c of the Statute. See also de Vit, G. (1995) *The Committee of Ministers of the Council of Europe,* Strasbourg: Council of Europe, pp 49–50.
[41] 'If the notification is given during the first nine months of the financial year [January to December], the withdrawal takes effect at the end of that year. If, however, the notification is given only during the last three months, it will take effect only at the end of the next financial year,' Klein, E. (2017) 'Membership and observer status', in S. Schmahl and M. Breuer (eds) *The Council of Europe: Its Law and Politics,* Oxford: Oxford University Press, p 66.

The statutory regulation explained in the previous paragraphs does not seem overly complex. However, in practice this framework led to some complications which we will now consider. Although there are very few cases when membership sanctions were in fact used, the CoE has issued a number of regulations and explanations elaborating on the rules provided in the Statute. On this basis, we identify two types of expulsion – phased and immediate. The phased expulsion may take place when the situation with human rights, democracy and the rule of law deteriorates slowly and the CoE still has hope that the member state will return to compliance with its CoE obligations. This type of expulsion received a formal regulatory status by the introduction of the so-called complementary joint procedure.[42] The immediate expulsion is more likely to be a response to a major crisis, such as a war of aggression.

As Chapter 4 explains, the complementary joint procedure came in response to a statutory crisis within the CoE that emerged after Russia's annexation of Crimea in 2014. The problem was compounded in 2017 when the Russian authorities decided to unilaterally suspend the payment of their contribution to the budget of the CoE until the full and unconditional restoration of the credentials of the delegation of the Federal Assembly of the Russian Federation within PACE.[43] Here, we need to be clear: Russia's conditioning of the payment of its unconditional statutory contributions on the full reconstitution of its rights in PACE was an act of blackmail and coercion and had no basis in law of the CoE.

Development of the complementary joint procedure was an attempt to resolve the standoff between Russia and PACE. However, it was also argued at the time that the new procedure was designed to develop synergies between PACE and the CM and to provide for joint action by them and the Secretary General in order to strengthen the organisation's ability to react more effectively in situations where a member state violates its statutory obligations while still respecting the autonomy of the two bodies.[44] This

---

[42] PACE Resolution 2319 (2020), 'Complementary joint procedure between the CM and the Parliamentary Assembly in response to a serious violation by a member State of its statutory obligations', available from: http://assembly.coe.int/nw/xml/XRef/Xref-XML2HTML-en.asp?fileid=28568&lang=en [Accessed 12 June 2024].

[43] See PACE report, Doc. 14396, 15 September 2017, 'Call for a Council of Europe summit to reaffirm European unity and to defend and promote democratic security in Europe', available from: https://pace.coe.int/en/files/24017#trace-1 [Accessed 12 June 2024] para 12.

[44] PACE Resolution 2186 (2017), 'Call for a Council of Europe summit to reaffirm European unity and to defend and promote democratic security in Europe', available from: https://pace.coe.int/en/files/24210/html [Accessed 12 June 2024], para 16.

means that the need for coordination between the bodies requires a lengthier process which implies less efficiency, not more.

We need to make an important clarification here that puts the procedures enshrined in the Statute and further developed by the CoE in context. Ultimately, the decision to expel is a political one and the scope of discretion is determined by political agreement between the overwhelming majority of the member states (in the CM) as to whether to expel or not. That is why even in the organisations that did not have a statutory provision for expulsion, such de facto expulsion was possible. At the same time, as we have indicated, although the legality of the procedure is crucially important, the legal regulations might be read creatively if there is a political consensus to that end. Lengthy, phased procedures risk justifying the continuing presence of a problematic state in the organisation if there is no immediate will to expel and there is a hope that the pressure of expulsion can improve the situation. There is a risk that phased expulsion would provide a convenient excuse for the CoE not to apply the ultimate membership sanctions to a problematic member if they have not yet crossed certain red lines.

3.1 Immediate expulsion

As discussed previously, Article 8 envisages a sequence of actions. First, the CM should decide on suspension of rights of representation, then the member state is invited to withdraw under Article 7, and if no withdrawal or no significant change of circumstances happens then the CM can decide to expel the state. The Statute is silent as to the time to be given to the member state to withdraw; however, there is no reason why the CM could not be prescriptive about the timeframe. For example, it could 'request' the *immediate* withdrawal of the state under Article 7, or give the state only a very short period of time within which to act. Setting a short time frame or deadline for actioning the request would allow the CM to move to expulsion on a time scale that it so decides.

The expulsion of Russia shows that although expulsion could not happen immediately, it could be progressed in a relatively short period of time, namely between 23 February and 16 March 2022. This time was primarily needed due to the practical requirement of convening an Extraordinary Session of PACE. For general understanding of the process of membership sanctions we need to describe the phased expulsion here too.

3.2 Phased expulsion ('complementary joint procedure')

The phased expulsion was elaborated in 2019 under the 'complementary procedure between the Committee of Ministers and the Parliamentary Assembly in response to a serious violation by a member State of its statutory obligations'[45] and has never been used yet. According to the wording of the decision of the CM, the procedure 'will address only the most serious violations of fundamental principles and values enshrined in the Statute of the CoE'.[46] It seems that this procedure could be triggered in response to an event or set of circumstances that represent a serious violation of Article 3 of the Statute of the CoE. For instance, it could potentially be triggered in response to the Court finding a violation under Article 46(4) ECHR (the ECtHR infringement procedure).[47] The complementary joint procedure risks being a prolonged process, leading to unpredictable outcomes depending on the level of consensus among the member states. The length of time for such sanctions to be applied arguably provides maximum scope for states to walk back from the brink, but it may also simply render the sanction ineffective, and there is no guarantee that any corrective action would be taken in the meantime. Ultimately, the choice to give latitude to an 'offending' member state to correct their course comes down to a political determination by the member states. Very limited practice on Article 46(4) ECHR shows that it has taken the CM more than two years after the initial judgment to send the Article 46(4) ECHR request to the Court.[48] In a suitable case, failure to implement an Article 46(4) judgment could be an appropriate trigger for the complementary joint procedure.[49] On 11 July 2022, the Grand Chamber of

---

[45] CM Decision CM/Del/Dec(2019)129/2, 'A shared responsibility for democratic security in Europe', available from: https://search.coe.int/cm/Pages/result_details.aspx?ObjectId=090000168094787e [Accessed 12 June 2024].

[46] CM Decision CM/Del/Dec(2019)129/2, n 45.

[47] According to Article 46(4) ECHR the Court upon request from the CM can rule if the Contracting Party to the Convention 'refuses to abide' by a previous judgment. This procedure is often called 'infringement procedure'. For more detail see de Londras, F. and Dzehtsiarou, K. (2007) 'Mission impossible? Addressing non-execution through infringement proceedings in the European Court of Human Rights', *International and Comparative Law Quarterly*, 66(2): 467–90; Keller, H. and Marti, C. (2016) 'Reconceptualizing implementation: the judicialization of the execution of the European Court of Human Rights' judgments', *European Journal of International Law*, 26(4): 829–50; Glas, L.R. (2019) 'The European Court of Human Rights supervising the execution of its judgments', *Netherlands Quarterly of Human Rights*, 37(3): 228–44.

[48] In *Ilgar Mammadov v. Azerbaijan* (infringement proceedings) [GC], no. 15172/13, 29 May 2019, the judgment under Article 46(4) was delivered in 2019, which is five years after the initial judgment delivered in 2014. The latter judgment concerned the events that took place in 2013. The Court referred the case of *Kavala v. Turkey*, no. 28749/18, 10 December 2019 on 2 February 2022 (see https://search.coe.int/cm/Pages/result_details.aspx?ObjectID=0900001680a56447 [Accessed 12 June 2024]), while the initial judgment of the ECtHR was delivered in 2019.

[49] See 'Practical modalities for a complementary procedure between the CM and the Parliamentary Assembly in response to a serious violation by a member state of its statutory obligations', available from: https://rm.coe.int/1366d01-7app/16809a59c4 [Accessed 12 June 2024].

the ECtHR found a violation of Article 46(4) ECHR in the case of *Kavala v. Türkiye*.[50] At the time of writing, this judgment has not yet triggered the complementary joint procedure.[51]

Another potential 'trigger' for the initiation of the phased expulsion process could be an inter-state judgment of the Court identifying mass violations of human rights in a situation which is still ongoing. A report by PACE or investigation by the Human Rights Commissioner describing mass violations of human rights could also arguably trigger the complementary joint procedure, but there is no practice to either support or undermine this suggestion.

The complementary joint procedure can be initiated by either of the main statutory bodies: the CM, PACE or the Secretary General. Once initiated, the Secretary General should develop a road map for the member state in question which is expected to be implemented within roughly a year. According to the timeline suggested by the CM, the complementary procedure cannot last for less than one year and three months. In practice it will probably last much longer. Considering that the trigger to this procedure can take a long time the whole procedure can take years to complete. The last step of this procedure is the following:

> if the Committee of Ministers through a decision, by a two-thirds majority … after consultations with the Parliamentary Assembly and the Secretary General, concludes that there has been no improvement of the situation, and a serious violation of Article 3 by the member State concerned continues to exist, a move to the third and final stage of the process could be agreed in that decision. A Committee of Ministers' decision based on Article 8 of the Statute would follow.[52]

One could argue that this procedure was created to prolong the expulsion procedure where the immediate expulsion is not realistic. An alternative reading is that the procedure provides an opportunity to develop a consensus among the CoE's statutory organs to provide a stronger basis for expulsion. That said, when the situation reaches the level of emergency, the CoE can act swiftly if required: the decision that established the complementary joint procedure did not amend the Statute of the CoE[53] and does not exclude the

---

[50] *Kavala v. Türkiye* (infringement proceedings) [GC], no. 28749/18, 11 July 2022.
[51] At the time of writing (26 April 2023), the CM was still attempting to pursue high-level dialogue with Türkiye in relation to this case. See Decision CM/Del/Dec(2023)1459/H46-27, available from: https://hudoc.exec.coe.int/ENG?i=004-55161 [Accessed 12 June 2024].
[52] 'Practical modalities for a complementary procedure', n 49.
[53] See Resolution 2319 (2020), n 42, para 4.2

possibility of using immediate expulsion when it is necessary and appropriate. The documentation was explicit in that it would 'not preclude the direct implementation by the CM of Article 8, as provided in the Statute'. It also noted that 'a decision to act under Article 8 of the Statute ... in all aspects lies with the Committee of Ministers'.[54] In other words, if the event or act is of a scale, order or magnitude that is manifestly contrary to Article 3 of the Statute of the CoE and no dialogue can lead to a positive outcome, then the phased expulsion can be omitted and the CM can immediately initiate Article 8. This is what happened in 2022, when Russia launched its full-scale war of aggression against Ukraine.[55]

4 Comparable cases in the CoE's history

On the surface it appears that because the provisions regulating membership sanctions are included in the Statute of the CoE it should make the application of these sanctions more legalistic, legitimate and grounded. This may be seen to limit the ability of the organisation to respond rapidly to an emerging crisis, though the experience of Russia's expulsion in 2022 suggests otherwise. If the CM wishes to move decisively, it can do so.

Since its formation, only two states have left the CoE, Greece and Russia, though both under different circumstances. In the late 1960s, Greece withdrew from the CoE. The complementary joint procedure did not exist at the time, so the exit of Greece prior to its suspension is a *sui generis* situation and significantly different to the expulsion of Russia. Although in the 1970s Türkiye was on the brink of membership sanctions, they were never initiated.[56] In 2022, the offensive military operation against Ukraine triggered an extraordinarily quick response from the CoE resulting in the expulsion of Russia. We will now consider the Greek and Turkish cases and then provide a detailed analysis of the Russian expulsion from the CoE.

4.1 Greece's exit from the CoE in 1969

Greece withdrew from the CoE in 1969. The events that led to the withdrawal, the process of withdrawal and its consequences are well

---

[54] CM Decision CM/Del/Dec(2019)129/2, n 45.
[55] See the comments by Roeland Böcker, who stated that the complementary joint procedure was not even contemplated in February–March 2022, Böcker, R. (2023) 'Een ongekend moment. Multilateralisme en de Raad van Europa', *Nederlands Tijdschrift voor de Mensenrechten*, 48: 179.
[56] The situation in Cyprus has, however, been a permanent item on the agenda of the CM since the 1970s.

documented and discussed in legal scholarship.[57] In this short section we merely highlight the key milestones in Greece's temporary departure from the CoE and underscore why the Greek example does not shed much light, nor does it provide guidance in relation to the Russian expulsion from the CoE.

On 21 April 1967, a coup d'état took place in Greece. A military dictatorship was established, and human rights were significantly curtailed. Among other things elections were cancelled, the opponents of the regime were sent to prison and censorship was introduced. In June 1967, the then Consultative Assembly (now PACE)[58] recommended that the governments of the ECHR member states refer the Greek case either separately or jointly to the European Commission of Human Rights in accordance with the former Article 24 ECHR.[59] Parallel to the inter-state proceedings, the Consultative Assembly chose to initiate its own procedure on the basis of Article 23 of the Statute of the CoE.[60]

On 20 September 1967, the Danish, Norwegian and Swedish governments submitted an inter-state application before the European Commission on Human Rights against Greece. The Netherlands lodged their application on 27 September 1967. The applications alleged violations of multiple Articles of the Convention[61] notwithstanding that Greece had issued derogation

---

[57] See, for example, Bates, E. (2010) *The Evolution of the European Convention on Human Rights,* Oxford: Oxford University Press, pp 264–70; Risini, I. (2018) *The Inter-State Application under the European Convention on Human Rights,* Leiden: Brill, pp 108–24; Kiss, A.-C. and Vegleris, P. (1971) 'L'affaire grecque devant le Conseil de l'Europe et la Commission europeenne des Droits de l'homme', *Annuaire français de droit international,* vol. 17, Paris: CNRS Editions, pp 889–931; Benedek, W. (2020) 'The effectiveness of the tools of the Council of Europe against democratic backsliding: what lessons can be learned from the "Greek Case"?', *Austrian Law Journal,* 7(1): 1–21; Leuprecht, P. (2019) 'Fighting a dictatorship in the "homeland of democracy"', in D. Huber (ed) *Europe: A Human Enterprise, 30 Stories For 70 Years Of European History,* Strasbourg: CoE Publishing, pp 31–6.

[58] The Parliamentary Assembly of the CoE was called as such in the 1960s. In July 1974 the Standing Committee of the Consultative Assembly decided that the name 'Parliamentary Assembly' should be used in place of 'Consultative Assembly' since it reflected more accurately the role and composition of the Assembly.

[59] Consultative Assembly Resolution 346 (1967), 23 June 1967, Yb 10 (1967), pp 94–6.

[60] Article 23 CoE Statute allows PACE 'to discuss and make recommendations upon any matter within the aim and scope of the CoE as defined in Chapter I'. One motivation was that it was not likely that the Assembly would be able to see or discuss the findings of the Commission in the inter-state proceedings, as the report was to be discussed by the political body of the CoE, the CM, not by the deliberative body, the Assembly, see Coleman, H. (1972) 'Greece and the Council of Europe: the international legal protection of human rights by the political process', *Israeli Yearbook of Human Rights,* vol. 2, p 121, with reference to interviews with members of the Consultative Assembly.

[61] Articles 5, 6, 8, 9, 10, 11, 13 and 14 ECHR, later Articles 3 and 7 ECHR and 1 and 3 of Protocol 1 ECHR were added.

notices under Article 15 ECHR.[62] These applications were considered by the European Commission of Human Rights, the body that functioned within the ECHR system until it was abolished by Protocol 11 in 1998.[63] These applications were quite unusual as the applicant states had no 'direct self-interest' in the outcome of the case.[64] In the majority of inter-state cases, the applicant has some identifiable 'selfish' reason, apart from ideals of human rights protection, to pursue: for instance, the citizens of the relevant state(s) are involved in the events leading to the application,[65] or there is/was a military confrontation between two Contracting Parties to the Convention.[66]

On 29 January 1969, the Assembly decided 'not to recognize the credentials of any Greek delegation purporting to represent the Greek parliament until such time as the Assembly is satisfied that the freedom of expression is restored and a free and representative parliament is elected in Greece'.[67] This decision amounted to a de facto exclusion of the Greek representatives from the Consultative Assembly. The deliberative organ was not ready to await the report of the Commission finding violations of the ECHR.

In November 1969, the European Commission of Human Rights concluded a report in which it described multiple, serious violations of the ECHR by Greece, including torture of political prisoners. Moreover, it declared that Greece's Article 15 derogation had not been valid as there was no 'threat to the life of the nation' required to trigger it.[68] This report became a catalyst for the CM to consider the suspension of Greece, as a draft resolution to that effect had been included on the CM's agenda. This followed a call from PACE (January 1969) for Greece's suspension from the CoE on the basis that it had violated its statutory obligations.[69] Risini describes the subsequent events:

> the Committee of Ministers met in December 1969 in order to discuss a possible suspension of Greece from the Council of Europe under

---

[62] See (1967) 'Greek Notice of Derogation of Obligations Under Article 15 of the European Convention on Human Rights', *International Legal Materials*, 6(4): 829.

[63] For more information about the European Commission on Human Rights, see Myers, D.P. (1956) 'The European Commission on Human Rights', *American Journal of International Law*, 50(4): 949–51.

[64] See Benedek, n 57, 2–3.

[65] *Latvia v. Denmark*, no. 9717/20, struck off the list on 16 June 2020.

[66] *Georgia v. Russia (II)* [GC], no. 38263/08, 21 January 2021.

[67] Consultative Assembly Resolution of 547 (1969), 30 January 1969, Yb 12 (1969), 126.

[68] *The Greek Case*: Report of the European Commission on Human Rights: Application no. 3321/67, *Denmark v. Greece*; Application no. 3322/67, *Norway v. Greece*; Application no. 3323/67, *Sweden v. Greece*; Application no. 3344/67, *Netherlands v. Greece*, 1970.

[69] This was under parallel proceedings taken up by PACE, separate from the Commission's report.

Article 3 of the Statute of the Council of Europe … On 12 December 1969, the Greek foreign minister announced the Greek withdrawal from the Council of Europe under Article 7 [of the Statute of the Council of Europe]. Formally, Greece was a member of the Council of Europe until 31 December 1970 … Greece also denounced the ECHR under ex-Article 65 ECHR. Greece ceased to be a member of the ECHR on 13 June 1970.[70]

According to a contemporary commentator, the Greek delegation anticipated that it would lose a vote on suspension, so it walked out of the relevant CM's meeting, that is, before suspension was considered, denouncing the Statute of the CoE and the Convention.[71] A Resolution passed by the CM found that Greece had 'seriously violated Article 3 of the Statute [of the CoE]', and that there was no need to consider procedures for suspension under Article 8 of the Statute, as Greece had withdrawn from the CoE.[72]

The relatively swift and decisive actions of the CM in this case were not universally praised. Bates explains:

> For Commissioner Sorensen[73] the Committee of Ministers' handling of events represented a 'lost opportunity'. He argued that the Committee played its last card (threat of suspension) too early, that this precipitated the Greek government's actions and thus foreclosed the opportunities that otherwise existed for providing a Convention-based solution.[74]

It will be pointed out in the subsequent sections that similar views were relied upon to argue against expulsion of Russia for many years. Although the context of the expulsion of Greece was different and Commissioner Sorensen's view was conditioned by such context, the idea that expulsion should only be used as the option of last resort sounds familiar to those who followed the Russia–CoE relations in the last decade. The argument of 'better in than out' discussed previously has a strong persuasive value.

Although the Greek case is the only other case where a state left the organisation, it is largely incomparable to the expulsion of Russia from the CoE. Also, the CoE was a different organisation with different ambitions, operating in a different geopolitical environment back in the 1960s. This

---

[70] Risini, n 57, 85.
[71] Beckett, J. (1970–1971) 'The Greek case before the European Human Rights Commission', *Human Rights*, 1: 107. See also Benedek, n 57, 2–3.
[72] Committee of Ministers, Resolution (69) 51, 'On Greece', 12 December 1969, available from: https://rm.coe.int/09000016804faa01 [Accessed 28 June 2024].
[73] Member of the Human Rights Commission.
[74] Bates, n 57, 268.

also explains why the geopolitical damage for the expulsion of Greece was incomparable to the expulsion of Russia. Although some loose parallels may be drawn with the Greek case, one must avoid conflating the two.

The first key difference between Greece leaving the Council and Russia being expelled from it is the fact that Article 8 of the CoE Statute was not triggered by the time Greece withdrew, whereas it had for Russia when it purported to do so. In the Greek case, the *threat* of triggering Article 8 prompted Greece to withdraw – in short, Greece got its move in first, exiting the CoE before the CM could debate suspension, and thus evading Article 8. However, this was *not* the case with Russia in March 2022. As will be noted later, the Article 8 process was triggered by the CM on 24 February 2022, when it *was* suspended from the CoE, and this process was followed through thereafter, culminating in the expulsion decision of 16 March 2022. The fact that Russia attempted to frustrate this process on 15 March, by its purported withdrawal from the CoE under Article 7, may raise some parallels with what occurred with Greece in the late 1960s but the process in the Greek case had not yet started properly, and so it could not have been interrupted.

In terms of the politics of these events there are some similarities between 1969 and 2022, when seen from the perspective of the sanctioned state. In both the Greek and Russian instances each state acted in anticipation of the likely application of the membership sanctions, by its purported unilateral withdrawal. Given the timings, and context, it may be assumed that the key reason for doing so in both cases was political. Being expelled from the CoE is a highly political and deeply humiliating act. It signals that the state has committed actions that are so repugnant to the CoE's values that its membership can no longer be tolerated. Withdrawal before expulsion would be an attempt to lessen the indignity of what was about to occur. It enables the state to *claim* – disingenuously – that it was not actually expelled but that it chose to leave. Such a strategy may also allow it to raise allegations of injustice and inappropriate procedures on the part of the CoE, potentially distracting from the illegality of its own actions which had led to the Article 8 processes in the first place.[75]

The circumstances were such that in 1969 Greece had the opportunity to withdraw while in 2022 Russia was immediately expelled under Article 8. Although as we have stated, there are important political differences between withdrawal and expulsion, the ultimate legal consequences are the same – the member state ceases to be the member of the organisation, its

---

[75] For example, in relation to Greece, the Commission's report had been leaked prior to the relevant meeting of the CM. The Greek government blamed the Commission and accused it of bias against Greece, arguing its report should be null and avoid. This was just before Greece withdrew from the Council of Europe.

rights and obligations vis-à-vis this organisation end. The legal conditions of such withdrawal or expulsion can be different. For instance, the timing is different, expulsion can arguably have an immediate effect as it did in the case of Russia, while the withdrawing state carries on being formally a member until the end of the 'notice period' (in accordance with Article 7) as in the case of Greece. However, and to reiterate, the most important differences are political and 'emotional'. Even despite the fact that Greece was a military dictatorship, and it was found to be in violation of the prohibition of torture, according to the Commission, it still had the opportunity to withdraw. The CM was moving through various procedural steps rather than jumping to the decisive point of expelling Greece. In the case of Russia, the intention of the CM was clear: given the gravity of its actions, Russia could not just leave, it had to be expelled from the organisation despite having to 'expedite' the process of expulsion as a result.

The second important difference between 1969 and 2022 is that, arguably, the consequences of Greek withdrawal were much less severe for the Strasbourg system than the expulsion of Russia. According to the text of the ECHR that was current in 1969, the Contracting Parties could choose to accept the jurisdiction of the ECtHR and the right of individual petition. In the 1960s, Greece did neither, so there were no pending cases against Greece except the inter-state applications at the Commission mentioned earlier. It is therefore impossible to draw meaningful parallels with the Greek situation in relation to how the ECtHR would deal with the over 18,000 applications pending against Russia at the moment of expulsion. Moreover, the budget of the CoE would shrink significantly, as Russia, unlike Greece, was one of the major financial contributors. These are just the illustrative examples among many others of the differences in impact between the Greek withdrawal and the Russian expulsion.

Having said all that, there are still important lessons that one can learn from the Greek case. It seems that although Russia does not engage with the ECtHR (post-expulsion), this should not shield it from being held to account for its human rights transgressions under the Convention. Here, the Greek case provides guidelines: the Commission in the second Greek case pointed out that the failure to participate in the proceedings before the Commission cannot absolve the respondent state of the responsibility under the Convention, but equally it argued that finding automatic violations should not happen.[76] This reasoning is important in the context of the Russian expulsion. It means that non-participation of the state cannot

---

[76] *Denmark, Norway and Sweden v. Greece*, no. 4448/70, Commission (plenary) decision of 16 July 1970; see also *Cyprus v. Turkey (IV)* [GC], no. 25781/94, ECHR 2001-IV, paras 10–12.

prevent the ECtHR from dealing with the applications that were submitted and not decided before expulsion takes effect.[77] Another important lesson which perhaps falls outside the legal realm is the fact that the return of the state is possible after a change in political regime in the country. It is hardly imaginable that Putin's Russia could be accepted back to the CoE, but one must not rule out the possibility of a democratic Russia, based on the rule of law seeking to return one day. Any possible return of Russia will almost certainly be much more complex than the return of Greece, which was admitted back only five years after withdrawal following a change of government. A key challenge in the case of Russia is that there is a significant number of judgments against Russia – including leading and inter-state cases – for which execution is pending and it would seem foolhardy to allow Russia back to the CoE without the new Russian government enforcing or at least clearly committing to enforce all of these judgments. This prospect is also likely to be contingent on Russia cooperating with accountability mechanisms for its alleged crimes in Ukraine.

4.2 Turkish military action in Cyprus (1974) and military coup (1980)

Two relevant examples when application of membership sanctions was arguably possible are the litigation relevant to Turkish occupation of Cyprus in the 1970s and the military coup in the 1980s. In this section we will review the key reasons why Türkiye was not suspended from the CoE when it occupied a part of Cyprus in 1974 and, subsequently, when a military coup took place in Türkiye in 1980, although one could plausibly argue that the membership sanctions could have applied.

This section does not aim to provide a detailed account of events, but rather lists the key relevant points and explains why, despite several attempts by PACE to trigger Article 8 of the Statute, this was not followed up by the CM.

The events in Cyprus started with the Greek-sponsored coup on the island on 15 July 1974 and the intervention by Türkiye five days later. As a result, Türkiye occupied around 40 per cent of the territory of Cyprus. This is how the outcomes of this invasion were described:

> The consequences of the Turkish intervention in Cyprus were devastating both in human and in material terms. Nearly half of the population of Cyprus was uprooted; some 4,000 Greek Cypriots, including civilians, were killed; 2,100 people were listed as missing, while seventy percent of Cyprus' economic output was under the

---

[77] This issue will be discussed in more detail in Chapter 6.

control of the Turkish army. Moreover, there was extensive documented evidence of rape, murder, torture, looting, forced detention and deportation of Greek Cypriots, confiscation of property, etc., by the Turkish army.[78]

Subsequently, the Cypriot government submitted four inter-state applications (in 1974,[79] 1975,[80] 1977[81] and 1994[82]). The litigation lasted for more than four decades. In the cases of *Cyprus v. Turkey (I)* and *(II)*, which were dealt with together, the CM – a political institution, not a court – was unable to reach any decision following the report of the Commission under old Article 32 ECHR. According to this Article, the CM had to vote whether there had been a violation of the Convention or not, and was effectively the decision-making organ in the absence of the jurisdiction of the Court to hear the case. The CM's only action with respect to the *Cyprus v. Turkey (III)* case was to decide to publish the Commission report in 1992.[83]

The Consultative Assembly[84] had established a working group on Cyprus as early as 5 September 1974 and had on various occasions adopted a number of Recommendations pertaining to humanitarian and political aspects of the situation on the island. However, it had not pursued any deeper engagement with the Cyprus issue, such as calling for action under Article 8, quite unlike in the so-called Greek case in the late 1960s.[85]

Only *Cyprus v. Turkey (IV)* reached the ECtHR, as Türkiye accepted the Court's jurisdiction in 1990; the fourth inter-state application led to a judgment in 2001.[86] The Court found multiple violations of the ECHR. Finally, in 2014, the Court rendered a judgment on just satisfaction[87] to the

---

[78] Coufoudakis, V. (1982) 'Cyprus and the European Convention on Human Rights: the law and politics of Cyprus v. Turkey, applications 6780/74 and 6950/75', *Human Rights Quarterly*, 4(4): 451.

[79] *Cyprus v. Turkey (I)*, no. 6780/74.

[80] *Cyprus v. Turkey (II)*, no. 6950/75.

[81] *Cyprus v. Turkey (III)*, no. 8007/77.

[82] *Cyprus v. Turkey (IV)*, n 76.

[83] Resolution DH (92)12 of the CM, 2 April, 1992, 13 HRLJ 181 (1992). In particular, the CM's ' "absolute inertia" with respect to the third inter-state application between Cyprus and Turkey met with criticism', Tomuschat, C. (1992) 'Quo Vadis, Argentoratum? The success story of the European Convention on Human Rights – and a few dark stains', *Human Rights Law Journal*, 13(11–12): 402.

[84] The Parliamentary Assembly of the CoE was called Consultative Assembly at the material time.

[85] Specific references in Coufoudakis, V. (1982) 'Cyprus and the European Convention on Human Rights: the law and politics of Cyprus v. Turkey, Applications 6780/74 and 6950/75', *Human Rights Quarterly*, 4(4): 465.

[86] *Cyprus v. Turkey (IV)*, n 76.

[87] *Cyprus v. Turkey (IV)* (just satisfaction) [GC], no. 25781/94, ECHR 2014.

victims of human rights violations. None of these events triggered suspension or expulsion of Türkiye from the CoE.

The second set of events worth mentioning here is the military coup that happened in Türkiye in 1980. This crisis can be compared to the Greek military coup of 1967 discussed earlier but, unlike in the case of Greece, the CoE has never come close to the suspension of Türkiye, although there were calls from the members of PACE to that effect. One commentator observes:

> As soon as the Parliamentary Assembly resumed sessions there were numerous moves that called for the suspension of Turkey's membership. Some parliamentarians, particularly socialists, were pressing for the suspension of Turkey's membership on the grounds that the Council did so when the Colonels' coup took place in Greece in 1967. Parallels could easily be found between the two cases. Since a democratic form of government was the prerequisite of membership according to the statute, expulsion would be a straightforward measure until democratic rule were restored. In the meeting of the Committee of Foreign Ministers, just a month after the coup, [the] Turkish Foreign Minister emphasized 'the government's determination' to restore parliamentary democracy in the shortest possible time and reaffirmed that Turkish government in this transition period would 'conform totally to the principles of the rule of law, and the respect for human rights'.[88]

In May 1981, PACE decided not to 'envisage the prolongation of the term of office of the Turkish delegation.'[89] This was clearly a reaction to the coup as PACE also noted that it 'looks forward to the time when developments in Türkiye will enable it to welcome back in its midst an elected and properly constituted Turkish delegation'.[90] However, the situation was not resolved quickly and the pressure from the CoE mounted. At one point, the Turkish Prime Minister threatened that Türkiye would be prepared to leave the CoE.[91] In 1982, PACE called the member states to bring an inter-state complaint against Türkiye under the ECHR. France, the Netherlands, Denmark and Sweden did so in 1982.[92]

In 1983, in Resolution 794, PACE decided 'to give serious consideration to making a recommendation to the CM aiming at application of Article

---

[88] Dagi, I.D. (1996) 'Democratic transition in Turkey, 1980–83: the impact of European diplomacy', *Middle Eastern Studies*, 32(2): 132.
[89] Term of office of the Turkish parliamentary delegation, doc 398, 14 May 1981, available from: https://pace.coe.int/en/files/13604 [Accessed 12 June 2024].
[90] Term of office of the Turkish parliamentary delegation, n 89.
[91] Dagi, n 88, 132.
[92] *Denmark, France, Norway, Sweden and the Netherlands v. Turkey*, no. 9940/82 to 9944/82.

8'.⁹³ However, no such Recommendation was passed. The political pressure at the level of PACE was exercised more cautiously here than in the case of Greece in the late 1960s.⁹⁴ It appears that on this occasion the Assembly decided to show a certain degree of deference towards the proceedings before the European Commission of Human Rights.⁹⁵

A commentator argued that 'the Committee of Ministers never gave a decision on suspension (Turkey's strategic position, between east and west, obviously made a diplomatic solution seem the better option)'.⁹⁶ This perhaps is a fair description of the events, politically speaking. For expulsion it is not enough to just seriously violate Article 3 of the Statute of the CoE, and if that was enough the CoE may have fewer member states than it does today. As discussed earlier, the magnitude of the alleged violations and the broader political context must also be taken into account. The balancing exercise between severity of the actions of the member state and geopolitical damage to the organisation played in Türkiye's favour. In the cases of Greece and Russia (albeit only in 2022), the political will and the magnitude of crises reached the tipping point required for resorting to suspension and expulsion, while in Türkiye's case they did not.

As with the debates surrounding the application of membership sanctions to Russia (and to Greece in the late 1960s), there were two camps in the CoE in relation to the issue of expulsion of Türkiye: those who pushed for suspension and expulsion, and those who were arguing in favour of continuing dialogue. In this case, the CoE chose a middle ground: 'At the end the prevailing view was that the Council should neither be too soft about the suspension of democracy and violation of human rights nor press too hard for the expulsion of Turkey. Therefore, Turkey's membership issue was kept on the agenda throughout the period.'⁹⁷

The inter-state litigation launched in the 1980s ended with a friendly settlement in December 1985⁹⁸ to the dissatisfaction of some commentators who pointed out that:

---

⁹³ Resolution 794 (1983), 'Situation in Turkey', available from: https://pace.coe.int/en/files/16205 [Accessed 12 June 2024].
⁹⁴ Pancracio, J.-P. (1984) 'La Turquie et les Organes Politiques du Conseil de L'Europe', *Annuaire Français de Droit International,* 30: 161; see also Kälin, W. (1987) 'Die Vorbehalte der Türkei zu ihrer Erklärung gem. Art. 25 EMRK', *EuGRZ,* 421.
⁹⁵ PACE Resolution 822 (1984) adopted on 10 May 1984, stating in para 15: 'Reaffirming its interest in the investigation currently in progress before the European Commission of Human Rights'.
⁹⁶ Benoît-Rohmer, F. and Klebes, H. (2005) *Council of Europe Law: Towards a pan-European Legal Area,* Strasbourg: CoE Publishing, p 41.
⁹⁷ Dagi, n 88, 134.
⁹⁸ Risini, n 57, 172–6.

Western European states, who had put forth detailed allegations based on specific cases reported by Amnesty International and victims, settled their complaint on the basis of Turkey's vague promises. They completely overlooked their own allegations concerning the violations of the right to fair trial, freedom of expression and freedom of association, accepted Turkey's vague expressions of the intention to lift martial law without addressing the question of derogations and let Turkey off the hook regarding serious allegations of torture.[99]

It is not impossible that the Turkish membership will be under threat in the near future.[100] The infringement proceedings in the case of Kavala found a violation of the Convention and the complementary joint procedure might be triggered. It is unlikely the CoE will have an appetite to expel another important member so soon after the expulsion of Russia, though on the other hand there may well be a renewed focus on good faith compliance with CoE standards and the integrity of the ECHR system. Furthermore, one cannot rule out the possibility of voluntary withdrawals, if political discussions in the direction of membership sanctions begin to intensify. However, a detailed analysis of this question falls outside the ambit of this monograph.

5 Analysing Russia's expulsion from the CoE

In this section we will first discuss the events leading up to the expulsion of Russia from the CoE and then consider the legality and legitimacy of the process. This story begins on 24 February 2022, when Russian President Putin launched a full-scale invasion of Ukraine.[101]

5.1 Russia's invasion and the CM's immediate triggering of Article 8 (24 February 2022)

On the very same day as the invasion, 24 February, the CM concluded that there had been a 'serious violation' of Article 3 of the CoE Statute – only the second time it had ever done so[102] – and immediately indicated its

---

[99] Kurban, D. (2020) *Limits of Supranational Justice,* Cambridge: Cambridge University Press, p 62.
[100] See Dzehtsiarou and Coffey, n 13.
[101] Ward, A., Toosi, N. and McLeary, P. (2022) 'Russia attacks Ukraine', *Politico*, available from: www.politico.com/news/2022/02/23/russia-invasion-ukraine-00011238 [Accessed 12 June 2024].
[102] In section 4.1 of this chapter, we explained that it was previously done in relation to Greece in the 1960s, albeit this was after Greece's withdrawal.

preparedness to trigger Article 8.[103] This it did, the next day, 25 February, when the CM decided to 'suspend the Russian Federation from its rights of representation in the CoE in accordance with Article 8 of the Statute of the CoE'.[104] For the first time ever, then, the CM acted under Article 8.

For an organisation which is not famous for its speed and decisiveness in response to ongoing events,[105] this decision and the way in which it was adopted were truly unprecedented. Although the voting in the CM is confidential it has been widely reported that only one country apart from Russia voted against: Armenia, while Türkiye abstained, Azerbaijan did not vote and Serbia was reportedly not present.[106] Although unanimity is not required for such a decision to be adopted[107] the voting result – if accurate – shows the overwhelming agreement among the member states of the Council that Russia had to be suspended. The CM stated that the suspension was effective immediately.

Also on 25 February 2022, Tiny Kox, the President of PACE stated that he was 'deeply appalled by the military attack of the Russian Federation against Ukraine',[108] and announced an extraordinary session of PACE on

---

[103] The CM issued a Decision (CM/Del/Dec(2022)1426bis/2.3) 'Situation in Ukraine – measures to be taken, including under Article 8 of the Statute of the Council of Europe', see https://search.coe.int/cm/Pages/result_details.aspx?ObjectID=0900001680a5a360 [Accessed 12 June 2024], in which it 'condemned in the strongest terms the armed attack on Ukraine by the Russian Federation in violation of international law' [para 1]. It decided 'to examine without delay, and in close co-ordination with the Parliamentary Assembly and the Secretary General, the measures to be taken in response to the *serious violation by the Russian Federation of its statutory obligations as a Council of Europe member State*' [para 2, emphasis added]. The Committee agreed to meet on the next day, 'with a view to considering measures to be taken, including under Article 8 of the Statute of the Council of Europe', para 7.

[104] The document referred, again, to the 'serious violation by the Russian Federation of its obligations under Article 3 of the Statute of the Council of Europe'. It also highlighted that there has been 'an exchange of views with the Parliamentary Assembly in the Joint Committee'. Decision (CM/Del/Dec(2022)1426bis/2.3), n 103.

[105] Drzemczewski and Lawson argued that the reaction of the organs to Russia's invasion stands 'in marked contrast to the internal divisions and hesitations with which various bodies reacted to the Russian annexation of Crimea in 2014 and the deterioration of human rights in Russia in general', Drzemczewski, A. and Lawson, R. (2022) 'Exclusion of the Russian Federation from the Council of Europe and the ECHR: an overview', *Baltic Yearbook of International Law*, vol. 21, p 41.

[106] See, for instance, Drzemczewski and Lawson, n 105, 43.

[107] According to Article 20d of the Statute, a two-thirds majority of the representatives casting a vote and of a majority of the representatives entitled to sit on the Committee is required to adopt such decision.

[108] PACE President reacts to Russian military attack on Ukraine (24 February 2022), available from: https://pace.coe.int/en/news/8610/le-president-de-l-apce-reagit-a-l-attaque-militaire-russe-contre-l-ukraine [Accessed 12 June 2024].

14–15 March 2022.[109] In response, the former Russian President and then Deputy Chairman of the Security Council of Russia, Dmitry Medvedev, immediately reacted by saying that 'suspension of the membership is a good opportunity to restore some important measures deterring the most heinous crimes'. He then confirmed that he meant the death penalty, which is in 'active use in the US and China'.[110] The Ministry of Foreign Affairs of Russia chose not to comment.

On 2 March 2022, the CM adopted a Resolution on legal and financial consequences of the suspension of Russia from the CoE.[111] In this Resolution the Committee highlighted that the suspension does not affect the participation of the Russian Federation in all treaties concluded under the auspices of the CoE or the work of the Human Rights Commissioner. In particular, it was stated that:

> The Russian Federation remains subject to its obligations under the European Convention on Human Rights. The judge elected to the European Court of Human Rights in respect of the Russian Federation remains a member of the Court, and any current and future applications introduced against or by this High Contracting Party will continue to be examined and decided by the Court. The Russian Federation may continue to participate in the meetings of the Committee of Ministers only when the latter exercises its functions in respect of the supervision of the execution of judgments under Article 46 of the Convention with a view to providing and receiving information concerning the judgments where it is the respondent or applicant State, without the right to participate in the adoption of decisions by the Committee nor to vote.[112]

The Russian Ministry of Foreign Affairs officially reacted to these events on 10 March 2022. In their statement they claimed that:

---

[109] Parliamentary Assembly – Extraordinary Session (14–15 March 2022), available from: https://search.coe.int/cm/Pages/result_details.aspx?ObjectID=0900001680a5a 457 [Accessed 12 June 2024].

[110] (2022) 'Медведев увидел в приостановке членства в СЕ повод вернуть смертную казнь' ('Medvedev sees the suspension of membership of the CoE as an opportunity to restore the death penalty'). (Translated by the authors), *RBC News*, available from: www.rbc.ru/politics/26/02/2022/6219ec289a79470d35420698 [Accessed 12 June 2024].

[111] Resolution CM/Res(2022)1, 'On legal and financial consequences of the suspension of the Russian Federation from its rights of representation in the Council of Europe', available from: https://rm.coe.int/2022-cm-resolution-1/1680a5b463.

[112] Resolution CM/Res(2022)1, n 111, para 7.

[u]nfriendly states of the EU and NATO, by abusing their majority in the Committee of Ministers of the Council of Europe, continue to destroy the Council of Europe and common legal and humanitarian space in Europe … Russia will not participate in the transformation by NATO, with the EU following it obediently, of the oldest organisation in Europe into another place for reading mantras about Western superiority and narcissism. They can enjoy each other's company without Russia.[113]

It was unclear what the Russian authorities implied when they said that they would not participate in the CoE. Some media even announced that this meant Russia's withdrawal from the CoE[114] but this was not officially confirmed. Moreover, some Russian officials opined that Russia *should* withdraw, for instance, on 11 March 2022 this was suggested by the Chairman of the State Duma's international affairs committee.[115] However, several days later, the Press Secretary of the President of Russia informed in the morning of 15 March 2022 that Putin had not yet made up his mind on that issue.[116] Later that day Russia did purport to withdraw from the CoE, under Article 7, a point we shall come back to shortly.

In the meantime, however, on 10 March, the CM had formally asked PACE (to meet in extraordinary session on 14–15 March) to provide its Opinion in relation to the potential further recourse of Article 8 of the Statute.[117] The Committee did so in a Decision considering the consequences of the aggression of Russia against Ukraine, which it described as 'a breach of peace

---

[113] (2022) 'Заявление МИД России о ситуации в Совете Европы' ('Statement of the [Ministry of Foreign Affairs] MFA of Russia about the situation in the Council of Europe'). (Translated by the authors), available from: https://mid.ru/ru/foreign_policy/news/1803555/ [Accessed 12 June 2024].

[114] Gotev, G. (2022) 'Russia leaves Council of Europe, avoiding being kicked out', *Euractiv*, available from: www.euractiv.com/section/global-europe/news/russia-leaves-council-of-europe-avoiding-being-kicked-out/ [Accessed 12 June 2024]; see also Leach, P. (2022) 'A time of reckoning? Russia and the Council of Europe', *European Human Rights Law Review*, 222(3): 219–27.

[115] *TASS* (2022) 'Russia must leave Council of Europe this year – Duma committee's chief', *TASS*, available from: https://tass.com/politics/1420649 [Accessed 12 June 2024].

[116] Постникова, Е. (2002) 'Решающий уход: в каких условиях Россия покидает Совет Европы' (Postnikova, E. (2002) 'Decisive exit: what are the conditions of Russia's withdrawal from the CoE'), *Izvestiya*. (Translated by the authors), available from: https://iz.ru/1305541/ekaterina-postnikova/reshaiushchii-ukhod-v-kakikh-usloviiakh-rossiia-pokidaet-sovet-evropy [Accessed 12 June 2024].

[117] Decision CM/Del/Dec(2022)1428bis/2.3 'Consequences of the aggression of the Russian Federation against Ukraine', section 9, available from: https://search.coe.int/cm/Pages/result_details.aspx?ObjectId=0900001680a5c619 [Accessed 12 June 2024].

of unprecedented magnitude on the European continent since the creation of the CoE'. The Committee stated that it:

> remained determined to act in close co-ordination with the Parliamentary Assembly in the context of further measures to be taken in response to the serious violations by the Russian Federation of its statutory obligations as a member State of the Council of Europe and agreed to consult the Parliamentary Assembly on potential further use of Article 8 of the Statute of the Council of Europe.[118]

5.2 PACE's emphatic response: 'the Committee of Ministers should request the Russian Federation to immediately withdraw' (14–15 March 2022)

On 14 and 15 March, PACE held its Extraordinary Session and adopted a unanimous[119] Opinion calling for Russia's expulsion under Article 8.

Opinion 300 referred to the 'continuation of the war of aggression waged by the Russian Federation against Ukraine since 20 February *2014*' (emphasis added), the year being a reference to the first invasion of Ukraine by Russia eight years previously. It then referred to the escalation of Russian aggression since 24 February 2022, Russia having chosen 'recourse to force over dialogue and diplomacy to achieve its foreign policy objectives, in violation of the legal and moral norms that govern the peaceful coexistence of States'. The Opinion described the conduct as showing *'disregard for the very essence of the Council of Europe, as enshrined in its Statute,* which is the conviction that the pursuit of peace based upon justice and international co-operation is vital for the preservation of human society and civilisation' (emphasis added).[120] The PACE's Opinion stated that what has occurred was in breach of core international standards such as the Charter of the United Nations, and that it was:

> a serious breach of Article 3 of the Statute of the Council of Europe and a violation of the obligations and commitments that the Russian Federation accepted upon becoming a member of the Organisation, including the commitments to settle international and internal disputes by peaceful means, rejecting resolutely any threats of force against its

---

[118] Decision CM/Del/Dec(2022)1428bis/2.3, n 117.
[119] 216 members voted in favour, 3 abstained and nobody voted against this opinion. PACE Opinion 300, 'Consequences of the Russian Federation's aggression against Ukraine', available from: https://pace.coe.int/en/files/29885 [Accessed 12 June 2024].
[120] PACE Opinion 300, n 119.

neighbours, and to denounce the concept of treating neighbouring States as a zone of special influence called the 'near abroad'.[121]

With specific reference to the request to provide an opinion to the CM under statutory resolution (51) 30, the Opinion went on:

> [T]he Assembly is convinced that the gravity of the actions committed by the Russian Federation and the profound breach of trust caused by them fully justify the further recourse to Article 8 of the Statute. Taking into account all of the above and that the Russian Federation has committed serious violations of the Statute of the Council of Europe that are incompatible with the status of a Council of Europe member State, does not honour its undertakings to the Council of Europe and does not comply with its commitments, the Assembly considers that the Russian Federation can therefore no longer be a member State of the Organisation.

This emphatic passage, which must be seen in the context of the Opinion overall, of course, was the most detailed explanation by any CoE body of the precise legal basis upon which Russia would be expelled.[122]

The Opinion concluded:

> The Assembly, therefore, is of the opinion that the Committee of Ministers should request the Russian Federation to *immediately withdraw* from the Council of Europe. If the Russian Federation does not comply with the request, the Assembly suggests that the Committee of Ministers determine the *immediate possible* date from which the Russian Federation would cease to be a member of the Council of Europe.[123]

The language used here echoed Article 8 in that the expectation was that a request would be made that Russia withdraw. However, it is worth highlighting that what was envisaged was '*immediate*' withdrawal. Likewise, the reference to an '*immediate* possible date' for departure, should Russia not comply with the request, underlined the intention that Russia's ejection, via Article 8, occur as soon as possible.

To appreciate why this was so, one may recall that there had already been some talk of Russia withdrawing under Article 7. Even if Russian press

---

[121] PACE Opinion 300, n 119.
[122] One may draw a contrast between this and the circumstances of Greece's withdrawal from the CoE in 1969.
[123] Opinion 300 (2022), n 119. Emphasis added.

reports on the morning of 15 March suggested that this would not occur,[124] Russia purported to withdraw under Article 7 later that day, that is, *during* the Assembly's Article 8 debate. Here the verbatim record of the debates shows that late in the day on the 15 March (in fact 18:54 hrs local time), Tiny Kox, President of PACE, announced that the Secretary General of the CoE 'has received a notification from the Russian Federation announcing that it withdraws from the CoE under Article 7'. However, President Kox added that Russia's actions would 'not intervene in our discussions'; as he put it, 'our process', by which he meant Article 8 'goes on'.[125]

5.3 Russia's purported withdrawal under Article 7, as the Assembly debates its expulsion (15 March 2022)

Before coming to the CM's response to PACE's Resolution, let us comment on Russia's purported reliance upon Article 7. As noted, on 15 March 2022, after PACE had started its debate, but before it had concluded it, the Russian authorities notified the Secretary General that Russia was withdrawing from the CoE.[126] If valid, the effect of this Article 7 withdrawal would have been that Russia would have left the CoE on 31 December 2022.[127]

On the same day, that is, 15 March 2022, the Secretary General of the CoE officially informed the chair of the CM of the decision of Russia to withdraw in accordance with Article 7 of the Statute. The Secretary General also informed the CM in the same letter that the Russian authorities intended to denounce the ECHR.[128] We shall come back to the legality, or otherwise, of this purported withdrawal but for now, however, the following points need to be made.

Evidently, Russia's attempt to withdraw under Article 7 came at a stage when it was a near certainty that it was about to be requested to withdraw under Article 8. As noted, it purported to withdraw in the latter half of 15 March, during the second day of the two-day Assembly debate. The

---

[124] See section 5.1 of this chapter.
[125] For the verbatim records of the meeting, see https://pace.coe.int/en/verbatim/2022-03-15/pm/en, Tuesday 15 March 2022, at 18:54:01 hrs.
[126] 'Заявление МИД России о запуске процедуры выхода из Совета Европы' ('Statement of the MFA of Russia on the commencement of the procedure of withdrawing from the Council of Europe'). (Translated by the authors), available from: https://mid.ru/ru/foreign_policy/news/1804379/ [Accessed 12 June 2024].
[127] Pursuant to Article 7 of the CoE Statute, 'Any member of the Council of Europe may withdraw by formally notifying the Secretary General of its intention to do so. Such withdrawal shall take effect at the end of the financial year in which it is notified.'
[128] The letter of the Secretary General of the CoE to the Chair of the CM of the CoE (on file with the authors).

draft opinion which was being debated had been tabled the day before, 14 March. It was written in unequivocal terms calling for Russia's ejection from the CoE. Moreover, it was clear by 15 March which way the debate was going.

By 15 March, Russia was about to be expelled under Article 8 – it therefore tried to 'jump' before it was 'pushed'. So, as with Greece in 1969, at the 11th hour, when Russia's CoE fate was almost certain, it 'got in first'. Or at least, it tried to do so. Indeed, the sense that there was a kind of race between the CoE and Russia in terms of a decisive move was in evidence in the Assembly debate. In this regard it is notable that the PACE Opinion called for an '*immediate*' withdrawal, and an '*immediate* possible date' for departure.

By purporting to rely on Article 7, it may be assumed that Russia was seeking to avoid the indignity of being expelled from the CoE under Article 8. It may also be assumed that it was laying groundwork for a narrative that it left of its own accord, rather than being *forced* out without its consent. Here some issues arise around the membership sanction effect of whether a state is able to say that it walked away (Article 7), or was expelled (Article 8). The former may be an attempt to gain a façade of respectability in a situation when expulsion is inevitable (perhaps from a propaganda perspective, for domestic consumption) by justifying exit from the CoE as a decision Russia itself took of its own accord. The CoE, on the other hand, was keen to demonstrate that Russia was expelled: PACE and the CM wished to emphasise that Russia was not in control, that Article 8 was about to be actioned against it, and to that extent its exit was *not* of its own accord.

What was at stake can be demonstrated by examining the reactions of certain members of PACE to the announcement of Russia's purported withdrawal. At issue were the perceived implications of such a step, in that it would deprive the CoE institutions of their opportunity to condemn wholeheartedly what Russia had done. So, as soon as the President of PACE had announced Russia's attempted withdrawal, the very first statement from a speaker was that:

> I don't think we should allow them to withdraw. I think we should force them to be kicked out and listen to this Assembly and listen to the Committee of Ministers. Listen to the voices here in this room today.
>
> I want to send a message to the people of Ukraine and let them know that we stand in solidarity with them and with their representatives …
>
> We stand with you. We support you. You are fighting not just for your country, your homes, and your freedom, but for values – values we share and values that I hope that we will stand together later this evening in opposition to Russia's – to Putin's tyranny on behalf of the Russian people.

I really hope that this Assembly does not allow them to withdraw, but kick them out.[129]

A subsequent speaker reacted to the Russian announcement in these terms:

They intend to withdraw by using Article 7.

They intend to do that to try and stop, to withdraw before we push them, and we must proceed to push them, to expel them. The Council [sic] of Ministers must expel them too, because in expelling them we defend the values of this organisation, we defend the values of Europe.[130]

The latter statement suggests that expulsion is viewed as a punitive statement of principle, which goes beyond merely stopping being a member of the Council: it shows the ultimate condemnation of the actions of the Russian authorities.

Internally, the Russian authorities both in legal documents and through its media outlets highlighted that they had left the CoE rather than they were expelled. In an explanatory note to the Law of the Russian Federation denouncing the majority of the treaties signed by Russia within the framework of the CoE, the Russian authorities stated that the Russian Federation had informed the Secretary General of their withdrawal from the organisation. Then it stated: 'However, on 16 March 2022, the Committee of Ministers of the Council of Europe, in gross violation of the Council of Europe Statute, adopted a Resolution of termination of membership of Russia in the Council of Europe effective immediately.'[131]

This document also explained that in this situation the Russian authorities had decided to pay the membership fee only until 16 March 2022 and not until the end of the financial year, which would have been the case if Russia withdrew in accordance with Article 7. So, in effect, the Russian authorities accepted the legal consequences of the fact that Russia was expelled on 16 March 2022.

---

[129] Mr Richard Holden, United Kingdom. For the verbatim records of the meeting, see https://pace.coe.int/en/verbatim/2022-03-15/pm/en, Tuesday 15 March 2022, at 18:54:59 hrs.

[130] Mr Dara Calleary, Ireland. For the verbatim records of the meeting, see https://pace.coe.int/en/verbatim/2022-03-15/pm/en, Tuesday 15 March 2022, at 19:20:04.

[131] 'Подписан закон о прекращении действия в отношении РФ международных договоров Совета Европы' ('The law on denouncing of international treaties concluded under the auspices of the Council of Europe has been signed') (28 February 2023). (Translated by the authors), available from: http://kremlin.ru/acts/news/70605 [Accessed 12 June 2024].

In the Russian media, Russia's departure from the CoE did not receive major prominence and was covered in terms of 'exit from the Council of Europe'[132] or 'inability to remain in the organisation',[133] emphasising the fact that this departure 'will not affect the rights and freedoms of the citizens'.[134]

5.4 The CM expels Russia under Article 8 (16 March 2022)

Returning to the chronology of expulsion, it may be recalled that by the end of 15 March 2022, Russia had been suspended from its rights of representation in the CoE (25 February 2022), and that PACE had unanimously called for its 'immediate' withdrawal (15 March). By this stage, then, certain procedures envisaged by Article 8 of the Statute had been followed, as had a political requirement to obtain the opinion of PACE.

In a relatively brief (less than three hundred words) Resolution of 16 March 2022, the CM '[r]eaffirm[ed] that the aggression of the Russian Federation' was a 'serious violation' of Article 3 of the Statute of the CoE; it '[r]ecall[ed] its 25 February 2022 decision' whereby it 'launch[ed] the procedure provided by Article 8 of the Statute and agreed to suspend' Russia from its rights of representation in the CoE; it also 'recall[ed]' its consultation of PACE and the latter's unanimous response that 'the Russian Federation can no longer be a member State of the Organisation'; it then '[n]oted' [rather than 'recalled'] Russia's 'communication' dated 15 March 2022 'of its withdrawal from the CoE in accordance with the Statute of the CoE and of its intention to denounce the European Convention on Human Rights'. It then 'Decided', 'in the context of the procedure launched under Article 8 of the Statute of the Council of Europe, that the Russian Federation ceases to be a member of the Council of Europe as from 16 March 2022'.[135]

The specific language employed here – 'ceases to be a member of the CoE [at date determined by CM]' – mirrored Article 8. However, the

---

[132] 'Выход из Совета Европы не повлияет на права и свободы россиян, заявил МИД' ('The MFA says that exiting the Council of Europe will not impact the rights and freedoms of the Russians') (15 March 2022). (Translated by the authors), available from: https://ria.ru/20220315/se-1778329554.html [Accessed 12 June 2024].

[133] 'В МИД заверили, что выход РФ из Совета Европы не повлияет на права и свободы россиян' ('The MFA insists that exit from the Council of Europe will not impact the rights and freedoms of the Russians') (15 March 2022). (Translated by the authors), available from: www.interfax.ru/russia/828377 [Accessed 12 June 2024].

[134] 'Выход России из Совета Европы: что изменится' ('Exit of Russia from the Council of Europe: what has changed?') (10 March 2022). (Translated by the authors), available from: www.vesti.ru/article/2687195 [Accessed 12 June 2024].

[135] Resolution CM/Res(2022)2, 'On the cessation of the membership of the Russian Federation to the Council of Europe', available from: https://rm.coe.int/0900001680a5da51 [Accessed 12 June 2024].

procedure adopted was not entirely faithful to Article 8. As noted previously, it stipulates that a state against whom Article 8 action is being taken should be 'requested' 'by the CM to withdraw under Article 7'. Under the terms of Article 8, it is only if 'such member does not comply with this request', that the Committee may proceed to 'decide that it has ceased to be a member of the Council'. We shall come back to this procedural anomaly in the expulsion of Russia later.

5.5 Russia's initial reaction to expulsion

Before analysing the various issues arising in connection with Russia's expulsion, one may note how Russia reacted to the CM's Resolution of 16 March. On 17 March 2022, the press-secretary of the Russian Ministry of Foreign Affairs (MFA), Maria Zakharova, made the following statement in response to this decision of the CM:

> [o]n 15 March this year, the Russian Federation submitted to the Secretary General of the Council of Europe the official notification of withdrawal from this organisation. Russia itself took this decision and started the relevant legal procedures. However, the next day, the Committee of Ministers of the Council of Europe in impotent rage (I cannot find any better way to describe that) adopted a unilateral decision expelling Russia as of 16 March of this year ... This demarche cannot change anything ... This belated decision of the hurriedly called Committee of Ministers just removes the necessity to comply with the remaining procedures and obligations.[136]

The statement made some general, yet undefined allegations of impropriety as regards the expulsion of Russia. In that connection, several points may be made: first, the emotional tone of the statement, and its factual inaccuracies. It referred to the CM acting with 'impotent rage', to its 'unilateral action', its 'belated' action and 'hurriedly' called meeting. However, as we have seen, in fact the CM had acted in a carefully planned process. Its Resolution stated that Article 8 action had been triggered on 25 February. Furthermore, it was endorsed by a unanimous PACE at an Extraordinary Session held by it.

---

[136] 'Брифинг официального представителя МИД России М.В.Захаровой, Москва, 17 марта 2022 года' ('Briefing of the official representative of the Russian MFA M.V. Zakharova, Moscow, 17 March 2022'). (Translated by the authors), available from: https://mid.ru/ru/foreign_policy/news/1804778/#11 [Accessed 12 June 2024]. See also Drzemczewski and Lawson, n 105, 53–4.

Second, the statement did not try to undermine the substantive merits of the decision of the CM itself. It seems that the Russian authorities were indeed unable to say that they did not violate Article 3 of the Statute and to claim that there was no good reason to expel Russia. Instead they had to focus on some alleged procedural irregularities in the actions of the CM.

Third, what, then, was the reason for the statement? In fact, the statement seemed to be an attempt to take charge of the narrative by generally discrediting the CM and the CoE and so by implication the general process of expulsion. Presumably this was for the purposes of internal media consumption. In that last connection, it may be noted that the representative of the Russian MFA made grossly unsubstantiated claims that the CoE had turned into an ideological machine that was led by NATO and the USA.[137] Moreover, she mentioned that the CoE did nothing to protect people in Donbass from the war.[138] At the same time the representative did not even refer to the war in Ukraine as the key reason for expulsion.

The fourth point is that the way in which Russia tried to leave the CoE – that is, via Article 7 – is noteworthy. As suggested previously, the most important aspect of it was reputation and face saving, and an attempt to maintain that it was Russia who was in control – 'Russia itself made this decision'– rather than it being *required* to leave. Of course, to be the first and only country ever to be expelled from the CoE is not an accolade that any state would wish to have. That indignity did not befall even Greece under the 'black colonels' in the 1960s, for, as noted earlier, in the circumstances then occurring it was able to withdraw.[139]

There is one last point to mention about the significance of the application of Article 7 or Article 8 here. As we indicated before, technical issues arise dependent on which Article was relied upon. So, as Philip Leach pointed out:

> Article 7 would allow a state's (voluntary) withdrawal to take effect at the end of the financial year (December) in which it is notified (where notification is given during the first nine months of the financial year) … If Russia had been permitted to use the art.7 withdrawal route, then in theory at least, it could have delayed matters, for quite a considerable period. Instead, the CM has applied the art.8 procedure, allowing it to decide that Russia ceased to be a member from 16 March.[140]

---

[137] Briefing of the official representative of the Russian MFA, n 136.
[138] Briefing of the official representative of the Russian MFA, n 136.
[139] See section 4.1 of this chapter. For a brief analysis of this statement, see Istrefi, K. (2022) 'Russia will no longer participate in the Council of Europe: a problematic Member State who could not commit to peace', *ECHR Blog* [Blog], available from: www.echrblog.com/2022/03/russia-will-no-longer-participate-in.html [Accessed 12 June 2024].
[140] Leach, n 114, 222.

In fact, then, from a technical point of view the decision of the CM (under Article 8) was beneficial to Russia as it stopped paying the membership fees from the moment of expulsion and stopped being a member of the organisation immediately, rather than at the end of the financial year. Since this was what the Russian authorities wanted, it is hardly a decision that led to a practical disadvantage for Russia, other than, it may be said, for the political reasons that we have discussed. Indeed, on 23 March 2022, the Committee published the Resolution on Legal and Financial Consequences of the cessation of membership.[141] According to this document Russia ceased to be a member of the CoE on 16 March 2022, as a result it stopped having all rights of representation in all of the statutory bodies of the Council. The document also made provision that the Russian Federation should pay its fees up to the moment of its expulsion on 16 March 2022, and so not up until 31 December 2022, as Article 7 withdrawal would have required.

5.6 Criticisms of the CM Resolution of 16 March 2022

Though there can be no criticism of the merits or legitimacy of the expulsion, let us now consider some of the possible criticisms that may be levelled regarding the procedure adopted by the CM, as reflected in its Article 8 exclusion Resolution of 16 March 2022. Two main issues arise here. First, whether Russia's purported withdrawal under Article 7 on 15 March 2022 precluded the CM's actions under Article 8, on 16 March 2022. Second, the extent to which the procedural flaw associated with the CM's Article 8 Resolution noted previously[142] is of relevance. In what follows we will examine these matters and offer some potential answers or explanations. It is impossible to offer definitive conclusions on certain aspects, in part because the relevant Resolution itself was far from clear on aspects of some points. Indeed, that itself can attract further criticism of the CM. It is understandable that the CM was acting under the time pressure, but the detailed official legal analysis was not published. Though it is not a legal requirement, it would certainly help to clarify the interpretation of Articles 7 and 8 of the Statute.[143]

---

[141] Resolution CM/Res(2022)3, 'On legal and financial consequences of the cessation of membership of the Russian Federation in the Council of Europe', available from: https://rm.coe.int/resolution-cm-res-2022-3-legal-and-financial-conss-cessation-membershi/1680a5ee99 [Accessed 12 June 2024].

[142] See section 5.4 of this chapter.

[143] Marko Milanovic called the wording of these articles 'a drafting mess', Milanovic, M. (2022) 'Russia's submission to the ICJ in the genocide case; Russia's withdrawal from the Council of Europe', *EJIL:Talk!* [Blog], www.ejiltalk.org/russias-submission-to-the-icj-in-the-genocide-case-russias-withdrawal-from-the-council-of-europe/ [Accessed 12 June 2024].

Before embarking on a discussion of these two matters, an important point must be made. The title of section 5.6 in this chapter employs the word 'criticism'. At the outset we need to clarify that what follows does not cast any doubt over the actual *validity* of Russia's expulsion from the CoE in mid-March of 2022. Further, whatever the weight of the criticisms that may be directed at the CM, and regardless of the explanation of this, or observations, one matter is abundantly clear: circumstances compelled the CoE to expel Russia in mid-March 2022. So, for example, even if one were to maintain that Russia did successfully withdraw under Article 7 (as it tried to on 15 March 2022), as is discussed further, it is self-evident that this only occurred against the backdrop of an inevitable, forthcoming Article 8 Resolution, which followed less than 24 hours later. Further, it is equally important to bear in mind that the CM had a legal right under the Statute to expel Russia on 16 March 2022, so here the only point of contestation is what effect the failure to 'request' Russia's withdrawal had as part of the expulsion.

Turning then to Articles 7 and 8, our examination should begin by noting that the CM is the main decision-making body of the CoE and 'the competence to write law and to establish and manage the legal, administrative, and budgetary framework of the Organisation is exclusively vested in the CM'.[144] However, this does not mean that the constraints of the Statute are not applicable to it. Therefore, the explanations of what happened on 16 March 2022 must be considered by reference to the text of the Statute: the text of Articles 7 and 8, as well as the context.

5.6.1 Relevance of Russia's notification of withdrawal under Article 7

Let us first consider the significance of Russia's notification of withdrawal on 15 March 2022 and why it might be deemed not effective to preclude the CM's action on Article 8. The Resolution was silent on this matter, so this leads us to speculate as to the possible legal answers to this issue. Here two, separate and unconnected propositions arise. First, that the notification of withdrawal on 15 March 2022 was not legally valid. Second, the notification was irrelevant as Article 8, which had been triggered on 24 February 2022, precluded Russia's independent resort to Article 7 on 15 March 2022.

Regarding the first proposition, one can argue that the note submitted to the Secretary General by the Russian MFA cannot be considered as a proper withdrawal procedure,[145] because it was arguably not effective

---

[144] Palmer, S. (2017) 'The Committee of Ministers', in S. Schmahl and M. Breuer (eds) *The Council of Europe: Its Law and Politics*, Oxford: Oxford University Press, p 137.

[145] Statement of the MFA of Russia, n 126. Relevant Russian legislation is also described in the Venice Commission report 'On the Domestic Procedures of Ratification and

according to domestic law. Pursuant to Article 37 of the Federal Russian Law on International Treaties,[146] international treaties that were adopted by the Federal Law can only be suspended and denounced by the Russian Parliament. The Russian Federation joined the Statute of the CoE by virtue of the Federal Law in 1996.[147] In case of necessity, the President of Russia can suspend or denounce a treaty but again the Russian parliament must give a subsequent agreement on this.[148] As far as it has been reported the intent to start the withdrawal process from the CoE was communicated by the Minister of Foreign Affairs of Russia[149] which can neither initiate nor finalise the process of withdrawal from the CoE.

The argument that Russia's request to withdraw lacks legal validity seems legally problematic and farfetched. Such a suggestion assumes that the CM should assess the compliance of the communications of the Russian MFA with the Russian law. Of course, the CM needs to receive the information about withdrawal from the proper source, but one should consider (and the CM must assume) the MFA as a proper representative of the state in this context. Moreover, pursuant to Article 67(2) Vienna Convention on the Law of Treaties (VCLT), from the perspective of international law the Minister for Foreign Affairs is deemed a representative of the state and hypothetical illegality of the act at the national level does not make it illegal internationally. Finally, if the CM would have wished to suggest that Article 7 could not be relied upon because it had not been validly executed by Russia (it is very unlikely that they did), surely it would have explicitly stated this in its Resolution on the matter.

Denunciation of International Treaties', available from: https://venice.coe.int/webforms/documents/?pdf=CDL-AD(2022)001-e [Accessed 12 June 2024], pp 47–9.

[146] Федеральный Закон 'О международных договорах Российской Федерации' (Federal Law on international treaties of the Russian Federation). (Translated by the authors), available from: www.consultant.ru/document/cons_doc_LAW_7258/ [Accessed 12 June 2024].

[147] Федеральный закон от 23 февраля 1996 г. N 19-ФЗ 'О присоединении России к Уставу Совета Европы' (Federal Law from 23 February 1996 No 19-ФЗ on Accession of Russia to the Statute of the Council of Europe). (Translated by the authors), https://base.garant.ru/105142/1cafb24d049dcd1e7707a22d98e9858f/ [Accessed 12 June 2024].

[148] Article 37(2). On 16 February 2023, however, the Russian Duma adopted the law which formally confirmed termination of the Statute of the Council of Europe in respect of Russia from 16 March 2022: Федеральный Закон 'О Прекращении Действия В Отношении Российской Федерации Международных Договоров Совета Европы' (Federal Law on Termination of International Treaties of the Council of Europe in respect of Russia). (Translated by the authors), available from: www.consultant.ru/document/cons_doc_LAW_440539/ [Accessed 12 June 2024].

[149] (2022) 'Россия приняла решение о выходе из Совета Европы' ('Russia made a decision to withdraw from the Council of Europe') *Interfax*. (Translated by the authors), available from: https://www.interfax.ru/russia/828367 [Accessed 12 June 2024].

In a similar vein, Lawson and Drzemczewski explored whether the fact that this notification came by fax would make it invalid. They rightly suggest that this is not a very convincing argument:

> Here, the argument would be that a fax is not a valid means of transmitting such an important document as a termination of membership. Indeed, Article 7 of the Statute requires a member State wishing to withdraw to 'formally notify the Secretary General'. A fax might not qualify as a formal notification. But on closer scrutiny this line of reasoning may not be convincing. President Kox, for one, referred to a 'notification from the Russian Federation' when, during its debate of 15 March, he informed PACE of the Russian withdrawal.[150]

If Russia's Article 7 withdrawal notification was not invalid on these bases, then the question arises as to why it was not considered effective by the CM.

We will provide two alternative possible answers. The first answer would be that it was not considered valid or effective under the regime provided for by the Statute of the CoE. Although, the CM's Resolution did not address this question directly, it did contain certain indications of what the answer was. So, within the text of the Resolution the notification supplied by the Russian government was referred to as being merely *'noted'*, rather than 'recall[ed]'. The precise language seemed significant in terms of its dismissive, passing reference to something that has happened, rather than an acknowledgement of its legal importance. And why would that be so? The Resolution was clear and unambiguous in that the CM was acting 'in the context of the procedure *launched* [past tense; emphasis added] under Article 8 of the Statute of the Council of Europe', an earlier paragraph referring to the Committee's decision to 'launch the procedure provided by Article 8 of the Statute', *on 25 February 2022*. From this it seems very clear that the CM saw itself as concluding, and *entitled* to conclude, what it had begun nearly three weeks earlier. Nonetheless, in itself that would not explain why Russia could not rely on Article 7. The explanation for this would be that Article 8 is arguably the 'superior' provision of the Statute dealing with expulsion, and that once an Article 8 procedure has been triggered for a particular state, that state's otherwise unimpeded unilateral right to withdraw under Article 7 is no longer applicable. The CoE's Director of Legal Advice and Public International Law explained: 'Article 8 [deals] with serious violations of the Statute. Once the procedure has been launched, the Committee of Ministers is in charge. It is not the suspended member,

---

[150] Drzemczewski and Lawson, n 105, 51.

but only the Committee that is entitled to fix the terms, including the date of cessation of membership.'[151]

Such an approach would be in keeping with a reading of Article 8 which sees its object and purpose as a provision which is a genuine political sanction available to the CM. That is, the place occupied by Article 8 in the CoE Statute needs to be understood in terms of it creating not just a *basis* to expel a state, but also the opportunity for the main organ of the CoE to protect that organisations' values by communicating a strong message of expulsion, and so, if necessary, the sanction of disapproval (by the other states) that this involves. Based on this understanding of Article 8, once that provision is triggered, a resort to Article 7 would serve only to frustrate if not evade one of the objects and purposes of Article 8, namely to inflict a membership sanction at the behest of other member states of the CoE, acting through the CM.[152] On this basis, it may be concluded Russia's expulsion from the CoE has set a new precedent as regards the operation of Article 7, *when* Article 8 has already been triggered.

Although this reading of the Statute is appealing, there are certain complications with it as there is nothing in the text of the Statute that would explicitly suggest the superiority of Article 8 over Article 7. Moreover, Article 8 does not say that if it is triggered the state in question cannot withdraw in the meantime. Such restriction on the use of Article 7 would be significant from the point of sovereign will of the withdrawing state and it would need to be clearly stated in the text of the Statute. The CM of the CoE is an ultimate interpreter of the Statute in this context and it is up to it to establish precedents; however, the CM should follow established legal procedures. One could plausibly argue that these procedures were drafted more than 70 years ago when it was not expected that breaches of the Statute of the order and magnitude committed by Russia in February 2022 would occur. The possibility of immediate expulsion was not explicitly reflected in the Statute, even if the ultimately executive authority of the CM is. So, an additional possible justification for why the notification of Russia was not deemed to be valid was due to the gravity of its violations

---

[151] Polakiewicz, J. (2022) 'Russia's expulsion from the CoE – communication to the 62nd meeting of the Committee of Legal Advisers on Public International Law (CAHDI)', available from: www.coe.int/en/web/dlapil/-/62nd-meeting-of-the-committee-of-legal-advisers-on-public-international-law-cahdi- [Accessed 12 June 2024]. On the legal issues related to the distinction between Articles 7 and 8 of the Statute, see also Vogiatzis, N. (2022) ' "No longer a member state of the organisation": the expulsion of Russia from the Council of Europe and Articles 7 and 8 of the Statute', *ECHR Blog* [Blog], available from: https://www.echrblog.com/2022/03/no-longer-member-state-of-organisation.html [Accessed 12 June 2024], and Drzemczewski and Lawson, n 105, 50.

[152] See Articles 13, 15(a) and 16 of the Statute of the CoE regarding the role of the CM.

of the foundational values of the organisation. From this angle, one might perhaps argue that the CM as a representative of the collective will of the members of the organisation can interpret the prescribed procedure and set aside the Article 7 notification from the state that violates the fundamental values of the organisation.

This, however, does not fully explain why the CM failed to request Russia to withdraw according to the wording of Article 8. This is now considered.

5.6.2 Failure of the CM to 'request' that Russia withdraw

Article 8 is written in terms which require[153] that the state concerned be requested to withdraw from the CoE, a step which was not adopted by the CM in March 2022. The failure to adhere to this step can be levelled as a criticism; however, for the reasons that follow, this should not call into doubt the validity of Russia's expulsion.

Under Article 8, the CM is the ultimate authority as regards expulsion from the CoE, and it is able to proceed on a footing which entails that a 'request' to withdraw is in fact an *instruction* to do so. In this last connection, note that the second sentence of Article 8 refers to the state concerned not 'comply[ing] with the request': this language is indicative of the request as in fact being an unconditional order to leave, and so not a polite invitation to do so. This puts into perspective the relative insignificance of the fact that no request was actually made to Russia. It underlines how the failure to do so made no substantial difference to the outcome;[154] it is (and was at the material time) abundantly clear that Russia's cessation of membership of the CoE was going to occur, no matter how Russia would react to the request.

It would not be difficult to identify why the CM would have been unwilling to make the request. Commentators have referred to the request as 'a polite invitation to withdraw',[155] one which would give the state concerned 'the opportunity for "saving face" and to declare its exit on its own decision'.[156] On this understanding the 'request' is not a legal condition for expulsion

---

[153] Unless the words 'may be' in the first part of the first sentence of Article 8 also apply to the request referred to in the second part of the first sentence. This seems an unlikely interpretation given that the second sentence of Article 8 refers to the 'request' which is expected to be sent by that stage. Here, the words 'may be' provide the Committee of Minister with the discretion to suspend *and* request to withdraw. In other words, even in a case of a serious violation of Article 3, the CM is not obliged to apply Article 8; however, if such application is deemed to be necessary the CM is expected to suspend and request to withdraw.

[154] See section 5.1 of this chapter.

[155] Makarczyk, n 32, 486.

[156] Klein, n 41, 3.67.

but reflective of a type of diplomatic showing the door to the state. It is a benefit granted to the state for it to avoid the disgrace of being ejected, but one that does not bite on the ability of the CM to expel. Furthermore, Article 8 of the Statute states that the CM's Article 8 'request' enables the state to 'withdraw under *Article 7*' (emphasis added), this would have meant that its withdrawal would not take effect until 31 December 2022. This in turn means that a state which had flouted (and was continuing to flout) fundamental values of the CoE would have remained within the organisation for a further ten months, which would seem to run contrary to the object and purpose of the organisation as stated in the Preamble to the Statute.[157] It is not very difficult to see why the thinking within the CM was very likely that Russia did not deserve the potential benefits that could attach to a 'request' to withdraw, and that a message had to be communicated that its departure should be immediate, since its continued presence was intolerable.

Perhaps the CM decided to expel by reading the Statute as a whole and bypassing aspects of the specific procedure enshrined in Article 8. This decision was politically justifiable due to the magnitude of the violation of Article 3 by Russia. Although the Vienna Convention on the Law of Treaties (VCLT) does not directly regulate interpretation of the Statute of the CoE as the latter chronologically preceded the former, Article 60 VCLT can be instructive here.[158] According to this Article, in the case of a material breach of a multilateral treaty[159] by one of the parties, other parties are entitled to suspend or terminate this treaty by unanimous agreement. The unanimous agreement was clearly present when the CM expelled Russia. Article 60 VCLT also defines the meaning of the material breach as 'the violation of a provision essential to the accomplishment of the object or purpose of the treaty'.[160] Presence of Russia in the CoE – the organisation that was designed to 'to achieve a greater unity between its members'[161] – would not make sense after launching an unjustified full-scale military operation against another member state. Arguably, the actions of Russia were directed against the very

---

[157] According to the Preamble, the member states of the CoE reaffirmed 'their devotion to the spiritual and moral values which are the common heritage of their peoples and the true source of individual freedom, political liberty and the rule of law, principles which form the basis of all genuine democracy'.

[158] Moreover, it has been argued that VCLT is a codification of customary international law and can be applicable as such. See Aust, A. (1969) 'Vienna Convention on the Law of Treaties', *Max Planck Encyclopaedia of Public International Law*, available from: https://spacelaw.univie.ac.at/fileadmin/user_upload/p_spacelaw/EPIL_Vienna_Convention_on_the_Law_of_Treaties_1969.pdf [Accessed 12 June 2024].

[159] The Statute of the CoE is a multilateral treaty for the purposes for the VCLT.

[160] Article 60(3)(b) VCLT.

[161] Article 1 of the Statute.

core of the Statute and such actions call for immediate expulsion on the basis of implied powers of the CM as a main decision-making body of the CoE.

6 Conclusion

Membership sanctions are controversial and extraordinary. There is no universal view on what is the best way to apply them or even whether they should be applied at all, this is particularly so when there may be various readings of statutory provisions underpinning them. They come with a lot of side-effects – they stop cooperation between the expelled state and the international organisation, and rights-holders in an expelled country might suffer more than their government or other authorities. Having said all this, it seems that in some circumstances using these sanctions is almost unavoidable. This is so, especially in the case of organisations designed to promote democracy, human rights and the rule of law such as the CoE, which relies on credibility and integrity in the furtherance of its normative mission. It is clear that launching a full-scale aggression against a fellow member state undermines the core foundations of this organisation and expulsion of Russia in 2022 was completely appropriate and justified. Russia was the first and only country that was expelled from the CoE. This expulsion is the end of a long period of complex and often controversial relationships and, as discussed in Chapter 4, followed decisive efforts by the CoE to accommodate and retain Russia in spite of its subversive tendencies. The CoE applied various membership sanctions to Russia in the past[162] but the magnitude of the violation of the core principles of the Council which happened on 24 February 2022 called for immediate expulsion.

The legal basis for suspension and expulsion of members of the CoE is provided in Articles 7 and 8 of the Statute of the CoE. Strictly speaking it provides a three stages process: suspension of the member state, request to withdraw and then expulsion if the state does not withdraw. Standing back, one may argue that the CM made a procedural shortcut in expelling Russia from the CoE, even if the expulsion is entirely justifiable when the Statute of the CoE is read as a whole. Although one might argue that the expulsion of Russia did not fully comply with the procedure established by Article 8, which states that the member state that violated Article 3 may be suspended *and* requested to withdraw from the Council, the validity of this act is not undermined by this procedural anomaly.

Nevertheless, the failure of the CM to formally 'request' Russia to withdraw remains the chief criticism of the Resolution of 16 March 2022. That failure is not so fundamental that the validity of expulsion is put into

---

[162] See Chapters 2, 3 and 4 of this monograph for detailed explanation.

doubt, and, as far as the authors are aware, no commentator has suggested as much, nor even Russia itself. However, the failure risks casting a shadow on the *perceived* legitimacy of what occurred. If so, one may respond by stating that if the legitimacy is to be the benchmark of assessment in relation to what occurred, then there are numerous arguments to be made as to why the actions of the CM were legitimate in the context of what occurred, and these eclipse the procedural shortcoming in question.

The expulsion of Russia from the CoE is an important example of practice that demonstrates that a state can be expelled if they harm the foundational principles of the organisation. Although the CM has clearly established that the membership of Russia in the CoE ended on 16 March 2022, it also explained that Russia continued being a party to the ECHR until 16 September 2022.[163]

---

[163] Resolution CM/Res(2022)3, n 141, para 7.

6

The Legacy of Russia's Expulsion on the European Court of Human Rights

1 Introduction

The legacy of Russia's expulsion from the Council of Europe (CoE) is multi-layered and multi-faceted. It can be considered from various angles: political, legal, historical, emotional and many others. After more than 25 years in the organisation Russia certainly made an impact. While the scale of this impact is a matter of perspective, the presence of Russia was felt in Strasbourg, as is its absence. We are not planning to be comprehensive in this chapter for two main reasons. First, some aspects of this influence have already been covered in the other chapters[1] and, second, to be comprehensive is likely to require writing another book. In this chapter, we only deal with the consequences of expulsion of Russia from the CoE from the perspective of the European Convention on Human Rights (ECHR).

Two aims are pursued here. First, we will explain the impact the ECHR had on Russia and argue that the European Court of Human Rights (ECtHR) was, in general, quite effective at the micro level, namely at the level of just satisfaction and individual measures.[2] It was also quite effective in relation to some technical (not politically sensitive) reforms of the national legal system in Russia. At the same time, it was much less impactful at a

---

[1] See, for example, the conclusion to Chapter 4, and also Chapter 7.
[2] Just satisfaction is a payment of sums of money awarded by the Court to the applicant. When mere monetary compensation cannot adequately erase the consequences of a violation, the CM makes sure that the authorities take any other individual measures which may be required to remedy the violation. This can include reopening of unfair criminal proceedings, revocation of expulsion orders and many others. See 'The supervision process', available from: www.coe.int/en/web/execution/the-supervision-process [Accessed 12 June 2024].

macro level where changes matter most. Here the Court needs to prevent the Contracting Parties, in particular, from democratic backsliding. Having said that, a caveat is that the Court has little control over how its judgments are effectuated, and for the system to work the Contracting Parties need to be willing to cooperate with the Court and the Committee of Ministers (CM) of the CoE in good faith. So, the chapter will demonstrate that Russia ceasing to be a party to the ECHR will have significant and tangible consequences on a micro level. However, we insist that this effect should not be overestimated as the Court has already proven to be unable to prevent curtailing of the key political freedoms in Russia, which as a matter of both scale and intensity, represent the more critical and systemic human rights concerns. The second aim of this chapter is to dive into the details of Russia's exit from the Convention and to see what will happen with the cases which are still pending before the Court. In order to achieve these two aims, this chapter proceeds as follows.

First, we will look at what impact the Court had on the legal system in Russia. In the decade preceding expulsion, Russia was the biggest 'client' of the ECtHR: it had the highest number of applications and, correspondingly, the highest number of judgments were delivered every year against it. Also, there was (and still is) the highest number of pending inter-state applications submitted against Russia, mostly in the context of the military confrontation between Russia and Ukraine. So, the second section of this chapter will demonstrate that the Court had significant impact on the legal system in Russia on the micro level, but failed to prevent a catastrophic shift from a potential democratic path to totalitarian rule on a macro level.

Second, we will point out that the Court will lose even the limited capacity to impact the ongoing litigations which it had before the Convention ceased to be applicable. In fact, the Court could only issue interim measures to try to impact such ongoing human rights violations while Russia remained party to the Convention. We argue that even when Russia was a member of the CoE, these tools were insufficient to stop major crises, and now when Russia is out, the Court's ability to issue interim measures in relation to Russia has ceased altogether. We will specifically consider whether these interim measures are capable of limiting the impact of war.

We then move to the second aim of this chapter and delve into the complexity of interpretation of Article 58 ECHR, which regulates how the Convention can be denounced, and so consider exactly when the ECHR stopped applying to Russia. The key issue of contention here is whether Russia should have stopped being the party to the Convention from the moment of expulsion by the CM on 16 March 2022, or six months later. The CM and the Court argued that it was the latter (that is, September 2022) but were vague as to their reasoning for this, leaving space for a legal argument that the proper interpretation of the Convention is that it should stop its application at the moment of expulsion, namely on 16 March 2022. Irrespective of whether or not one agrees with the Court and the CM on this matter, it seems that expulsion of Russia has created a precedent that has clarified the interpretation of Article 58 ECHR.

Although Russia ceased to be a member of the CoE on 16 March 2022, the ECtHR is competent to deal with a high number of cases in relation to the violations that happened when Russia remained a Contracting Party to the Convention. Since the Court is in uncharted waters here we suggest a number of solutions that the Court had at its disposal;[3] we consider their advantages and drawbacks and analyse their operationalisation. We argue that the Court could continue 'business as usual', namely it could deal with all pending applications. The Court could also resort to the 'pick and choose' model and select the most sensitive or representative cases and dispose of the rest. Finally, the Court could use the radical approach and either freeze all the pending applications against Russia or even strike them out of the list of cases. It seems that the radical solution has clearly been rejected, at least for the time being. It also seems that the Court decided to apply the combination of 'business as usual' and 'pick and choose' to the pending Russian applications.

Finally, in this chapter we will consider potential implementation of the judgments which are still pending execution before the CM. We point out that Russia has stopped all communication with the CoE and as things stand now it is almost certain that the Russian authorities will not voluntarily enforce any of the judgments. The CM decided to continue their process of execution, but this will unlikely bear fruit under the current political regime in Russia. It needs to be stated that the strategy adopted by the CM is realistic and tries to use the available avenues to persuade the Russian authorities to enforce the judgments of the ECtHR. However, some more creative approaches can be considered.

2 The ECtHR and its impact on the legal system in Russia

It is worth noting, statistically at least, that at the time of Russia's expulsion, a total of 1,358 cases (out of 3,851) in which Russia was the respondent were considered by the CM to have been satisfactorily implemented,[4] even though some 17,450 applications were still pending against Russia before

---

[3] It is worth reiterating that this study looks at the situation as it was on 16 March 2023 at the latest. Since then, the Court has somewhat qualified its approach.

[4] See Factsheet on Russian Federation and the CoE, Department of Execution of Judgments, available from: www.coe.int/en/web/execution/russian-federation [Accessed 12 June 2024].

the Court as of 16 September 2022.[5] Regardless of any possible outcome of these pending cases, Russia almost certainly will not act on any of the Court's findings. So, the overall number of unexecuted cases will only increase.

The CoE and some academics argued that the ECtHR had a significant and positive impact on the Russian legal system.[6] We are not going to repeat what has already been said, but the ECtHR has delivered a high number of very important judgments, some of which were implemented. This has had tangible effects on the specific victims, who at least received some monetary compensation for the violation of their rights; moreover, in technical areas these judgments when implemented[7] created useful changes on the micro level.[8] In terms of just satisfaction, Russia has not paid it in 1,300 cases, owing over €2.7 billion. That said, the largest part of this comes from the unpaid just satisfaction in *Yukos v. Russia* (€1.87 billion)[9] also a significant proportion was awarded in the inter-state case of *Georgia v. Russia* (€10 million).[10] It means that although the debt of Russia is very significant, in a large proportion of cases just satisfaction has, in fact, been paid by the authorities.

Now we will try to articulate the obstacles to effective impact of the ECtHR on the macro level. The first and the most obvious one is the lack of political will of the Russian authorities to implement the ECtHR

---

[5] See Press Release of the European Court of Human Rights, ECHR 286 (2022), 16 September 2022.

[6] See, for example, 'Russia and the European Convention on Human Rights: 20 years together: 20 cases that have changed the Russian legal system', available from: https://rm.coe.int/russia-and-the-european-convention-on-human-rights-20-years-together-b/16808b3b38 [Accessed 12 June 2024]; Kovler, A. (2016) 'Russia: European Convention on Human Rights in Russia: fifteen years after', in I. Motoc and I. Ziemele (eds) *The Impact of the ECHR on Democratic Change in Central and Eastern Europe: Judicial Perspectives*, Cambridge: Cambridge University Press, pp 351–72.

[7] See *Burdov v. Russia (no. 2)*, no. 33509/04, ECHR 2009. On the point of failure to fix broader challenges associated with Russian judiciary, see Leach, P., Hardman, H. and Stephenson, S. (2010) 'Can the European Court's pilot judgment procedure help resolve systemic human rights violations – Burdov and the failure to implement domestic court decisions in Russia', *Human Rights Law Review*, 10: 346–59.

[8] See Chapter 4, section 3.2.1.

[9] *OAO Neftyanaya Kompaniya Yukos v. Russia* (just satisfaction), no. 14902/04, 31 July 2014. See Chapter 4, section 4.2. This amount increased to €2,523,385,527 (including interest) in 2024.

[10] *Georgia v. Russia (I)* (just satisfaction) [GC], no. 13255/07, 29 January 2019. See CoE leaders profoundly concerned about Russia's non-execution of judgments of the European Court of Human Rights, including the non-payment of just satisfaction, available from: www.coe.int/en/web/portal/-/council-of-europe-leaders-profoundly-concerned-about-russia-s-non-execution-of-judgments-of-the-european-court-of-human-rights-including-the-non-payment-of-just-satisfactio [Accessed 12 June 2024]. This amount increased to €12,584,945 (including interest) in 2024.

judgments. Moreover, in the period prior to its expulsion, the government of Russia was actively undermining the standards adopted by the ECtHR as well as efforts to make the system more efficient and effective (as also discussed in Chapter 4). There are multiple examples that instead of the releasing of political prisoners and liberalising of certain legislation, the Russian authorities did exactly the opposite. The examples of such cases are too numerous to provide a comprehensive overview here but they range from repressions against the LGBTI community,[11] free speech and assembly to the labelling of human rights organisations as 'foreign agents'[12] and the almost outright banning of political dissent.[13] This reason corresponds with the inability of the CM to 'force' the authorities of Russia to make the necessary changes. Numerous Resolutions issued in many of these cases failed to produce a desired result.

The second obstacle for the effective impact of the ECtHR is far from being unique to Russia: the complexity of resource-intensive reforms required as a result of the ECtHR judgments. For instance, there has been a litany of cases condemning Russia's conditions of detention and medical care in Russian prisons, from *Kalashnikov v. Russia*,[14] which centred on sanitary conditions and healthcare, to *Ananyev and Others v. Russia*, on pretrial detention centres,[15] right up to the high-profile *Magnitsky v. Russia*[16] case which highlighted the acute problems of detention conditions, ill-treatment and failure to provide medical care. Russia proposed action plans to the CM which focussed on legislative amendment and access to remedies, rather than practical and effective initiatives to improve the material situation of prisoners. That said, these cases require long and complex reforms backed up by investment of significant resources. These challenges to the effectiveness of the ECtHR judgments in Russia were often combined with a lack of political will. As a result, the judgments of the Court remained unimplemented.

Finally, a significant obstacle of the effectiveness of the Court was the length of proceedings in Strasbourg leading to key judgments. This by no means exonerates the Russian authorities of their responsibility for non-implementation, but in many crucial cases the Court took too much time to reach its (often fairly obvious) conclusion. Very often the Court made clear and forceful condemnations of the Russian authorities at the end of years of waiting, but crucial time when the situation could have been

---

[11] *Alekseyev v. Russia*, nos. 4916/07 and 2 others, 21 October 2010.
[12] *Ecodefence and Others v. Russia*, nos. 9988/13 and 60 others, 14 June 2022.
[13] *Navalnyy and Yashin v. Russia*, no. 76204/11, 4 December 2014.
[14] *Kalashnikov v. Russia*, no. 47095/99, ECHR 2002-VI.
[15] *Ananyev v. Russia*, no. 20292/04, 30 July 2009.
[16] *Magnitskiy and Others v. Russia*, nos. 32631/09 and 53799/12, 27 August 2019.

potentially reversed was lost. In Chapters 2–4, we highlighted some of the cases which signposted the democratic decline of Russia. For instance, the application in *Khodorkovskiy v. Russia* was submitted in February 2004 and the judgment was delivered in November 2011 (over 7 years);[17] the application for cases related to the brutal dispersal of a political rally in Bolotnaya Square took 4 years to decide;[18] the case about the ban of 'gay propaganda' in Russia took more than 8 years to adjudicate;[19] while the so-called 'foreign agents' case took almost 10 years, the judgment being pronounced after Russia had already been expelled from the CoE.[20] Undoubtedly, the Court's proceedings cannot be quick, especially in complex cases, but the length of proceedings can clearly undermine the Court's ability to prevent anti-democratic backsliding. Having said that, the Court has also attempted to influence the ongoing human rights violations via interim measures, but this tool has its own significant limitations which the following section will examine.

3 The ECtHR and its continued engagement with the ongoing human rights violations

The ECtHR is no longer competent to adjudicate on alleged human rights violations that the Russian authorities commit, at home or abroad, after 16 September 2022. One of the consequences of Russia's expulsion from the CoE, for example, is that the ECtHR will no longer be able to try to impact the actions of the Russian authorities in Ukraine. Although, in general, the ECtHR has limited ability to influence the ongoing human rights violations in cases of armed conflict, this limited possibility to influence is rendered entirely ineffective in the current circumstances.

In the majority of cases of individual applications,[21] the Court deals with the consequences of such violations: it can award monetary compensation to the victims or their relatives and indicate measures aiming to prevent the repetition of these violations. In cases when the violation is continuing at the moment of delivery of the relevant judgment, it can have some tangible individual effects.[22] As we just argued, the time gap between the violation and the judgment of the ECtHR reduces the effectiveness of such judgments.

---

[17] *Khodorkovskiy v. Russia*, no. 5829/04, 31 May 2011.
[18] *Frumkin v. Russia*, no. 74568/12, 5 January 2016.
[19] *Bayev and Others v. Russia*, nos. 67667/09 and 2 others, 20 June 2017.
[20] *Ecodefence and Others v. Russia*, n 12.
[21] Article 34 ECHR.
[22] See, for example, *Ilgar Mammadov v. Azerbaijan*, no. 15172/13, 22 May 2014.

The same can be said about inter-state applications: they take many years to adjudicate.[23]

In order to prevent violations of human rights in select (very defined) circumstances, the ECtHR developed the tool of interim measures which requires the Contracting Parties to refrain from certain actions or undertake some actions that can stop human rights violations in a particular case or prevent the worsening of the situation. Initially, the Court used interim measures where there was a risk of clearly identifiable harm, especially in Article 3 deportation contexts, but then the application of such measures was significantly expanded, though still maintaining considerable restraint, issuing measures only in the contexts which presented risks of serious violations of the ECHR. The latter type of interim measure was predominantly used in inter-state cases, but not only. Although there is some connection between inter-state cases and interim measures of general application, not all interim measures in inter-state cases are of general character. In fact, the very first interim measure was requested in the context of inter-state litigation,[24] but it was of a specific nature and was used to prevent clearly identifiable harm, namely execution of the death penalty.[25] An example of more general interim measures can be found in *Georgia v. Russia (II)* litigation concerning the five-day war in August 2008: 'On 12 August 2008 the President of the Court … decided to apply Rule 39 of the Rules, calling upon both the High Contracting Parties concerned to honour their commitments under the Convention, particularly in respect of Articles 2 and 3 of the Convention.'[26] Here, the Court effectively reiterates that the Convention has to be complied with, arguably something that has already been known before issuing these measures. The development of interim measures from clear and limited use to more general usage led to an academic debate. Some scholars pointed out that general interim measures are unlikely to be complied with and the Court goes too far in this respect,[27] while some others have argued that the Court does not go far enough.[28]

---

[23] See, for example, *Georgia v. Russia (II)* [GC], no. 38263/08, 21 January 2021. The application was lodged on 11 August 2008. The judgment on merits was delivered on 21 January 2021.

[24] See *Greece v. United Kingdom*, no. 176/56, 26 September 1958, para 34.

[25] For discussion of general and specific interim measures, see Dzehtsiarou, K. (2016) 'Can the European Court of Human Rights prevent war? Interim measures in inter-state cases', *Public Law*. 254–71.

[26] *Georgia v. Russia (II)*, n 23, para 5.

[27] See the discussion in Dzehtsiarou, K. and Tzevelekos, V. (2021) 'Interim measures: are some opportunities worth missing', *European Convention on Human Rights Law Review*, 2(1): 1–10.

[28] See, for example, Lieblich, E. (2022) 'Not far enough: the European Court of Human Rights' interim measures on Ukraine', *Just Security*, available from: www.justsecurity.org/80482/not-far-enough-the-european-court-of-human-rights-interim-measures-on-ukraine/ [Accessed 12 June 2024].

The Court issued interim measures in 2014 in the context of the conflict in the eastern part of Ukraine, for instance. Here, the Court called upon both Contracting Parties:

> to refrain from taking any measures, in particular military actions, which might entail breaches of the Convention rights of the civilian population, including putting their life and health at risk, and to comply with their engagements under the Convention, notably in respect of Articles 2 (right to life) and 3 (prohibition of inhuman or degrading treatment).[29]

Needless to say, these interim measures were not particularly effective. Nor is it surprising that on 28 February 2022 the government of Ukraine submitted a request to the ECtHR to issue interim measures in the context of the new phase of aggression that began on 24 February 2022. The President of the Court agreed to indicate these measures on 1 March 2022. In the Court's press release[30] the ECtHR ordered:

> the Government of Russia to refrain from military attacks against civilians and civilian objects, including residential premises, emergency vehicles and other specially protected civilian objects such as schools and hospitals, and to ensure immediately the safety of the medical establishments, personnel and emergency vehicles within the territory under attack or siege by Russian troops.[31]

Three issues are worth highlighting in relation to these interim measures. First, the Court decided to use these measures only in relation to Russia (in the past, in 2014, the Court had requested both parties to the conflict to refrain from violating the ECHR).[32] Second, the Court used the language

---

[29] 'Interim measure granted in inter-State case brought by Ukraine against Russia', 13 March 2014, available from: https://hudoc.echr.coe.int/eng-press?i=003-4699472-5703982 [Accessed 12 June 2024].

[30] The text of the decision is not officially published by the ECtHR.

[31] 'The European Court grants urgent interim measures in application concerning Russian military operations on Ukrainian territory', 1 March 2022', available from: 'https://hudoc.echr.coe.int/app/conversion/pdf/?library=ECHR&id=003-7272764-.9905947&filename=The%20Court%20grants%20urgent%20interim%20measures%20in%20application%20concerning%20Russian%20military%20operations%20on%20Ukrainian%20territory.pdf [Accessed 12 June 2024].

[32] See, for example, interim measures in the context of the Nagorno–Karabakh conflict, available from: (https://hudoc.echr.coe.int/app/conversion/pdf/?library=ECHR&id=003-7528728-10337270&filename=Interim%20measures%20in%20the%20case%20Armenia%20v.%20Azerbaijan%20(no.%204).pdf) [Accessed 12 June 2024]. See also

of international humanitarian law when it talked about 'civilians and civilian objects'. For international human rights law, it matters much less whether the victim is a civilian or not. Finally, in the judgment in *Georgia v. Russia (II)*[33] that was issued slightly over a year before Russia attacked Ukraine, in a much-criticised interpretation of the scope of Article 1, the ECtHR effectively acknowledged that it does not have jurisdiction over the active phase of an ongoing military conflict. The Court stated there that:

> the very reality of armed confrontation and fighting between enemy military forces seeking to establish control over an area in a context of chaos not only means that there is no 'effective control' over an area as indicated above (see paragraph 126), but also excludes any form of 'State agent authority and control' over individuals.[34]

The interim measures issued in the context of the war between Russia and Ukraine might be just a sign that the Court is considering the revision of this position. As Marko Milanovic eloquently pointed out: 'The Court is now actively managing the chaos, or at least trying to do so'.[35] This approach is particularly surprising because President of the ECtHR Robert Spano, who indicated interim measures in relation to the war in Ukraine, was also a part of the majority in *Georgia v. Russia (II)*.

On 4 March 2022, the President of the Court repeated the same interim measures in individual cases from those civilians who are 'taking refuge in shelters, houses and other buildings, fearing for their lives due to ongoing shelling and shooting, without or with limited access to food, healthcare, water, sanitation, electricity and other interconnected services essential for survival, in need of humanitarian assistance and safe evacuation'.[36]

The third update of interim measures from the ECtHR in the context of this conflict was released on 1 April 2022. The government of Ukraine asked the Court to request the Russian Federation to stop using certain types of weapons, to cease attacking nuclear power plants and to stop operations against the Ukrainian civilian leadership. The ECtHR ruled that these

---

    previous interim measures indicated in the context of the conflict between Ukraine and Russia, n 29.

[33] *Georgia v. Russia (II)*, n 23.
[34] *Georgia v. Russia (II)*, n 23, para 137.
[35] Milanovic, M. (2022) 'Update on ECtHR interim measures concerning Russia and Ukraine', *EJIL:Talk!* [Blog], available from: www.ejiltalk.org/update-on-ecthr-interim-measures-concerning-russia-and-ukraine/ [Accessed 12 June 2024].
[36] 'Decision of the Court on requests for interim measures in individual applications concerning Russian military operations on Ukrainian territory', 4 March 2022, available from: https://t.co/AwcJf6b9oQ [Accessed 12 June 2024].

requests are covered by the previously indicated interim measures. However, the Court accepted the request of the Ukrainian authorities to allow the evacuation of civilians to the safer regions of Ukraine.[37] An interesting legal question, albeit of limited practical importance, is whether the Court can indicate Rule 39 measures to Russia after 16 September 2022, when its jurisdiction ended, in the context of cases which are still pending before it: for instance, in a case where the health of a victim of ill-treatment in prison has deteriorated and they request to be transferred to a civil hospital. Without going into details, one can argue that the Court should be able to issue such measures as they are connected to the case which falls within its jurisdiction and interim measures are the extension of such jurisdiction irrespective of when they are indicated.

It seems that the Russian authorities were responding to the Court's communications up until 16 March 2022 when Russia was expelled from the CoE, but after that almost all communications stopped. In effect, interim measures remain in force until the Court lifts them or the judgment within which the measures were indicated comes into force. The interim measures that were indicated during the war between Russia and Ukraine continue to be valid and applicable. In the fullness of time the ECtHR perhaps will find another violation of the ECHR for not complying with these measures, but unfortunately for now the real-life effects of the interim measures are negligible and remain little more than symbolic. In the following section we will consider how Russia's expulsion affected its other obligations under the ECHR.

4 The legal aspects of Russia ceasing to be a party to the ECHR

4.1 Interpretation of Article 58 ECHR adopted by the ECtHR and the CM

Before considering the future of the relations between Russia and the ECtHR, we need to discuss the process of denunciation of the ECHR which has already generated some academic commentary and proved to be far from being straightforward.[38] The CM was clear that the suspension of rights of representation of Russia at the CoE on 25 February 2022 did not

---

[37] 'Expansion of interim measures in relation to Russian military action in Ukraine', 1 April 2022, available from: https://hudoc.echr.coe.int/app/conversion/pdf/?library=ECHR&id=003-7300828-9953996&filename=Expansion%20of%20interim%20measures%20in%20relation%20to%20Russian%20military%20action%20in%20Ukraine.pdf' [Accessed 12 June 2024].

[38] See, for example, Dzehtsiarou, K. and Helfer, L.R. (2022) 'Russia and the European human rights system: doing the right thing ... but for the right legal reason?', *EJIL:Talk!*

affect the rights and obligations of Russia under the ECHR;[39] however, the expulsion of Russia on 16 March 2022 did. On the same day that Russia was expelled, the Court suspended examination of all applications against it.[40] At that point it was not certain whether the ECHR should immediately stop applying to Russia as a result of expulsion. Article 58 is instructive in this respect but not necessarily clear:

1. A High Contracting Party may denounce the present Convention only after the expiry of five years from the date on which it became a party to it and after six months' notice contained in a notification addressed to the Secretary General of the Council of Europe, who shall inform the other High Contracting Parties.
2. Such a denunciation shall not have the effect of releasing the High Contracting Party concerned from its obligations under this Convention in respect of any act which, being capable of constituting a violation of such obligations, may have been performed by it before the date at which the denunciation became effective.
3. Any High Contracting Party which shall cease to be a member of the Council of Europe shall cease to be a Party to this Convention under the same conditions.[41]

Before the ECtHR and the CM declared the legal position on the interpretation of Article 58, Dzehtsiarou and Helfer pointed out that there are at least three plausible interpretations of this Article in connection with the situation with Russia. They wrote:

[Blog], available from: www.ejiltalk.org/russia-and-the-european-human-rights-system-doing-the-right-thing-but-for-the-right-legal-reason/ [Accessed 12 June 2024]; Leach, P. (2022) 'A time of reckoning? Russia and the CoE', *Strasbourg Observers*, available from: https://strasbourgobservers.com/2022/03/17/a-time-of-reckoning-russia-and-the-council-of-europe/; Vogiatzis, N. (2022) ' "No longer a member state of the organisation": the expulsion of Russia from the Council of Europe and Articles 7 and 8 of the Statute', *ECHR Blog* [Blog], available from: www.echrblog.com/2022/03/no-longer-member-state-of-organisation.html [Accessed 12 June 2024]; Drzemczewski, A. and Lawson, R. (2022) 'Exclusion of the Russian Federation from the Council of Europe and the ECHR: an overview', *Baltic Yearbook of International Law*, vol. 21(1), pp 38–98.

[39] Resolution CM/Res(2022)1, 'On legal and financial consequences of the suspension of the Russian Federation from its rights of representation in the Council of Europe', available from: https://search.coe.int/cm/Pages/result_details.aspx?ObjectId=0900001680a5b15f [Accessed 12 June 2024].

[40] 'The European Court of Human Rights decides to suspend the examination of all applications against the Russian Federation', 16 March 2022, available from: https://echr.coe.int/Documents/Resolution_ECHR_cessation_membership_Russia_CoE_ENG.pdf [Accessed 12 June 2024].

[41] Article 58 ECHR; Article 58(4) is not relevant in this context.

First, the 'conditions' mentioned in section 3 may refer to both sections 1 and 2 of Article 58. Under this interpretation the Convention continues to apply in relation to the expelled party for six months. In effect, the same conditions ... apply to an expulsion precisely as they do for a voluntary withdrawal from the Convention.

Second, section 3 of Article 58 may refer only to section 2 of that Article. Under this interpretation, the Convention ceases to apply from the moment of expulsion. Read this way, Article 58 confirms that the expelled party remains responsible under international law for Convention violations that occurred only prior to that date.

Third, the 'conditions' under section 3 may refer to the condition ceasing of being a member state of the Council of Europe. In this view, the conditions are those established by the Statute of the Council and the Committee of Ministers as that organization's executive body.[42]

In reality the ECtHR and the CM chose the first interpretation of the Convention. Under the second and third interpretation the Convention would have ended its application on 16 March 2022, while in fact the Convention operated vis-à-vis Russia until 16 September 2022.

On 22 March 2022, the plenary[43] of the Court lifted the suspension of examination of Russian cases which was previously set by the President of the Court and opined that the Convention should apply to Russia until 16 September 2022.[44] The ECtHR argued that this reading of the Convention is in line with its object and purpose which calls for 'interpretation and application of its provisions so as to ensure practical and effective protection to those subject to the High Contracting Parties' jurisdiction'.[45]

The CM echoed this decision in its Resolution from 23 March 2022:

> The Russian Federation shall cease to be a High Contracting Party to the European Convention on Human Rights on 16 September 2022. In line with the Resolution of 22 March 2022 of the European

---

[42] Dzehtsiarou and Helfer, n 38.

[43] In accordance with the Rules of Court, the plenary of the Court consists of all elected judges of the Court. According to Rule 20, '[t]he quorum of the plenary Court shall be two-thirds of the elected judges in office'.

[44] Resolution of the European Court of Human Rights 'on the consequences of the cessation of membership of the Russian Federation to the Council of Europe in light of Article 58 of the European Convention on Human Rights', available from: https://echr.coe.int/Documents/Resolution_ECHR_cessation_membership_Russia_CoE_ENG.pdf [Accessed 12 June 2024].

[45] Resolution of the European Court of Human Rights, n 44.

Court of Human Rights, the Court remains competent to deal with applications directed against the Russian Federation in relation to acts or omissions capable of constituting a violation of the Convention provided that they occurred until 16 September 2022. The Committee of Ministers will continue to supervise the execution of the judgments and friendly settlements concerned and the Russian Federation is required to implement them.[46]

We need to break the chronology here and note that as early as on 15 March 2022, the Secretariat of the CM prepared a confidential memorandum on legal and financial consequences of the cessation of membership in the CoE under Article 8 of its Statute, which was only made public after the CM considered the issue of expulsion.[47] The memoranda of the Secretariat are not binding on the CM but represent highly influential interpretations of the Statute and other relevant legal documents. In the memorandum of 15 March 2022, it was argued that the ECHR should apply to Russia for six months after expulsion. The document stated:

> The ECtHR will retain its competence to deal with applications directed against a State, or introduced by it against another member State, if the acts in question took place no later than six months after the date upon which the withdrawal/expulsion of the State became effective. The final judgments and decisions of the Court continue to bind the State in question even after it has ceased to be a Party to the ECHR or a Council of Europe member and the obligation to abide by the judgments will thus persist. Therefore, the withdrawing/expelled State is not automatically freed from its obligations under the ECHR. Moreover, the Committee of Ministers continues to enjoy a supervisory role in relation to any cases concerning acts preceding the date on which the withdrawing/expelled State ceased to be Party to the ECHR.[48]

The memorandum also explained what their preferred interpretation of Article 58 is:

---

[46] Resolution CM/Res(2022)3, 'On legal and financial consequences of the cessation of membership of the Russian Federation in the Council of Europe', available from: https://rm.coe.int/resolution-cm-res-2022-3-legal-and-financial-conss-cessation-membershi/1680a5ee99 [Accessed 12 June 2024]. See section 4.2.3 of this chapter for more detail.

[47] Memorandum on 'consequences of the aggression of the Russian Federation against Ukraine', available from: https://search.coe.int/cm/Pages/result_details.aspx?ObjectId=0900001680a5d7d3.

[48] Memorandum, n 47.

Article 58 (3) ECHR provides that when a State ceases to be a member of the Council of Europe it will also cease to be a Party to the ECHR and those Protocols it has ratified, under the same conditions as those stipulated for the denunciation of the Convention under Article 58 (1) and (2) of the ECHR. Thus, Article 58 (3) ECHR assimilates the withdrawal/expulsion from the Council of Europe with the denunciation of the Convention: in both cases the member State in question will cease to be a Party to the ECHR six months after the notification of denunciation or the date on which the withdrawal/expulsion took effect.[49]

The CM followed this advice from the Secretariat. It is not entirely clear why the President of the Court suspended consideration of all Russian cases on 16 March 2022. This suspension could have been a holding measure pending a detailed consideration of what the next steps should be by the plenary of the Court. However, the situation was unfolding very rapidly and arguably this suspension did not make much of a difference. This could be an unexplained symbolic gesture from the Court, but due to the fact that it was quickly reversed its symbolic value is also not very clear. Whatever the rationale for this suspension was, it was lifted by the plenary and the Court continued dealing with the applications directed against Russia.

4.2 Legal analysis of the chosen solution and alternative perspectives on Article 58

It seems that the ECtHR and the CM chose one interpretation of the Convention from a range of legally plausible solutions in a vacuum of previous legal practice.[50] In what follows, while explaining that the selected solution is a legally valid and legitimate interpretation of Article 58(3), we will also highlight why alternative readings are also possible.

Article 58 ECHR is problematic and, as we identified earlier, open to interpretation. The preferred interpretation might depend on relevant policy considerations. We will now identify why one can plausibly argue that the ECHR could no longer apply to Russia from the moment when expulsion took place. Although this position was ultimately rejected by the CM and the ECtHR, it is still worth articulating it here. Article 58(3) ECHR provides that any Contracting Party 'which shall cease to be a

---

[49] Memorandum, n 47, para 34. This, however, is not the only possible reading of Article 58, see Dzehtsiarou and Helfer, n 38.
[50] Greece withdrew from the CoE rather than being expelled (see Chapter 5), and therefore, the interpretation of Article 58 was more straightforward as Article 58(1)–(2) applied.

member of the CoE shall cease to be a Party to this Convention *under the same conditions*' (emphasis added).[51] This reference to 'conditions' may be read as a reference back to Article 58(2) alone, namely that the exiting party cannot benefit from being released from its obligations under the Convention that existed at the point of its departure. If this reading is accepted, then the phrase *'under the same conditions'* has nothing to do with the timing of ceasing to be a party to the Convention; it only explains that departure from the CoE does not absolve the party from its pre-existing obligations. The timing of the ceasing is governed by the phrase: 'any High Contracting Party which shall cease to be a member of the CoE shall cease to be a Party to this Convention'. This means both events happen simultaneously: when the party ceases to be a CoE member, it ceases to be a party to the Convention at the same time.

The Convention is authentic in two languages – English and French. The French version of Article 58(3) states that 'Sous la même réserve cesserait d'être Partie à la présente Convention toute Partie contractante qui cesserait d'être membre du Conseil de l'Europe'. The part of this Article that reads as 'under the same conditions' in English can be translated from French as 'subject to the same reservation'. The fact that the word 'reservation' is used in singular rather than in plural suggests that this section refers only to Article 58(2), not to all other conditions enshrined in the previous sections of the Article. This in turn means that expulsion from the CoE and ceasing to be a member state to the Convention should happen at the same time.

The six-months residual jurisdiction mentioned in Articles 58(1)–(2) seems more applicable when the affected party is withdrawing from the CoE under Article 7 of the Statute and its membership of the latter also continues for at least six months.[52] Here, the Convention applies while the state still remains a member of the CoE. The ECHR is a closed treaty, a state cannot be a party to this treaty unless it is a member of the CoE with one (as we now know) noticeable exception – when a state is expelled from the organisation, it still continues to be a party for further six months. However, this exception does not unambiguously follow from the text of the Convention and one can argue that the Convention should only apply to the members of the CoE.

The ECtHR and the CM chose a different interpretation, namely that the Convention applies to Russia for six more months from the moment of expulsion. In *Fedotova v. Russia,* the ECtHR explained:

---

[51] Article 58(3).
[52] This was the case with Greece which withdrew from the CoE in 1960s. See Chapter 5 for more detail.

It appears from the wording of Article 58, and more specifically the second and third paragraphs, that a State which ceases to be a Party to the Convention by virtue of the fact that it has ceased to be a member of the Council of Europe is not released from its obligations under the Convention in respect of any act performed by that State before the date on which it ceases to be a Party to the Convention.[53]

This means that for the jurisdiction of the ECtHR it is important when the ECHR ceased its application and not when the state left the organisation. We will now offer three key arguments why this solution can be justified. First, it is easy to understand why this was done from a moral and policy perspective, particularly given that major rights violations were being perpetrated on Ukrainian territory, *de jure* within the jurisdiction of the ECHR. Both the Court and the CM aimed to avoid the situation when the expulsion of Russia, which was supposed to stigmatise it, could at the same time remove its responsibility for human rights violations between 16 March and 16 September 2022. The President of the ECtHR, Síofra O'Leary, emphasised exactly this point in her speech on 27 January 2023:

> More than anything, the Court's exercise of its residual jurisdiction reflects the fact that a State cannot take advantage of its expulsion from the Council of Europe to avoid responsibility for violations of the Convention. This is all the more vital given that some of the cases in question are of great significance in terms of Russia's responsibility under international law.[54]

Our second argument is textual, which was also deployed by the ECtHR and the CM. It is indisputable from Article 58(1) and (2) that the six months rule applies for a Contracting Party which denounces the ECHR. So, this is a model according to which, even if a Contracting Party declares its intention to leave the ECHR, it cannot do so with immediate effect. If that was the model chosen and if Article 58(3) was to differ from that, one would have expected it to clearly state so. In other words, there is a presumption that the model described in Article 58(1) applies to other circumstances unless it is explicitly overruled by the subsequent sections.

Finally, there is a further human rights related argument. It seems that the ECHR should not be read as unnecessarily restricting the scope of human

---

[53] *Fedotova and Others v. Russia* [GC], nos. 40792/10 and 2 others, 17 January 2023, para 71.
[54] 'Speech by Síofra O'Leary, President of the European Court of Human Rights, available from: www.echr.coe.int/Documents/Speech_20230127_OLeary_JY_ENG.pdf [Accessed 12 June 2024].

rights protection of the people under its jurisdiction. Withdrawing from the Convention removes a level of protection: the ECHR provides a special accountability regime in Europe with a collective enforcement mechanism. The ECtHR had compulsory jurisdiction over the Russian Federation, and the withdrawal has limited the scope of rights of people under the jurisdiction of Russia. Therefore, the Convention should not be interpreted in any way that would facilitate or accelerate the limitation of the scope of rights. With this in mind one can argue that the Convention should be read as much in favour of human rights protection as it is rationally possible. This is what perhaps the ECtHR and the CM did on this occasion.

As we have demonstrated, there are good legal and policy reasons to conclude that the decision of the CM and the ECtHR to extend the application of the ECHR to Russia for six more months was the correct one. The Russian authorities, however, did not interpret it as such and for internal purposes they considered the Convention ceased its application to Russia on 16 March 2022. Moreover, the Russian authorities declared that they will only enforce the ECtHR judgments that came into force before 16 March 2022, which is obviously groundless. On 11 June 2022, President Putin signed the Federal Law in accordance to which Russia will only enforce those judgments of the ECtHR that entered into force before 16 March 2022. Moreover, the law provides that payments of just satisfaction should be made in Russian roubles as opposed to euros, which is the default currency used by the Court.[55] This law does not provide any justification for this interpretation of the process of denouncement of the Convention.

The Russian authorities ceased almost all engagement with the ECtHR and the CM on 16 March 2022, but the question remains what the Court is going to do with the massive number of applications against Russia pending before it. The following section will investigate this question.

5 Adjudication of the pending cases

Although the ECtHR and the CM settled the question of the applicability of the ECHR to Russia, this approach is clearly not shared by Russia[56] and

---

[55] (2023) 'Putin signed laws on non-enforcement of the judgments of the ECtHR' (Путин подписал законы о неисполнении решений ЕСПЧ), *Vedomosti*, available from: www.vedomosti.ru/politics/news/2022/06/11/926200-reshenii-espch [Accessed 12 June 2024].

[56] The Russian Ministry of Foreign Affairs (MFA) stated that the extension of the application of the Convention was arbitrary in order to accept applications in the context of the Special Military Operation in Ukraine. (2023) 'On the withdrawal from the CoE' ('О выходе России из Совета Европы'), available from: www.mid.ru/ru/foreign_policy/rso/1834254/ [Accessed 12 June 2024].

it is unlikely that it will implement any of the rulings of the Court or indeed cooperate with the CoE. The anecdotal evidence shows that the Russian authorities have stopped almost any communications with the ECtHR and the CM of the CoE. For instance, in the judgment in *Svetova and Others v. Russia*, delivered on 24 January 2023, the Court already noted that the Russian authorities failed to submit their observations that were due on 13 May 2022.[57] No extension was requested or further explanation provided.

Neither the CM nor the ECtHR in their communication on 24–25 March 2022 were explicit as to how the Court should deal with the pending cases against Russia:

> The present Resolution is without prejudice to the consideration of any legal issue, related to the consequences of the cessation of the Russian Federation's membership to the Council of Europe, which may arise in the exercise by the Court of its competence under the Convention to consider cases brought before it.[58]

Therefore, plenty of questions remained at that point in relation to the cases against Russia alleging violations that happened before 16 September 2022. At the end of 2022, there were 16,750 pending applications from Russia.[59] Although the vast majority of these cases are repetitive or inadmissible, there are some complex and high-profile cases, including several major inter-state cases.[60] As has been argued earlier, this is a *sui generis* situation because when Greece withdrew from the CoE in the 1960s there were hardly any cases against it.[61] At the time, Greece had not accepted the right of individual petition, which was only done in 1985.[62] So, the ECtHR was in completely uncharted waters here. The ECtHR had a few plausible solutions to this challenging problem, which involved some complex procedural matters. We discuss these solutions in turn here.[63]

---

[57] *Svetova and Others v. Russia*, no. 54714/17, 24 January 2023, para 9.
[58] Resolution, n 39.
[59] ECtHR (2022) 'Analysis of statistics 2022', 7, available from: www.echr.coe.int/Docume nts/Stats_analysis_2022_ENG.pdf, [Accessed 12 June 2024].
[60] For the list of inter-state cases, see www.echr.coe.int/Pages/home.aspx?p=caselaw/int erstate&c [Accessed 12 June 2024]. See Chapter 4, section 4.
[61] See Chapter 5 for more detail.
[62] Greece's recognition of the right to individual petition took effect on 20 November 1985. See, for instance, *Philis v. Greece*, no. 15264/89, 10 February 1993, para 21.
[63] This section draws and develops the ideas presented in Dzehtsiarou, K. (2023) 'The range of solutions to the Russian cases pending before the European Court of Human Rights: between "business as usual" and "denial of justice"', *ECHR Blog* [Blog], available from: www.echrblog.com/2022/08/the-range-of-solutions-to-russian-cases.html [Accessed 12 June 2024].

5.1 The 'business as usual' model

Under the *'business as usual'* model the Court could have continued dealing with *all* pending Russian cases that fall within its jurisdiction in the manner it would have done so if the expulsion of Russia had never happened. The ECHR operates on the basis that the Court must consider every application that is submitted to it, subject to the admissibility criteria and jurisdictional requirements, albeit it in accordance with its Priority Policy. This rule has some other exceptions (for instance, the applications that do not comply with certain formal requirements are not even accepted and registered[64]) and the decision-making process by the Court is not restricted by any external timeframe. So, the Court can adjudicate these cases for many years.

The ECtHR will be able to dispose of clearly inadmissible applications fairly easily and quickly. This process does not normally involve the respondent state and it is done by the single judge, or committee in more complex cases. However, dealing with more important meritorious applications will be much more difficult under the 'business as usual' model for the following reasons: first, it is clear that the Russian authorities will not collaborate with the Court. This lack of collaboration should be considered from two angles: legality and legitimacy. From the formally legal perspective, the ECtHR can continue adjudicating cases when one of the parties fails or refuses to participate in the proceedings.[65] Although in the majority of judgments against Russia considered until the book's cut off point of 16 March 2023 the government of Russia had submitted their observations,[66] in the case of *Svetova* they did not. The Court here concluded that

> The cessation of a Contracting Party's membership of the Council of Europe does not release it from its duty to cooperate with the Convention bodies. This duty continues for as long as the Court remains competent to deal with applications arising out of acts or omissions capable of constituting a violation of the Convention, provided that they took place prior to the date on which the respondent State ceased to be a Contracting Party to the Convention. Since the events in the instant case which the applicants complained about had occurred before 16 September 2022 and the Court is competent to deal with the application, the respondent Government's failure to engage with the proceedings cannot be an obstacle for its examination.[67]

---

[64] See Rule 47 of the Rules of Court.
[65] See Rule 44C(2) of the Rules of Court.
[66] See, for instance, *B v. Russia*, no. 36328/20, 7 February 2023 and *Ossewaarde v. Russia*, no. 27227/17, 7 March 2023.
[67] *Svetova and Others v. Russia*, n 57, para 31.

The legitimacy angle of this issue is more complex. The cooperation of the respondent state is crucial not only because it increases the worth of the judgments and ensures compliance with the principle of equality of arms, but because the respondent government can clarify certain issues that the applicant might have no knowledge or access to. As Koroteev rightly pointed out, the Court 'should be cautious when deciding cases based on the submissions of only one party'.[68] It will not be the first time that states refused to collaborate with the Court, but in the case of Russia the authorities will not comment on any of the thousands of applications pending before the Court. If there is an expectation that these judgments are to be implemented at some stage, then the Court's commitment to the rule of law and equality of arms is crucial for the legitimacy of these judgments.

Secondly, the 'business as usual' model is problematic because currently there is no sitting 'Russian judge' on the ECtHR. After 16 September 2022, Judge Lobov ceased to be a member of the Court,[69] and according to Article 20 ECHR the Court shall consist of a number of judges equal to that of the Contracting Parties.

Article 26(4) states that:

> There shall sit as an *ex officio* member of the Chamber and the Grand Chamber the judge elected in respect of the High Contracting Party concerned. If there is none or if that judge is unable to sit, a person chosen by the President of the Court from a list submitted in advance by that Party shall sit in the capacity of judge.[70]

Effectively this Article mandates the Court to include the national judge in the composition in the case against their state or if this is impossible appoint someone from the list of ad hoc judges. Rule 29(2) of the Rules of Court regulates the situation when the President of the Chamber can appoint another sitting judge to sit as ad hoc judge:

> (a) … the Contracting Party concerned has not supplied the Registrar with a list as described in paragraph 1 (a) of this Rule, or (b) the President of the Chamber finds that less than three of the persons

---

[68] Koroteev, K. (2022) 'Moving on in Strasbourg', *Verfassungsblog* [Blog], available from: https://verfassungsblog.de/moving-on-in-strasbourg/ [Accessed 12 June 2024].

[69] See the Court's 'press release', available from: https://hudoc.echr.coe.int/eng-press?i=003-7435446-10180882 [Accessed 12 June 2024].

[70] Article 24(4) ECHR.

indicated in the list satisfy the conditions laid down in paragraph 1 (c) of this Rule.[71]

The Court also noted that the current list of ad hoc judges submitted by Russia is not valid.[72] Although none of the exceptions in Rule 29(2) strictly speaking are applicable, the Court has chosen to use it by analogy and keep appointing ad hoc judges among the sitting judges to fulfil the role of the national judge.[73] Even before the Russian judge left the Court, the ECtHR used this approach in some of the cases where Judge Lobov recused himself.[74] It is understandable why the Court decided to follow this path – declaring that an absent judge can stop the Court's adjudication can have negative consequences on the whole system of human rights adjudication. However, the requirement that a national judge sits on the bench is stipulated in the ECHR text for a reason: it is assumed that the national judge can provide clarifications and explanations to the bench on the issues of national law. Continuing appointment of ad hoc judges from the list of siting judges elected in respect to other states means that in case of significant inconvenience in the operationalisation of a procedural provision of the ECHR the ECtHR can be significantly reinterpret them. To some, this approach can be seen as an unjustifiable extension of the Court's competences.

The third reason why the 'business as usual' model presents challenges for the Court is practical in nature: it will take a lot of resources from the Court in circumstances when the budget of the organisation is under pressure as a result of the departure of Russia.[75] The necessary resources will have to

---

[71] Rule 29(2).
[72] *Kutayev v. Russia*, no. 17912/15, 24 January 2023, para 7.
[73] See, for example, *Kogan and Others v. Russia*, no. 54003/20, 7 March 2023 (procedure).
[74] *Ecodefence and Others v. Russia*, nos. 9988/13 and 60 others, 14 June 2022.
[75] See text accompanying n 11 in Chapter 5. The Ministers of the remaining states agreed to fill the gap in the 2022 budget. They stated that '[i]n order to ensure the organisation's sustainability and its ability to carry out its mission and mandate effectively, the Ministers decided to collectively ensure the financial resources to fill the gap in its 2022 Budget, following Russia's exclusion on 16 March', see 'Condemnation of Russia, Council of Europe's priorities, assistance for Ukraine – Foreign Affairs Ministers' meeting concludes in Turin' (2022), available from: www.coe.int/en/web/cm/news/-/asset_publisher/hwwluK1RCEJo/content/condemnation-of-russia-council-of-europe-s-priorities-assistance-for-ukraine-foreign-affairs-ministers-meeting-concludes-in-turin/16695?inheritRedirect=false&redirect=https%3A%2F%2Fwww.coe.int%2Fen%2Fweb%2Fcm%2Fnews%3Fp_p_id%3D101_INSTANCE_hwwluK1RCEJo%26p_p_lifecycle%3D0%26p_p_state%3Dnormal%26p_p_mode%3Dview%26p_p_col_id%3Dcolumn-4%26p_p_col_pos%3D1%26p_p_col_count%3D2 [Accessed 12 June 2024].

be taken from other cases where the Court can still have significant and meaningful impact.

The final reason why 'business as usual' raises issues is that the Russian authorities will not implement any of the judgments that entered into force after 16 March 2022. The binding nature of the judgments of the Court is beyond doubt.[76] However, the fact that a judgment is binding is not sufficient in itself: it needs to be accepted, preferably by the entity that is supposed to execute such judgment. Execution of the ECtHR judgments in cases against member states of the CoE can be tricky, execution of the judgments against uncooperative former member states is almost impossible. We will look into the issues surrounding execution of the final judgments against Russia in the following section. Here, it suffices to say that it is highly improbable that the Russian authorities will voluntarily execute any of the ECtHR judgments.

The argument that execution of these judgments can be used as a condition for admitting Russia back into the organisation[77] is not particularly convincing as it assumes that Russia will apply to join the CoE in the near future. At the moment, it seems that the 'gap' between Europe and Russia is becoming wider.[78]

The validity of this argument depends significantly on how soon Russia will apply to re-join. If this happens relatively soon, then this argument has some appeal, otherwise there are more reasons against it than for it. For instance, the judgments of the Court will inevitably reflect the situation that may not be current any longer. Though some rule of law issues of a systemic nature have been observable for years, the situation with human rights protection in Russia deteriorates very rapidly. The Court's judgments will deal and assess the violations that happened before the situation got even worse.

The victim-centric approach would perhaps support the 'business as usual' model, as in this case the ECtHR will at least confirm that human rights violations have taken place. Jörg Polakiewicz argued that 'accountability of the Russian Federation for its action and the rights of the applicants to get their voices heard have a weight that must not be ignored'.[79] Finding

---

[76] See Article 46 ECHR.
[77] See, for example, Kurnosov, D. (2022) 'Russia without Strasbourg and Strasbourg without Russia: a preliminary outlook', *Strasbourg Observers* [Blog], available from: https://strasbourgobservers.com/2022/09/20/russia-without-strasbourg-and-strasbourg-without-russia-a-preliminary-outlook/ [Accessed 12 June 2024].
[78] See Chapter 7 for more detail.
[79] Polakiewicz, J. (2022) 'Russia's expulsion from the CoE – communication to the 62nd meeting of the Committee of Legal Advisers on Public International Law (CAHDI)', available from: www.coe.int/en/web/dlapil/-/62nd-meeting-of-the-committee-of-legal-advisers-on-public-international-law-cahdi- [Accessed 12 June 2024].

of violation by the ECtHR will provide some satisfaction to the victims. Having said that, this acknowledgement is unlikely to lead to any tangible changes on the ground in Russia: the applicants are unlikely to even receive the monetary compensation from the respondent state. This might increase the feeling of frustration and hopelessness.

In her blog post, Julia Emtseva suggested that the Court was going to adopt the 'business as usual' model.[80] The two main reasons for this are that, according to her, the Court decided that it is capable of dealing with Russian cases without the Russian judge, and without the participation of the Russian authorities in the proceedings. It seems that this conclusion is plausible but premature, and although the Court can use this model, at the moment this cannot be proven conclusively.

Between 16 September 2022[81] and 16 March 2023,[82] the Court delivered 14 judgments in which Russia was a respondent state. Many of them are on highly sensitive topics such as persecution of human rights defenders,[83] LGBTI people[84] and religious groups.[85] Just to compare, between 16 September 2020 and 16 September 2021[86] the Court delivered twice as many judgments in relation to Russia, many of which were concerned with the right to property and the right to a fair trial. Moreover, communicated cases can also indicate the Court's approach. Between 16 September 2022 and 16 March 2023 the Court communicated to the Russian authorities ten cases. These cases are related to the conflict in Ukraine, the 'foreign agents' law and the declaration of some organisations in Russia as 'undesirable'. Again, these are highly sensitive cases. In comparison, between 16 September 2020 and 16 September 2021 the Court communicated 101 cases: ten times more than in 2022–2023.[87] This might at least suggest that the Court has changed its approach to Russian cases but there has not been any official announcement to this effect.

---

[80] Emtseva, J. (2023) 'The withdrawal mystery solved: how the European Court of Human Rights decided to move forward with the cases against Russia', *EJIL:Talk!* [Blog], available from: www.ejiltalk.org/the-withdrawal-mystery-solved-how-the-european-court-of-human-rights-decided-to-move-forward-with-the-cases-against-russia/ [Accessed 12 June 2024].

[81] On this day Russia left the Convention.

[82] This is the 'cut-off day' for this book, see Chapter 1, section 6.

[83] *Kogan and Others v. Russia*, n 73.

[84] *Fedotova and Others v. Russia*, n 53.

[85] *Ossewaarde v. Russia*, n 66.

[86] These dates are taken because on 24 February 2022 Russia started the full-scale invasion of Ukraine and the normal adjudication in Strasbourg was interrupted. During the same period in 2018–2019 – 32 judgments were delivered; in 2019–2020 – 33.

[87] During the same period in 2018–2019 – 85; 2019–2020 – 90.

5.2 The 'pick and choose' model

The Court could also adopt a *'pick and choose'* model. This way, the Court will select a number of leading cases which would include interstate cases, important and potentially sensitive political cases and the cases exemplifying the structural legal problems in Russia and deliver judgments in these cases.

Within this model, having delivered a leading judgment, the Court can use the so-called *Burmych* precedent. The judgment in *Burmych v. Ukraine*[83] was a follow-up judgment to the pilot case of *Ivanov v. Ukraine*.[89] In this case the Court ruled that non-execution of the final national judgments is a violation of Article 6 of the ECHR and that the delay in execution should be covered by an appropriate compensation. In *Burmych* the Court decided that there is no point to give judgments in clone cases and transferred all applications dealing with the same issue to the CM without making a judgment. The Court can also pick the key cases on particular broadly defined themes, attach similar applications to this leading case and then transfer these cases to the CM.

This model would highlight the key problematic areas and give limited satisfaction to some victims. It would also be less resource-intensive, but this approach would not be able to solve other problems highlighted in the previous paragraph such as lack of state involvement and the short-term non-implementation of such judgments. It also creates a new challenge: the risk of generating a perception of selection-bias. The Court will have to justify why some cases are selected while others are not. This will absorb some resources and can open the ECtHR up to criticism. This approach might resemble the Court's priority policy,[90] but a more extreme version of it: those applications which do not fall within the priority category will not be in effect considered.

As Koroteev argues, the *Burmych* approach works as a follow-up to a vast number of cases which would fall within the well-established case law (WECL) category.[91] In other words, this approach will work with simple cases which can be decided on the basis of the principle established in a leading case. Not all pending Russian cases can be categorised as WECL cases. It still means that many other cases would need to be dealt with outside this approach.

---

[88] *Burmych and Others v. Ukraine* (striking out) [GC], nos. 46852/13 et al, 12 October 2017.
[89] *Yuriy Nikolayevich Ivanov v. Ukraine*, no. 40450/04, 15 October 2009.
[90] The Court's Priority Policy, available from: www.echr.coe.int/documents/d/echr/priority_policy_ENG [Accessed 12 June 2024].
[91] Koroteev, n 68.

5.3 The 'radical' model

The Court could use the *'radical approach'*. Under the 'radical approach' we mean either the total freeze of all applications against Russia or even striking them out. From the most recent Court's practice and speeches of its Presidents,[92] we can gather that it was decided not to resort to this extreme stance. We will now consider what these two solutions are and why they have been rejected.

Total freeze would have been one of the quicker and immediately available solutions for the ECtHR. The Court could have suspended the adjudication of all applications against Russia until the situation changes and Russia would either return to the CoE or at least it would agree to comply with the judgments. This solution was possible as the ECtHR has already briefly suspended examination of Russian cases before this suspension was lifted by the plenary of the Court.[93] This suspension could have taken two forms – either total freeze of all pending applications or a rejection of all clearly inadmissible applications and then the freezing of all meritorious ones. Both of these solutions would have saved a lot of resources for the Court, would remove the need for a 'deemed to fail' cooperation of Russia with the Court and would not require the Court to select the 'lucky' applications to deal with. However, no victim would have obtained even moral satisfaction from the fact that the ECtHR found their rights violated.

The clearest and most 'radical approach' would be striking out all the cases against Russia pending before the ECtHR. As politically controversial as this option would be, pursuant to Article 37(1)c ECHR the Court can strike out any application for any reason if it is no longer justified to continue the examination of the application. The Convention provides very wide discretion to the Court here. The ECtHR can decide that in the current situation the delivery of judgments will make no impact and therefore all the applications should be excluded from the list of pending cases. It is hard to imagine that this option has been seriously considered by the Court especially since the plenary of the Court ruled that Article 58 should be interpreted as allowing for an additional six months of the residual jurisdiction of the Court. It is perhaps unwise to allow applications to be submitted to the Court only to then reject them altogether. That said and depending on how quickly the Court will be dealing with the backlog of Russian cases,

---

[92] See, for example, Speech by Síofra O'Leary, n 54.
[93] Resolution of the European Court of Human Rights, 'On the consequences of the cessation of membership of the Russian Federation to the CoE in light of Article 58 of the European Convention on Human Rights', available from: https://echr.coe.int/Documents/Resolution_ECHR_cessation_membership_Russia_CoE_ENG.pdf [Accessed 12 June 2024].

the Court might use this approach to the remaining applications in some years from now.

As things stand at the moment, it seems safe to suggest that the Court has rejected this 'radical approach' as it continues issuing judgments against Russia. It does not mean that the Court cannot go back to this option in the future. It seems that the approach that the Court is applying at the moment is a combination between the 'business as usual' and 'pick and choose' models. It is perhaps this approach that President O'Leary calls the 'middle ground'[94] that the Court accepted in dealing with pending applications against Russia.

6 Execution of the judgments against Russia

There are 2,227 cases[95] that are pending execution by the Russian Federation. Execution of ECtHR judgments is supervised by the CM and takes place on three different levels.[96]

The first level is known as just satisfaction and includes monetary compensation for the human rights violation paid to the victim.[97] Here, Russia has a relatively adequate record[98] and if one does not take into account the cases with a very high level of compensation such as *Yukos v. Russia*,[99] or some politically sensitive cases,[100] the Russian authorities largely honoured the monetary compensation.[101] However, no monetary compensation has been paid by Russia for any judgments that entered into force after 16 March 2022.

The other two levels are those of individual and general measures, namely that the respondent state is obliged to make certain changes to fix the violations committed in relation to a particular victim (for instance, release the applicant from incarceration or review their case on the domestic level) or make changes that would prevent similar violations from happening (for

---

[94] 'Exchange of views with the CM. Speech by Síofra O'Leary', available from: www.echr.coe.int/documents/d/echr/speech_20230413_oleary_exchange_views_committee_ministers_coe_bil [Accessed 12 June 2024].
[95] 'Strategy paper regarding the supervision of the execution of cases pending against the Russian Federation', 8 December 2022, available from: https://search.coe.int/cm/Pages/result_details.aspx?ObjectID=0900001680a91beb [Accessed 12 June 2024].
[96] de Londras, F. and Dzehtsiarou, K. (2017) *Great Debates on the European Convention on Human Rights,* London: Palgrave, chapter 8.
[97] See Article 41 ECHR.
[98] See section 2 of this chapter for a detailed discussion of the debt of the Russian authorities in terms of compensation for human rights violations.
[99] *OAO Neftyanaya Kompaniya Yukos v. Russia*, n 9.
[100] See, for instance, *Catan and Others v. the Republic of Moldova and Russia* [GC], nos. 43370/04 and 2 others, ECHR 2012.
[101] See Chapter 4, section 3.2.1 and earlier in this chapter for more detail.

instance, initiate a legal reform or change legal practice). It is on these levels that the majority of cases against Russia are still not enforced.[102]

On 11 June 2022, Russian President Putin signed a law that amended relevant legal provisions from various domestic Russian laws. By this law most references to the ECtHR judgments and their execution were removed from the legislation of Russia. Prior to 11 June, for example, a criminal case could be reviewed on the basis of the ECtHR judgment; however, now the provision empowering national courts to do that has lost its legal force. Among other things the law of 11 June 2022 provided:

> Judgments of the European Court of Human Rights that entered into force after 15 March 2022 cannot be enforced by the Russian Federation. The amounts of monetary compensation awarded in the judgments of the European Court of Human Rights that entered into force before 15 March 2022 can be transferred only in Russian Roubles to the accounts in Russian credit organisation and cannot be transferred to the accounts in foreign credit organisations located in the foreign states that commit unfriendly actions towards the Russian Federation.[103]

This law clearly states that the Russian authorities have their own approach to interpretation of the ECHR which is significantly different to the one of the ECtHR and the CM. It seems that for Russia the Convention no longer applied as of 15 March 2022 and, moreover, it considers that the judgments are sufficiently implemented when the monetary compensation is paid; no other measures seem to be necessary. As a result, Russia paid some of the remaining monetary compensation and dissolved the department that dealt with the representation of Russia before the ECtHR. From the perspective of the Russian authorities, their obligations under the ECHR have conclusively ended. Unsurprisingly, the CM was of a different view

---

[102] See 'Russian Federation and the CoE', available from: www.coe.int/en/web/execution/russian-federation [Accessed 12 June 2024]. The data summarised by the European Implementation Network (EIN) states that there are 217 leading judgments pending implementation. Average time leading cases have been pending: 8 years, 15 days. Percentage of leading cases from the last 10 years still pending: 90 per cent. 'EIN Russia', available from: www.einnetwork.org/russia-echr [Accessed 12 June 2024].

[103] Article 7 of the Federal Law on 'Amending Certain Legislative Acts of the Russian Federation and Declaring Certain Legislative Acts of the Russian Federation as No Longer in Force' (Федеральный закон от 11 июня 2022 г. № 183-ФЗ 'О внесении изменений в отдельные законодательные акты Российской Федерации и признании утратившими силу отдельных положений законодательных актов Российской Федерации'). (Translated by the authors), available from: www.garant.ru/products/ipo/prime/doc/404720365/ [Accessed 12 June 2024].

because, as Koroteev rightly pointed out, 'a respondent State cannot choose, under whatever criteria, the judgments of the Court it abides by and those it does not'.[104]

On 8 June 2022, prior to the entry into force of the Russian Law on non-execution, the CM adopted a decision regarding its supervisory role and practices in respect to Russian cases.[105] In this decision, the CM recalled its own resolution from 23 March 2022 in which it invited the Russian authorities to participate in the meetings of the Committee in which the execution of judgments against Russia are discussed. Russia, however, has not done so. The CM stated that it can receive communications on the state of execution from the NGOs and other sources. Finally, the CM called on the Russian Federation to comply with its international obligations, namely execute the judgments of the ECtHR.

On 8 December 2022, the CM presented the strategy of execution of judgments against Russia.[106] This is a realistic strategy that takes into account the unfortunate fact that Russia is not going to collaborate with the CoE under the current political regime. The CM emphasised the need for collaboration with the Russian civil society and other international organisations of which Russia is still a member, taking stock of the pending cases and amounts of just satisfaction and communicating this to the public. The Committee also decided not to alter its approach to execution. However, it remains to be seen in the longer run how this approach can be maintained as the CM relies to some extent on the documents received from the state, such as action plans and various reports.

As one of the consequences of this strategy the Secretary General of the CoE wrote a letter to the Minister of Foreign Affairs of Russia on 9 December 2022, urging him to execute some of the judgments including *Georgia v. Russia (I)*[107] and *(II)*,[108] *Catan v. Russia and Moldova*[109] and *Mozer v. Republic of Moldova and Russia*,[110] *Jehovah's Witnesses of Moscow v. Russia*,[111] *Navalnyy and Ofitserov v. Russia*[112] and *Volodina v. Russia*.[113] The reaction of

---

[104] Koroteev, n 68.
[105] CM Decision, CM/Del/Dec(2022)1436/A2 on 'cases pending against the Russian Federation', available from: https://search.coe.int/cm/pages/result_details.aspx?objectid=0900001680a6cfe8 [Accessed 12 June 2024].
[106] Strategy paper, n 95
[107] *Georgia v. Russia (I)*.
[108] *Georgia v. Russia (II)*, n 23.
[109] *Catan and Others v. the Republic of Moldova and Russia*, n 100.
[110] *Mozer v. the Republic of Moldova and Russia* [GC], no. 11138/10, 23 February 2016.
[111] *Jehovah's Witnesses of Moscow and Others v. Russia*, no. 302/02, 10 June 2010.
[112] *Navalnyy and Ofitserov v. Russia*, nos. 46632/13 and 28671/14, 23 February 2016.
[113] *Volodina v. Russia*, no. 41261/17, 9 July 2019.

the Russian Ministry of Foreign Affairs (MFA) to this letter was remarkable. The press officer of the ministry stated:

> Before I comment on the letter, it is necessary to study it in detail. Unfortunately, the Council of Europe has taken the path of 'megaphone diplomacy' when communicating with us. Strasbourg rushed to make the letter public, as they published it almost at the same time as they sent it to the official Russian representatives.
>
> This clearly shows that it is not about a desire to begin a constructive dialogue with our country, but about yet another propaganda campaign. The point is apparently to show that the Council of Europe allegedly cares about human rights in Russia while we try to wriggle out of fulfilling our international obligations. In the meantime, they overlook the fact that this organisation has destroyed the common cooperation in humanitarian law on the continent with their own hands to please a Russophobic majority, thus making Russia's membership in the Council of Europe and participation in its main conventions impossible.[114]

Leaving the emotional tone of this statement aside, one needs to note that it seems that no communication from the CoE to Russia will have any intended effect at the moment. It seems unlikely that the fact that the letter was made public made any difference to its influence on human rights in Russia. That said, it shows that public statements might trigger at least some reaction and therefore it is perhaps wise to continue making statements on the situation of execution of cases against Russia.

Overall, it is safe to conclude that the situation with execution of the judgments against Russia is not very hopeful. The individual and general measures required by judgments currently pending execution before 15 March 2022 will not be implemented. These included the demand of the Committee to free Alexei Navalnyy – one of the leaders of the opposition in Russia, who tragically lost his life in detention in February 2024. Moreover, none of the judgments that have been delivered after 15 March 2022 will be executed, including in terms of just satisfaction. Many important judgments are still pending, including inter-state applications. Hundreds of unenforced ECtHR judgments will be one of the key legacies of Russia of its 26-year membership in the CoE.

---

[114] 'Comment by Foreign Ministry spokeswoman Maria Zakharova on the letter from the Secretary General of the Council of Europe Marija Pejcinovic Buric to Foreign Minister Sergey Lavrov', available from: www.mid.ru/ru/foreign_policy/news/1843582/?lang=en [Accessed 12 June 2024].

One can argue that this unprecedented situation requires unprecedented approaches and creative solutions. The CoE has never experienced a situation like this; never has a state with a high number of pending applications and pending unenforced judgments left the organisation. This creates a challenge but can also be seen as an opportunity to try new approaches. The *sui generis* nature of this situation can justify the ways to enforce judgments which are impossible to current members. For instance, one can consider using the frozen assets of Russian state companies to pay at least some of the compensation awarded by the ECtHR. This as well as other suggestions such as a trust fund for compensation[115] are ripe with legal difficulties but it is an opportunity for the CM to set a strong precedent here.

7 Conclusion

This chapter demonstrated that Russia's expulsion had a deep impact on the Strasbourg system of human rights protection. The Court lost its largest and most challenging respondent state, which from a purely administrative perspective and knowing the scale of the Court's backlog might not be necessarily a negative development going forward. However, from the perspective of human rights protection in Europe, this is a dramatic and clearly negative event. We established that among other things, the Court will not be able to make any meaningful impact on ongoing human rights violations that take place under the jurisdiction of Russia, inside and outside of the Russian borders. Moreover, the Court will be unable to impact the situation in Russia even on the micro level: this was possible prior to expulsion.

The expulsion of Russia gave the CM and the Court an opportunity to elaborate on the interpretation of Article 58 ECHR, which had never been used in the same context in the past, and now its meaning and effects have been clarified. Despite the fact that the text of Article 58 is not very clear, it seems that the ECtHR will retain six months of residual jurisdiction irrespective of how a state has left the CoE. This is not the only possible reading of Article 58 but it has now been confirmed by the CM and the plenary of the ECtHR.

The Court and the CM are left with a large number of applications and judgments against Russia; the former need to be adjudicated, and the latter have to be enforced. It is unlikely that the current Russian authorities will implement any of the judgments of the Court. The Court had a range of solutions at its disposal and it seems that the Court has chosen a middle ground between the 'pick and choose' and 'business as usual' models. This

---

[115] Koroteev, n 68. See Chapter 4, section 4.2.

approach, however, can be amended depending on how the situation develops. The CM's strategy for execution of ECtHR judgments accepts the reality of the lack of cooperation with Russia and tries to find meaningful ways of impacting the Russian authorities.

7

Conclusion: A Legacy of Bad Faith

1 Introduction

When Mikhail Gorbachev addressed the Parliamentary Assembly of the Council of Europe (PACE) in 1989, he cited Victor Hugo's European aspiration that the day would come when all the nations of the continent would form a European brotherhood and 'the only battlefield would be markets open for trade and minds open to ideas'.[1] These words resonated throughout European capitals which were, by that time, desperate to break down the physical and metaphorical barriers that had divided the continent for half a century. The rapid integration of some post-Soviet states into the family of European democracies seemed to be the *right* thing to do, morally and politically, and this also seemed true in the case of Russia. The prospect of integration was also seen as a unique opportunity, so there was a certain urgency attached to the process.

By virtue of its size, population and geopolitical importance, Russia's admission to the Council of Europe (CoE) in 1996 transformed the organisation, significantly enhancing its profile by giving it an overwhelmingly pan-European character,[2] allowing it ostensibly to fulfil the illustrious accolade of becoming a 'vast area of democratic security' as mooted at the 1993 Vienna Summit.[3] Although some commentators were suspicious that Russia was seeking to 'readjust' the CoE to its own ends,[4] Russia appeared

---

[1] Speech made by Mikhail Gorbachev, as President of the Supreme Soviet of the Soviet Union to the Assembly, 6 July 1989, available from: www.cvce.eu/en/obj/address_given_by_mikhail_gorbachev_to_the_council_of_europe_6_july_1989-en-4c021687-93f9-4727-9e8b-836e0bc1f6fb.html [Accessed 13 June 2024].

[2] CM Resolution (96) 2, 'Invitation to the Russian Federation to become a member of the Council of Europe', 8 February 1996.

[3] Council of Europe Vienna Declaration, Vienna, 9 October 1993.

[4] Massias, J.-P. (2007) *Russia and the Council of Europe: Ten Years Wasted?*, France: Institut Français des Relations Internationales, Russia/NIS Research Programme, pp 4–17.

to double-down on the spirit of European unity when it chaired the CoE Committee of Ministers (CM) for the first and only time from May to November 2006 on the theme 'Towards a united Europe – without dividing lines'.[5] However, by this stage Russia's commitment to the CoE was already weakening significantly on a domestic level and, soon after, populist politics, the erosion of democracy and the revival of aggressive nationalism in Russia not only eliminated the early idyll associated with membership, but thrust the CoE into an unprecedented crisis which has cast a long shadow over the organisation.

This book has sought to provide a unique and comprehensive overview of Russia's membership of the CoE. It traced Russia's journey from hopeful accession all the way through to full-scale military aggression against a fellow member state, ultimately leading to its expulsion. In parallel, the monograph has highlighted systemic weaknesses of the CoE in particular when faced with Russia's aggression against its neighbours, its repeated breaches of accession commitments, democratic backsliding, persistent non-compliance and so its general bad faith towards (if not contempt for) the CoE and its values. Despite some initial progress in certain areas – such as supporting the development of a nascent, but deeply committed, civil society and human rights defender movement – it is regrettably the issues of non-compliance and bad faith that emerge as the prevailing legacies of Russia's membership of the CoE from 1996 to 2022, in great contrast to its stated aspiration in the 1990s that it would become a committed member of the European 'family of nations'.

However, the analysis of Russia's membership has also served to triage several serious political, resourcing and organisational challenges facing the organisation. It is clear that if the CoE is to play a meaningful role in addressing future challenges and to help secure peace and prosperity in Europe, the institutional weaknesses exposed during Russia's membership should serve as a blueprint for the reform and normative revival of the CoE, subject to the will of the member states.

In this final chapter, our aim is not to summarise the book, but rather to offer a more reflective overall assessment, identifying the more dominant aspects of Russia's legacy on the CoE in the light of our key arguments. To do so, we present an analysis of some of the factors compounding the damage done by Russia to the CoE, including through its egregious breaches of the Statute. We refer to this convergence of systemic failures as the 'Triple Fault'. We then cast an eye to the future, which is fraught with risk and

---

[5] Chairmanship of Committee of Ministers: Russian Federation presents its priorities, 19 May 2005, available from: http://wcd.coe.int/ViewDoc.jsp?p=&id=1002429&Site=COE&direct=true, [Accessed 14 June 2024].

uncertainty, in the hope that the member states might seize their statutory responsibilities and empower the CoE to build back stronger.

2 The core argument of the book

Set against a dramatic and still-unfolding international legal and geopolitical context, this book set out to comprehensively examine the legacy of Russian membership of the CoE and its expulsion from the organisation. The purpose was to offer a chronicle of the key developments – as we see them – and to identify certain systematic challenges which deserve further consideration if the CoE is to be prepared for the future. The narrative of the book centres on Russia's attempted transition towards European liberal democratic standards within the CoE framework, and its gradual but dramatic retreat from that path into authoritarianism. The core arguments set out are therefore strongly linked to the concept of good faith.

Russia was admitted to the organisation in 1996 based on a promise of good faith.[6] Irrespective of how one views Moscow's original intentions regarding membership, the overall evidence shows that, especially after the early 2000s, it did not fully engage in good faith – indeed, often quite the opposite – and instead adopted an increasingly ritualistic approach to its membership.

The decision to admit Russia in the first place gives rise to many legitimate questions about the appropriateness of balancing a unique historical opportunity to encourage alignment with the European normative agenda, on the one hand, with the risks of turning a blind eye to serious deficits in human rights law, policy and practice by rushing the process, on the other. This was, as we describe it, the 'therapeutic' logic that prevailed, admitting Russia in spite of the objective shortcomings and risks based on a presumption that accession would help to create conditions for conformity with CoE standards.

One's view on the appropriateness of admitting Russia as a member state is largely influenced by the weight one attaches to *realpolitik* considerations, on the one hand, or idealist aspirations, on the other. From a political perspective, the decision to admit Russia was entirely consistent with the political mood in Europe at that time to capitalise on the fall of communism and to embrace the momentum building behind the ideas of open borders, markets and minds. It was also in step with the direction of travel with the organisation itself. By then the CoE had steadily consolidated its membership base, readmitting democratic Greece in 1974, inviting Portugal in 1976 and

---

[6] See Chapter 2.

Spain in 1977, San Marino in 1988 and Finland in 1989.[7] In the mid-1980s, the Colombo Commission on the long-term future of European cooperation emphasised the possibilities of European cooperation across the frontiers of the different economic and political systems, setting the stage for a broader easterly integrationist policy to develop within the CoE.[8] The difficulties, however, emanated from normative considerations. As former Secretary General Daniel Tarschys observed, 'Russia is an incomplete democracy, not yet being fully governed by law'.[9] While not wishing to cast aspersions on those who took the calculated risk to admit Russia for good reasons in 1996, our analysis shows this presumption of 'therapeutic' membership was ill-advised.

As the political leadership in Russia actively eroded the rule of law and democracy at home, internationally it misused its power, including to seek to limit the effectiveness of the CoE through, for example, its filibuster tactics regarding Protocol 14 and its non-execution of judgments of the European Court of Human Rights (ECtHR). Although a core aspect of our argument emphasises that the overarching responsibility for Russia's retreat into authoritarianism lies with the Russian political leadership, the failure of the CoE to appropriately respond to overt challenges to the integrity of the system ultimately became the prelude to Russia's cataclysmic violation of the Statute of the CoE. In other words, the CoE was not only fully aware of the democratic backsliding taking place in Russia over a considerable period of time, it observed gross violations of the CoE Statute in the cases of Chechnya and Crimea without meaningful follow-up, let alone sanction.

3 A dominant legacy of bad faith?

Tracing the experience of Russian membership of the CoE paints a picture full of contrasts, curiosities and inconsistencies. The story is one which

---

[7] CM Resolution (74) 34, 'Invitation to Greece to rejoin the Council of Europe', 28 November 1974; CM Resolution (76) 37, 'Invitation to Portugal to become a member of the Council of Europe', 20 September 1976; CM Resolution (77) 32, 'Invitation to Spain to become a member of the Council of Europe', 18 October 1977; CM Resolution (88) 14, 'Invitation to the Republic of San Marino to become a member of the Council of Europe', 24 October 1988; CM Resolution (89) 1, 'Invitation to Finland to become a member of the Council of Europe', 31 January 1989.

[8] Final Report of the Commission of Eminent European Personalities (Colombo Commission), June 1986.

[9] Tarschys, D. (1996) 'Enlargement: the Russian chapter', in Council of Europe (ed) *The Challenges of a Greater Europe: The Council of Europe and Democratic Security*, Strasbourg: Council of Europe Publishing, pp 59–61.

began with opportunities, but transpired to be replete with micro-successes and profound macro-failures. Here we build on the reflections offered in the conclusion to Chapter 4, concerning Russia's persistent breach of CoE obligations and its damaging membership.

Russia's CoE membership lasted for 26 years, but cooperation between the Soviet Union and the CoE spans almost five decades, with engagement in the spheres of youth policy and environmental protection as early as the 1970s.[10] During its term of membership, Russia signed or ratified 83 out of more than two hundred CoE treaties, eight out of thirteen partial agreements,[11] and actively participated in the elaboration of new standards. Membership facilitated a level of interaction and trust-building across the European continent, including at government,[12] inter-parliamentary,[13] local government,[14] civil society and judicial levels,[15] the value of which is impossible to fully assess but certainly bore important dividends. Russian experts and civil servants participated in cooperation projects, trainings, seminars and conferences to share their experiences, to learn more about CoE standards and to engage with their European counterparts. It is impossible to know precisely how many people were spared from the death penalty due to the moratorium of the late 1990s. Membership also created a platform for, or at least encouraged the development of, democratic forces, including civil society in Russia. A permanent Russian diplomatic presence in Strasbourg allowed for engagement on a continuous basis with European counterparts which

---

[10] See 'History of the Russian Federation's participation in the Council of Europe', Archived site of the Permanent Representation of Russia to the Council of Europe, 15 March 2022, available from: https://coe.mid.ru/en_GB/istoria-ucastia-rossii-v-sovete-evropy [Accessed 14 June 2024].

[11] See CoE Treaty Office website: www.coe.int/en/web/conventions/by-non-member-states-of-the-coe-or-the-european-union?module=treaties-full-list-signature&CodePays=RUS&CodeSignatureEnum=&DateStatus=03-10-2024&CodeMatieres= [Accessed 13 June 2024].

[12] 'Political dialogue' between Russia and the Committee of Ministers has been established since 7 May 1992. See PACE Opinion 193 (1996), 25 January 1996, para 7.2.

[13] The Russian Parliament received special guest status at the Parliamentary Assembly on 14 January 1992. Opinion 193 (1996), para 2.

[14] One of the last major interventions by Russia at the CoE Congress of Local and Regional Authorities prior to expulsion in 2022 was by Deputy Minister of Justice Sergei Bystrevskii in October 2019, see https://rm.coe.int/cg37-2019-12-en-written-questions-deputy-minister-of-justice-sergei-by/1680989a26, [Accessed 14 June 2024].

[15] Russia was a driving force behind the aspiration to create a common pan-European space in the development of direct cooperation between the supreme legal (judicial) bodies of member states. This was a key priority of its 2006 chairmanship of the Committee of Ministers, and the initiative later developed into the CoE Superior Courts Network which was officially launched on 5 October 2015.

created a unique platform for dialogue, doubtlessly relevant to matters well beyond the scope of the CoE itself.[16]

In the early years Russia's substantive contribution to the organisation tended to focus on issues in the fields of linguistic minority rights, culture, education, science, youth and sports.[17] It sought, and with some success, to advance certain agendas, such as that of intercultural dialogue.[18] Perhaps somewhat curiously, Russia was to the fore in pushing for a comprehensive Memorandum of Understanding between the CoE and the European Union to establish clear principles of cooperation between the two main European inter-governmental organisations.[19] Membership also had some important, though as discussed in Chapters 4 and 6 largely superficial, effects domestically through a process of standards 'socialisation'.[20] In his 2005 report, the Commissioner for Human Rights observed that up to that point 'a series of major transformations' had taken place, including that 'legislation governing the country had been substantially reformed'.[21] After the first ten years of membership, former Secretary General Terry Davis pointed to four discreet areas in which the CoE membership had already had a positive influence on Russia.[22] He argued that membership led directly to a moratorium on the death penalty which prevented tens, if not hundreds, of people from being executed. He emphasised the value of Russians having the opportunity to seek and receive protection from the ECtHR, and he pointed to the importance of the Russian authorities being subjected to regular and often critical reporting resulting from different CoE monitoring mechanisms. Finally, he noted the benefits of having access to CoE expert

---

[16] For discussion of the influence that Russia had on the day-to-day functioning of the ECtHR, see Fura, E. and Maruste, R. (2018) 'Russia's impact on the Strasbourg system, as seen by two former judges of the European Court of Human Rights', in L. Mälksoo and W. Benedek (eds) *Russia and the European Court of Human Rights: The Strasbourg Effect*, Cambridge: Cambridge University Press, pp 222–51.

[17] See, by way of illustration, Chairmanship priorities from 2006, available from: https://rm.coe.int/1680720ecc [Accessed 13 June 2024].

[18] The International Conference 'Dialogue of Cultures and Inter-Faith Cooperation' (the so-called Volga Forum), Nizhniy Novgorod/Russian Federation, 7–9 September 2006, significantly advanced the focus on intercultural dialogue, which led to the white paper entitled 'Living Together as Equals in Dignity', launched by the Council of Europe Ministers of Foreign Affairs at their 118th Ministerial Session, Strasbourg, 7 May 2008.

[19] Memorandum of Understanding between the Council of Europe and the European Union, 23 May 2007.

[20] See generally Mälksoo, L. and Benedek, W. (2018) *Russia and the European Court of Human Rights: The Strasbourg Effect*, Cambridge: Cambridge University Press, p 228.

[21] Report by Mr Alvaro Gils-Robles, Commissioner for Human Rights, on his visit to the Russian Federation, 15 – 30 July 2004, CommDH(2005)2, 20 April 2005.

[22] Op-ed by Terry Davis, *New York Times*, 24 May 2006, available from: www.nytimes.com/2006/05/24/opinion/24iht-eddavis.html [Accessed 14 June 2024].

advice and cooperation. The fact that Russia was still embroiled in the Second Chechen war at the time of writing was largely overlooked by the Secretary General's op-ed, save for a loose reference to just satisfaction for victims and the development of an action plan to prevent future violations.

However, what one can see from this vantage point is the inescapable fact that Russia's membership of the CoE was always carried out on Russia's terms, with an overbearing sense of Russian exceptionalism,[23] and its preparedness to use its clout and 'big payer' status as a basis to potentially weaken its accountability. The case law of the ECtHR and the reports of monitoring bodies over several years paint a clear picture of weak effectiveness and shallow penetration of CoE standards, often cosmetic approximation of laws (and in later years, direct challenges to them) and a progressive deterioration of compliance with the standards of the CoE.[24] Following its refusal to be held to account in relation to Chechnya in breach of explicit accession commitments, Russia's obfuscation and dilatory tactics regarding the ratification of Protocol 14,[25] which had initially opened for signature in 2004 but was not accepted by Russia until 2010, can all be seen as acts of profound bad faith, undermining critical efforts to improve the effectiveness of the Court. However, this was eclipsed by the direct defiance of the CoE witnessed over the 2010s, Russia's contempt for the CoE Statute being in evidence in relation to its actions in Georgia in (and since) 2008 and, later, even more glaringly, in Crimea. These actions were then compounded by its non-cooperation with the CoE after 2016, and how after that it used its stature and influence to serve its own interests, resulting in its ritualistic reintegration into the CoE in 2019.[26]

Meanwhile, within Russia itself, the government's deliberate misuse of the rule of law is a particularly insidious aspect of its democratic decay. The so-called 'foreign agents' law and related legislation is an example in this regard, where despite the best efforts of the CoE in highlighting inconsistencies between Russian legislation and practice and European

---

[23] Antonov describes 'a great deal of exceptionalism in legal matters' on Russia's part, particularly as concerns human rights. See Antonov, M. (2018) 'Philosophy behind human rights: Valery Zorkin vs. the West?', in L. Mälksoo and W. Benedek (eds) *Russia and the European Court of Human Rights: The Strasbourg Effect*, Cambridge: Cambridge University Press, p 152.

[24] See details of cases pending execution in which Russia is the respondent, available from: www.coe.int/en/web/execution/russian-federation and https://hudoc.exec.coe.int/eng#%22execidentifier%22:[%22HEXEC(2023)12-RUS-MEASURES-REQUIRED-IN-PENDING-CASES-ENG%22]} [Accessed 14 June 2024]. On execution of judgments, see further Chapter 4, section 3.2.1 and Chapter 6, section 2. On the prospects of execution, post-expulsion, see Chapter 6, section 6.

[25] See Chapter 3, section 3.3.3.

[26] See Chapter 4, sections 2.2–2.4.

standards, the Russian authorities refused to change course, as discussed in Chapter 4. In January 2006, immediately prior to Russia assuming the chairmanship of the CM, new legislative amendments concerning the non-governmental sector in Russia were enacted and these were seen as having the potential to have a chilling effect on civil society in Russia.[27] Despite intensive engagement by the Commissioner for Human Rights[28] and some initial indications of progress in 2009 which simplified the reporting and registration requirements, further legislative changes came into force up to 2015 which progressively restricted the freedom of civil society organisations to operate in Russia through the imposition of financial reporting obligations, limits on foreign funding and/or other requirements that impeded their operation. The law on 'undesirable foreign and international organisations'[29] was subject to detailed review by the Venice Commission[30] and engagement by the Secretary General among others.[31] The ECtHR also ruled that a 2012 law, the 'foreign agents' law, violated Article 11 interpreted in the light of Article 10 in the case of *Ecodefence and Others v. Russia*.[32] The Venice Commission also reviewed the 2012 Act. To add insult to injury, the CoE itself was not immune from laws restricting civil society space, as on 22 December 2020 the General Prosecutor's Office of the Russian Federation and the Ministry of Justice categorised the CoE Association of Schools of Political Studies as an undesirable organisation in the territory of the Russian Federation.[33]

---

[27] Federal Law No. 18-FZ of 10 January 2006, 'On introducing amendments to certain legislative acts of the Russian Federation'. For discussion of the context, see Chapter 3, section 4.

[28] See Opinion of the Commissioner for Human Rights on the Legislation of rhe Russian Federation on Non-Commercial Organisations in light of Council of Europe Standards, CommDH(2013)15, 15 July 2013; and Opinion of the Commissioner for Human Rights on the Legislation of the Russian Federation on Non-Commercial Organisations in light of Council of Europe Standards, An Update, CommDH(2015)17, 9 July 2015.

[29] Federal Law No. 129-FZ 'On Amending Certain Legislative Acts of the Russian Federation'.

[30] CDL-AD(2016)020-e, Russian Federation – Opinion on Federal Law No. 129-FZ 'On Amending Certain Legislative Acts' (Federal Law on Undesirable Activities of Foreign and International Non-Governmental Organisations), adopted by the Venice Commission at its 107th Plenary Session, Venice, 10–11 June 2016.

[31] See, for example, the report by the Secretary General of the Council of Europe (2016), 'State of Democracy, Human Rights and the Rule of Law: A Security Imperative for Europe', Strasbourg: Council of Europe, p 65 *inter alia*.

[32] *Ecodefence and Others v. Russia*, nos. 9988/13 and 60 others, 14 June 2022.

[33] The CoE Schools of Political Studies are a cooperative scheme funded by the CoE to strengthen the democratic leadership potential of young political and social leaders and to develop their competences for democratic culture. As of 2021, the Moscow School of Political Studies has been dissolved.

Then there is the non-execution of cases related to the conflict in Chechnya, the detention and repression of political opposition figures such as Alexei Navalnyy in flagrant disregard for the judgments of the European Court of Human Rights (ECtHR), the shrinking civil society space and deliberate targeting of human rights organisations, and the de facto limitation of the work of the CoE itself, including the Commissioner for Human Rights.[34] Despite an enormous and growing portfolio of unimplemented cases and the well-documented deterioration of human rights[35] and democracy in Russia, it was the illegal annexation of the territory of another sovereign state in 2014 and its subsequent hostility toward the CoE that confirmed that Russia's enduring legacy during its membership of the CoE is one of sustained bad faith, breaches of its international legal obligations and repeated broken promises.

4 Democratic decay, aggressive military actions and the 'Triple Fault' scenario

The experience of Russia's membership and ultimate expulsion from the CoE has highlighted the extent to which a member state can retreat from its commitments, on the one hand, but it also shines a light on a number of major system failures, on the other. These failures relate to the ineffectiveness of post-accession supervision, the inadequacy of the process of execution of ECtHR judgments, the lack of effective and accessible membership sanctions, and the accountability gap between monitoring processes and the work of the CM, all of which have been exacerbated by persistent resourcing deficiencies and political apathy at the highest level of member state governments over many years.

At risk of labouring the point, Russia's decision to launch a war of aggression on Ukraine and, before that, its illegal annexation of Crimea in 2014 were entirely and exclusively of its own doing, and indicative of the

---

[34] See, among others, 'Council of Europe's Rights Chief Decries Abuses, Says Russia "Only Country Not Cooperating"', available from: www.rferl.org/a/muizneks-russia-chechnya-azerbaijan-crimea-council-europe/28760684.html, 27 September 2017 [Accessed 14 June 2024].

[35] By way of illustration, under Article 10 (2) of the European Convention for the Prevention of Torture and Inhuman or Degrading Treatment or Punishment, if a state party 'fails to co-operate or refuses to improve the situation in the light of the Committee's recommendations, the Committee may decide, after the Party has had an opportunity to make known its views, by a majority of two-thirds of its members to make a public statement on the matter'. Up to 2022, the CPT has made ten such statements, four of which relate to Russia (2001, 2003, 2007, 2019). See Brummer, n 43 at 263–4. In 2019, the CPT focussed on the torture of detained persons in the Chechen Republic, which it described as 'a deep-rooted problem'. See text accompanying n 81.

acute political, legal and moral failure of the Russian political leadership. However, other factors contributed to the progressive weakening of the CoE as a pan-European system for the protection of human rights, the rule of law and democracy over a number of decades. These factors directly affected the form, function and effectiveness of CoE interventions vis-à-vis Russia, and they represent a significant risk to the organisation going forward.

Generally speaking, actors within the CoE (most notably PACE and the Commissioner) highlighted human rights, democracy and rule of law concerns effectively and sometimes even in a timely manner, while the ECtHR was able to elaborate a rich and diverse portfolio of judgments, albeit often many years later and therefore too late. However, overall, the CoE failed to prevent democratic decline in Russia and lacked effective tools to deal with bad faith in an appropriate manner, a fact which was understood and seems to have been exploited by Russia. As a consequence, the CM moved from accepting an uneasy status quo, lasting many years, where Russia was largely non-compliant (and latterly, defiant), to expelling it in a dramatically short period of time. A confluence of system failures was apparent politically, legally and structurally, which fundamentally undermined Europe's human rights protection architecture. One can observe three separate but partially inter-dependent failures which we will refer to as the 'Triple Fault':

(1) The original failure relates to Russia's observable pattern of bad faith. The willingness of the Russian authorities to actively breach the fundamental values of the CoE in flagrant, premeditated and deliberate ways demonstrates its incontrovertible failure to comply in good faith with its obligations under Statutory Article 3, the general commitments it made upon accession, and with respect to individual CoE treaties, most notably the ECHR (including Article 46(1)).

(2) The second failure relates to the inability or unwillingness (or both) of the CM to effectively safeguard the Statute. In other words, the abject failure of political leadership of the CoE (that is, the member states exercising collective responsibility in the CM format) to calibrate responses of maximum utility, proportionate to observable transgressions of the Statute, in a timely manner in accordance with the CoE Statute.

(3) The third dimension is the conditional failure of the CoE system to effectuate compliance with CoE values and standards (including judgments and interim measures of the ECtHR, recommendations of monitoring and advisory bodies, including relevant findings by PACE) despite evidence of a progressive pattern of democratic decay, verified deterioration of human rights and rule of law standards and increasing hostility towards the international human rights legal framework.

Russia is responsible for the aggression and its consequences. However, if the CoE is to reaffirm its role 'as the leading intergovernmental organisation in Europe for all matters relating to human rights, democracy and the rule of law',[36] there is a need to critically reflect on the functioning of the system and to identify key weaknesses which must be addressed to strengthen the system for the future. We will now consider each aspect of this Triple Fault, in turn.

4.1 Original fault: Russia's bad faith and rejection of CoE values

Turning firstly to the original fault, the failure of Russia to comply in good faith with its commitments under Statutory Article 3, numerous accession commitments and Article 46 ECHR is evident. This failure is attributable exclusively to Russia as a sovereign state with authority over its own decisions.[37] As discussed in Chapter 5, for the purpose of triggering suspension or expulsion proceedings, the question of whether or not a member state has 'seriously violated' Article 3 of the Statute is the reserved prerogative of the CM.[38] It is difficult to conceive of a credible legal argument diminishing Russia's responsibility for its actions in Ukraine. In its Opinion 300 (2022), PACE noted that the armed attack on Ukraine in 2022 qualifies as a 'crime against peace' under the Charter of the International Military Tribunal (Nuremberg Charter) and constitutes an 'aggression' under the terms of Resolution 3314 (XXIX) of the United Nations General Assembly.[39] Any decision by a sovereign government to launch an aggressive war is unjustifiable and patently incompatible with Article 3 of the Statute of the CoE. However, not every situation may be as clear-cut and enjoy such a resounding consensus within the CM, which is, after all, a political institution. A margin of discretion necessarily applies to any determination of what constitutes a 'serious breach' of Article 3, and in this regard the role of PACE in offering its views on the matter could be decisive. As we argued in Chapter 5, the decision by the CoE to expel Russia was consistent with the scale and nature of the transgression and the CM acted decisively and although not exactly in accordance with the procedure provided to it by the Statute, the deviations cannot undermine the validity of the process.[40] The decision to expel Russia was explicitly and exclusively

---

[36] PACE Recommendation 2245 (2023), para 11.
[37] This does not preclude the possibility that crimes committed in Ukraine may be attributable to others who have facilitated, aided or abetted Russia, such as Belarus.
[38] Council of Europe Statute, 5 May 1949, Article 8.
[39] PACE Opinion 300 (2022), para 3.
[40] See Dzehtsiarou, K. and Tzevelekos, V.P. (2025) '"Don't bother quitting, because you're fired": Russia's expulsion from the Council of Europe' (forthcoming) *International Organizations Law Review*.

related to the aggression against Ukraine, and so it creates an exceptionally high threshold for its actual use. In other words, all we can deduce from this experience in terms of precedent is that a full-scale invasion of another member state of the CoE triggers Article 8 as far as the CM is concerned. It cannot, however, be definitively concluded that persistent bad faith or non-compliance with membership obligations represent a trigger even if it is arguable that this too *should* engage Article 8 of the Statute which regulates expulsion from the organisation. Here it is striking that the CM Resolution[41] does not refer to a pattern of bad faith behaviour, its backlog of unexecuted cases or the democratic decay in Russia even if all of these points, arguably, could be considered to be aggravating factors in its decision to exercise the ultimate sanction. The experience of Russia, therefore, may not necessarily serve as a particularly useful precedent if the CoE faces serious, but less acute, violations of Article 3 in the future. In such a scenario, a longer-term, more holistic assessment of the situation regarding human rights and democracy in a member state is warranted, as such an exercise would allow the CoE to identify patterns of behaviour indicative of democratic decline over a period of time. The Reykjavík Principles for Democracy adopted in May 2023 at the Fourth Summit of Council of Europe Heads of State and Government provides a useful yardstick in this regard. However, what seems clear is that there were convincing reasons why the CM should have at least considered triggering Article 8 before 2022, in particular after the illegal annexation of Crimea in 2014, but perhaps also in light of the conflict in Georgia, if not earlier still in relation to Chechnya.[42]

4.2 Abject failure of the CoE political leadership

At the CoE level, the key problematic systemic weakness lies in the inability or unwillingness (or both) of the broader political leadership of the CoE (that is, the member states exercising collective responsibility in the CM format) to calibrate appropriate and timely responses to democratic decay in Russia and fundamental breaches of the CoE Statute.[43] This book has laid bare the asymmetric nature of responses to the scale and scope of well-documented transgressions by Russia. To illustrate this point, one may look at the striking differences between the speed and decisiveness of the CoE's response to Russia's full-scale invasion of Ukraine in February 2022 and its comparatively weak reaction to the illegal annexation of Crimea in 2014

---

[41] Resolution CM/Res(2022)1.
[42] On Russia's breach of its CoE obligations generally, see Chapter 4, section 5.1.
[43] Brummer discusses the partial inability but mostly unwillingness to sanction in Brummer, K. (2024) 'The Council of Europe, Russia, and the future of European cooperation: any lessons to be learned from the past?', *International Politics*, 61: 258–78.

which constituted a clear breach of the territorial integrity and sovereignty of Ukraine, and a breach of the Statute of the CoE. It is the CM, and so the states, which come under the spotlight here.[44]

As the situation in Crimea developed early in 2014, on 11–14 March the CM merely 'expressed grave concern regarding the intention to hold a referendum on the status of Crimea not authorised by Ukraine'.[45] Then on 19–20 March the CM condemned the referendum, deplored Russia's formal annexation and 'urged' Russia to 'enter into direct dialogue with the Government of Ukraine and called on both sides to use all relevant international mechanisms to find a peaceful and negotiated solution to the current crisis'.[46] By 2–3 April the CM was stressing that the referendum held in Crimea on 16 March 2014 was 'illegal' as was the subsequent annexation by Russia and that it 'cannot form the basis for any alteration of the status of the Autonomous Republic of Crimea and the city of Sevastopol'.[47] Notably, there was still no reference to a possible breach of the Statute. It was not until the session of the CM held in Vienna on 6 May 2014 that the Chair's Conclusions finally unequivocally 'condemned the annexation of Crimea as contravening international law and the Statute of the CoE'.[48] Importantly, this was not a formal Decision of the CM, and even then there was no suggestion of any sanction being applied to Russia, let alone the triggering of the Statutory Article 8 procedure. The events that followed this over the period from 2014 to 2019 and how Russia was able to prevail on the Crimea issue, remaining in the CoE despite being in continuing breach of Article 3 (and there being no plan to meaningfully address the Crimea issue), have been set out in detail in Chapter 4. We suggested then that through this pattern of behaviour, no state has done more harm to the CoE than Russia.

As argued at the end of Chapter 3, it was very clear by the mid-2010s that Russia was on an authoritarian path. The CM was well-appraised of the decline of democracy in Russia through, *inter alia*, the reports of various monitoring mechanisms, which acted in a timely fashion.[49] The Ministers' Deputies will also have undoubtedly witnessed how the bad faith of Russia manifested itself in the CM Chamber on a weekly basis. The unexecuted case-load, the filibuster tactics related to Protocol 14, the refusal of access to

---

[44] See further Chapter 4, sections 5.2–5.4. Further for criticism of the CM in relation to Chechnya, see Chapter 3, sections 2.1.1 and 2.3.2.

[45] CM/Del/Dec(2014)1194, 17 March 2014. See Chapter 4, section 2.1.

[46] CM Decision CM/Del/Dec(2014)1195, 21 March 2014.

[47] CM Decisions at 1196th meeting, 2–3 April 2014, available from: https://search.coe.int/cm/Pages/result_details.aspx?ObjectId=09000016805c5f7f [Accessed 14 June 2024].

[48] CM/Inf(2014)15, 124th Session of the Committee of Ministers (Vienna) – Conclusions of the Chairman, 6 May 2014, para 7.

[49] See Chapter 3, section 4.

the Commissioner for Human Rights and the brazen rejection of multiple public statements by the European Committee for the Prevention of Torture (CPT), including those related to impunity for crimes in Chechnya,[50] are but a snapshot of a pattern of bad faith behaviour that was all too obvious. And this was even before the illegal annexation of Crimea in 2014, which was patently in violation of the CoE Statute, Russia's financial blackmailing and its threat of Ruxit. Yet, the CM chose a path of least political resistance, which, at best, represented a failure of their collective statutory responsibility and directly undermined the integrity of the CoE, and at worst may have emboldened an already belligerent Russia.[51]

One must also consider the formal role of the member states in supervising the execution of judgments, which itself has been bedevilled with delays and difficulties. Though the Contracting Parties undertake to abide by the final judgment of the Court in any case to which they are parties in accordance with Article 46 ECHR, the challenge of supervising the implementation of judgments lies with the Committee of Ministers Human Rights (CMDH),[52] typically consisting of Ambassadors or their Deputies. Often the most complex or politically sensitive cases are those least likely to be executed in a timely manner, if at all. This large and growing backlog of complex cases makes the work of the CMDH appear inefficient and often ineffective. The effectiveness of the execution supervision process is best measured in outcomes both in terms of cases under supervision and those cases for which supervision has concluded. Ultimately, implementation depends on the relevant respondent state executing any final judgment addressed to them, in good faith. The overall effectiveness of the system is dependent upon a harmonious interplay between the Court ruling in a timely manner, the CM considering cases efficiently and the member state in question discharging their responsibilities in accordance with Article 46 ECHR. The CMDH often issues strongly worded Decisions on unexecuted cases, but it is unable to force the respondent state to execute.[53]

The tragic case of Alexei Navalnyy, Russian opposition politician and prominent anti-corruption advocate, provides a stark illustration of the weaknesses of the supervision process. The ECtHR found violations of Articles 5, 6, 11 and 18 in a variety of cases related to Mr Navalnyy's

---

[50] See Chapter 3, text accompanying n 47–9.
[51] Despite all this, for some arguments in favour of Russia remaining in the CoE in 2019, see Chapter 4, sections 2.1.3 and 3.1.
[52] Here we refer to the quarterly CM Human Rights ('CMDH') meetings.
[53] See, for example, Interim Resolution CM/ResDH(2023)35 'On execution of the judgments of the European Court of Human Rights in respect of *Navalnyy and Ofitserov group against Russian Federation*' (9 March 2023), where, *inter alia*, the Committee 'deeply deplored' that the authorities have not responded to the Committee's repeated calls for information and 'exhorted' once again the authorities to release him immediately.

conviction and continued detention.[54] The CMDH called for the applicant's release in no fewer than two interim Resolutions and six Decisions which were flatly ignored by the Russian authorities. Furthermore, in February 2021, the ECtHR granted an interim measure requiring the Russian government to release Mr Navalnyy with immediate effect, 'having regard to the nature and extent of the risk to [Mr Navalnyy's] life ... and seen in the light of the overall circumstances of [his] current detention'. In its most recent communication of an Action Report regarding the implementation of the cases of *Navalnyy and Ofitserov*[55] and *Navalnyye*,[56] the Russian government bluntly accused the CM of seeking to operate beyond its authority and that Russia would decide what measures were most appropriate to achieve *restitutio in integrum*.[57] Mr Navalnyy tragically died while illegally incarcerated in early 2024, and the CM has explicitly blamed Russia for his death.[58]

The Article 46(4) infringement procedure was introduced as an exceptional measure to try to address the situation of non-execution, though not as a sanction per se. It is not, in principle, designed to further distance a member state from the CoE or even from the CMDH. On the contrary, it is designed to focus the mind of the non-compliant state and to prompt follow-up to a non-executed judgment. The provision states:

> [i]f the Committee of Ministers considers that a High Contracting Party refuses to abide by a final judgment in a case to which it is a party, it may, after serving formal notice on that Party and by decision adopted by a majority vote of two-thirds of the representatives entitled to sit on the committee, refer to the Court the question whether that Party has failed to fulfil its obligation under paragraph 1.[59]

At the time of writing, it had been only resorted to on two occasions, first in the case of *Mammadov v. Azerbaijan*[60] in 2017 and *Kavala v. Türkiye* in

---

[54] See, for example, *Navalnyy and Ofitserov v. Russia*, nos. 46632/13 and 28671/14, 23 February 2016 and *Navalnyye v. Russia*, no. 101/15, 17 October 2017.

[55] *Navalnyy and Ofitserov v. Russia*, n 54. On Navalnyy, see also Chapter 4, n 155.

[56] *Navalnyye v. Russia*, n 54.

[57] See Action Report (19/10/2021) Communication from the Russian Federation concerning the cases of *Navalnyy and Ofitserov v. Russian Federation* (No. 46632/13) and *Navalnyye v. Russian Federation* (No. 101/15), 1419th meeting (December 2021) (DH).

[58] Statement of the CM Chair on the Death of Alexei Navalnyy, 16 February 2024, available from: www.coe.int/en/web/portal/-/death-of-alexei-navalnyy-statement-by-committee-of-ministers-president [Accessed 14 June 2024].

[59] Article 46(4) ECHR.

[60] *Ilgar Mammadov v. Azerbaijan*, no. 15172/13, 22 May 2014.

2022.⁶¹ The *Mammadov* case illustrates that this procedure can be effective under certain conditions in ad hoc cases, but the ability of this procedure to be successful consistently is doubtful.⁶² In the *Mammadov* case, though, the official Communication from the Government Agent of Azerbaijan clearly indicated that Azerbaijan's decision to quash Mr Mammadov's conviction was directly linked to the procedure: 'Having regard to the Court's judgment of 29 May 2019 concerning the proceedings under Article 46 § 4 in the case of Ilgar Mammadov v. Azerbaijan and the conclusions thereof, the Plenum decided to quash the convictions of Ilgar Mammadov and Rasul Jafarov.'⁶³

Nevertheless, the procedure is itself a gap-fill in lieu of any other sanction mechanism provided under the ECHR. It is a flawed remedy to the issue of non-execution, because it is neither a sanction nor is it a convincingly effective procedure.⁶⁴ Worse still, it is extremely resource-intensive, further absorbing the limited resources of the ECtHR⁶⁵ by forcing the Court to pronounce on facts that are either repetitive or blindingly obvious based on documentary evidence available to the CM. An important question now facing the CM is whether a violation of Article 46(4) will eventually lead to the triggering of Article 8 of the Statute.

4.3 Conditional failure of the CoE system

The final level of failure relates to the effectiveness of the broader CoE system, beginning with the Secretary General.⁶⁶ It is important to acknowledge that failure here is contingent on several important objective limitations, the most

---

61   *Kavala v. Türkiye* (infringement proceedings) [GC], no. 28749/18, 11 July 2022. See Çalı, B. (2023) 'The present and the future of infringement proceedings: lessons learned from Kavala v. Türkiye', *European Human Rights Law Review*, 2: 156–62.
62   See de Londras, F. and Dzehtsiarou, K. (2017) 'Mission impossible? Addressing non-execution through infringement proceedings in the European Court of Human Rights', *International and Comparative Law Quarterly*, 66(2): 467–90.
63   Action Report (23/04/2020) Communication from Azerbaijan concerning the cases of *Ilgar Mammadov v. Azerbaijan (*No. 15172/13) and *Rasul Jafarov v. Azerbaijan* (No. 69981/14), Doc DH-DD(2020)365 27/04/2020, 1377th meeting (June 2020) (DH), available from: https://search.coe.int/cm/Pages/result_details.aspx?ObjectID=09000016809e3fa4 [Accessed 14 June 2024].
64   The Kavala case demonstrates the challenges of Article 46(4) procedure which were highlighted by commentators. See de Londras and Dzehtsiarou, n 62.
65   For criticism of the CoE states' failure to resource the Court properly, and related issues, see Chapter 4, section 5.3.
66   Forde argues that the Council of Europe System comprises a matrix of mutually reinforcing judicial and non-judicial institutions for which Member States have a collective responsibility, rather than a hierarchy of autonomous institutions. See Forde, A. (2024) *European Human Rights Grey Zones: The Council of Europe and Areas of Conflict*, Cambridge: Cambridge University Press, pp 20–33.

significant of which is that the Secretary General is politically in a significantly weaker position than the other two statutory institutions; indeed, the Secretary General is responsible directly to the CM.[67] They obviously therefore depend upon cooperation with member states, and so must strike a balance between neutrality, advocacy and normative activism. Too much of any of these elements risks undermining the Secretary General's mandate, which may have wider consequences for the organisation. However, an imbalance between political expediency and normative willingness became particularly apparent after Russia's annexation of Crimea in 2014 when the Secretary General appeared excessively diplomatic, even seeming reluctant to criticise Russia directly.

In his 2014 annual report, the Secretary General referred to the annexation as a 'unilateral action clearly in contradiction with the Constitution of Ukraine', which has 'provoked a fully-fledged crisis in Europe'.[68] The asymmetry is particularly obvious in that the reference appears in a paragraph focussed principally on the deficiencies in the parliament, judiciary and media *in Ukraine* with no similar reference to Russia, whose parliament and Constitutional Court had endorsed the annexation and validated the results of the illegally held referendum in Crimea respectively. The 2015 report of the Secretary General does little to change the perception that the focus was more on Ukraine than on Russia by noting:

> The crisis in Ukraine is another case in point. Changing borders unilaterally and through force — as happened in Crimea — is never justified: it always leads to crisis and often war. Yet, recognising this should not prevent us from understanding that Ukraine's problems did not begin or end with this act. Widespread corruption, a lack of independent institutions and the mismanagement of power weakened the country too.[69]

It is difficult to comprehend why the Secretary General was so reluctant to address at least similarly pointed criticism to Russia as it did to Ukraine. Contrast this, with the language of PACE, which condemned 'without reservation the violation of the territorial integrity and sovereignty of

---

[67] In accordance with Article 37.b of the CoE Statute.
[68] 'State of democracy, human rights and the rule of law in Europe' (2014), Strasbourg: Council of Europe, p 5, available from: https://edoc.coe.int/en/fundamental-freedoms/5949-state-of-democracy-human-rights-and-the-rule-of-law-in-europe.html [Accessed 14 June 2024].
[69] 'State of democracy, human rights and the rule of law in Europe – a shared responsibility for democratic security in Europe' (2015), Strasbourg: Council of Europe, available from: https://search.coe.int/cm/Pages/result_details.aspx?ObjectID=090000168058e01e [Accessed 14 June 2024].

Ukraine by the armed forces of the Russian Federation in early March 2014', and expressed their 'gravest concern that members of the Upper House of the Russian Parliament unanimously authorised such action in advance'.[70] It went on to note the 'serious violation of the basic principles of the CoE mentioned in Article 3 of, and the preamble to, the Statute'.[71] It was not until 2017 that a Secretary General's annual report explicitly noted the annexation of Crimea as being illegal:

> Three years have passed since the illegal annexation of Crimea, and the question of how the CoE's monitoring structures can function there still remains open. This underlines the importance of identifying viable solutions to ensure that the 2.5 million people living in Crimea are effectively covered by our human rights mechanisms.[72]

Annual reports do not represent the formal position of the member states, nor do they offer a comprehensive picture of the work of the Secretariat, but the importance of the Secretary General taking a principled, public stance when it comes to matters fundamental to the CoE Statute cannot be underestimated. Failing to do so risks undermining the office of the Secretary General and may run contrary to the solemn pledge to 'have regard exclusively to the interests of the CoE'.[73] Demir-Gürsel suggests that former Secretary General Thorbjørn Jagland's policy preferences with regard to Russia's annexation of the Crimea and Türkiye's state of emergency prioritised political expediency at the expense of the CoE's normative mission.[74]

Again, we stress, one must also be cognisant of the inherent limitations associated with the mandate of the Secretary General. The CM, PACE and the Secretary General are very different statutory institutions, each with their own powers and limitations. The Secretary General must actively balance political and normative considerations, as well as the operational requirements

---

[70] PACE Resolution 1990 (2014), para 1. See Chapter 4, section 2.1.
[71] PACE Resolution, n 70.
[72] 'State of democracy, human rights and the rule of law' (2017), Strasbourg: Council of Europe, available from: https://edoc.coe.int/en/an-overview/7345-pdf-state-of-democracy-human-rights-and-the-rule-of-law.html [Accessed 14 June 2024].
[73] As per the Solemn Statutory Declaration of the Secretary General. See, for instance, CM/Del/Dec(2019)1353bis/1.3-app, 18 September 2019, available from: https://search.coe.int/cm/Pages/result_details.aspx?ObjectID=0900001680973077 [Accessed 14 June 2024].
[74] Demir-Gürsel, E. (2021) 'The former Secretary General of the Council of Europe confronting Russia's annexation of the Crimea and Turkey's state of emergency', *European Convention on Human Rights Law Review*, 2(2): 303–5.

of the organisation, including importantly the need to maintain budgetary stability, which depends upon cooperative member states. Here again, we see that the long-standing policy of zero nominal budgetary growth is a relevant context which certainly contributed to weakening the institution. PACE, conversely, is impeded only by the will of its members which means it can be significantly more agile in its positions, as discussed in detail in Chapter 4. Nevertheless, it is difficult to reconcile the apparent asymmetry in approach of the Secretary General, and indeed the CM discussed earlier, when faced with the annexation of one member state's territory by another.

The effectiveness of other parts of the CoE system is unfortunately no more encouraging. As mentioned earlier, Russia effectively cut cooperation with the CoE Commissioner for Human Rights after September 2014,[75] during the tenure of Commissioner Nils Muižnieks, neither allowing on-site visits nor engaging in any meaningful formal communication.[76] The situation hardly improved under Dunja Mijatović, whose work regarding the human rights situation in Chechnya was openly criticised by Russia as being biased, with it threatening that its cooperation with the Commissioner's office could be built up pragmatically but this depended on her 'rid[ding] herself of the selective and discriminatory' approach.[77]

Engagement with CoE monitoring mechanisms was an accession commitment made by Russia in 1996, and is a cornerstone of cooperation with the CoE and can be considered a fundamental requirement of membership. Indeed, it is explicitly provided for under Article 6.1 of Resolution (99) 50, establishing the institution of the Commissioner for Human Rights such that: 'Member States shall facilitate the independent and effective performance by the Commissioner of his or her functions. In particular, they shall facilitate the Commissioner's contacts, including travel, in the context of the mission of the Commissioner and provide in good time information requested by the Commissioner.' Yet, the stone-walling of the Commissioner was never meaningfully discussed, let alone condemned by the CM. The problem of access was similar in areas of protracted conflict

---

[75] See Muižnieks, N. (2022) 'Human rights in contested European areas'. Presentation at a conference organised by the Ireland presidency of the Council of Europe entitled 'Lighting the Shade: Effective Application of ECHR in Contested European Territories', 1 September 2022.

[76] Final Report of Engagement by Nils Muižnieks, Commissioner for Human Rights of the Council of Europe, following his mission in Kyiv, Moscow and Crimea from 7 to 12 September 2014, CommDH(2014)19. See further Chapter 3, section 4.2.

[77] See Russian Assessment of Council of Europe Commissioner for Human Rights Performance, 26 March 2021, available from: https://coe.mid.ru/en_GB/-/o-rossijs kih-ocenkah-deatel-nosti-komissara-soveta-evropy-po-pravam-celoveka [Accessed 14 June 2024].

effectively controlled by Russia including Abkhazia, South Ossetia (Georgia) and Transnistria (Moldova). PACE proposed an approach whereby states are presumed to have consented to visits by human rights monitoring bodies in circumstances where there is reason to believe that there are serious violations of fundamental human rights and dignity such as threats to life, torture, inhuman or degrading treatment or denial of basic humanitarian needs,[78] but the CM just ignored this proposal.[79]

The final example we would offer here to illustrate the conditional failure of the CoE system is the deeply unsatisfactory engagement by Russia with the CPT. Russia ratified the CPT in 1998 and by the time of its expulsion the Committee had carried out thirty visits to Russia.[80] It had also been subjected to an unprecedented four public statements in line with Article 10(2) of the European Convention on the Prevention of Torture which provides that the Committee may issue a public statement if a party to the Convention 'fails to co-operate or refuses to improve the situation in the light of the Committee's recommendations.' The statements are reserved for the most egregious cases of non-cooperation by member states with the CPT, and only ten such statements have ever been issued across all CoE member states. That 40 per cent of all such statements were issued just to Russia is a damning indictment in its own right. In its most recent public statement in 2019, the CPT issued a blistering criticism of the Russian authorities' inaction regarding ill-treatment particularly in Chechnya:

> [I]t is of grave concern that, notwithstanding the efforts it has made over the last 20 years, torture of detained persons in the Chechen Republic has remained a deep-rooted problem. This speaks not only to a dereliction of duty at the level of the Republic's authorities, but also to a failure of effective oversight and control at the federal level.[81]

The statement went on to note that the problem was general in nature, not only confined to Chechnya such that '[t]he widespread practice of police ill-treatment, including torture, is not unique to this republic of the Russian Federation' and concluded that '[s]uch a state of affairs can only be qualified as an ongoing failure to co-operate with the CPT'. The

---

[78] PACE Recommendation 2140 (2018) 'Unlimited access to member States, including "grey zones", by Council of Europe and United Nations human rights monitoring bodies', para 3.
[79] Reply to Recommendation, PACE Doc. 15033, 20 January 2020.
[80] Eight periodic visits and 22 ad hoc visits, according to the CPT, see www.coe.int/en/web/cpt/russian-federation [Accessed 14 June 2024]. See Chapter 3, section 2.1.1.
[81] See CPT Public Statement, 11 March 2019, available from: https://rm.coe.int/16809371ee and www.coe.int/en/web/cpt/-/-1 [Accessed 14 June 2024].

relationship between Russia and the CPT requires further examination, as Russia remains party to the European Convention for the Prevention of Torture, post-expulsion.[82]

The lamentable state of execution of judgments of the ECtHR and the poor record of engagement and follow-up with monitoring body recommendations highlights some of the systemic weaknesses facing the system. The system failure is conditional because it is necessarily limited in its potential to affect change in member states; it relies on the good faith of the contracting parties. If member states choose not to execute a judgment, not to follow a recommendation, or to take action based on the narrowest possible interpretation of recommendation or a judgment, the system is effectively powerless.

5 Limiting scope for repetition and adapting to post-peace Europe

The CoE is currently experiencing a profound challenge, transitioning from a phase of largely peaceful expansion, cooperation and consolidation to a 'post-peace' Europe. This new phase is hoped to be marked by ensuring accountability for international crimes and seeking to strengthen security (including democratic security) with a view to reducing the risk of further conflict in Europe as well as finding an effective antidote to the democratic decay in some member states.

Since February 2022, the CoE has been in a reactive state, dealing with a truly cataclysmic situation. Although this book demonstrated that in 2022 the member states came together in the face of the existential threat of violence coming from Russia and acted quickly and decisively, how long will this unity of purpose for the CoE remain? Despite this uncertainty, the CoE must take stock of the experience of 2022 and be ready for the future to maximise its effectiveness as the leading regional human rights system. The CoE must be prepared politically and legally to deal with the consequences of conflict or with serious or systemic non-compliance more effectively in the future. This requires leadership, first and foremost, from the member states, which must properly resource CoE institutions, and live up to their rhetoric of appreciation for them.[83] The Reykjavík Declaration is, perhaps, the first step in this process as it articulates a new vision for the organisation which prioritises, among other issues, accountability for serious breaches of international law.

---

[82] See Statement from CPT President, 31 March 2022, available from: www.coe.int/en/web/cpt/-/-1 [Accessed 14 June 2024].
[83] See Chapter 4, Conclusion, especially section 5.4.

5.1 Dealing with the past

One can perhaps draw some lessons from the domain of transitional justice in considering how the CoE might seek to adapt following the experience of one member state pursuing an aggressive war against another. To deal with the past, there is a need firstly to establish the facts and acknowledge shortcomings on the part of the organisation before putting in place institutional reforms which limit the potential for repetition and improve future responses to bad faith.

In the field of transitional justice, it is now well-established that non-repetition is inextricably linked to institutional reflection and reform.[84] Boraine notes, for instance, that '[f]or truth and reconciliation to flourish, serious and focused attention must be paid, not only to individuals but also to institutions',[85] and while, of course, such reform is understood within the context of a country transitioning from conflict, some of the underpinning principles seem no less relevant for the CoE. In this monograph we documented the key highlights of the Russian membership but also we have offered a detailed analysis of what challenges the CoE faced in addressing the polycrisis caused by Russian bad faith. It is imperative that the CoE learns from this experience to strengthen its ability to handle belligerence, backsliding and bad faith.

The CoE would benefit from addressing recent experiences in a systematic and holistic manner through, for instance, a comprehensive review of the CoE membership of Russia. Such a process ideally would take the form of an ad hoc Commission of Inquiry mandated by the CM under the terms of Statutory Article 17 which provides that the CM 'may set up advisory and technical committees or commissions for such specific purposes as it may deem desirable'.[86] Whether such an inquiry takes a long term or a more limited review, for example from 2014 to 2022, would be a matter for the CM to determine, but the purpose of such a review could be to examine the practice of statutory, non-statutory and other CoE actors and infer key, actionable learnings. Depending on the nature of follow-up required, the CM could consider other actions to further the aim of the CoE under the terms of Article 15(a) of the Statute.

This can be a historical inquiry of some of the complex and multilayered challenges which may include what we have referred to earlier as the 'Triple Fault'. Comparable inquiries and investigation are not uncommon both on

---

[84] United Nations (2023) *Transitional Justice: A Strategic Tool for People, Prevention and Peace: Guidance Note of the Secretary-General*, New York: United Nations.
[85] Boraine, A. (2006) 'Transitional justice: a holistic interpretation', *Journal of International Affairs*, 60(1): 17–27.
[86] Article 17, CoE Statute.

the domestic level[87] and at the level of the CoE.[88] In this inquiry the CoE can take stock of what happened, what was done and what was not done, and consider how to make sure that this will not happen again. Of course, some events and examples will be *sui generis* and only relevant to the situation with Russia, but some challenges have broader implications and the CoE can indeed learn from an inquiry such as this.

5.2 Political renewal based on standards and realism

In reflecting on how the CoE has approached the actions and transgressions of Russia, one must be realistic about the capabilities and limits of the organisation as well as the prevailing macro-political context in Europe. Despite the conviction that 'the pursuit of peace based upon justice and international cooperation is vital for the preservation of human society and civilisation',[89] the annexation of Crimea and the full-scale aggression against Ukraine by Russia show that the CoE is incapable of preventing or stopping war.[90] This in no way diminishes its relevance, but it does point to objective and systemic weakness. It also struggles to meaningfully influence the situation of human rights, the rule of law and democracy in member states which are determined to defy it, and there are several CoE member states which appear to be on a path of democratic backsliding.

This being said, the CoE has a chance to play a significant role even within the scope of objective political limitations such as lack of membership sanctions, lack of infrastructure to influence domestic affairs of the member states and inability to force any standards on the members. The main statutory bodies – the CM, PACE and the Secretary General – can help to empower

---

[87] A commission of investigation is a type of ex-post facto inquiry, usually based in law, into a matter of general public concern. Such commissions typically provide recommendations for reparation, as well as for legal and policy changes to prevent repetition. See, for example, Hart's report as a result of Historical Institutional Abuse Inquiry, available from: www.hiainquiry.org/sites/hiainquiry/files/media-files/Chapter%203%20-%20Findings.pdf [Accessed 14 June 2024].

[88] Though extremely rare, the CoE has set up at least one independent investigation. In 2017 the Bureau of the PACE established an independent investigative body to examine allegations of corruption within the Assembly. See http://assembly.coe.int/Communication/IBAC/IBAC-GIAC-Report-EN.pdf [Accessed 14 June 2024].

[89] CoE Statute, Preamble.

[90] It is also evident in a non-international armed conflict sense when one considers, for example, Azerbaijan's military operation in Nagorno-Karabakh in 2020 and beyond. See, *inter alia*, Forde, A. (2021) 'Nagorno Karabakh – a stark reminder of the Council of Europe's operational "grey zones"', *OpinioJuris*, 11 February 2021, available from: https://opiniojuris.org/2021/02/11/nagorno-karabakh-a-stark-reminder-of-the-council-of-europes-operational-grey-zones/ [Accessed 14 June 2024].

domestic democratic frameworks, strengthen the quality of national laws, assist in the development of strong, pluralist civil societies and media, and provide a platform for peer engagement between member states. They can also monitor compliance through judicial and non-judicial processes. These are roles no other organisation currently fulfils and so represent a unique comparative advantage. However, it must never compromise on standards, and here is where there is scope for improvement both politically and from an internal/system perspective.

Forde has discussed the notion of the 'normative will' as a form of antidote or counter-force to the prevailing and dominant 'political will' of member states, particularly if the political will risks undermining the values of the CoE.[91] The notion is based on the premise that the Secretary General in particular is a statutory institution in its own right, duty-bound to simultaneously serve member states *and* the object and purpose of the CoE. That means ensuring the system is animated to the maximum extent possible particularly in situations of critical human rights, the rule of law and democracy concern such as democratic backsliding or conflict. The monitoring and advisory mechanisms can serve as an early-warning system, but it is a matter for the political leadership of the organisation whether it wishes to heed these warnings or not.

How the CoE is to approach engagement with democratic backsliding,[92] bad faith and conflict will be among the most significant political and operational challenges the organisation faces in the future. The CoE showed unprecedented unity and values-based decisiveness in the immediate aftermath of Russia's aggression on Ukraine in February 2022, culminating in a decision to expel Russia under Article 8 of the Statute on 16 March. It complemented this political commitment with expertise and other support relevant for Ukraine, and has committed to the urgent need to ensure a comprehensive system of accountability for serious violations of international law arising out of the Russian aggression against Ukraine in order to avoid impunity and to prevent further violations.[93] The CoE must, of course, maintain this focus, and ensure it has the political mandate, statutory framework and resources to allow it to adapt to a new political and security reality in Europe. Member states took the first steps in this direction through the Reykjavík Declaration in May 2023.

In spite of the existence of the statutory defence clause which provides that '[m]atters relating to national defence do not fall within the scope of the Council of Europe',[94] the CoE has maintained a legitimate interest in

---

[91] Forde, n 66, pp 206–8.
[92] Bermeo, N. (2016) 'On democratic backsliding', *Journal of Democracy*, 27(1): 5–19.
[93] CM/Del/Dec(2023)1457bis/2.3 Consequences of the aggression of the Russian Federation against Ukraine, 24 February 2023.
[94] Article 1.d of the CoE Statute.

conflict prevention and peacebuilding since at least the 1990s, in particular due to the risk conflicts pose to 'security, unity and democratic stability'.[95] In January 2019, referring to the annexation of Crimea and the conflict in eastern Ukraine, Secretary General Thorbjørn Jagland noted that 'under the current international order it is not for us to solve these conflicts' but that 'should not prevent [the CoE] from protecting people's rights'.[96] He went further to suggest that it is precisely 'because there is an open conflict, we should deploy all our instruments in these areas [of conflict]'.[97] The CoE is generally well-placed to support verification, accountability and confidence-building in post-conflict contexts, but it faces an acute challenge in relation to how it engages with areas still occupied, under the effective control or decisive influence of Russia. The organisation must work closely with the states to find innovative ways to engage with those regions wherever and however possible, and in a status-neutral manner to maximise strategic communication and to pursue confidence-building processes. This could include, for instance, engaging with civil society, media, academia and de facto human rights institutions in a more decisive manner. The CoE must not fall into the trap of assuming other organisations are better-placed to work in conflict-affected territories. The reality on the ground in Europe has profoundly changed – so too should the approach of the CoE. As the High-Level Reflection Group noted, that '[a]t a time in which war has returned to Europe, the CoE – the continent's main pan-European organisation – must adapt in order to remain fit for purpose'.[98]

5.3 Future relationship with Russia

There has never been a more rapid and expansive deterioration of relations with a member state in the CoE's history than the 2022 experience with Russia. The expulsion was entirely justified, but the events which triggered the expulsion, the years immediately before, and the multiple issues arising from Russia's troubled membership as set out in this book have cast a long shadow on the CoE as a whole. The inescapable fact remains that Russia is now a non-member state with no formal intergovernmental relationship with the CoE, even if it remains (at the

---

[95] Warsaw Declaration, 16–17 May 2005, Warsaw: Council of Europe, Preamble.
[96] Address by Thorbjørn Jagland to the Parliamentary Assembly of the Council of Europe, 22 January 2018.
[97] Jagland, n 96.
[98] Report of the CoE High-Level Reflection Group, p 5, available from: https://rm.coe.int/report-of-the-high-level-reflection-group-of-the-council-of-europe-/1680a85cf1 [Accessed 14 June 2024].

time of writing) party to some CoE Treaties. At some point, though, circumstances might change and the guns will fall silent in Ukraine. Later still, the politics in Russia may also change, perhaps creating scope for enhanced interaction and, eventually, a rapprochement might be possible. Consideration must be given to how and in what circumstances formal relations with Russia can be pursued, and to what ends. The inter-state cases concerning Russia,[99] and matters such as the register of just satisfaction,[100] the register of damages for Ukraine and the possible establishment of an Internationalised Tribunal within the framework of the CoE will be important in this regard.

Following the expulsion of Russia, the CM adopted a Resolution which noted that the organisation will take initiatives to support and engage with human rights defenders, democratic forces, free media and independent civil society in Russia.[101] This approach has also been endorsed by PACE, which emphasised the need to engage with Russian human rights defenders and civil society under the same conditions as their counterparts from CoE member states.[102] This is an important channel which should be cultivated and expanded further. In practice, cooperation, if any, is likely to remain relatively sporadic, superficial and ad hoc for some time. There needs to be profound change in Russian political culture and decisive and meaningful steps to ensure full accountability and maximal remedy for its actions in Ukraine before more formal engagement could recommence. Even if political conditions become more favourable, the parameters required to consider a deepening of relations with the CoE must be stringent. People in Russia and in particular the many democratic forces, human rights defenders, free media, lawyers, academics, civil society actors and others who have been so profoundly betrayed by their political leadership must understand that, someday, the protection provided by the CoE systems, and the ECHR in particular, can be restored. However, any rapprochement depends on formal accountability for the crimes in Ukraine, a profound political transformation in Russia and on Russian society coming to terms with its legacy of aggression.

---

[99] See Chapter 4, section 4.
[100] See Chapter 4, text accompanying n 197.
[101] Resolution CM/Res(2022)3, 'On legal and financial consequences of the cessation of membership of the Russian Federation in the Council of Europe', Adopted by the Committee of Ministers on 23 March 2022 at the 1429bis meeting of the Ministers' Deputies, 23 March 2022.
[102] PACE Recommendation 2228 (2022) 'Consequences of the Russian Federation's continued aggression against Ukraine: role and response of the Council of Europe', para 6.1.

6 Conclusion

The dominant legacy after Russia's twenty-six years of membership of the CoE is one of bad faith. Superficial progress in some areas has been comprehensively overshadowed by a pattern of belligerence and bad faith. This book has sought to highlight this, both for the inherent importance of doing so and so that lessons may be learned for the future. Of course, now that Russia has been expelled, and attention has rightly turned to ensuring accountability for its aggression, its pattern of bad faith during membership may seem like a matter of secondary importance. Indeed, looking ahead the central concern for all who are seeking an effective human rights legal and institutional system in Europe is the systemic weaknesses the experience of membership has highlighted. In particular, the tolerance of democratic backsliding and the asymmetry of the responses of the CM to the observable pattern of bad faith by Russia over many years, culminating in the egregious breaches of the CoE's values, should serve as catalysts for further reflection and action by the CM.[103]

The expulsion of Russia in March 2022 marked a decisive milestone for the CoE, though one could say that it was more a necessity than a decision. Article 8 was triggered when one member state launched a neo-imperial invasion on another. If the CM had not shown unity of purpose then, when would it?

Though we firmly believe this is avoidable, Russia's expulsion *could* also mark the point from which the most sophisticated regional human rights system in the world slowly slips into further decline. The taboo of expulsion or withdrawal has been definitively broken, and this forces the CoE to reassess its added-value proposition as well as its approach to dealing with non-compliance. To maintain relevance and to avoid further decline requires a sober appraisal of the confluence of factors that led to Russia's most egregious breach of the CoE Statute since the treaty was signed in 1949. Given that much of the literature around the effectiveness of the European human rights system focusses on the Court, the non-compliance of states could deceptively be portrayed as a problem for the ECtHR alone, when the reality is that this is principally a political matter within the scope of the CM. As the then President of the ECtHR, Síofra O'Leary, stated at the opening of the judicial year in 2023:

> [m]uch ink has rightly been devoted in recent years to the European Convention's rule of law guarantees and to the frontal challenges to

---

[103] Muižnieks and Patrício previously cautioned against innovation or the propagation of new mechanisms without a proper impact assessment of existing ones. See Muižnieks, N. and Patrício, R. (2023) 'Using the summit to breathe new life into the Council of Europe', *European Human Rights Law Review*, 2: 126–34.

judicial independence which Europe has been witnessing. In contrast, a misplaced complacency may have installed itself in certain States over the last decades regarding the Convention's success in supporting and preserving democracy itself.[104]

Since 2010, successive chairmanships of the CM have focussed much attention on the concept of 'shared responsibility', though the progressive disempowerment of the CoE's bodies by the member states over many years of cosmetic reform, the budgetary policy of zero-nominal growth as well as sub-optimal engagement at the highest levels of government seems more focussed on burden-reduction than burden-sharing. In several cases, engagement by member state governments appeared declaratory or performative in nature.

This is a point of inflection for the member states of the CoE, whose collective will is deterministic of the future of the organisation. Do they wish to see the bulwark of human rights, democracy and the rule of law slip into further decline, or will they seize this moment to reflect and rebuild in line with the object and purpose intended when the organisation was established?

---

[104] Speech by Síofra O'Leary, President of the European Court of Human Rights, Dialogue between Judges 2023, 27 January 2023. See further Chapter 4, section 5.3.

Index

A

accession commitments 18–19, 21–8, 32–3, 55, 57, 65, 71, 81, 130, 217, 222
accession to CoE by Russia 28–33
authoritarianism 8, 71, 84, 115, 121, 131, 134–5, 138, 218–19
Azerbaijan 26–7, 99, 146, 152, 165, 230–1, 238

B

backsliding (democratic) 10, 14, 25, 71, 92, 109, 112, 142, 155, 186, 190, 217–19, 237–9, 242
bad faith 3–7, 12–14, 25, 35–6, 71, 99, 109, 111, 216–19, 222–9, 237–9, 242
better in than out 27–9, 36, 107, 113, 132–4, 141, 143, 157
Bolotnaya Square 190
Burmych 208
business as usual 187, 202–7, 210, 215

C

chaos 193
challenge to credentials (PACE) 9, 23, 26–7, 36, 46, 57–63, 70, 95–9, 100–3, 106–9, 130, 146–7, 150, 156
Chechnya 3, 12, 21, 26–34, 42–55, 61–5, 112, 121, 129, 131–2, 134, 136–7, 219, 222–4, 227–9, 234–5
  impunity for grave human rights violations in 42–55
CM *see* Committee of Ministers
CoE (Council of Europe)
  failure of political leadership 227–30
  importance of human rights actors' role 134
  monitoring (general) 18, 21, 23–6, 29, 36

CoE financing
  blackmail (financial by Russia) 18, 102, 112, 131, 136, 150
  budget 18, 45, 60, 102, 106, 112, 136, 142, 150, 159, 177, 205, 234, 243
  contributors 18, 102, 136, 142, 159
  non–payment (or threats of) by Russia 18, 45, 60, 99, 102–5, 107, 110, 112
  precarious financial situation 136
Colombo Commission 219
Commission of Inquiry 237
Commissioner for Human Rights 42, 53, 66, 68–9, 83, 85, 98, 101, 112, 135–6, 166, 221, 223–5, 228, 234
Committee of Ministers (CM) 6–9, 13–14, 25–8, 42–9, 52–6, 62–4, 132–7, 140–1, 147–54, 156–62, 164–7, 169–84
  and Article 58 ECHR 194
  and execution of Russian judgments post–expulsion 210–14
  failure of leadership 227–31
  impunity re Chechnya 51–5
  power but lack of political will 62
  'Triple Fault' scenario 224–35
complementary joint procedure 108–9, 150–4, 164
conditions of detention 20, 72–3, 115, 189
consensus 139, 141, 145–6, 151–3
Consultative Assembly 155–6, 161
Council of Europe
  failure of political leadership 227–30
  importance of human rights actors' role 134
  monitoring (general) 18, 21, 23–6, 29, 36

244

INDEX

Council of Europe, statute 1, 4, 6–7, 9, 13–14, 18, 25–7, 57–64, 95–100, 105–6, 108–111, 130–3, 146–7, 151–8, 162–5, 168–83, 196–7, 225–9, 231, 233, 237, 239, 242
 Article 3 17–19, 25, 36, 64, 91–7, 100, 106, 110–11, 117, 130–1, 136, 144, 146–8, 152–4, 156–7, 163–5, 168, 173, 175, 191–3, 225–8, 233
 Article 4 19
 Article 7 147–9, 151, 157–9, 167, 169, 170–2, 174–82
 Article 8 4, 19, 25–6, 45, 53, 58, 60–2, 71, 95–6, 98, 109–10, 117, 123, 140–1, 147–9, 151, 153–4, 157–8, 160–1, 164–82, 197, 227–8, 231, 239, 242
 Article 9 18, 102–3
Court's budget 136
CPT (Committee for Prevention of Torture) 15, 20, 47, 53, 79, 224, 229, 235–6
Crimea 91–135, 227–9, 232–4, 238, 240
Cuba 145
Cyprus v. Turkey 159, 161

D

damaging membership 36, 111, 130–1
death penalty 33, 220–1
Declaration on Compliance with Commitments (1994) 22, 26, 37, 44–5, 48–9, 62, 70, 108, 132
democratic security 17, 22, 30, 38, 93, 102, 105–6, 137, 150–2, 216, 219, 232, 236
denunciation 194–5, 198
Duma 30, 33, 45, 74–8, 82–4, 86, 88, 100–1, 118, 120, 167, 178
Dzehtsiarou and Coffey 109, 113, 132, 144

E

early concerns and forewarnings 33
ECHR *see* European Convention on Human Rights
ECtHR *see* European Court of Human Rights
ending of the non-participation crisis 104
European Commission 155–6, 163

European Convention on Human Rights (ECHR)
 Article 1 *see* jurisdiction
 Article 46 26, 52, 62–4, 73, 88, 133, 152
 Article 52 44, 59
 Article 58 13, 194–201, 214
 constitutional amendment in Russia to limit influence 87, 120
 early concerns 33–4
 execution of judgments 72, 114, 187–90, 210
 infringement procedure 10, 26, 64, 152–3, 164, 230–1
 limited influence on Russia/significant violations 114–17, 187–90
 Protocol 6 20, 33
 ratification by Russia 33
European Court of Human Rights (ECtHR) 92, 94, 98, 101, 104, 114–16, 119–36, 143–4, 152, 159, 161
 Article 58 (ECHR) 194
 budget 136
 Chechnya cases 49–51
 continued engagement post expulsion 190–4
 critique of 135–6
 early cases (Russia) 72–4
 envisaged role re Russia 29
 execution of judgments generally 72–5, 114–15, 187–90
 execution of judgments post expulsion 210–14
 just satisfaction (Russia cases) *see* just satisfaction
 last hope/resort re Chechnya 49, 129
 last resort for inter-state cases 121, 129
 limitations of 70
 pending/remaining cases 201–10
 strained relations after 2005 75
exceptionalism 222
expulsion
 comparable cases to Russia 154–63
 from international organisations 141–5
 process (CoE) 145–54
 Russia's analysed 164–83

F

Federal Law 34, 83–4, 178, 201, 211, 223
Finland 1, 219

foreign agents (Act/law) 84, 86, 118–19, 120, 135, 189–90, 207, 222–3

G

geopolitical importance 7, 17, 29, 31, 127, 139, 142, 144, 145
Georgia 41–2, 48, 50, 55–62, 64, 68–70, 83, 90, 92–3, 100, 105, 114, 122, 125–30, 134–8, 222, 227, 235
Georgia v. Russia inter-state cases 57, 125–8, 156, 188, 191, 193, 212
good faith 218, 225–6, 229, 236
Gorbachev, Mikhail 1–2, 216
Grand Chamber 152
Greece 140, 154–60, 162–4, 169, 171, 175, 218–19
gross violations 145

I

immediate expulsion 140, 151
impact (of ECHR on Russia) 72, 114–17, 185–90, 205, 209, 214
infringement procedure 152, 164, 230–1
interim measures 186, 190–4
internal sanctions 97, 100–1, 106
International Humanitarian Law 193
inter-state cases 121, 153, 155, 159–61, 163, 191, 202, 208, 213
  brought by Georgia 125
  brought by Ukraine 122

J

jurisdiction 193–4, 196, 200–1, 203, 214
just satisfaction 53–6, 71, 88–9, 185, 188, 201, 210, 212

K

Kavala 10, 152–3, 164, 230–1
Kohl, Helmut 2
Koroteev, K. 204, 208, 212, 214
Kovler 56, 74–6, 79–80, 188
Kox, Tiny 165, 170, 179

L

Lavrov 59, 60, 98, 101, 102
Lawson and Drzemczewski 179
Leach, P. 51–2, 63, 136, 167, 175
legitimacy 139–40, 144–5, 164, 184
LGBTI 77–8, 115, 189, 207

M

macro level 186, 188
Magnitsky, S. 116, 119, 189
Mammadov v. Azerbaijan 10, 152, 190, 230–1
medical care 189
membership sanctions 139–46, 149–51, 154, 158, 160, 163–4, 183
memorandum 197
micro level 185–6, 188, 214
Moldova 21, 48, 55–6, 62, 68, 77, 138, 210, 212, 235
Muižnieks, N. 234

N

NATO *see* North Atlantic Treaty Organization
Navalnyy 5, 119, 189, 212–13, 224, 229–30
Nemtsov, B. 119
normative will 232, 239
North Atlantic Treaty Organization (NATO) 167, 175
notification of withdrawal 174, 177
Nuremberg Charter 226

O

O'Leary, S. 137, 199, 200, 209–10, 242
Organisation for Security and Cooperation in Europe (OSCE) 146
Organization of American States 145

P

Parliamentary Assembly of the Council of Europe (PACE) 155, 170
  boycott of 85, 93, 98–9, 101, 106
  challenge to credentials procedure 9, 23, 26–7, 45–6, 57–8, 61–2, 70, 84, 96–7, 100–3, 106–9, 117, 119, 121, 130, 146–7, 150, 156
  delegation's credentials 26
  denial of voting rights 27, 45–6, 58, 97–8, 106, 111
  guardian of CoE values 9, 26, 43, 61, 138
  monitoring (human rights) 21–9, 39–40, 58–9, 61–2, 66–70, 74, 81–6, 95, 99, 101–8, 116–18
  opinion (accession) 30–2
  opinion on expulsion 168–9
  position on expulsion 168–9
  weakened 112

INDEX

participatory rights 139
pending applications 187, 202, 209–10, 214
pending cases 188, 202, 209, 212
phased expulsion 150–1, 153–4
pick and choose 187, 208, 210, 215
plenary of the Court 198, 209
Polakiewicz, J. 206
President of the Court 191–3, 196, 198, 204
priority policy 208
protection of National Minorities 20
Putin, V. 8, 160, 164, 167, 171

R

'radical approach' 187, 209–10
RCC *see* Russian Constitutional Court
realpolitik 142, 145, 218
register of damages 15, 126
register of just satisfaction 125–6, 128, 241
residual jurisdiction 199–200, 209, 214
Reykjavík Declaration 137–8, 227, 236, 239
ritualism 91–3, 113–15, 118, 121, 129, 132
role of the CoE's human rights actors 134
Rules of Court 196, 203–4
Rules of Procedure 148–9
Russia
  bad faith membership 111–12, 219–24, 226
  'big payer' status 18
  and the ECtHR after 2005 75
  and the ECHR, initial room for positivity 72
  persistent breach of CoE obligations 130
Russian Constitutional Court (RCC) 33–4, 72, 74, 76, 80, 87, 88–9, 120, 232
Russian Ministry of Foreign Affairs 166, 175, 178
Russian PACE delegation's credentials 96–7, 119
Russophobism 65, 75, 98–9, 104, 213
Ruxit
  threat of 102–4, 109–11, 113, 122, 131

S

same conditions, the 195–6, 198–9
sanctions 26
Secretary General 44, 59, 77, 79, 84, 143, 147, 149–50, 153, 165, 170, 172, 174, 177, 179, 195, 212
statutory bodies 139
Serbia 146, 165
Sorensen, Commissioner 157
Soviet Union 1, 8, 220
Spain 219
Statute *see* Council of Europe Statute
statutory bodies 139
strategy of execution 212
subversive influence (Russia) 3, 41, 79, 111–12, 133, 183
suspension 194–6, 198, 209

T

Tarschys, D. 219
therapeutic admission 17, 28, 31, 34, 37
torture 50–2, 73, 94, 116, 156, 159, 161, 164
transitional justice 237
Transnistria 21, 55–6, 62
triggers 152–3, 156, 160, 165
'Triple Fault' 217, 225, 237
Trojan horse 41, 60
Türkiye 140, 142, 153–4, 160–3, 165, 230–3

U

Ukraine 91, 93–6, 108–9, 122–5, 128–30, 137, 140, 143, 165, 168, 171, 175, 205, 208, 224, 226–8, 232, 238–41
  inter-state cases brought by 122–5
unexecuted cases 188
United Nations General Assembly 226
USA 175

V

VCLT *see* Vienna Convention on the Law of Treaties
Venice Commission 77, 83–4, 86, 88, 118, 120, 135–6, 177, 223
victims 188, 190, 206, 208
Vienna Convention on Law of Treaties (VCLT) 178, 182
Vienna Declaration 2, 11, 17, 22, 29, 93, 138, 216
voting rights 97–9, 105–6, 111

W

war 186, 193–4
war of aggression 142, 150, 154, 168
well established case law (WECL) 208

Y

Yeltsin, B. 17, 19, 22, 30, 32
Yukos 71, 78, 89, 117, 126, 188, 210

Z

Zorkin, V. 34, 77, 87, 222

www.ingramcontent.com/pod-product-compliance
Lightning Source LLC
Chambersburg PA
CBHW071154070526
44584CB00019B/2780